MW00719517

NOVELL'S®

NetWare® 4.1 Administrator's Handbook

NOVELL'S®

NetWare® 4.1 Administrator's Handbook

KELLEY J. P. LINDBERG

NOVELL PRESS®

Novell Press, San Jose

Novell's NetWare® 4.1 Administrator's Handbook

Published by
Novell Press
2180 Fortune Drive
San Jose, CA 95131

Library of Congress Catalog Card No.: 95-81100

ISBN: 1-56884-737-8

Printed in the United States of America

10 9 8 7 6 5 4 3

1A/SS/RS/ZV

Distributed in the United States by IDG Books Worldwide, Inc.

Distributed by Macmillan Canada for Canada; by Computer and Technical Books for the Caribbean Basin; by Contemporantea de Ediciones for Venezuela; by Distribuidora Cuspide for Argentina; by CITFC for Brazil; by Ediciones ZETA S.C.R. Ltda. for Peru; by Editorial Limusa SA for Mexico; by Transworld Publishers Limited in the United Kingdom and Europe; by Al-Maiman Publishers & Distributors for Saudi Arabia; by Simron Pty. Ltd. for South Africa; by IDG Communications (HK) Ltd. for Hong Kong; by Toppan Company Ltd. for Japan; by Addison Wesley Publishing Company for Korea; by Longman Singapore Publisher Ltd. for Singapore, Malaysia, Thailand, and Indonesia; by Unalis Corporation for Taiwan; by WS Computer Publishing Company, Inc. for the Philippines; by WoodsLane Pty. Ltd. for Australia; by WoodsLane Enterprises Ltd. for New Zealand.

For general information on Novell Press books in the U.S., including information on discounts and premiums, contact IDG Books at 800-434-3422 or 415-655-3000. For information on where to purchase Novell Press books outside the U.S., contact IDG Books Worldwide at 415-655-3021 or fax 415-655-3295. For information on translations, contact Waterside Productions, Inc., 2191 San Elijo Avenue, Cardiff, CA 92007-1839, at 619-632-9190. For sales inquiries and special prices for bulk quantities, call IDG Books Worldwide at 415-655-3200. For information on using Novell Press books in the classroom, or for ordering examination copies, contact Jim Kelly at 800-434-2086.

John Kilcullen, *President & CEO, IDG Books Worldwide, Inc.*
Brenda McLaughlin, *Senior Vice President & Group Publisher, IDG Books Worldwide, Inc.*

Rosalie Kearsley, *Publisher, Novell Press, Inc.*

Welcome to Novell Press

Novell Press, the world's leading provider of networking books, is the premier source for the most timely and useful information in the networking industry. Novell Press books cover fundamental networking issues as they emerge—from today's Novell and third-party products to the concepts and strategies that will guide the industry's future. The result is a broad spectrum of titles for the benefit of those involved in networking at any level: end-user, department administrator, developer, systems manager, or network architect.

Novell Press books are written by experts with the full participation of Novell's own technicians and are published only on the basis of final released software, never on prereleased versions. Novell Press at IDG is an exciting partnership between two companies at the forefront of the knowledge and communications revolution. The Press is implementing an ambitious publishing program to develop new networking titles centered on the current version of NetWare and on Novell's GroupWise and other popular groupware products.

Novell Press books are translated into 12 languages and are available at bookstores around the world.

Rosalie Kearsley, Publisher, Novell Press, Inc.
David Kolodney, Associate Publisher, IDG Books Worldwide, Inc.

Novell Press

Publisher
Rosalie Kearsley

Associate Publisher
David Kolodney

Market Development Manager
Colleen Bluhm

Associate Acquisitions Editor
Anne Hamilton

Communications Project Specialist
Marcy Shanti

Managing Editor
Terry Somerson

Development Editor
Vicki Van Ausdall

Copy Editor
Vicki Van Ausdall

Technical Editors
Larry Biggs
Roger Dayton
Todd Grant
Craig Oler
Howard Olson
Jill Ostrie
Jan Provan

Editorial Assistant
Jean Leitner

Production Director
Beth Jenkins

Supervisor of Project Coordination
Cindy L. Phipps

Supervisor of Page Layout
Kathie S. Schnorr

Production Systems Specialist
Steve Peake

Pre-Press Coordination
Tony Augsburger
Patricia R. Reynolds
Theresa Sánchez-Baker

Media/Archive Coordination
Leslie Popplewell
Michael Wilkey

Project Coordinator
Valery Bourke

Graphics Coordination
Shelley Lea
Gina Scott
Carla Radzikinas

Production Staff
Dominique DeFelice
Mark Owens
Laura Puranen
Anna Rohrer

Proofreaders
Melissa D. Buddendeck
Christine Meloy Beck
Gwenette Gaddis
Dwight Ramsey
Carl Saff
Robert Springer

Indexer
Richard T. Evans

Cover Design
Archer Design

Cover Photographer
Richard Elkins

About the Author

Kelley J. P. Lindberg, a Certified Novell Engineer (CNE), joined Novell in 1986. As senior project manager, she has managed projects such as NetWare 3.12, NetWare 4.1, and other Novell products. She has also written four other books about NetWare products, including the award-winning *Novell's Guide to Managing Small NetWare Networks*. She lives in Salt Lake City, Utah.

For Andy

Acknowledgments

With a final digital flourish, I click the Send button on my e-mail, and this book's creation process comes to a close. As with every book I've written, this one has been an adventure that has taught me more than I thought I had the time to learn, and not just about NetWare 4.1. I've met new people, tapped into new sources, and explored the boundaries of those pesky physical limitations of time. (Twenty-four hours in a day is a woefully short period of time.)

This is always my favorite part of writing a book — when I get to thank the people who helped me get through the last few months.

First, genuine thanks go to Novell, for allowing me to spend the last decade of my life helping make NetWare the most superior networking system in the world. I also thank Novell for allowing me to spend my so-called spare time writing about NetWare products.

Next, I want to thank the people at IDG Books, who somehow managed to get my book edited and produced while simultaneously setting up a new department and partnership with Novell Press. Vicki Van Ausdall, my editor, is probably one of the best editors I've worked with in quite some time. I wish her well in her new venture. Thanks also go to Anne Hamilton for working out the contract details, David Kolodney for knowing I had another book in me, Carolyn Welch for tying up the loose editing ends, and Ron Hull for putting up with all the e-mails.

Rose Kearsley, at Novell Press, deserves my thanks for her encouragement and enthusiasm (as well as my congratulations on the successful completion of her own project — a beautiful baby boy). Colleen Bluhm and Marcy Shanti also helped me with their encouragement and quick attention to details.

A huge vote of appreciation goes to Doug Hascall and Cindy Eckerman at the Compaq-Novell Enterprise Computing Partnership, who supplied me with a couple of great machines (a Proliant and a Prosignia VS) to help with my research. In addition, they sent me a copy of Compaq's SmartStart package, which includes NetWare 4.1 and other software products, and I was impressed with their implementation of NetWare 4.1's installation program. Thanks again to everyone at Compaq.

My technical reviewers for this book were terrific. First, I want to thank Howard Olson. As always, he came through with patience, answers, suggestions, and a ready sense of humor whenever I showed up at his door. Despite the fact that he was already working long hours on his own project, he still found time to review several key chapters for me, as well as supply me with the occasional doughnut, poster, or other motivational prop.

Craig Oler is another friend and technical expert who helped ensure that I wasn't straying from the mark in several chapters. Jan Provan, Jill Ostrie, Todd Grant, Roger Dayton, and Larry Biggs also helped keep me honest by graciously reviewing chapters in their respective areas of expertise. This book is much stronger for all of their efforts, and I can't thank them enough.

Of course, I am very grateful to my friends and family, who think I've chosen an odd way to spend my evenings and weekends, but who put up with me anyway. Above all, I want to thank my husband, Andy, for being the best thing that ever happened to me.

(IDG Books Worldwide would like to give special thanks to Patrick J. McGovern, founder of International Data Group, who made this book possible.)

Preface

As the administrator of a NetWare 4.1 network, you are responsible for ensuring that the network is installed correctly and runs smoothly. To do this, you may arm yourself with a variety of information sources: manuals, online documentation, magazines, books, and maybe even the phone numbers of a few knowledgeable friends. Because there is so much flexibility and functionality built into NetWare 4.1, there is a tremendous amount of information available to help you manage your network.

Sometimes, however, all you really want is a quick way to find just the information you need. You don't need a full-scale discussion of every aspect of managing the network. You don't want to wade through stacks of magazines or hypertext your way through two dozen manuals to find the information you know you saw once before. What you really want is a brief refresher, if necessary, and instant access to the command, utility, syntax, or parameter setting you want. This book was written with you in mind.

Filled with lists, tables, and installation checklists, this handbook will be a vital tool in your administrator's bag of tricks. The Instant Access pages at the beginning of each chapter will help you immediately identify the utilities or commands you use to complete a specific task. If you, like most other busy network administrators, don't have a lot of time to spend looking for information, you'll want to keep this book handy.

What You Need to Know

This book is designed to provide quick-reference access to essential data and facts about setting up, reconfiguring, managing, and troubleshooting your NetWare 4.1 network. While the explanations provided throughout the book equip you with the basic concepts behind each NetWare feature, you should be somewhat familiar with how a NetWare 4.1 network operates.

You should also have access to the online documentation that came with your NetWare 4.1 operating system, in case you need more detailed instructions or explanations of concepts that are unfamiliar to you.

You should also be familiar with the operating systems that run on the workstations you'll be maintaining, such as DOS, Windows, OS/2, or Macintosh System.

Using Windows-Based vs. DOS-Based NetWare Utilities

In many cases, NetWare 4.1 provides you with more than one way to complete the same task, usually by supplying you with two utilities: one that runs in DOS, sometimes referred to as a character-based utility, and one that runs in Windows, often called a GUI (graphical user interface) utility.

The primary utility that network administrators use to manage a NetWare 4.1 network is the NetWare Administrator utility, which runs in Windows. There is a DOS-based utility, called NETADMIN, which allows you to perform many of the same tasks as the NetWare Administrator utility. However, NetWare Administrator has more features than NETADMIN, and because of its graphical interface, NetWare Administrator can be easier to use in some situations. In addition, due to conventional memory limitations, NETADMIN may have difficulty working with NDS Directories that contain several thousand objects in a single context. Therefore, most people prefer to use the NetWare Administrator instead. For this reason, NETADMIN is not discussed in this book.

What This Book Contains

All of the major components of NetWare 4.1 are explained in the chapters and appendices of this book.

- Chapter 1 describes the network topologies and network cabling architectures that you can use when setting up a NetWare 4.1 network.
- Chapter 2 explains how to install a NetWare 4.1 server, and how to upgrade a server from a previous version of NetWare.
- Chapter 3 discusses the various ways you can manage, maintain, and monitor the performance of a NetWare 4.1 server and its storage devices.
- Chapter 4 describes how to install and upgrade network workstations running DOS, Windows, OS/2, or Windows NT.
- Chapter 5 provides an overview of NetWare Directory Services (NDS), including explanations of how to set up and manage NDS objects, bindery services, NDS partitions and replicas, and NetSync. It also explains how to merge NDS trees and how to troubleshoot your NDS setup.

- Chapter 6 includes instructions for creating and managing users and groups on the network. It describes how to create a user template to simplify the creation of users. It also explains how to set up login scripts and menus to automatically set up your users' access to network directories and applications.

- Chapter 7 covers the various security tools provided in NetWare 4.1, which you can use to make sure your network is as secure as you need it to be.

- Chapter 8 discusses file management, including tips on how to plan the directory structure, conserve the server's disk space, manage volumes, back up and restore files, and protect databases using NetWare's Transactional Tracking System (TTS). It also covers the utilities you can use to work with files and directories, and explains features such as data migration and file compression.

- Chapter 9 covers both the Quick Setup and the Custom methods for setting up NetWare print services.

- Chapter 10 explains how to connect Macintosh workstations to your NetWare 4.1 network, as well as how users can share PC and Macintosh files.

- Chapter 11 provides an overview of the protocols supported by NetWare 4.1 (IPX, TCP/IP, and AppleTalk) and explains the utilities you can use to configure them.

- Chapter 12 explains how to set up and use the online documentation that came with your NetWare 4.1 network operating system.

- Chapter 13 provides tips on disaster planning and recovery.

- Appendix A lists all the available parameters that can be used in each workstation's NET.CFG file.

- Appendix B lists all the available SET parameters that can be used to modify your server's performance.

- Appendix C describes a variety of additional resources you can turn to for more help or information (such as user groups, Novell's Internet site, Novell publications, and so on).

- Appendix D supplies you with a variety of worksheets you may want to use to document information about your network, such as its hardware inventory, configuration settings, and backup schedules.

This book also includes a glossary and an index to help you quickly get to the information you need.

Contents at a Glance

Table of Contents

Chapter 5 • Managing NetWare Directory Services 117

CHAPTER 1

Network Topologies and Architectures

Planning the Network Architecture

- Ethernet, currently the most common network architecture, provides good performance at a reasonable cost, and it is relatively easy to install.
- ARCnet is a relatively simple and inexpensive network architecture. However, its performance is not generally as fast as that of other network architectures.
- Token Ring generally works well in situations that involve heavy data traffic because Token Ring is reliable. It is also fairly easy to install, but it is more expensive than either ARCnet or Ethernet networks.
- AppleTalk networks can run on several different network architectures: LocalTalk, EtherTalk, and TokenTalk. AppleTalk, a networking protocol suite built into every Macintosh, provides peer-to-peer networking capabilities between all Macintoshes and Apple hardware.
- High-speed network architectures, the newest generation of architectures, are capable of supporting speeds up to 100 Mbps. Most of these architectures use fiber-optic cabling.

The format in which a network is laid out is called its *topology*. For example, a network can be laid out in a bus format (see Figure 1.1), a ring format (see Figure 1.2), or a star format (see Figure 1.3). Variations or combinations of these topologies are also commonly used.

The cabling scheme that connects the nodes together into these topologies can be called the *network cabling architecture*, or just network architecture. The most common network architectures are Ethernet, ARCnet, Token Ring, and AppleTalk. High-speed architectures, such as Fiber Distributed Data Interface (FDDI), Thomas Conrad Network System (TCNS), Fast Ethernet, and ARCnet Plus, are becoming more and more prevalent.

Because each of these network architectures handles data in a different way, each requires a unique type of network hardware.

FIGURE 1.1

Bus Topology

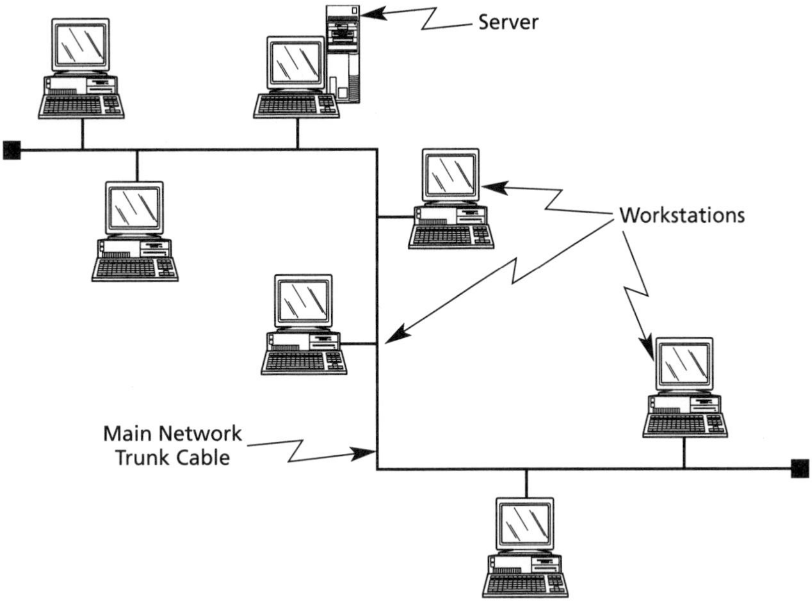

FIGURE 1.2

Ring Topology

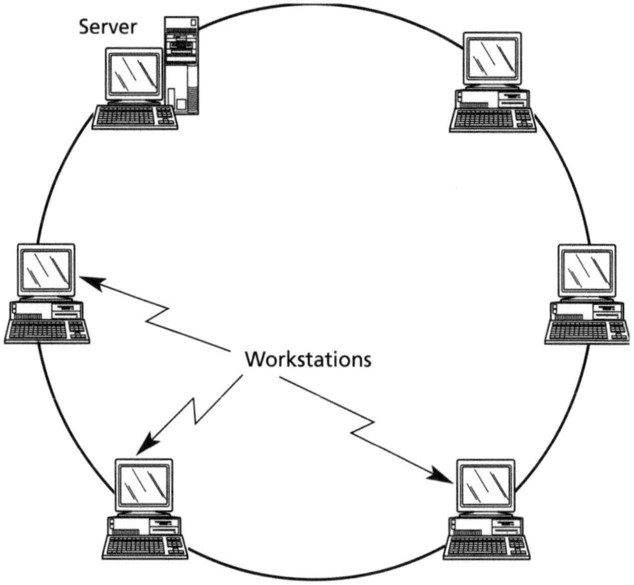

FIGURE 1.3

Star Topology

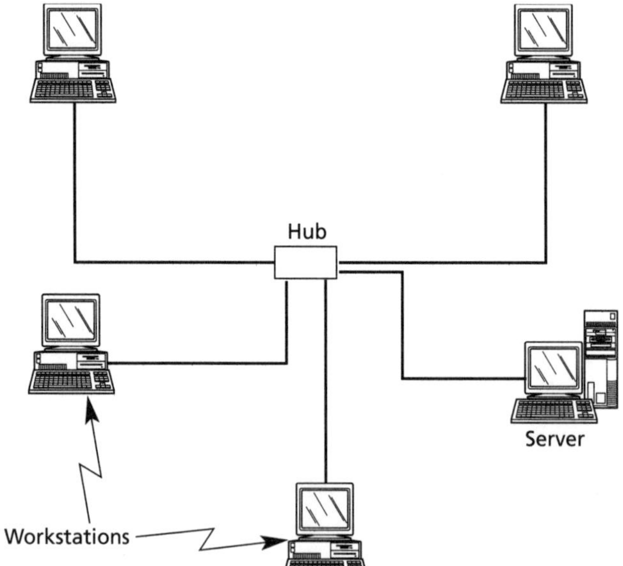

Network Hardware — An Overview

Networking hardware consists of the following:

- *Network boards.* These special circuit boards, installed in each workstation or server, connect the computer to the network cables.
- *Cables.* Network cables connect each workstation and server to the network. These cables can be coaxial (also called coax), unshielded twisted-pair, shielded twisted-pair, or fiber-optic. The type of cable you use depends on the restrictions of the topology you install.
- *Connectors and terminators.* Each type of cable requires different types of connectors to join cables together or connect them to other pieces of hardware (such as network boards). Some types of cable also require special connectors known as terminators to be attached to the open ends of any cables. Terminators keep stray signals from causing interference on the network.
- *Hubs.* Some network architectures require that the cables attached to workstations all feed into a separate piece of hardware before being connected to the main network cable. *Passive hubs* simply gather the signals and relay them. *Active hubs* actually boost the signals before sending them on their way. (The terms active hub and concentrator are often used interchangeably.)

Ethernet Network Architecture

Ethernet is currently the most commonly used network architecture. Ethernet is relatively easy to install at a moderate cost. Because it has been so widely used for many years, its technology has been well tested. Ethernet networks can use either bus or star topologies.

There are several variants of Ethernet, each of which package *data packets* (units of information packaged into a sort of electronic envelope and sent across the network) in different ways. These different types of Ethernet packet formats are called *frame types.* In most cases, a given network will support only one Ethernet frame type. However, NetWare allows you to support more than one frame type by configuring the LAN driver for the server's network board to recognize two or more types.

ETHERNET FRAME TYPES

The four Ethernet frame types are shown in Table 1.1.

TABLE 1.1

Ethernet Frame Types

FRAME TYPE	DESCRIPTION
Ethernet II	This is the original "official" Ethernet frame type. It is used on networks that use AppleTalk Phase 1 addressing (explained in Chapter 10) or TCP/IP, and on networks that communicate with DEC minicomputers.
Ethernet 802.3	This is the default frame type supported by NetWare 3.11 and earlier versions of NetWare. This frame type can support either a bus or star topology. It is also called the *raw frame type*, because it uses only the defined 802.3 header and doesn't include the standard header extensions defined by the 802.2 and SNAP variants of Ethernet. Ethernet 802.3 is not a standard IEEE 802.2 frame type, and it was used primarily by Novell in earlier versions of NetWare. Don't use this frame type on networks that use protocols besides IPX.
Ethernet 802.2	This frame type can support either a bus or star topology. Because it is an IEEE standard, NetWare 3.12 and NetWare 4.1 use this frame type by default. If you are upgrading a NetWare 3.11 (or earlier) network to NetWare 4.1, or adding a NetWare 4.1 server to an existing 3.11 network, you have two choices. You can either make the LAN drivers in the 4.1 server recognize both frame types, or you will have to change all LAN drivers in the older servers and workstations so they will recognize 802.2 instead of 802.3. The latter solution is preferred because it allows for easier growth in the future and it doesn't generate as much packet traffic on the network as supporting two frame types. Ethernet 802.2 packet frames have both the 802.3 header and the 802.2 header extension.

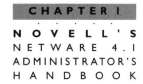

TABLE 1.1

Ethernet Frame Types (continued)

FRAME TYPE	DESCRIPTION
Ethernet SNAP	This is a variant of the 802.2 packet format. It is used on networks that have workstations using protocols such as AppleTalk Phase 2 addressing (explained in Chapter 10). Ethernet SNAP packet frames have both the 802.3 header and the SNAP header extension. SNAP stands for Sub-Network Access Protocol.

ETHERNET CABLE OPTIONS

In an Ethernet topology, the cables that connect the machines together are laid in out a specific fashion. The cables you use will fall into three general types of functions. These are described in Table 1.2.

TABLE 1.2

Categories of Cable Functions in an Ethernet Network

CABLE'S FUNCTION	DESCRIPTION
Trunk cable	The trunk cable is the backbone of the network. All other nodes (workstations, servers, and so on) are connected to this trunk.
Drop cable	The drop cable can be used to connect a node to the trunk cable in a thick Ethernet network.
Patch cable	The patch cable can be used to connect two hubs.

How these types of cables are laid out depends on the cabling hardware (physical wiring) you select. Ethernet networks can be wired using any of the following types of physical cables:

- Thin coaxial cable (also called Thin Ethernet cable)
- Thick coaxial cable (also called Thick Ethernet cable)
- Twisted-pair cable

These types of cables are explained in the following sections.

Thin Ethernet Cable

Thin Ethernet cable is RG-58 (50-ohm) coaxial cable. It is 3/16 inch in size. It is also called ThinNet, CheaperNet, and 10Base2. Thin Ethernet cabling is more popular than Thick Ethernet cable because it is less bulky, more flexible, and relatively easy to handle.

Thin Ethernet, like most coaxial cable, is covered with PVC, so it can be run through air conditioning and heating ducts. However, PVC-covered cable cannot be used in the space between a false ceiling and the next floor (called the *plenum space*) because PVC is quite toxic if it burns. Another type of cable, called *plenum cable,* must be used in those areas.

If you use thin Ethernet, you will need the following types of hardware components:

- Ethernet network boards are necessary for each workstation and server.
- BNC barrel connectors are used to connect lengths of the trunk cable together into one trunk segment.
- BNC T-connectors are used to connect each node to the network cable.
- BNC terminators are used to terminate one end of each trunk segment.
- BNC grounded terminators are used to terminate and ground the other end of each trunk segment.
- Repeaters, if needed, regenerate the signal and pass it on to another trunk segment, thereby extending the normal limits of the network.

Thin Ethernet cable, like all cable, has limits and restrictions (described in Table 1.3) that will affect how you can set up the network.

TABLE 1.3

Limits and Restriction of Thin Ethernet Cable

NETWORK ITEM	LIMITS AND RESTRICTIONS
Trunk segments	Maximum segment length (segments can consist of several shorter cables linked with BNC barrel connectors) is 607 feet (185 meters).
	Maximum number of segments per network (linked by repeaters) is 5, for a total of 3035 feet (925 meters). Only 3 of the segments can be populated with nodes, however.
	All trunk segments must be terminated at one end and terminated and grounded at the other end.
Nodes	Maximum number of nodes per trunk segment (including repeaters, which count as nodes) is 30.
	Maximum number of nodes (including repeaters) on the entire network is 90.
	Minimum cable distance between nodes is 1.6 feet (0.5 meters).

Thick Ethernet Cable

Thick Ethernet cable is RG-8 (50-ohm) coaxial cable. It is 3/8 inch in size. It is also called ThickNet, Standard Ethernet, or 10Base5. Because Thick Ethernet cable is bulkier, stiffer, and more difficult to handle than Thin Ethernet cable, it is usually used as the trunk cable, with twisted-pair drop cables used to connect the nodes to the thick Ethernet trunk.

Thick Ethernet, like most coaxial cable, is covered with PVC, so it can be run through air conditioning and heating ducts. However, as previously mentioned, PVC-covered cable cannot be used in the space between a false ceiling and the next floor because PVC is toxic if it burns. Another type of cable, called plenum cable, must be used in those areas.

If you use thick Ethernet, you will need the following types of hardware components:

- Ethernet network boards are necessary for each workstation and server.
- N-series barrel connectors are used to connect lengths of the trunk cable together into one trunk segment.
- Transceivers (one for every node) connect the nodes' drop cables to the trunk segment.

- N-series T-connectors or vampire taps attach the transceivers to the trunk cable.
- Drop cables (also called transceiver cables) connect the network board in the node to the transceiver. The drop cable must have DIX connectors on each end.
- N-series terminators are used to terminate one end of each trunk segment.
- N-series grounded terminators are used to terminate and ground the other end of each trunk segment.
- Repeaters, if needed, regenerate the signal and pass it on to another trunk segment, thereby extending the normal limits of the network.

Thick Ethernet cable, like all cable, has limits and restrictions (described in Table 1.4) that will affect how you can set up the network.

TABLE 1.4

Limits and Restrictions of Thick Ethernet Cable

NETWORK ITEM	LIMITS AND RESTRICTIONS
Trunk segments	Maximum segment length (segments can consist of several shorter cables linked with N-series barrel connectors) is 1640 feet (500 meters).
	Maximum number of segments per network (linked by repeaters) is 5, for a total of 8200 feet (2500 meters). Only 3 of the segments can be populated with nodes, however.
	All trunk segments must be terminated at one end and terminated and grounded at the other end.
Nodes	Maximum number of nodes per trunk segment (including repeaters, which count as nodes) is 100.
	Maximum number of nodes (including repeaters) on the entire network is 300.
	Every node must have its own drop cable connected to its own transceiver to connect to the trunk.
	Minimum cable distance between transceivers is 8 feet (2.5 meters).
	Maximum drop cable length between node and transceiver is 165 feet (50 meters).

Twisted-Pair Cable

There are two types of twisted-pair cabling: unshielded and shielded. *Unshielded twisted-pair* cable is commonly used as telephone wire. *Shielded twisted-pair* uses heavier-gauge wire and is protected with insulation and foil shielding.

Unshielded twisted-pair, although commonly found in abundance in buildings, is a poorer choice for network cabling because it can be very susceptible to electromagnetic interference from sources such as fluorescent lights, elevators, and telephone ring signals. This type of cable is also called UTP Ethernet or 10BaseT.

Shielded twisted-pair is a better choice for networks because of its extra insulation and foil shielding.

If you use twisted-pair cabling, you will need the following types of hardware components:

- Ethernet network boards are necessary for each workstation and server.
- Wiring hubs can be used to connect nodes to the network. All nodes must be connected to a wiring hub, either directly (through a cable) or through a wallplate or concentrator. The maximum distance between a node and a wiring hub is 330 feet (100 meters). *Stand-alone hubs* are devices with their own power supply. *Peer hubs* are boards that can be installed in one of the computers on the network and physically connected to that computer's network board. A twisted-pair network can have up to four linked wiring hubs.
- Twisted-pair cables connect the nodes to wiring hubs.
- An external concentrator, if needed, connects nodes that use coaxial or fiber-optic cable to the network.
- Punch-down blocks, if desired, make cable termination easier to change.
- RJ-45 connectors are used to connect the cables to wallplates, network boards, and wiring hubs.

ARCnet Network Architecture

ARCnet has been used for many years and is a relatively simple and inexpensive network architecture. Because its performance is not generally as fast as other network architectures (its transmission rate is only 2.5 Mbps, or megabytes per second), it is typically used in smaller networks. ARCnet Plus is a newer version of ARCnet; its transmission rate is 20 Mbps.

ARCnet can use either a star or a bus topology, but the star topology usually provides better performance. ARCnet can use coaxial (usually RG-62 with 93-ohm impedance, although others can be used), twisted-pair, or fiber-optic cable.

If you use ARCnet, you will need the following types of hardware components:

- ARCnet network boards are necessary for each workstation and server. These boards have jumpers (pins) that you must set to specify an address for the node in which the card will be installed. Each node must have a unique address (from 1 to 255). You must also set the interrupt (IRQ) and I/O address on each board. Most ARCnet boards have a low-impedance transceiver on them, which is used for a star topology. Some boards have high-impedance transceivers; these are best for a bus topology.

- If twisted-pair or fiber-optic cable is used, a hub or adapter must connect that cable to a coaxial cable.

- A terminator must terminate the last node in the ARCnet network (93-ohm for coaxial networks and 105-ohm for twisted-pair networks).

- Terminators must be attached to all unused ports on a passive hub.

- BNC connectors are used to connect lengths of coaxial cable together. Twisted-pair cables are connected using either RJ-11/RJ-45 connectors or the D-shell connectors used for standard serial and parallel ports.

- Active links are devices used to connect two cable segments that both have high-impedance network boards connected to them.

- Baluns (a piece of hardware that adjusts impedances in order to connect different types of cable) are used to connect coaxial and twisted-pair cables together.

- Wiring hubs can be used to connect nodes to the network. Active hubs have their own power supply, and they clean and boost the signal to extend the network past its normal limits. Passive hubs collect and relay signals, but do not boost them or extend the network. Passive hubs cannot be connected to other passive hubs in a series; they must be connected to an active hub or server. *Intelligent hubs* are active hubs that also monitor the status of a connection. (Passive hubs cannot be used on a high-impedance network.)

ARCnet cable, like all cable, has limits and restrictions (described in Table 1.5) that will affect how you can set up the network.

TABLE 1.5

Limits and Restrictions of ARCnet Cable

NETWORK ITEM	LIMITS AND RESTRICTIONS
Hubs	Active hubs must be within 2000 feet (610 meters) of another active hub or a node.
	Passive hubs must be within 100 feet (30 meters) of an active hub.
	Passive hubs cannot be used on a high-impedance network.
Cabling	The cabling cannot loop back on itself.
	Each cable segment must be terminated at both ends by either a terminator or a hub.
	Maximum length of a cable segment is as follows: Coaxial is 1500 – 2000 feet (450-600 meters). Unshielded twisted-pair is 330 feet (100 meters). Shielded twisted-pair is 660 feet (200 meters).
	Maximum number of cable segments in a series is 3 (making the maximum length 1000 feet for coaxial and 450 feet for unshielded twisted-pair).
	Maximum length of the entire network, end to end, is 20,000 feet (6000 meters).

(continued)

TABLE 1.5

Limits and Restrictions of ARCnet Cable (continued)

NETWORK ITEM	LIMITS AND RESTRICTIONS
Nodes	Maximum number of nodes in a series with no intervening hubs is 8 for coaxial, 10 for twisted-pair. Maximum number of nodes on the network (including active hubs, which count as a node) is 255. On a high-impedance network, nodes must be connected to T-connectors that have at least 3.25 feet (1 meter) of cable distance between them.

Token Ring Network Architecture

A Token Ring network is cabled like a star, but it acts like a ring. Data flows from workstation to workstation around the ring. Because the network is cabled like a star, however, the data ends up going through the central point between each workstation on the trip around the ring.

Token Ring networks can run on twisted-pair (either shielded or unshielded) or fiber-optic cables. They generally work well in situations that involve heavy data traffic because Token Ring is reliable. It is also fairly easy to install, but it is more expensive than either ARCnet or Ethernet networks.

Unshielded twisted-pair cabling is a poorer choice for network cabling because it can be very susceptible to electromagnetic interference from sources such as fluorescent lights, elevators, and telephone ring signals.

Shielded twisted-pair is a better choice for networks because of its extra insulation and foil shielding.

There are two different versions of Token Ring — one that supports a 4 Mbps transmission speed and one that supports 16 Mbps. A single network can run only one or the other, but networks of differing speeds can be connected through a bridge or router.

If you use Token Ring, you will need the following types of hardware components:

- Token Ring network boards are necessary for each workstation and server.

- *Multistation Access Units* (MAUs) are wiring concentrators. Nodes connect to these MAUs, which are in turn are connected to other MAUs to form the ring. The wiring inside a MAU forms a ring of the attached nodes.

- Cabling is necessary to connect the MAUs in the main ring.

- Patch cables are used to connect the nodes to the MAUs.

- Repeaters, if needed, regenerate the signal and pass it on, thereby extending the normal limits of the network.

IBM defined different types of cabling for use in Token Ring networks. These cabling types are as follows:

- Type 1 cable is shielded twisted-pair cable. It has two pairs of 22-gauge solid wire, and can supply data-quality transmission. It can be used for the main ring (similar to a trunk cable in an Ethernet network) or to connect nodes to MAUs.

- Type 2 cable is a hybrid cable, containing four pairs of unshielded 22-gauge solid wire for voice transmission, and two pairs of shielded 22-gauge solid wire for data transmission.

- Type 3 cable is unshielded twisted-pair cable, which is only required to support voice-quality transmission. It can have two, three, or four pairs of 22-gauge or 24-gauge solid wire, with each pair having at least two twists per foot. This cable is not recommended for Token Ring networks.

- Type 4 cable is undefined.

- Type 5 cable is fiber-optic cable, with two glass fiber cores. Type 5 cables are used to cable the main ring in a Token Ring network and can also be used to extend the distance between MAUs or to connect network segments between buildings.

- Type 6 cable is shielded twisted-pair cable, with two pairs of 26-gauge stranded wire. Type 5 cables are commonly used as an adapter cable to connect a node to a MAU.

- Type 7 cable is undefined.
- Type 8 cable is shielded twisted-pair cable, with two pairs of flat, 26-gauge solid wire. It is designed to run underneath carpeting.
- Type 9 cable is shielded twisted-pair cable, with two pairs of 26-gauge solid or stranded wire. It is covered with a plenum jacket and is used to go between floors.

Token Ring cable, like all cable, has limits and restrictions (described in Table 1.6) that will affect how you can set up the network.

TABLE 1.6

Limits and Restrictions of Token Ring Cable

NETWORK ITEM	LIMITS AND RESTRICTIONS
MAUs	Maximum number of MAUs on a network that uses Type 1 or 2 cabling is 33. Maximum number of MAUs on a network that uses type 6 or 9 cabling is 12.
Cabling	Maximum distance between a node and a MAU is as follows: For Type 1 and 2 cable: 330 feet (100 meters) For Type 6 and 9 cable: 220 feet (66 meters) For unshielded twisted-pair: 150 feet (45 meters) Maximum distance between MAUs is as follows: For Type 1 and 2 cable: 660 feet (200 meters) For Type 6 cable: 140 feet (45 meters) For unshielded twisted-pair: 400 feet (120 meters) For fiber-optic cable: 0.6 miles (1 km) Maximum number of cable segments (separated by repeaters) in a series is 3. All cable segments must be terminated at one end and terminated and grounded at the other.
Nodes	Maximum number of nodes is as follows: For networks using Type 1 and 2 cable: 260 For networks using Type 6 and 9 cable: 96 For networks using unshielded twisted-pair: 72 Minimum cable distance between a node and a MAU is 8 feet (2.5 meters).

AppleTalk Network Architectures

AppleTalk is the networking protocol suite developed by Apple Computers. It provides peer-to-peer networking capabilities between all Macintoshes and Apple hardware. AppleTalk capability is automatically built into every Macintosh.

AppleTalk can run with several types of architectures:

- LocalTalk was Apple's built-in architecture in most older Macintoshes. A Macintosh doesn't need a separate network board to communicate over LocalTalk cables, but does need a separate network board to use other topologies.
- EtherTalk is Apple's implementation of Ethernet. EtherTalk Phase 1 was based on the Ethernet II version of Ethernet. EtherTalk Phase 2 is based on the Ethernet 802.3 version. EtherTalk Phase 2 has replaced LocalTalk as the built-in networking architecture in most newer Macintoshes.
- TokenTalk is Apple's Token Ring implementation.
- FDDITalk is Apple's implementation of the 100 Mbps FDDI architecture.

For more information about using AppleTalk with NetWare 4.1, see Chapters 10 and 11.

High-Speed Network Architectures

Several new types of high-speed network architectures are currently being developed. These architectures are capable of supporting speeds up to 100 Mbps. Most of them use fiber-optic cabling. Because fiber-optic technology is relatively new and still evolving, most knowledgeable people in the industry recommend hiring a qualified, experienced vendor to take care of the network hardware installation. It's also important to get your vendor to guarantee that the components it installs will work together.

The following are some of the new high-speed architectures that are gaining in popularity:

- Fiber Distributed Data Interface (FDDI) is a new network architecture for using fiber-optic cables at very high speeds. It supports speeds of up to 100 Mbps, and it uses a dual-ring topology in which data can travel in opposite directions.
- Thomas Conrad Network System (TCNS) can use coaxial, shielded twisted-pair, or fiber-optic cabling. It, too, can support speeds of up to 100 Mbps.
- Fast Ethernet is being designed to transmit 100 Mbps over unshielded twisted-pair cable.
- ARCnet Plus, released by Datapoint, is a 20 Mbps version of ARCnet. It is backward compatible with regular ARCnet, and it can use the same RG-62 cable.

CHAPTER 2

Installing and Upgrading Servers

Installing

- To install a new server using default options (the quick and easy way), run INSTALL from the *NetWare 4.1 Operating System* CD-ROM and select the Simple Installation of NetWare 4.1 option.
- To install a new server using advanced features, run INSTALL from the *NetWare 4.1 Operating System* CD-ROM and select the Custom Installation of NetWare 4.1 option.

Upgrading from NetWare 4.0x

- To upgrade a NetWare 4.0x server, use INSTALL.NLM and choose the Upgrade to NetWare 3.1x or 4.x option.

Upgrading from NetWare 3.1x

- To upgrade an existing server without moving any data off the server, use INSTALL.NLM and choose the Upgrade to NetWare 3.1x or 4.x option. (This is the simplest upgrade option.)
- To transfer all the NetWare 3.1x server's data to a new machine on which NetWare 4.1 has already been installed, use the Across-the-Wire Migration feature of the MIGRATE workstation utility.
- To remove all the NetWare 3.1x server's data, upgrade the machine to NetWare 4.1, move the data back to the server, and then use the Same-Server Migration feature of the MIGRATE workstation utility.

Upgrading from NetWare 2.x

- To transfer all the NetWare 2.x server's data to a new machine on which NetWare 4.1 has already been installed, use the Across-the-Wire Migration feature of the MIGRATE workstation utility.

- To remove all the NetWare 2.x server's data, upgrade the machine to NetWare 4.1, move the data back to the server, and then use the Same-Server Migration feature of the MIGRATE workstation utility.

- To upgrade an existing NetWare 2.x server without moving any data off the server, use the In-Place Upgrade. The In-Place Upgrade is more hazardous because the file system itself must be changed, and there is some risk to existing files. An In-Place Upgrade requires the 2XUPGRDE utility, followed by INSTALL.NLM. Because the other two methods are more secure, and because this option is seldom used, the In-Place Upgrade isn't covered in this book.

How you install your NetWare 4.1 server depends on whether you are installing a new server or upgrading one from an earlier version of NetWare. This chapter discusses four different scenarios:

- Installing a new server
- Upgrading from NetWare 4.0x
- Upgrading from NetWare 3.1x
- Upgrading from NetWare 2.x

Before you begin installing or upgrading your server, you need to make sure you're prepared with all the necessary information, as described in the next section.

Preparing to Install or Upgrade a Server

Regardless of whether you are upgrading or installing a new server, there are several decisions you have to make about your server. You may want to refer to the worksheets "Server Installation and Configuration" and "Volumes" in Appendix D to help you plan your server's installation. If you answer all the questions on these worksheets before you tackle the actual installation procedure, the process may go more smoothly.

Before starting the installation or upgrade, you should have the following information about the server:

- *The server's name.* The name can be between 2 and 47 characters long, using letters, numbers, hyphens, or underscores.
- *The server's memory.* Theoretically, a NetWare 4.1 server should have a minimum of 8MB of RAM, but a minimum of 16MB is greatly preferable for most situations. Depending on the size of the network (the number of servers, number of users on the server, total disk space on the server, and so on), you may want even more memory.

- *The server's internal IPX network number.* One will be generated randomly for you, or you can specify your own. Each server on the network must have a unique internal IPX network number. (IPX, for Internetwork Packet Exchange, is NetWare's native network protocol.)

- *The server's Directory tree.* You must know the name of the Directory tree into which the server will be installed. For more information about NetWare Directory Services, see Chapter 5.

- *The server's type of time synchronization.* You may have Single Reference, Reference, Primary, or Secondary time servers. By default, the installation program will make the first server in the tree into a Single Reference time server, and all others will be Secondary time servers. For more information about time synchronization services, see Chapter 3.

- *The server's time zone.* You'll need to know the acronym for the server's time zone and whether that time zone supports Daylight Saving Time.

- *The server's location (name context) in the Directory tree.* Before you install the server, be sure you are familiar with NetWare Directory Services and how you want your network to be laid out in the Directory tree. In the Custom Installation, you'll need to specify to which Organization object or Organizational Unit object this server belongs. In the Simple Installation, you are simply asked for the name of your organization (for instance, your company name). This Organization object name will become the tree name, as well. For more information about NetWare Directory Services, see Chapter 5.

You should also know the following information before starting the installation or upgrade:

- *The protocol you will use on the network.* See Chapter 11 for more information about protocols. IPX/SPX is the default and is required. TCP/IP and AppleTalk are optional.

- *The types of network boards you will install in the server.* You'll need to know the type of board, the name of its corresponding LAN driver, its settings, and the frame type you will use (such as Ethernet 802.2, Ethernet 802.3, Ethernet SNAP, Ethernet II, Token Ring, or Token Ring SNAP). NetWare 4.1's default Ethernet frame type is Ethernet 802.2. For TCP/IP only, you will also need the board's IP address and subnet mask.

- *The amount of hard disk space you will allocate for a DOS disk partition.* The DOS partition is the portion of the hard disk that is reserved for DOS system files and other DOS files that you want to store on the server. The rest of the disk becomes a NetWare partition, which stores the NetWare files and network data. A 15MB minimum DOS partition is recommended, but a rule of thumb is to add 1MB to the DOS partition for every MB of server RAM installed. The first hard disk will have a DOS partition and a NetWare partition. All other disks can have only one NetWare partition each. (Each NetWare disk partition can have up to eight volumes on it, however.) You should create the DOS disk partition before running the installation program. (The installation process will create the partition for you if you want, but it's generally easier to do it yourself so that you can avoid having to reinstall the CD-ROM drive's drivers and other configuration information.)

- *Whether or not you want to mirror or duplex the hard disks.* Disk mirroring and duplexing let two disks store identical copies of network files so that if one disk fails, the other will keep working. Disk mirroring mirrors two disks. Disk duplexing mirrors the disks plus uses duplicate disk controller boards and cables. (For more information about disk mirroring and duplexing, see Chapter 3.)

- *Whether you want to install SFT III.* SFT III lets you set up two identical servers so that if one fails, the other continues to operate. For information on how to install SFT III, see Chapter 3.

- *The name of the disk controller board.* You must know the disk controller board's settings and the name of its corresponding disk driver.

- *The size of NetWare volume SYS.* A volume named SYS is mandatory for NetWare system and utility files. You should allocate at least 75MB of hard disk space for SYS, or if you plan to install the NetWare online documentation, at least 135MB for SYS.

- *The size and names of any additional NetWare volumes.* It's often a good idea to reserve SYS for NetWare files only, and create a separate volume for regular applications and data files. In addition, if you will be supporting Macintosh files, you may want to create a volume just for those files.

  If you choose to let NetWare create your volumes automatically, NetWare will assign the entire NetWare disk partition on the first hard disk to SYS. Each additional disk will have its own volume named VOL1, VOL2, and so on. You must choose the Custom Installation if you want the option of changing the sizes and names of the volumes before NetWare creates them. If you want to create more volumes than just SYS, you should use the Custom Installation.

- *Whether you want to use file compression on any volumes.* File compression can save up to 60 percent of your hard disk space by compressing unused files. By default, all NetWare volumes are enabled for file compression. However, just because a volume is enabled for compression doesn't mean the files will be compressed — you must turn on file compression for specific directories. For more information about file compression, see Chapter 8.

- *Each volume's block size and whether you want the volume to use block suballocation.* A *block* is a unit of disk space that is allocated to store a file. *Block suballocation* divides a block into 512-byte suballocation blocks, so that several smaller files can share a single block. By default, block suballocation is turned on. (For more information about block suballocation, see Chapter 8.) The default block size depends on the volume's size, as shown in the following list.

Volume Size	**Block Size**
0 to 31MB	4 or 8K
32 to 149MB	16K
150 to 499MB	32K
500MB or more	64K

- *Whether you want data migration turned on.* Data migration lets little-used files be migrated off the server's hard disk onto an external storage device, such as a tape, hard disk, or optical disk. These files are automatically "demigrated" back onto the server's hard disk when a user accesses them. For more information about data migration, see Chapter 8.
- *Whether you want any volumes to support non-DOS files.* Non-DOS files include Macintosh, Unix, or OS/2 extended files. Because non-DOS files support longer file names and different file formats, you must load a special type of program, called a *name space module,* on the server. Then you must assign that name space to the volume that you want to store those files.

Installing a New Server

If you are setting up a new NetWare 4.1 server, you have two choices. You can either use the Simple Installation, which will set up a basic NetWare server with default choices and a simple NetWare Directory Services implementation, or you can choose the Custom Installation, which will let you configure more aspects of your network.

SIMPLE NETWARE 4.1 INSTALLATION

The Simple Installation method will work very well in most smaller networks (fewer than 100 users). If you have a larger network, you probably want to use the Custom Installation to specify more details about your server and volumes.

The Simple Installation's Default Settings

When you use the Simple Installation procedure to install NetWare 4.1, the server and NetWare Directory Services are set up with the following default characteristics. If you want different characteristics than these, use the Custom Installation described later in this chapter.

- The server has a name that you specify.
- The server has a randomly generated internal IPX network number.

- If this was the first server in the Directory tree, it becomes a Single Reference time server. If it was installed into an existing tree, it becomes a Secondary time server. See Chapter 3 for more information on time servers.

- The Directory tree has only one Organization object, named with your organization's name. The server, its volumes, and a user named ADMIN will be created under this Organization object. (The Organization object's name is also the name of the Directory tree.) For more information about NetWare Directory Services, see Chapter 5.

- The server is set up to use the protocol IPX/SPX.

- The LAN drivers you select will be bound to the network boards in the server. Ethernet boards are set to use the default frame type Ethernet 802.2. If this server is being installed into an existing network, the existing frame type will be automatically detected.

- The DOS disk partition you set up on the server's first hard disk before running the installation program still exists. (A minimum of 15MB is recommended.) The rest of the hard disk's space is created as a NetWare partition.

- Disk partitions are not set up to support disk mirroring or duplexing.

- SFT III is not installed.

- The NetWare disk partition on the server's hard disk is set up to be a single volume, named SYS. All NetWare files are copied into this volume, and all other applications and data files are stored in this volume as well.

- The server supports DOS files by default.

- File compression is enabled for all volumes, but it is not turned on for any directories yet. For more information about file compression, see Chapter 8.

- Block suballocation is turned on, and block sizes are set to the default size, which is based on the volume's size. (See the preceding table.) For more information about block suballocation, see Chapter 8.

- Data migration is turned off. For more information about data migration, see Chapter 8.

The Simple Installation Procedure

The following is a checklist of the steps you perform for the Simple Installation of NetWare 4.1.

1 • Set up the server hardware.

a. Install and configure the network boards in the server. Refer to the network board manufacturer's documentation for configuration instructions.

b. Using the DOS FDISK and FORMAT commands, create a DOS disk partition of at least 15MB. Leave the rest of the disk space free.

c. Install the CD-ROM drive as a DOS device on the server, following the manufacturer's instructions.

d. Using the DOS DATE and TIME commands, verify that the computer's time and date are set correctly, and change if necessary.

2 • Install the NetWare operating system.

a. Insert the *NetWare 4.1 Operating System* CD-ROM into the computer's CD-ROM drive.

b. Change to the CD-ROM drive's letter (usually D), and enter the following command:

```
INSTALL
```

c. If you are using the International version of the NetWare 4.1 CD-ROM, choose the language you want to use.

d. Choose NetWare Server Installation, choose NetWare 4.1, and then choose Simple Installation of NetWare 4.1.

e. Enter a name for this server.

f. In some cases, you may be asked to specify the country code, code page, and keyboard mapping for your server. (To select these, press Enter and choose the correct selections from the lists that appear.) If you're using United States English DOS, you usually won't see this screen.

3 • Select the disk drivers for your server's hard disk controller board and CD-ROM drive controller board, and specify their settings.

4 • Select the LAN drivers for your server's network boards, and specify their settings.

5 • Select whether to access the CD-ROM as a DOS device or a NetWare volume. To avoid a possible driver conflict, you should allow INSTALL to mount the CD-ROM as a NetWare volume. If the keyboard locks up, repeat the installation and choose Continue Accessing the CD-ROM via DOS option instead.

6 • If you are asked whether to delete any existing nonbootable partitions, select Yes.

7 • Insert the License diskette when prompted, and the installation program will begin copying files to the server.

8 • If you are installing this server into an existing NetWare Directory tree, select the correct tree. (To create a new tree, press Insert.) If this is the first server in the tree, select "Yes, this is the first NetWare 4 server."

9 • Select the time zone in which this server will exist.

10 • If this is the first server in the Directory tree, enter the name of your organization (such as your company name). Keep the name short. This will become the name of your Directory tree and your only Organization object.

11 • Enter a password for the ADMIN user. If this is the first server in the tree, enter any password you want. If this server is being installed into an existing NDS tree, type in the ADMIN password that has already been assigned.

12 • After the remaining files are copied to the server, choose Create DOS/MS Windows/OS2 Client Install Diskettes to make a set of diskettes you can use to install workstations on your network. See Chapter 4 for more information about installing workstations.

13 • If you want to install the online documentation, choose Install Online Documentation and Viewers. Then see Chapter 12 for more information about installing the NetWare online documentation and the DynaText viewers (which allow you to read the online documentation).

CUSTOM NETWARE 4.1 INSTALLATION

The Custom Installation method lets you specify exactly how your server is set up, how partitions are created and mirrored, what frame types to use, what volumes to create, and so on. The following is a checklist of the steps you perform for the Custom Installation of NetWare 4.1.

1 • Set up the server hardware.

a. Install and configure network boards in the server. Refer to the network board manufacturer's documentation for configuration instructions.

b. Using the DOS FDISK and FORMAT commands, create a DOS disk partition of at least 15MB. Leave the rest of the disk space free.

c. Install the CD-ROM drive as a DOS device on the server, following the manufacturer's instructions.

d. Using the DOS DATE and TIME commands, verify that the computer's time and date are set correctly, and change if necessary.

2 • Install the NetWare operating system.

a. Insert the *NetWare 4.1 Operating System* CD-ROM into the computer's CD-ROM drive.

b. Change to the CD-ROM drive's letter (usually D), and enter the following command:

```
INSTALL
```

c. If you are using the International version of the NetWare 4.1 CD-ROM, choose the language you want to use.

d. Choose NetWare Server Installation, choose NetWare 4.1, and then choose Custom Installation of NetWare 4.1.

e. Enter a name for this server.

f. Either accept the default IPX internal network number, or enter your own.

g. Accept or change the default destination path for the NetWare server startup (boot) files so that they are copied to the DOS partition on the server.

h. Choose the country code, code page, and keyboard mapping for your server, and then press F10 to continue. (To select these, press Enter and choose the correct selections from the lists that appear.)

i. Select the DOS file name format.

j. If you want to add any SET parameters to the server's startup files now, select Yes and enter them. Otherwise, select No.

k. Specify whether you want the AUTOEXEC.BAT file to automatically load the server (SERVER.EXE). If you do not add this command to AUTOEXEC.BAT, you will have to load the server by entering the command

```
SERVER
```

at the DOS prompt any time the server is rebooted.

3 • Select the disk drivers for your server's hard disk controller board and CD-ROM drive controller board, and specify their settings.

4 • Select the LAN drivers for your server's network boards, and specify their settings. If you want to load protocols besides IPX, choose Select/Modify Driver Parameters and Protocols, and select the protocols you want. Also specify an IP address and IP mask numbers if you are using TCP/IP. If you want to select the frame type for your LAN driver, press F3 and choose the frame type. Press F10 to save your settings.

5 • Select whether to access the CD-ROM as a DOS device or a NetWare volume. To avoid a possible driver conflict, you should allow INSTALL to mount the CD-ROM as a NetWare volume. If the keyboard locks up, repeat the installation and choose Continue Accessing the CD-ROM via DOS option instead.

6 • Press Enter to bind IPX to the LAN driver listed. (If you selected specific frame types in step 4, you may need to enter the IPX external network number for each frame type.)

7 • Select whether you want to create disk partitions automatically or manually.

- The automatic option assigns all space on the first hard disk to volume SYS, and creates separate volumes named VOL1, VOL2, and so on, on any additional disks. If you choose the automatic method, skip to step 10.

- Use the manual option if you want to set up disk mirroring, assign more than one volume per hard disk, or assign one volume to span multiple hard disks.

8 • (This step covers manual disk partitioning only.) Select the Create, Delete, and Modify Disk Partitions option, choose the disk you want to partition, and then choose Create NetWare Disk Partition. Specify the partition size and the Hot Fix redirection area.

9 • (This step covers manual disk partitioning only.) If you want to set up disk mirroring, choose Mirror and Unmirror Disk Partition Sets. Select the disk partition you want to mirror and press Enter. Then press Insert to choose an available disk partition to mirror to the first partition. Press F10 when you are finished mirroring partitions.

10 • The Manage NetWare Volumes screen shows the volumes that the installation will create for you.

- To change the volume's name, block size, or other status, select the volume, press Enter, and make the desired changes.

- To change the volume's size, press Insert or F3, select the volume, and change the volume's size.

- To add an additional volume, first decrease another volume's size, and then select the "free space" that will be shown, press Enter, and specify the new volume's information.

- To accept the proposed volumes, press F10.

11 • Insert the License diskette when prompted.

12 • Verify the source path, and press Enter so the installation program will begin copying files to the server.

13 • Select the utility sets you want to install on the server. Press Enter to select or eliminate file sets. (An "X" means the set is selected and will be copied.) Press F10 to start copying the files.

14 • If you are installing this server into an existing NetWare Directory tree, select the correct tree. (To create a new tree, press Insert.) If this is the first server in the tree, select "Yes, this is the first NetWare 4 server."

15 • Select the time zone in which this server will exist, and accept or change the time synchronization information that appears. ("DST offset from standard time" means the number of hours you are ahead or behind Greenwich Mean Time.) See Chapter 3 for more information about time synchronization.

16 • Create a name context for the server. By entering the name of the organization (such as your company) and the names of descending levels of Organizational Units (such as a division and a department), you actually create the branch of the NDS tree that will contain this server if the branch doesn't already exist. If a branch already exists, press Enter on each field and select the Organizational Unit objects you want. You can enter up to three Organizational Unit names by typing the names in the available fields. If you want to create more, use the Server Context field, and type in the server's full name, with periods delimiting each Organizational Unit.

17 • Enter a password for the ADMIN user. If this is the first server in the tree, enter any password you want. If this server is being installed into an existing tree, type in the ADMIN password that has already been assigned or enter the name and password of another User object already in the NDS tree. This User object must have enough NDS trustee rights to add the server to the context specified. See Chapter 7 for more information about NDS trustee rights.

18 • Review the STARTUP.NCF file that appears on the screen. Information you entered during the installation process so far is already placed into this file. Press F10 to save the file and continue.

19 • Review the AUTOEXEC.NCF file that appears on the screen. Information you entered during the installation process so far is already placed into this file. If necessary, add any additional commands to the AUTOEXEC.NCF file. For example, you can add a command to mount all the server's volumes automatically whenever the server boots (MOUNT ALL), and you can add commands to load NLMs (NetWare Loadable Modules) automatically. Press F10 to save the file and continue.

20 • After the remaining files are copied to the server, choose Create DOS/MS Windows/OS2 Client Install Diskettes to make a set of installation diskettes that you will need to install workstations on your network. See Chapter 4 for more information about installing workstations.

21 • If you want to install the online documentation, choose Install Online Documentation and Viewers. Then see Chapter 12 for more information about installing DynaText viewers and the NetWare online documentation.

22 • Choose any other installation options or additional products you want to install, or exit the installation program.

23 • If you want the server to be able to store Macintosh files or other non-DOS files that use longer names than DOS allows, you must load the name space on the server, and then add the name space to one or more volumes.

a. To allow the server to store Macintosh files, enter the following command:

```
LOAD MAC
```

at the server's console. To allow the server to store OS/2, NT, or Windows 95 files with long names, enter the following command:

```
LOAD OS/2
```

b. Then specify a particular volume that will store the non-DOS files by entering the ADD NAME SPACE command in the following format (replace *name* with either MAC or OS2, and replace *volumename* with the name of the volume, such as SYS or VOL1):

```
ADD NAME SPACE name TO VOLUME volumename
```

For Macintosh files, you will also need to install NetWare for Macintosh to provide Macintosh support on the network. See Chapter 10 for more information about installing NetWare for Macintosh.

24 • Make a backup of the new NetWare 4.1 server.

Upgrading from Previous Versions of NetWare

There are several methods for upgrading servers from previous versions of NetWare to NetWare 4.1. The method you use depends on the version of NetWare you're currently running and the type of data transfer method you prefer.

UPGRADING FROM NETWARE 4.0X

To upgrade an existing NetWare 4.01 or 4.02 server to NetWare 4.1, you will use INSTALL.NLM and choose the Upgrade to NetWare 3.1x or 4.x option. This is the most simple way to upgrade a server. With this option, INSTALL.NLM will copy new NetWare files and the new NetWare 4.1 operating system onto the existing server. It will also upgrade NetWare Directory Services. (This option can also be used to upgrade NetWare 3.1x servers to NetWare 4.1.)

In most cases, it's best to upgrade all NetWare 4.0x servers to NetWare 4.1 as soon as possible, to avoid maintaining a mixed network. NetWare 4.1 fixed several problems with the older versions of NetWare Directory Services, and it is easier to maintain NDS if all servers are operating at the same level.

For a checklist of steps to follow to upgrade a NetWare 4.01 or 4.02 server, see the section "Simple Upgrade."

UPGRADING FROM NETWARE 3.1X

There are three options for upgrading a NetWare 3.1x server to NetWare 4.1:

- Upgrade an existing NetWare 3.1x server to NetWare 4.1 without moving any data off the server. This is the simplest way to upgrade a server, and you use INSTALL.NLM to do it, just as you do if you are upgrading from NetWare 4.0x. See the section "Simple Upgrade" for a checklist of upgrade steps.

- Transfer all the NetWare 3.1x server's data to a new machine on which NetWare 4.1 has already been installed. This is called an Across-the-Wire Migration and it requires the MIGRATE workstation utility. See the section "Across-the-Wire Upgrade" for a checklist of upgrade steps.

- Remove all the NetWare 3.1x server's data, upgrade the machine to NetWare 4.1, and then move the data back to the server. This is called a Same-Server Migration, and it also requires the MIGRATE workstation utility. Although it is possible to use this method for NetWare 3.1x upgrades, in most cases, it is probably easier to use INSTALL.NLM (described above) and upgrade the server without moving data across the network. See the section "Same-Server Upgrade" for a checklist of upgrade steps for using the Same-Server Migration.

When upgrading a NetWare 3.11 or 3.12 server, the server's existing bindery data is upgraded into a NetWare Directory Services (NDS) database. All of the server's bindery objects become NDS objects, and they are all placed in the same location (name context) in the Directory tree as the server. In fact, the server itself will appear as a Server object in the Directory tree.

Binderies are specific to particular servers. This means that if you want user John to access three different NetWare 3.1x servers, you have to create John as a separate user on all three servers. With NDS, a single NDS database is common to all servers in the network. Therefore, you only need to create John once, and then just give him trustee rights to files on those three servers.

Keep this in mind if you are upgrading several NetWare 3.1x servers into a NetWare 4.1 Directory tree. If you have multiple instances of user John on different NetWare 3.1x servers, they will all be merged into one user John if you install all three servers into the same location (name context). If one of the NetWare 3.1x users named John is actually a different person than the other two Johns, you will need to rename one of them before starting the upgrade to ensure that they don't merge.

UPGRADING FROM NETWARE 2.X

There are three options for upgrading a NetWare 2.x server to NetWare 4.1:

- Transfer all the NetWare 2.x server's data to a new machine, on which NetWare 4.1 has already been installed. This is called an Across-the-Wire Migration and it requires the MIGRATE workstation utility. See the section "Across-the-Wire Upgrade" for a checklist of upgrade steps.

- Remove all the NetWare 2.x server's data, upgrade the machine to NetWare 4.1, and then move the data back to the server. This is called a Same-Server Migration, and it also requires the MIGRATE workstation utility. See the section "Same-Server Upgrade" for a checklist of upgrade steps for using the Same-Server Migration.

- Upgrade an existing NetWare 2.x server without moving any data off the server. This method, called an In-Place Upgrade, is more hazardous because the file system itself must be changed, and there is some risk to existing files. An In-Place Upgrade requires the 2XUPGRDE utility, followed by INSTALL.NLM. Because the other two methods are more secure, and because this option is seldom used, the In-Place Upgrade isn't covered in this book.

Like NetWare 3.1x, the NetWare 2.x server's existing bindery (the database of network objects) is upgraded into an NDS database. All of the server's bindery objects become NDS objects, and they are all placed in the same location (name context) in the Directory tree as the server. This means that, just as with NetWare 3.1x, you must ensure that any identical user names on separate NetWare 2.x servers belong to the same person so that they can be merged without creating confusion. If there are identical names (such as Mary) on separate servers, but they belong to two different users who are both named Mary, rename one of the users so that the two won't be merged.

SIMPLE UPGRADE

INSTALL.NLM can be used to upgrade NetWare 3.11, 3.12, 4.01, and 4.02 servers to NetWare 4.1. With this utility, new files are copied from the CD-ROM to the existing server to upgrade it.

The following is a checklist of the steps you use to upgrade a NetWare 3.1x or 4.0x server to NetWare 4.1.

1 • Because deleted files in NetWare 3.1x and 4.x remain on the server in a salvageable state, you may want to see whether there are any deleted files you want to salvage before you upgrade the server. The upgrade process will purge any deleted files still on the server.

2 • Make two backups of all network files.

3 • If necessary, edit the existing AUTOEXEC.NCF file to specify the Ethernet frame type you want. NetWare 4.1 uses Ethernet 802.2 by default.

4 • Bring down the existing server by entering the command

```
DOWN
```

and then the command

```
EXIT
```

5 • Back up the existing server's boot files to another directory or diskette.

6 • Create a new directory, called SERVER.41, on the C drive. This directory will be the new server's boot directory.

7 • If you are using a third-party disk driver or LAN driver that did not come in the NetWare package, copy that driver to the newly created SERVER.41 directory so that it will be available when you need it.

8 • Insert the *NetWare 4.1 Operating System* CD-ROM into the computer's CD-ROM drive, change to the CD-ROM drive's letter (usually D), and enter the following command:

```
INSTALL
```

9 • Choose NetWare Server Installation, choose NetWare 4.1, and then choose Upgrade NetWare 3.1x or 4.0x to 4.1.

10 • Specify the destination directory, which is the new directory you created for the server boot files (SERVER.41).

11 • When prompted, enter the location of the existing SERVER.EXE file (the older server boot directory). The server boot files are now copied to the new directory.

12 • If necessary, change the country code, code page, and keyboard mapping for this server. (To select these, press Enter and choose the correct selections from the lists that appear.)

13 • Select the DOS file name format.

14 • Select the disk drivers for your server's hard disk controller board and CD-ROM drive controller board, and specify their settings.

15 • Select the utility sets you want to install on the server. Press Enter to select or eliminate file sets. (An "X" means the set is selected and will be copied.) Press F10 to start copying the files.

16 • When the message appears describing a temporary AUTOEXEC.NCF file, continue with the installation.

17 • Select the LAN drivers for your server's network boards.

18 • If you are installing this server into an existing NetWare Directory tree, select the correct tree. (To create a new server, press Insert.) If this is the first server in the tree, select "Yes, this is the first NetWare 4 server."

19 • Select the time zone in which this server will exist, and accept or change the time synchronization information that appears. See Chapter 3 for more information about time synchronization.

20 • Create a name context for the server. By entering the name of the organization (such as your company) and the names of descending levels of Organizational Units (such as a division and a department), you actually create the branch of the NDS tree that will contain this server if the branch doesn't already exist. If a branch already exists, press Enter on each field and select the Organizational Unit objects you want. You can enter up to three Organizational Unit names by typing names in the available fields. If you want to create more, use the Server Context field, and type in the server's full name, with periods delimiting each Organizational Unit.

21 • Enter a password for the ADMIN user. If this is the first server in the tree, enter any password you want. If this server is being installed into an existing tree, type in the ADMIN password that has already been assigned or enter the name and password of another User object already in the NDS tree. This User object must have enough NDS trustee rights to add the server to the context specified. See Chapter 7 for more information about NDS trustee rights.

22 • Review the STARTUP.NCF file that appears on the screen. Information you entered during the upgrade process so far is already placed into this file. Press F10 to save the file and continue.

23 • Review the AUTOEXEC.NCF file that appears on the screen. Information you entered during the upgrade process so far is already placed into this file. If necessary, add any additional commands to the AUTOEXEC.NCF file. For example, you can add a command to mount all the server's volumes automatically whenever the server boots (MOUNT ALL), and you can add commands to load NLMs (NetWare Loadable Modules) automatically. Press F10 to save the file and continue.

24 • After the remaining files are copied to the server, choose Create DOS/MS Windows/OS2 Client Install Diskettes to make a set of installation diskettes that you will need to install workstations on your network. See Chapter 4 for more information about installing workstations.

25 • If you want to install the online documentation, choose Install Online Documentation and Viewers. Then see Chapter 12 for more information about installing DynaText viewers and the NetWare online documentation.

26 • Choose any other installation options or additional products you want to install, or exit the installation program.

27 • If you assigned random passwords, print the NEW.PWD file and give users their new passwords. Tell them to change their passwords immediately.

28 • Make a backup of the new NetWare 4.1 server.

ACROSS-THE-WIRE UPGRADE

MIGRATE.EXE can be used to upgrade NetWare 2.1x, 2.2, and 3.1x servers to NetWare 4.1. You can use the Across-the-Wire feature of MIGRATE if you want to replace your old server computer with a new computer.

To migrate a server this way, you actually install a new NetWare 4.1 server elsewhere on the network (using the procedure described in the section "Installing a New Server"). Then the MIGRATE utility transfers the old server's bindery information to a workstation, where the old bindery information is converted into a format NDS can understand. Next, MIGRATE transfers the converted bindery information from the workstation to the new NetWare 4.1 server. Finally, MIGRATE copies all of the regular network data files from the old server to the new server.

When you've evaluated the new server's final state, you can erase all the information from the old server and convert it into a workstation.

The following is a checklist of the steps you use to upgrade a NetWare 2.x or 3.1x server to NetWare 4.1.

1 • (This step is for NetWare 3.1x only.) Because deleted files in NetWare 3.1x remain on the server in a salvageable state, you may want to see whether there are any deleted files you want to salvage before you upgrade the server. The upgrade process will purge any deleted files still on the server.

2 • (This step is for NetWare 2.x only.) Because NetWare 2.2 allowed directories and files to have names up to 14 characters long, and NetWare 4.1 only supports the DOS convention of 8-character names with 3-character extensions, rename any long file or directory names to meet this requirement.

3 • Run BINDFIX on the old server to delete any MAIL directories for users who no longer exist.

4 • Make two backups of all network files.

5 • Install the NetWare 4.1 server on a new machine. See "Installing a New Server" earlier in this chapter.

6 • On the workstation, make sure the NET.CFG file contains the following commands:

```
PROTOCOL IPXODI
IPX RETRY COUNT=60
```

7 • From a workstation, log in as SUPERVISOR with a bindery connection to the NetWare 4.1 server. This ensures that the new server's Directory tree will look like a familiar bindery to the old server. To log in with a bindery connection, specify the server's name and use the / b option. For example, to log in to server MKTG, enter the command:

```
LOGIN MKTG/SUPERVISOR /B
```

8 • If the workstation has a CD-ROM drive, insert the *NetWare 4.1 Operating System* CD-ROM and change to the CD-ROM drive's letter (usually D), and then change to the MIGRATE subdirectory. If the workstation doesn't have a CD-ROM drive, create a MIGRATE subdirectory on the workstation and copy the files from the MIGRATE subdirectory on the newly installed NetWare 4.1 server to the workstation.

9 • Start the migration utility by entering the following command:

```
MIGRATE
```

and choosing Across-the-Wire Migration.

10 • Select the source LAN type (the old server) and the destination LAN type (NetWare 4.1).

11 • When the Migration Utility Configuration screen appears, accept the default working directory and specify whether you want the utility to pause after every warning or error.

12 • Select the source (old) server and use the F5 key to mark the information and the volumes you want to migrate.

13 • Select the destination (NetWare 4.1) server and specify destinations to which the volumes will be migrated. (Press Insert to see a list of volumes and directories on the NetWare 4.1 server. Press F10 when you've finished assigning volume destinations.)

14 • Select whether you want to assign random passwords to all users or no passwords. If you choose random passwords, they will be listed in the file NEW.PWD in SYS:SYSTEM on the NetWare 4.1 server. You can print the file and tell the users what their new passwords are. Tell them to change their passwords immediately.

15 • Press F10 to save all the information on the screen.

16 • Select the Start the Migration option.

17 • When the migration is finished, you can read a report about the process by selecting View Migration Reports or you can exit the MIGRATE utility.

18 • You have the option of upgrading print services. Use the following steps to do so:

a. Map a search drive to the NetWare 4.1 directory SYS:SYSTEM\NLS.

b. Change back to the MIGRATE directory (on the CD-ROM or workstation) and add the following command in which *source* is the old server and *destination* is the new NetWare 4.1 server:

```
MIGPRINT /S=source /D=destination
```

If you don't want to migrate print queues to the default volume (SYS), add the option:

```
/VOL=volume
```

to the end of the command, specifying a new volume for the print queues.

c. Follow the instructions displayed until the print services migration is complete.

d. Use PCONSOLE from the new NetWare 4.1 server to update print queues and print servers.

19 • If you assigned random passwords, print the NEW.PWD file and give users their new passwords. Tell them to change their passwords immediately.

20 • Make a backup of the new NetWare 4.1 server.

21 • When you've verified that the new server is functioning correctly and all files have been migrated, you can delete NetWare from the old server and set up the machine as a workstation.

SAME-SERVER UPGRADE

MIGRATE.EXE can be used to upgrade NetWare 2.1x, 2.2, and 3.1x servers to NetWare 4.1. You can use the Same-Server feature of MIGRATE if you don't want to run the server on a new machine. The Same-Server upgrade lets you remove data from the old server, upgrade the old server to NetWare 4.1, and then move the data back onto the upgraded server.

The Same-Server feature is primarily useful for NetWare 2.x upgrades. Most NetWare 3.1x upgrades can use the simple upgrade process in INSTALL.NLM instead of the Same-Server feature of MIGRATE.

In a Same-Server Migration, you first must back up all of the network data on the server. The Same-Server Migration will only migrate bindery information. After the migration is complete, you will have to replace the network data onto the newly upgraded server by restoring the files from your backup tapes or disks.

To perform a Same-Server Migration, the MIGRATE utility transfers the old server's bindery information to a workstation, where the old bindery information is converted into a format NDS can understand. Next, you install NetWare 4.1 on the old server. Then, MIGRATE transfers the converted bindery information from the workstation to the new NetWare 4.1 server. Finally, you restore all of the regular network data files from the backup you made to the new server.

The following is a checklist of the steps you use to upgrade a NetWare 2.x or 3.1x server to NetWare 4.1.

1 • (This step is for NetWare 3.1x only.) Because deleted files in NetWare 3.1x remain on the server in a salvageable state, you may want to see whether there are any deleted files you want to salvage before you upgrade the server. The upgrade process will purge any deleted files still on the server.

2 • (This step is for NetWare 2.x only.) Because NetWare 2.2 allowed directories and files to have names up to 14 characters long, and NetWare 4.1 only supports the DOS convention of 8-character names with 3-character extensions, rename any long file or directory names to meet this requirement.

3 • Run BINDFIX on the old server to delete any MAIL directories for users who no longer exist.

4 • Make two backups of all network files.

5 • On the workstation, make sure the NET.CFG file contains the following commands:

```
PROTOCOL IPXODI
IPX RETRY COUNT=60
```

6 • From a workstation, log in as SUPERVISOR to the old server.

7 • If the workstation has a CD-ROM drive, insert the *NetWare 4.1 Operating System* CD-ROM and change to the CD-ROM drive's letter (usually D), and then change to the MIGRATE subdirectory. If the workstation doesn't have a CD-ROM drive, insert the CD-ROM into the server's CD-ROM drive and load INSTALL.NLM by using the following command:

```
LOAD INSTALL
```

Select the option to create migration diskettes, and insert blank diskettes when requested. Then insert the first migration diskette into the workstation's diskette drive, change to the diskette drive's letter, and then change to the MIGRATE subdirectory.

8 • Start the migration utility by entering the following command:

```
MIGRATE
```

and choosing Same-Server Migration.

9 • Select the source LAN type (the old server) and the destination LAN type (NetWare 4.1).

10 • When the Migration Utility Configuration screen appears, accept the default working directory and specify whether you want the utility to pause after every warning or error.

11 • Select the source (old) server you want to migrate and use the F5 key to mark the source volumes you want to migrate. Press F10 when finished.

12 • Select Migrate to the Working Directory and press Enter. Now all the old server's bindery information is migrated to the workstation.

13 • Install NetWare 4.1 on the old server, using the instructions under the section "Installing a New Server" earlier in this chapter.

14 • Restore the network files from your backup device to the newly installed NetWare 4.1 server.

15 • At the workstation, restart MIGRATE and select the Same-Server Migration option.

16 • Select the source LAN type (the old server) and the destination LAN type (NetWare 4.1), just as you did in step 9.

17 • Specify the destinations on the NetWare 4.1 server to which the bindery information will be migrated. Press F10 when finished specifying the destination server and volumes.

18 • Select whether you want to assign random passwords to all users or no passwords. If you choose random passwords, they will be listed in the file NEW.PWD in SYS:SYSTEM on the NetWare 4.1 server. You can print the file and tell the users what their new passwords are. Tell them to change their passwords immediately.

19 • Press F10 to save all the information on the screen.

20 • Select the Migrate from Working Directory option.

21 • When the migration is finished, you can read a report about the process by selecting View Migration Reports or you can exit the MIGRATE utility by pressing Esc and selecting Exit.

22 • If you assigned random passwords, print the NEW.PWD file and give users their new passwords. Tell them to change their passwords immediately.

23 • Make a backup of the new NetWare 4.1 server.

CHAPTER 3

Managing the Server

Optimizing Performance

- To monitor performance, use MONITOR.NLM.
- To optimize performance, use SCHDELAY.NLM, SET parameters, and SERVMAN.NLM.
- To manage server memory, use the MEMORY, MEMORY MAP, and REGISTER MEMORY console utilities.
- To see a history of errors that have occurred with the server, the volume, or TTS, use a text editor or EDIT.NLM to read the error log files: SYS$LOG.ERR, VOL$LOG.ERR, TTS$LOG.ERR.

Protecting the Server

- To use an uninterruptible power supply (UPS) to protect the server from power outages, use UPS.NLM, the UPS STATUS console utility, and the UPS TIME console utility.
- To protect the server and network from virus infections, use a virus detector, assign executable files the Execute Only file or Read-Only attributes, and warn users against loading files from external sources.

Maintaining the Server

- To display a server name, use the NAME console utility.
- To display the server's hardware information, use the CONFIG and SPEED console utilities.

- To display the server's version information, use the VERSION console utility.
- To display a list of the server's volumes, use the VOLUMES console utility.
- To bring down the server, use the DOWN console utility, followed by the EXIT console utility.
- To reboot the server, use the DOWN console utility, followed by the RESTART SERVER console utility.
- To obtain patches, use NetWire (Novell's online service on both CompuServe and the Internet).
- To control the server from a workstation, use the Remote Console feature. Load REMOTE.NLM and either RSPX.NLM or RS232.NLM on the server, and then run the RCONSOLE.EXE workstation utility.
- To control server startup activities, use the server startup files: AUTOEXEC.NCF and STARTUP.NCF. (Edit these files by using EDIT.NLM and SERVMAN.NLM.)
- To manage workstation connections, use MONITOR.NLM and the ENABLE LOGIN and DISABLE LOGIN console utilities.
- To manage protocols, use INSTALL.NLM and INETCFG.NLM. (See also Chapter 11.)
- To charge for server usage, use the accounting services in the NetWare Administrator utility and ATOTAL.
- To synchronize time, use TIMESYNC.NLM, the SYSTIME workstation utility, and the TIME, SET TIME, and SET TIME ZONE console utilities.
- To work with NLMs, use the LOAD, UNLOAD and MODULES console utilities, and DOMAIN.NLM.

Managing Storage Devices

- To add a new hard disk or replace an existing one, use INSTALL.NLM.
- To protect network data by mirroring hard disks, use INSTALL.NLM and the MIRROR STATUS, REMIRROR PARTITION, and ABORT REMIRROR console utilities.
- To protect network data by mirroring complete servers, use the NetWare SFT III feature. Install SFT III by using INSTALL.NLM, and manage SFT III with SERVMAN.NLM, INSTALL.NLM, and the HALT console utility.
- To protect network data from bad blocks on the hard disk, use the Hot Fix feature. (Set up Hot Fix in INSTALL.NLM. Monitor the number of bad blocks found with MONITOR.NLM.)
- To manage CD-ROMs, use CDROM.NLM and the CD console utility.
- To manage High-Capacity Storage Systems (HCSS), use INSTALL.NLM, HCSS.NLM, and the NetWare Administrator utility.

Managing Routing Between Servers

- To list networks, use the DISPLAY NETWORKS console utility.
- To list servers, use the DISPLAY SERVERS console utility.
- To execute protocol configuration commands made using INETCFG.NLM, use the INITIALIZE SYSTEM and REINITIALIZE SYSTEM console utilities.
- To configure protocols, use INETCFG.NLM.
- To configure IPX, AppleTalk, and TCP/IP protocols, use INETCFG.NLM.

- To configure RIP/SAP packet filtering, use FILTCFG.NLM.
- To display routing information, use the TRACK ON and TRACK OFF console utilities.

Managing a NetWare 4.1 server involves many different types of tasks, from monitoring performance to adding new hard disks to charging customers for their usage. This chapter explains how you can accomplish these tasks.

Console Utilities and NLMs

There are two types of tools you can use when you work with the NetWare 4.1 server: console utilities and NetWare Loadable Modules.

Console utilities are commands you type at the server's console (keyboard and monitor) to change some aspect of the server or view information about it. These console utilities are built into the operating system, just as internal DOS commands are built in to DOS. To read online help for console utilities, enter

```
HELP
```

at the server console.

NetWare Loadable Modules (NLMs) are software modules that you load into the server's operating system to add or change functionality. Many NLMs are automatically installed with the NetWare 4.1 operating system. Others are optional, which you can load if your particular situation requires them. There are four different types of NetWare Loadable Modules that you can use to add different types of funtionality to your server: NLMs, name space modules, LAN drivers, and disk drivers. These NLMs are described in Table 3.1. Many third-party software manufacturers create different types of NLMs to work on NetWare 4.1.

TABLE 3.1

Different Types of NLMs

TYPE OF NLM	FILENAME EXTENSION	DESCRIPTION
NLM	.NLM	Changes or adds to the server's functionality. Such an NLM might allow you to back up network files, add support for another protocol, or add support for devices such as a CD-ROM drive or a UPS (uninterruptible power supply).

TABLE 3.1

Different Types of NLMs (continued)

TYPE OF NLM	FILENAME EXTENSION	DESCRIPTION
Name space module	.NAM	Allows the operating system to store Macintosh, OS/2, or NFS files, along with their long file names and other characteristics. Name space modules support file naming conventions other than the default DOS file names.
LAN driver	.LAN	Enables the operating system to communicate with a network board installed in the file server.
Disk driver	.DSK	Enables the operating system to communicate with a disk controller board installed in the file server.

You can load and unload NLMs while the server is running. Many NLMs have their own status screen that displays on the server. To move between NLM screens on the server's console, use Alt-Esc to cycle through the available NLM screens and use Ctrl-Esc to bring up a list of available screens, from which you can select one.

To work with NLMs, you can use the commands shown in Table 3.2 from the server console. (The server console may be either the physical console or the Remote Console, as explained in the next section.)

TABLE 3.2

NLM Commands

COMMAND	DESCRIPTION
LOAD *nlmname*	Loads the NLM. You do not need to type the NLM's filename extension. In most cases, if an NLM requires other NLMs to also be loaded, it will automatically load them.
UNLOAD *nlmname*	Unloads the NLM.
MODULES	Lists all the currently loaded NLMs.
DOMAIN	Allows you to load an NLM in a protected memory domain (called OS_PROTECTED) so that it cannot corrupt the operating system memory. If you are testing an NLM for proper behavior, first load DOMAIN.NLM from the STARTUP.NCF file

(continued)

TABLE 3.2

NLM Commands (continued)

COMMAND	DESCRIPTION

DOMAIN (continued)	when you boot the server. Then you can load an NLM in the protected domain by entering
	`DOMAIN=OS_PROTECTED`
	Then load the NLM you're testing. When you are satisfied that the NLM is using memory correctly, you can unload it, enter
	`DOMAIN=OS`
	and reload it so that it runs in the regular domain. To see where all NLMs are currently loaded, just enter
	`DOMAIN`

Controlling the Server from a Workstation with Remote Console

To control the server from a workstation, you can temporarily transform your workstation into a "remote console." With the Remote Console feature running, you can enter console utilities and load NLMs, and the commands you execute will work just as if you were using the server's real keyboard and monitor. Using Remote Console allows you to access the server from any workstation on the network, which gives you greater freedom when administering your network.

You can use Remote Console over a direct connection to the network or via asynchronous lines through a modem.

To run Remote Console over a direct network connection, you must first load REMOTE.NLM on the server. When you load REMOTE.NLM, you are asked for a password. Enter any password you choose. (You will have to supply this same password when you use Remote Console from the workstation.) After loading REMOTE.NLM, you must next load RSPX.NLM on your server. Then, from a workstation, map a search drive to SYS:SYSTEM to give the workstation access to the Remote Console files. Finally, to execute the Remote Console on the workstation, enter

```
RCONSOLE
```

at the workstation's DOS prompt and enter the Remote Console password you assigned when you loaded REMOTE.NLM.

To run Remote Console via a modem connection, load REMOTE.NLM on the server. When you load REMOTE.NLM, you are asked for a password. Enter any password you choose. (You will have to supply this same password when you execute Remote Console from the workstation.) After loading REMOTE.NLM, you must next load RS232.NLM, AIO.NLM, and a communications port driver, such as AIOCOMX.NLM, onto your server. Then copy the following files from SYS:SYSTEM to a directory on the workstation to give the workstation access to Remote Console files:

- RCONSOLE.EXE
- RCONSOLE.HEP
- RCONSOLE.MSG
- IBM_RUN.OVL
- _RUN.OVL
- IBM_AIO.OVL
- _AIO.OVL
- TEXTUTIL.HEP
- TEXTUTIL.IDX
- TEXTUTIL.MSG

Finally, to execute Remote Console on the workstation, enter the command

```
RCONSOLE
```

at the workstation's DOS prompt and enter the Remote Console password you assigned when you loaded REMOTE.NLM.

When using Remote Console, you cannot load NLMs directly from your workstation's local drive. You can, however, load NLMs from the SYS:SYSTEM network directory. Therefore, when you are running Remote Console, press Alt-F1 and select the Transfer Files to Server option. With this option, you can copy files from your local drive to SYS:SYSTEM. Once they are in SYS:SYSTEM, you can load the NLMs with Remote Console as usual.

The keystrokes shown in Table 3.3 let you navigate through the Remote Console screen after you've executed RCONSOLE.

TABLE 3.3

Remote Console Keystrokes

KEYSTROKE	DESCRIPTION
F1	Displays help.
Alt-F1	Displays the Available Options menu.
Alt-F2	Quits the Remote Console session.
Alt-F3	Moves you forward through the current server screens.
Alt-F4	Moves you backward through the current server screens.
Alt-F5	Shows this workstation's address.

Monitoring and Optimizing Server Performance

When you monitor the server's performance, you look for key indicators that the server is functioning at an optimal level. Some of the things you should monitor include the utilization percentage of the server's processor, the number of cache buffers being regularly used, and the server's memory allocation.

Every network has different needs and usage patterns. By default, server parameters are set so that the server will perform well on most networks, but it's a good idea to monitor the server's performance periodically anyway. By doing so, you can track how your server performs under different conditions, discover potential problems, and make improvements.

Server parameters, also called SET parameters, are aspects of the server that control things such as how buffers are allocated and used, how memory is used, and so on. You can change these parameters by loading SERVMAN.NLM, or by typing the full SET command at the server's console prompt. Using SERVMAN.NLM is much easier, because you can select the SET parameters you want from menus, and SERVMAN will automatically save the command in the correct server startup file. For more information about SET parameters, see Appendix B.

The server will optimize itself over a period of time by leveling adjustments for low-usage times with peak-usage bursts. Over a day or two, the server will have allocated an optimal number of buffers for each parameter, such as packet receive buffers. If you bring down the server and reboot it, the server will automatically be reset to the default allocation for all parameters.

To speed up the optimization period, record the allocations after one or two days of server usage, and then set the given parameters to the recorded values. To set these parameters, use SERVMAN.NLM to select the parameters and change them. Then, when you exit SERVMAN, it will ask you if you want to save the new settings in the STARTUP.NCF and AUTOEXEC.NCF files. Say Yes, so that these settings will be executed by those files the next time the server is booted.

The following sections describe some of the ways to monitor and optimize your server's performance.

MONITORING PROCESSOR UTILIZATION

If one or more server processes monopolize the server's CPU, the server's performance can be degraded, or other processes may have trouble running appropriately.

To see the total percentage utilization of the processor, load MONITOR.NLM and note the percentage in the Utilization field. (This field is in the General Information screen that appears when MONITOR is first loaded.) If the utilization is high, one or more processes may be monopolizing CPU time.

Use MONITOR's Scheduling Information screen to list all server processes and see which ones have consistently high Load values. Then use the SCHDELAY console utility to prioritize server processes, schedule the processes to use less of the server's CPU, or slow processes down when the server is very busy. Experiment with SCHDELAY times until the CPU load value is acceptable.

Put the SCHDELAY command in the server's AUTOEXEC.NCF file to keep it in effect if you reboot the server.

MONITORING CACHE BUFFERS

If directory searches are slow, you may need to change some SET parameters to increase the allocation and use of directory cache buffers. Use SERVMAN.NLM to change the following SET parameters that relate to directory cache buffers: Directory Cache Allocation Wait Time, Maximum Directory Cache Buffers, and Minimum Directory Cache Buffers parameters.

If disk writes are slow, use MONITOR's General Information screen to see if more than 70 percent of the cache buffers are "dirty" cache buffers. Dirty cache buffers are the file blocks in the server's memory that contain information that has not yet been written to disk, but needs to be. Then use SERVMAN.NLM to increase the Maximum Concurrent Disk Cache Writes, Maximum Concurrent Directory Cache Writes, Dirty Directory Cache Delay Time, or Dirty Disk Cache Delay Time parameters.

See Appendix B for more information about these SET parameters.

MONITORING PACKET RECEIVE BUFFERS

If the server seems to be slowing down or losing workstation connections, use MONITOR's General Information screen to see how many packet receive buffers are allocated and how many are being used. If the allocated number is higher than ten but the server doesn't respond immediately when rebooted, or if you are using EISA or microchannel bus master boards in your server and "No ECB available" error messages appear after the server boots, you may need to increase the minimum number of packet receive buffers. To do this, use SERVMAN.NLM to increase the SET parameter Minimum Packet Receive Buffers so that each board can have at least five buffers.)

You can also increase the Maximum Packet Receive Buffers parameter in increments of ten until you have one buffer per workstation. (Again, if you are using EISA or microchannel bus master boards in your server increase this parameter until each board can have at least five buffers.

See Appendix B for more information about these SET parameters.

MONITORING MEMORY USAGE

One of the most common causes of server performance problems is a lack of adequate memory in the server. If the network seems to be operating slowly, or if you don't have enough memory to load NLMs, you may need to simply add more RAM to the server.

Use MONITOR's Cache Utilization screen to track the percentage of Long Term Cache Hits. If Long Term Cache Hits shows less than 90 percent consistently, add more RAM to the server.

You can use the MEMORY and MEMORY MAP console utilities to see how much memory the server is using.

To provide more memory to NLMs without adding RAM, you use SERVMAN.NLM to change the Minimum File Cache Buffers and Maximum Directory Cache Buffers parameters, which limit the memory for file and directory caching. Then reboot the server. However, only use this as a temporary solution until you can add more RAM to the server.

If you're using an ISA bus or PCI bus in the server, remember to use the REGISTER MEMORY console utility to register any memory above 16MB for an ISA bus or 64MB for a PCI bus.

MONITORING THE ERROR LOG FILES

There are four different error log files that you can monitor to see if any error messages have been generated by your network. You should make a practice of reviewing these files on a regular basis to ensure that nothing out of the ordinary is happening to your network.

- SYS$LOG.ERR logs error messages for the server. It is stored in the server's SYS:SYSTEM directory. All of the messages or errors that appear on the server's console are stored in this file.

- VOL$LOG.ERR logs error messages for a volume. Each volume has its own log file, which is stored at the root of the volume. Any errors or messages that pertain to the volume are stored in this file.

- TTS$LOG.ERR logs all data that is backed out by the NetWare Transaction Tracking System (TTS). This file is stored in the SYS: volume. To allow this file to be created, use SERVMAN.NLM to turn the TTS Abort Dump Flag parameter to On.

- CONSOLE.LOG is a file that can capture all console messages during system initialization. To capture messages in this file, load CONLOG.NLM in the AUTOEXEC.NCF file. CONSOLE.LOG is stored in the SYS:ETC directory. To stop capturing messages in this file, enter the command

  ```
  UNLOAD CONLOG
  ```

  at the server console.

To view any of these error log files, you can either use a text editor from a workstation, or you can use EDIT.NLM from the server. To use EDIT.NLM, enter the command

```
LOAD EDIT
```

and then specify the path and name of the desired log file.

To limit the size of the CONSOLE.LOG file, you can specify its maximum size in the command that loads CONLOG.NLM. In addition, you can specify that the previous CONSOLE.LOG file be saved under a different name. For example, to specify that the previous file be saved and named LOG.SAV, and to limit the new CONSOLE.LOG file to be no more than 100K in size, you would use the following command:

```
LOAD CONLOG SAVE=LOG.SAV MAXIMUM=100
```

To limit the size of the other three error log files (SYS$LOG.ERR, VOL$LOG.ERR, and TTS$LOG.ERR), use SERVMAN.NLM to change the appropriate SET parameters. Server Log File Overflow Size=*number* lets you specify the maximum size (in K) that the SYS$LOG.ERR file can become. Likewise, Volume Log File Overflow Size=*number* sets the maximum size for VOL$LOG.ERR and Volume TTS Log File Overflow Size=*number* sets the maximum size for TTS$LOG.ERR.

To specify what happens to a log file when it reaches the maximum size, use SERVMAN.NLM to change the Server Log File State=*number* parameter, the Volume Log File State=*number* parameter, or the Volume TTS Log File State=*number* parameter. With these parameters, replace *number* with 0 (leaves the log file in its current state), 1 (deletes the log file), or 2 (renames the log file and starts a new one). The default is 1.

Protecting the Server

Protecting the server is a very important safeguard that cannot be overlooked. Damage to the server can affect the entire network. The following types of activities can help you protect your server. In addition, see Chapter 7 for information about preventing other types of problems, such as unauthorized access of files.

PROTECTING THE SERVER FROM PHYSICAL HARM

If the server is in an exposed public area where anyone can have access to it, accidents may happen. For example, someone might unplug the power cord or turn off the server thinking it had been left on accidently.

Be sure to store the server in a locked room. In fact, you may also want to remove its keyboard and monitor, and access it only with the Remote Console feature when necessary.

Secure the server to a desk or counter if you are in an earthquake-prone area. Even a small shake can knock a computer to the floor.

PROTECTING THE SERVER FROM ELECTRICAL POWER PROBLEMS

Because electrical power is not always consistent, you need to ensure that your server will not be damaged and files won't be corrupted should a brownout, surge, spike, or outage occur.

Use a UPS for the server. This provides the server with a backup battery in case of a power outage, which allows enough time for the UPS to shut down the server cleanly, leaving no open files exposed to corruption.

If possible, attach each workstation to a UPS, too. If a UPS isn't feasible, at least use surge suppressors on the workstations and peripherals (such as printers) to prevent electrical surges from damaging the equipment.

Typically, UPS manufacturers provide software to manage their UPS products. Use the manufacturer's software to manage your UPS whenever possible. However, if you don't have software from the UPS manufacturer, you can use NetWare 4.1's UPS.NLM to support the UPS on the server.

The following is a checklist of the steps to install a UPS on a server using Novell's UPS.NLM.

1 • Attach the UPS to the server using the manufacturer's instructions.

2 • Load the UPS hardware driver on the server.

3 • If you are using a disk coprocessor board (DCB) to connect the UPS to the server, load the DCB.DSK driver on the server.

4 • Load UPS.NLM on the server, specifying the correct parameters in the following format:

`LOAD UPS TYPE=`*`type`* `PORT=`*`number`* `DISCHARGE=`*`time`* `RECHARGE=`*`time`* `WAIT=`*`time`*

In this format, *type* is a possible board type. The port *number* available is dependent on the type of board you use. (See Table 3.4.)

The discharge *time* is the number of minutes that the server can operate on battery power (check the battery manufacturer's documentation). The default value is 20 minutes, but values can range from 1 to 3976821 minutes.

The recharge *time* is the number of minutes the battery needs to fully recharge. The default value is 60 minutes, but values can range from 1 to 3976821 minutes.

The wait *time* is the number of seconds the UPS should wait after a power outage before it takes over. The default value is 15 seconds, but values can range from 1 to 300 seconds.

If you want the UPS to be configured the same way every time the server is rebooted, put the LOAD UPS command in the server's AUTOEXEC.NCF file.

TABLE 3.4
UPS Board Types

BOARD TYPE	PORT NUMBERS
Stand-alone	240, 231
Mouse	No port is required.
Keycard	230, 238
ECDB	380, 388, 320, 328
DCB (default)	346, 34E, 326, 32E, 286, 28E
Other	Refer to the manufacturer's documentation.

To see the UPS's status after UPS.NLM has been loaded, use the UPS STATUS console utility by entering

```
UPS STATUS
```

at the server's console.

To change the UPS's recharge or discharge times, use the UPS TIME console command. The general format of this command is as follows:

```
UPS TIME DISCHARGE=time RECHARGE=time
```

The discharge *time* is the number of minutes that the server can operate on battery power (check the battery manufacturer's documentation). The default value is 20 minutes, but values can range from 1 to 3976821 minutes.

The recharge *time* is the number of minutes the battery needs to fully recharge. The default value is 60 minutes, but values can range from 1 to 3976821 minutes.

PROTECTING THE SERVER FROM VIRUSES

Unfortunately, software viruses are a fact of life. Use a third-party product to check for viruses and to disinfect your network if one is found. Several companies are manufacturing virus detectors for NetWare networks.

Because new viruses are continually being created, keep your virus detection software up-to-date (get all available updates of the software, follow manufacturer's procedures for updating, and so on).

If necessary, establish policies against users loading their own software on the network or downloading software from outside online sources or e-mail messages, or provide diskless workstations to the users.

To prevent viruses from infecting executable files, you can assign those files the Execute Only file attribute, or you can remove users' Modify right from the directory that contains the executable files and assign the Read-Only attribute to the executables. If a user still has the Modify right to a file, the virus can change the Read-Only attribute to Read-Write, infect the file, then change the attribute back. Therefore, it's important to remove the Modify right from the user if you are going to use the Read-Only attribute for virus protection.

PROTECTING THE SERVER FROM HARDWARE FAILURES

To protect your server from hard disk problems, the NetWare feature called Hot Fix monitors any bad blocks that develop on the hard disk. (Hot Fix is explained in the section "Using Hot Fix," later in this chapter.) For more protection, you can use disk mirroring and disk duplexing to store identical copies of all network files on two disks so that if one disk goes bad, the data is still available from the other. This protection feature is explained in the section "Using Disk Mirroring and Duplexing," later in this chapter.

For extremely mission-critical data, duplicating the entire server may be necessary. This feature, called *System Fault Tolerance Level III* (SFT III) lets you set up two identical servers that mirror each other's data. Should one server fail for any reason, the other takes over seamlessly. This provides more protection than disk duplexing because all of the server's hardware is duplicated, including network boards, hard disks, cables, and so on. SFT III is explained in the section "Managing SFT III (Duplicate Servers)," later in this chapter.

Performing Server Maintenance

From time to time, you may find you need to perform some type of maintenance on your server. For example, you may need to add a new hard disk, load the latest patches (bug fixes or enhancements) on the server, or clear a workstation connection. The following sections explain how to do some of these common maintenance tasks.

DISPLAYING INFORMATION ABOUT THE SERVER

You can see information about the server by executing various console utilities at the server's console. Table 3.5 lists the types of information about the server that you can see and the console utilities you use to display that information.

TABLE 3.5

Console Utilities Used to Display Server Information

TYPE OF INFORMATION	CONSOLE UTILITY TO USE
The server's name	NAME
The server's Directory tree	CONFIG
The server's bindery context	CONFIG
The server's hardware information	CONFIG
All currently loaded NLMs	MODULES
The server's processor speed	SPEED
The server's version number and license information	VERSION
A list of all volumes mounted on the server	VOLUMES

BRINGING DOWN AND REBOOTING THE SERVER

If you need to bring down the server or reboot it, you can use the methods listed in Table 3.6.

TABLE 3.6

Utilities Used to Bring Down or Reboot the Server

TASK	HOW TO DO IT
Bring down the server, but leave it connected to the network so that it continues to receive packets.	Enter the command `DOWN`
Bring down the server, and exit to DOS. (This disconnects the server from the network.)	Enter the command `DOWN` then enter `EXIT`

(continued)

TABLE 3.6

Utilities Used to Bring Down or Reboot the Server (continued)

TASK	HOW TO DO IT

Reboot the server.	Enter the command
	`DOWN`
	then enter
	`RESTART SERVER`

Reboot the server from a Remote Console.	First, make sure the server's AUTOEXEC.BAT file automatically executes SERVER.EXE. Then enter the command
	`REMOVE DOS`
	then enter
	`DOWN`
	then enter
	`EXIT`

INSTALLING PATCHES

As with almost all software products, no matter how thoroughly the product is tested, there is always some flaw or unexpected behavior that crops up after the product has shipped. Usually, these types of flaws show up when the product is used in a customer configuration that varies from the testing configurations used within the manufacturer's labs.

To fix these problems, Novell releases software patches, which are modules that can be installed on your NetWare 4.1 server. Not all patches are needed in most customers' configurations, but it's often a good idea to get the patches and install them anyway, just to ensure that you protect your server from possible problems or down time.

Novell releases these patches in a variety of ways. Users with CompuServe accounts can obtain the patches through the NetWire forum (GO NETWIRE). The patches are also available via the Internet:

- World Wide Web: http://www.novell.com
- Gopher: gopher.novell.com
- File Transfer Protocol (FTP): anonymous FTP to ftp.novell.com

If you are accessing these areas from Europe, use .de instead of .com.

The patches are also released on the Novell Support Encyclopedia (NSEPro), which is updated monthly and sent out to subscribers.

For more information about all of these sources, see Appendix C.

MONITORING WORKSTATION CONNECTIONS

Some types of server maintenance require you to break a workstation's connection to the server or to prevent users from logging in while you're completing the maintenance task. Use the methods listed in Table 3.7 to perform these tasks.

TABLE 3.7

Utilities Used to Monitor Workstation Connections

TASK	UTILITY TO USE
See what workstations are connected and what files they have open.	MONITOR.NLM's Connection Information screen
Clear the workstation connection if the work-station has crashed and left files open on the server.	MONITOR.NLM's Connection Information screen (select the connection and press the Delete key)
Prevent users from logging in.	DISABLE LOGIN console utility
Allow users to log in again after you've disabled login.	ENABLE LOGIN console utility

BINDING PROTOCOLS AND LAN DRIVERS TOGETHER

Whenever you load a LAN driver to support a network board, you must also bind a protocol to the LAN driver.

During installation, the LAN driver and the IPX protocol are automatically bound together by the INSTALL program. After the initial installation, you can load additional LAN drivers and bind protocols to them by using either INSTALL.NLM or INETCFG.NLM.

INSTALL.NLM lets you load drivers for additional network boards, load drivers reentrantly (more than once for the same board) to support multiple frame types, and bind IPX to a LAN driver. INSTALL.NLM automatically detects network addresses on the boards to help reduce possible network address conflicts. INSTALL.NLM stores the commands to load the LAN drivers and bind IPX in the AUTOEXEC.NCF file.

Use INETCFG.NLM if you want to bind AppleTalk, TCP/IP, or another non-IPX protocol to the LAN driver. You can also use it to bind IPX to a LAN driver. When you first load INETCFG.NLM, you are asked if you want to transfer all the commands that load LAN drivers and bind protocols to them into the file that INETCFG.NLM uses (NETINFO.CFG) instead of AUTOEXEC.NCF. Once you use INETCFG.NLM and transfer the commands to NETINFO.CFG, you must always use INETCFG.NLM to configure drivers and protocols.

Working with Hard Disks

One of the most annoying problems that can happen to a server is a hard disk failure. There are several NetWare features, explained in the following sections, that can help you monitor and work with your server's hard disks. (For information about volumes, see Chapter 8.)

USING HOT FIX

NetWare provides a feature called Hot Fix, which monitors the blocks that are being written to on a disk. When NetWare writes data to the server's hard disk, NetWare writes the data, then verifies that the data was written correctly by reading it again (called read-after-write verification). When a bad block is encountered, the data that was being written to that block is redirected to a separate area on the disk, called the *disk redirection area,* and the bad block is listed in a bad block table.

Some manufacturers' hard disks maintain their own version of data redirection and do not need to use NetWare's Hot Fix feature. If your disk does use Hot Fix, the size of the redirection area is set up by default when you first create a volume on the disk.

Periodically, you should monitor the NetWare Hot Fix statistics to see if a disk is showing a high number of bad blocks and is filling up the allocated redirection area. To see the number of redirection blocks being used, use MONITOR.NLM's Disk Information screen. Track the number of bad blocks being found over time so that you can see if the disk suddenly starts to generate bad blocks at an undesirable frequency. (You may want to use a worksheet such as "Hot Fix Bad Block Tracking" worksheet in Appendix D.) If more than half of the redirection space has been used for redirected data, or if the number of redirected blocks has increased significantly since the last time you checked it, the disk may be going bad. Use the manufacturer's documentation to try to diagnose the disk problem.

USING DISK MIRRORING AND DUPLEXING

Another way to protect your network data from possible disk corruption is to implement disk mirroring, which ensures that data is safe and accessible even if one disk goes down. When you mirror disks, both disks are updated simultaneously with network data so that both disks contain identical copies of all network files. If one disk fails, the other takes over so that the network operates normally. Users don't typically see any difference in services.

If the mirrored disks are using the same disk controller board, it's simply called *disk mirroring.*

If the mirrored disks are using separate disk controller boards, it's called *disk duplexing.* Disk duplexing provides more security than disk mirroring because it duplicates not just the disk, but also the controller channel as well. Disk duplexing also increases the data reads and writes because the server will send reads and writes to both controllers. Whichever controller is least busy services the requests.

With mirrored or duplexed disks, if a disk problem causes the server to stop, you should turn off the server, remove the bad disk, and restart the server. Then replace the bad disk as soon as possible. When you install the new disk, the server will remirror the new drive with the existing one, which also means the server will copy all the data onto the new disk automatically.

Having disk mirroring or duplexing does not eliminate the need for keeping regular backups of your network. Be sure you always have a current backup of your network data before you change disks or change the server's hardware configuration.

Managing Mirrored or Duplexed Disks

You can use the utilities shown in Table 3.8 to work with mirrored disks.

TABLE 3.8

Utilities Used to Manage Mirrored Disks

TASK	UTILITY TO USE
Set up, monitor, and change disk mirroring or disk duplexing.	INSTALL.NLM
Show the status of mirrored disk partitions.	MIRROR STATUS console utility
Stop the server from remirroring a disk partition.	ABORT REMIRROR console utility
Restart the remirroring process if something halted the server's remirroring task.	REMIRROR PARTITION console utility

Recovering Files from an Out-of-Sync Disk

Usually, when a mirrored disk partition becomes unmirrored, its status in INSTALL (under Disk Options) is listed as Not Mirrored.

If the disk is listed as Out of Sync, NetWare does not recognize any volume information on the disk. To salvage the data from this partition, you must rename the partition so that it can be mounted as a separate volume. To do this, complete the steps in the following checklist.

1 • At the server's console, load INSTALL.NLM.

2 • Choose Disk Options, and then choose Mirror/Unmirror Disk Partitions.

3 • Select the out-of-sync partition and press F3.

4 • If another volume of the same name exists on another disk, you'll receive a warning that the partition you selected contains the name of a volume that is already defined. Press Esc to continue.

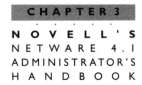

5 • When asked if you want to rename the volume segment, answer Yes.

6 • Enter a new, unique name for this volume segment.

7 • Answer Yes when asked if you want to salvage the volume segment.

8 • Mount the segment as an independent volume.

ADDING A HARD DISK TO A SERVER

The following is a checklist of the steps required to install a new hard disk in a server.

1 • Bring down the server and turn off its power (or the power to the disk's subsystem).

2 • If necessary, install a new disk controller board.

3 • Install the hard disk and cable it to the server as necessary.

4 • If necessary, configure the computer to recognize the new disk.

5 • Reboot the server.

6 • Load INSTALL.NLM to load the disk driver and create a new NetWare partition for the disk.

7 • Use INSTALL.NLM to either mirror the disk to another existing disk, create a new volume on it, or add its partition to an existing volume.

REPLACING A HARD DISK IN A SERVER

The following is a checklist of the steps required to replace an existing hard disk in a server.

1 • Back up the files on the existing hard disk.

2 • If the disk is mirrored, use INSTALL.NLM to dismount all of the disk's volumes and to unmirror the disk.

3 • Bring down the server and turn off its power (or the power to the disk's subsystem).

4 • Remove the original disk.

5 • Install the new disk and cable it to the server as necessary.

6 • If necessary, configure the computer to recognize the new disk.

7 • Reboot the server.

8 • Load INSTALL.NLM to load the disk driver.

9 • Use INSTALL.NLM to delete any existing partitions on the new disk and to create a new NetWare partition on it.

10 • Use INSTALL.NLM to either remirror the disk to the original disk's partner or re-create the volumes that were on the old disk (then restore the files from a backup).

Working with CD-ROM Drives and Other Storage Devices

With NetWare 4.1, a CD-ROM mounted in a drive that is attached to the server can appear as a NetWare volume. Users on the network can access the CD-ROM just like any other volume, except that it is read-only.

Because a CD-ROM is read-only, do not enable file compression or block suballocation on the CD-ROM volume, or you will corrupt the CD-ROM's volume index data. (If you do, use the CD console utility to rebuild the CD-ROM's volume index file.)

To mount a CD-ROM as a NetWare volume, you use CDROM.NLM. This NLM supports the High Sierra and ISO 9660 formats, but does not support HFS (Apple) file systems.

To work with the CD-ROM after it is mounted as a volume, use the CD console command. For help using the CD command, enter

```
CD HELP
```

The following is a checklist of the steps necessary to install a CD-ROM and mount it as a NetWare volume.

1 • Install a NetWare-compatible *host bus adapter* (HBA) that supports CD-ROM drives.

2 • Boot the server and make sure volume SYS is mounted.

3 • Load the HBA's disk driver and any other associated driver on the server.

4 • If your driver automatically loads the ASPITRAN.DSK driver, you must also load either ASPICD.DSK or CDNASPI.DSK on the server.

5 • Load NWPA.NLM (the NetWare Peripheral Architecture driver) on the server.

6 • Load CDROM.NLM on the server.

7 • Use the CD DEVICE LIST console utility to see the ID number of the CD-ROM, or use the CD VOLUME LIST console utility to see the CD-ROM's volume name.

8 • Using either the CD-ROM's volume name or ID number, mount the CD-ROM volume using the following command format:

CD MOUNT *volume or number*

9 • If you want the CD-ROM to be mounted as a volume every time the server is rebooted, put the commands that load the drivers (steps 3, 4, and 5) in the STARTUP.NCF file, and put the commands that load and mount the CD-ROM (steps 6 and 8) in the AUTOEXEC.NCF file.

Increasing the Server's Storage Capacity by Using HCSS

One way to expand your server's storage capacity is to use NetWare's *High-Capacity Storage System* (HCSS) to integrate an optical disc jukebox into the NetWare file system. (An *optical disc jukebox* is a storage device that holds several optical discs. The jukebox uses an autochanger to mount and dismount the discs as needed.) With HCSS, lesser-used files are migrated off the server's hard disks onto the optical disks. When accessed, the files on the optical disk are "demigrated" back onto the hard disks.

Users are seldom aware that the files they are accessing are on the optical disk system.

HCSS also lets you archive files by removing the optical disks with the files on them and storing the disks in another location.

To set up HCSS on your server, you install a jukebox, then you create an HCSS volume, complete with its own file system structure, on the server's hard disk. The HCSS file system consists of the HCSS volume, which can contain one or more domain directories. Each domain directory contains pairs of directories that correspond to the media labels on each side of an optical disk.

You will set up a workstation to use the HCSS "snap-in" module for the NetWare Administrator utility, and then you must use this utility to manage HCSS directories and activities. Do not use other utilities to change HCSS directories, or you may corrupt the HCSS file system.

To see and modify the status of HCSS once it's set up, you can use either NetWare Administrator or the HCSS console utility.

The following is a checklist of the steps for setting up HCSS support on your network.

1 • Install the jukebox and its SCSI adapter board according the manufacturer's documentation.

2 • Load the jukebox's driver on the server, specifying any necessary options as described in the manufacturer's documentation.

3 • Load HPCHGR.NLM (Novell's driver) on the server.

4 • To register the jukebox with the NetWare operating system, enter the

```
SCAN FOR NEW DEVICES
```

command at the console.

5 • Use INSTALL.NLM to create a volume on the server's hard disk specifically for HCSS. This volume should be at least 10 percent of the total capacity of the jukebox.

6 • With INSTALL.NLM, set whether you want file compression turned off or on. Then turn on data migration. Finally, set the volume block size.

7 • Mount the volume.

8 • Load HCSS.NLM on the server.

9 • If the jukebox begins ejecting media, remove the media and enter

```
MEDIA REMOVED
```

at the console, then enter

```
HCSS EJECT MEDIA OVERRIDE=ON
```

to prevent it from ejecting more media.

10 • At a workstation, log in as ADMIN and edit the NWADMIN.INI file to add the following lines under the heading [Snapin Object DLLs]:

```
Vis HCSSDecider=hdecsnap.dll
Vis HCSSObject=hobjsnap.dll
Vis HCSSMedia=hmedsnap.dll
```

11 • Begin creating the HCSS directory structure by opening the NetWare Administrator utility and selecting the HCSS volume.

12 • From the Tools menu, select HCSS Create and type in the name you want to give the first domain directory in the HCSS Directory field. If you want to create additional domain directories, select Create Another Directory. Then click on the Create button to create the directory.

13 • Next you will assign labeled media to the domain, so make sure the cartridges are labeled with the names of the two media-label directories you plan to create.

14 • From the Tools menu, choose HCSS Media, then choose Import Media.

15 • Insert the media into the jukebox and choose OK.

16 • (This step is optional.) If the media is unformatted, choose Format, enter the media label names, and choose OK. (If the media already contains files you want to keep, do not format it.)

17 • From the HCSS Assign Media screen, select an HCSS directory from the HCSS Directory field, then choose OK.

18 • To add more media, repeat steps 14 through 17.

Modifying Server Startup Activities

When you start up or reboot the NetWare server, its boot files execute in the following order:

1 • AUTOEXEC.BAT can be set to automatically execute SERVER.EXE.

2 • SERVER.EXE runs the NetWare 4.1 operating system on the computer, which turns the computer into the NetWare server.

3 • STARTUP.NCF automates the initialization of the NetWare operating system. It loads disk drivers, name space modules to support different file formats (Macintosh, OS/2, or NFS), and executes some SET parameters that modify default initialization values.

4 • AUTOEXEC.NCF loads the server's LAN drivers, specifies the server name and internal network number, mounts volumes, loads any NLMs you want automatically loaded (such as MONITOR), and executes additional SET parameters.

The STARTUP.NCF and AUTOEXEC.NCF files are automatically created during the installation process. They contain commands that reflect the selections you make during installation.

You can edit these .NCF files after installation to add new commands or modify existing ones. Table 3.9 has a description of these utilities you can use to edit the .NCF files.

TABLE 3.9

Utilities Used to Edit Server Startup Files

UTILITY	DESCRIPTION
EDIT.NLM	A text editor on the server that lets you manually edit the files. To use EDIT.NLM, enter `LOAD EDIT` then enter the name of the desired file.
INSTALL.NLM	Lets you modify the same options you set during installation. Automatically updates the appropriate file with the new information you've specified.
SERVMAN.NLM	Lets you add, delete, or modify SET parameters by selecting them from menus. Automatically updates the appropriate file with the new information you've specified.

Managing Connections Between Servers

With NetWare, multiple segments of a network or multiple networks can all be connected and communicate with each other. (Multiple networks connected together form an internetwork.) These network segments can all use the same topology and protocol (such as IPX, the NetWare default protocol), or they can use differing protocols, such as AppleTalk and TCP/IP.

NetWare uses *routing* software to enable these different segments of the network to communicate. Routing software in the NetWare server receives packets of data from a segment of the network, determines how to handle that packet, then sends it along the most efficient path to its destination.

Each server's routing software keeps track of the internetwork's configuration in a routing table, and each server updates the rest of the internetwork's configuration information by periodically broadcasting Router Information Protocol (RIP) and Service Advertising Protocol (SAP) information. RIP and SAP broadcasts are used to determine which servers are up and running and which routes will be the most efficient for transferring packets. Time servers also advertise their services using SAP broadcasts.

NetWare Link Services Protocol (NLSP) is another type of routing that NetWare supports. Instead of broadcasting routing and service information periodically, NLSP sends out this information only when a route or service on the network changes.

You can use the utilities listed in Table 3.10 to help you monitor the status of your internetwork and routers.

TABLE 3.10

Utilities Used to Manage Routers and Protocols

UTILITY	DESCRIPTION
DISPLAY NETWORKS console utility	Lists all networks that the server's router sees.
DISPLAY SERVERS console utility	Lists all servers advertised with SAP.
INITIALIZE SYSTEM console utility	Executes commands in NETINFO.CFG at server startup to enable the multiprotocol router configuration.
REINITIALIZE SYSTEM console utility	Reenables the multiprotocol router configuration after you've made changes to NETINFO.CFG.
INETCFG.NLM	Configures AppleTalk and TCP/IP packet routing across network segments. Configures IPX/SPX parameters. Loads LAN drivers and binds protocols to them. Enables NLSP.

TABLE 3.10

Utilities Used to Manage Routers and Protocols (continued)

UTILITY	DESCRIPTION
FILTCFG.NLM	Configures RIP/SAP packet filtering.
RESET ROUTER console utility	Resets the router table on the server if it has become corrupted.
TRACK ON console utility	Display the routing information that your server is broadcasting and receiving.
TRACK OFF console utility	Turns off the display of routing information.

Managing SFT III (Duplicate Servers)

NetWare 4.1 SFT III (System Fault Tolerance Level III) is a form of NetWare 4.1 that lets you install the operating system on two identical servers that work in concert with each other. If one server fails, the other takes over seamlessly and continues to run the network. Although the SFT III capability is built into NetWare 4.1, you cannot enable SFT III functionality unless you have purchased an SFT III license.

SFT III duplicates all of the server hardware, including monitor, keyboard, disks, network boards, and cables. It joins the two servers with a special high-speed network link to ensure that all data is instantly duplicated between the two servers. The network boards that form this high-speed link are called *mirrored server link* (MSL) boards. For a list of MSL boards that have been certified for use with NetWare 4.1, use one of the following numbers:

- Fax Back information (to get information automatically faxed to you): 801-429-2776 or 800-414-5227
- Hotline: 801-429-5544

With SFT III, the operating system is split into two pieces: the *mirrored server engine* (MSEngine) and the *I/O engine* (IOEngine). The MSEngine is the portion of the operating system that mirrors all the network data and operations. The IOEngine is the portion of the operating system that handles the hardware input and output for this particular server computer. The IOEngine is not mirrored.

The following is a checklist of the steps for installing NetWare 4.1 SFT III on your servers.

1 • Make sure the two servers you intend to mirror are identical, or nearly so, in terms of model, memory, disk space, hardware, and so on.

2 • Attach a CD-ROM drive to the first server, and install regular NetWare 4.1 on it, as explained in Chapter 1.

3 • On the second server, create a DOS partition that is the same size as the DOS partition on the first server.

4 • Format three high-density diskettes and label them Disk 1, Disk 2, and Disk 3.

5 • Install the MSL boards in both servers and cable the boards directly to each other according to the manufacturer's instructions. Record the MSL boards' addresses and interrupt numbers. (You can record the boards' information in a worksheet such as those in Appendix D.) For more protection, you can install a second pair of MSL boards in the servers, too.

6 • Insert the *NetWare 4.1 Operating System* CD-ROM in the CD-ROM drive on the first server and boot DOS on the first server.

7 • From the CD-ROM's root directory, run the installation program by entering the command

```
INSTALL
```

at the first server's console.

8 • Select NetWare Server Installation, then choose NetWare 4.1 SFT III Installation, then choose Convert NetWare 4.1 to SFT III.

9 • Enter the MSEngine name (you can use the name you first gave the server, or you can change it now).

10 • Assign IPX internal network numbers for all three engines (the MSEngine, and each of the two IOEngines). You can either accept randomly-assigned numbers by selecting Continue with Installation, or you can assign your own numbers by choosing Modify Network Numbers.

11 • Specify the first server's DOS boot directory and the location of the AUTOEXEC.BAT file. (Because SERVER.EXE will be changed to MSERVER.EXE, the installation program checks to see if SERVER.EXE is executed from AUTOEXEC.BAT and, if so, it changes the command to execute MSERVER.EXE instead.)

12 • Insert Disk 1 into the first server's disk drive and press Enter so that it will copy SFT III files onto it. Insert the other two diskettes as prompted.

13 • Specify the driver for the MSL board installed in the first server. (If you've installed a second MSL board in the server, specify that one, too.)

14 • Now that the first server is up and running, boot DOS on the second server.

15 • Insert Disk 1 in the second server's disk drive, change to that drive letter, and run the installation program from that diskette by entering

```
INSTALL
```

INSTALL copies the SFT III files onto the second server. (Insert the other two diskettes when prompted.)

16 • Specify the driver for the second server's MSL board. (If you installed two MSL boards, specify the driver for the second one, too.)

17 • Select the LAN and disk drivers for the second server, then select Continue Installation.

18 • Press Enter two more times to continue the installation.

19 • Create a NetWare partition on the second server's hard disk. If the two servers' hard disks are the same size, you can choose Automatically, and

the program will create the NetWare partition and mirror it to the partition on the first server. If the disks are different sizes, choose Manually and create the NetWare disk partition to the size you want and mirror it to the first server's disk. Then continue with the installation.

20 • When prompted, insert the license diskette.

21 • Exit the installation program. SFT III is now installed and the disks are being mirrored. The status of the mirroring is displayed on the screen.

The startup files for the SFT III servers are different from the regular NetWare startup files. Instead of a single STARTUP.NCF file and a single AUTOEXEC.NCF file, SFT III requires two of each: one for each server's MSEngine, and one for each server's IOEngine. These files are explained in Table 3.11.

TABLE 3.11

SFT III Server Startup Files

FILE	DESCRIPTION
IOSTART.NCF	Specifies the IOEngine's name and IPX internal network number, loads the disk drivers and MSL board drivers, executes IOEngine SET parameters, and loads NLMs that run in the IOEngine and don't need the MSEngine running.
MSSTART.NCF	Executes commands and SET parameters that affect the MSEngine.
MSAUTO.NCF	Executes commands after the servers are mirrored and volume SYS is mounted. This file includes commands that can execute in or affect network services that run in the mirrored portion of the operating system. For example, it loads most NLMs, loads NetWare Directory Services, initializes time synchronization, and so on.
IOAUTO.NCF	Loads LAN drivers and binds protocols to them. Loads NLMs that must run in the IOEngine but require the MSEngine to be running (such as backup and print services).

Once SFT III is up and running, any problem on one server will cause the second server to seamlessly take over network operations. The first server installed is the primary server, and the second server is the secondary one. If the primary server fails, the secondary server will become the primary server. When you bring the failed server back online, it will mirror itself to the "new" primary server and become the secondary server.

To manage your SFT III servers, you can use the utilities shown in Table 3.12.

TABLE 3.12

Utilities Used for Managing SFT III Servers

UTILITY	DESCRIPTION
MSERVER.EXE	Starts the server (replaces SERVER.EXE).
SERVMAN.NLM	Allows you to configure SFT III options by changing SET parameters.
HALT console utility	Stops the IOEngine in one server, forcing the other server to take over.
RESTART console utility	Reloads a stopped IOEngine while the IOEngine in the other server continues to run, or forces a server to switch from being primary to secondary.
INSTALL.NLM	Allows you to recover orphaned disk partitions.

Charging Customers for Server Usage

With NetWare, you can charge users for using a server's resources. You can charge them by the following criteria:

- The number of minutes that they are connected to your server
- The number of service requests they make to the server
- The total number of blocks they read
- The total number of blocks they write to
- The total number of blocks of disk storage they use per day

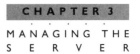

Bear in mind that the accounting feature tracks these items by the server. It does not support NetWare Directory Services, so if you want to charge for a user's activities across the network, you'll have to set up accounting on each server the user might access.

To manage accounting on a server, you use two utilities: the *NetWare Administrator utility*, which runs in Windows, and the *ATOTAL utility*, which is a command-line utility.

To set up accounting, use the NetWare Administrator utility from a workstation. (See Chapter 6 for instructions on setting up the NetWare administrator utility on a workstation.) First select the Server object. From the Object menu, choose Details. Then open the Accounting page and set up accounting information, such as the charge rate. The accounting charge rate is the amount you will charge for each unit used. To obtain the charge rate, you divide the total amount of money you want to accrue by the total amount of units you expect to be used. For example, if you want to charge a total of $1000 per month for your disk storage, and you expect users to use a total of 50,000 disk blocks per month, the formula would be:

100,000 (cents) / 50,000 (blocks) = 2 cents per block

If you set the multiplier to 0, the charge amount will be "No Charge."

To display daily and weekly totals for each of the items that are tracked by accounting services, use the ATOTAL utility by entering the command

```
ATOTAL
```

at the workstation's DOS prompt. To redirect the display to a text file that you can read with a text editor, use the following command format:

```
ATOTAL > filename
```

Synchronizing the Servers' Time

Because NetWare 4.1 maintains a networkwide database of network objects and information, all servers on the network must maintain the same time so that all updates to that database happen in the correct order, regardless of the server that originated the update.

To ensure that the servers are keeping the same time, a NetWare feature called Time Services is implemented on each NetWare 4.1 server. With Time Services, certain servers are designated to be the main timekeepers. The other servers all synchronize their times with these timekeepers.

When you install NetWare 4.1 on a server, you designate how you want this server to participate in Time Services with the other servers on the network.

Table 3.13 describes the four different time server designations you can give a server:

TABLE 3.13

Time Server Types

TIME SERVER	DESCRIPTION
Single Reference	The sole server that maintains the network time, a Single Reference server is often used on small networks. All other servers are Secondary time servers. Single Reference servers provide the time to workstations and Secondary servers.
Primary	A Primary server synchronizes its time by polling one or more Primary or Reference servers. Together, the Primary servers determine an average time, then adjust their time to approach that average. If a Reference server exists, the Primary servers approach the Reference server's time.
Reference	Similar to a Single Reference server, a Reference server is used on larger networks where additional Primary servers are desired. Reference servers participate with other Primary servers to determine the correct time, but they do not adjust their own time. Instead, Primary servers migrate their time to match the Reference server's time. If more than one Reference server exists, they must all be synchronized with the same external time source, such as an atomic clock.
Secondary	A Secondary server obtains the time from one of the other time servers. Secondary servers do not participate in determining the time; they merely obtain it for their own use and to provide the time to their workstations.

You set up time services on the server during installation, and time services are controlled by TIMESYNC.NLM, which is loaded automatically when the server is started up. If you want to modify the time synchronization after installation, you can edit the TIMESYNC.CFG file to modify its SET parameters.

You can use SERVMAN.NLM to change the SET parameters, but SERVMAN.NLM will not add the parameters to the TIMESYNC.CFG file. You must still edit the TIMESYNC.CFG file if you want the time synchronization parameters to be in effect the next time you reboot the server.

You can use EDIT.NLM to edit TIMESYNC.CFG.

Time synchronization uses, by default, SAP broadcasts to keep all time servers synchronized. This should be adequate in most cases. However, if you find that the SAP traffic is too heavy or that you frequently have servers joining and leaving the network (for testing or other purposes), you might want to turn the SAP synchronization off and tell the server exactly which time servers you want it to use.

To do this, edit the TIMESYNC.CFG file and add the following commands to it:

TYPE= *server type*

SERVICE ADVERTISING=OFF

CONFIGURED SOURCES=ON

For *server type*, specify whether this server is a Reference, Single Reference, Primary, or Secondary server. For example, enter

TYPE=PRIMARY

Then add the list of the time servers you want this server to contact, in order of priority. Add the following commands:

TIME SOURCE= *server1*

TIME SOURCE= *server2*

TIME SOURCE= *server3*

For *server1*, *server2*, *server3*, and so on, indicate the name of the time servers you want this server to contact.

Additional utilities you can use to work with a server's time are described in Table 3.14.

TABLE 3.14

Utilities Used to Manage Time Services

UTILITY	DESCRIPTION
TIME console utility	Displays the server's date, time, daylight saving time status, and time synchronization information.
SET TIME console utility	Lets you change the server's date and time.
SET TIME ZONE console utility	Lets you change the server's time zone information.
SYSTIME workstation utility	Lets you synchronize a workstation's time with the server's time.

CHAPTER 4

Installing Workstations

Instant Access

Installing

- To install DOS or Windows workstations, use the NetWare DOS Requester.
- To install OS/2 workstations, use the NetWare Client for OS/2.
- To install Windows NT workstations, use the NetWare Client for Windows NT.
- To install Macintosh workstations, use NetWare MacNDS Client. (See Chapter 10.)

Managing

- To configure network support, use VLM files and NET.CFG files. (See also Appendix A.)
- To manage NetBIOS support, use NETBIOS.EXE.
- To manage Token Ring source routing support, use ROUTE.COM and ROUTE.NLM.
- To manage support for the IBM LAN Support Program, use LANSUP.COM.

On a NetWare 4.1 network, you can have any combination of the following types of workstations:

- DOS and Windows (included in NetWare 4.1)
- OS/2 (included in NetWare 4.1)
- Windows NT (available on the NetWire CompuServe forum and Novell's Internet site)
- Macintosh (included in NetWare 4.1)

The following sections explain how to set up DOS and Windows, OS/2, and Windows NT workstations. See Chapter 10 for instructions on setting up Macintosh workstations.

Installing NetWare Client Software on a DOS or Windows Workstation

To allow a workstation to communicate with a NetWare 4.1 network, you must install NetWare client software on the workstation. (On a NetWare network, workstations are often called *clients* because they request services from the server.) The NetWare client software for DOS-based or Windows-based computers is called the *NetWare DOS Requester*. You must install the NetWare DOS Requester on every DOS-based or Windows-based workstation that will connect to the NetWare 4.1 network.

The NetWare DOS Requester consists of several files, which together regulate how the workstation communicates with the network and how tasks are accomplished. These files, called *Virtual Loadable Modules* (VLMs), each control a different aspect of the workstation's activities, such as the workstation's connections to servers, user authentication, backward compatibility with older client software, and so on. The VLMs are all managed by a single executable file, called VLM.EXE.

Along with the NetWare DOS Requester, the workstation also needs additional files to boot the machine and connect it with the network. Some of these files are regular DOS boot files that the workstation already has, but which need to be edited to provide NetWare support. Other files are provided by NetWare, such as the protocol files and LAN drivers for network boards.

The NetWare DOS Requester installation program automatically copies all necessary NetWare files to the workstation, and edits any DOS or Windows files that require modifications. In addition, the NetWare DOS Requester also installs User Tools (a NetWare utility that users can use to work with the network) on the workstation automatically.

PREPARING TO INSTALL THE NETWARE DOS REQUESTER

Before you can install a new workstation, you need to decide how you will install the client software. You have three choices: You can install the software from diskettes, from the *NetWare 4.1 Operating System* CD-ROM, or from a network directory (if you're upgrading the workstation only).

To use diskettes, you must make client installation diskettes from the *NetWare 4.1 Operating System* CD-ROM. To make the diskettes, format five high-density diskettes (and label them Disk 1 through Disk 5). Then run INSTALL.NLM at the server and select the Create DOS/MS Windows/OS2 Client Install Diskettes option. Choose the set of diskettes you want to create (3.5 inch DOS/MS Windows Client Install) by making sure its check box is marked with an "X," and then press F10. This process then automatically copies the needed files to the diskettes, prompting you when to swap diskettes.

You can install the client software directly from the *NetWare 4.1 Operating System* CD-ROM if the workstation has a CD-ROM drive installed in it.

If the workstation already has an older version of NetWare client software installed on it, and you are updating the workstation, you can run the client installation program from a network directory instead of from diskettes, if you selected the Set Up a Network Directory for Client Install option during the installation of the NetWare 4.1 server.

INSTALLING THE NETWARE DOS REQUESTER

The following is a checklist of the steps necessary to install the NetWare client software on a DOS or Windows workstation.

1 • Install a network board in the workstation according to the manufacturer's documentation. Be sure to record the board's configuration settings, such as its interrupt and port address. (You may want to use a worksheet such as the "Workstation Installation and Configuration" worksheet in Appendix D.)

2 • Cable the network board to the network, using the correct cabling hardware, including terminators, hubs, or any other hardware required by your topology. See Chapter 1 and your hardware manufacturer's documentation for more information about limitations and guidelines for installing network hardware.

3 • Boot DOS. If the workstation has Windows, make sure Windows is installed but is not running.

4 • Move to the appropriate directory from which you will install the client software and start INSTALL:

- If you are installing from diskettes, insert Disk 1 into the workstation's floppy disk drive, change to that drive letter, and enter

  ```
  INSTALL
  ```

- If you are installing from the CD-ROM, insert the *NetWare 4.1 Operating System* CD-ROM in the workstation's CD-ROM drive, change to the CD-ROM's drive letter, and enter

  ```
  INSTALL
  ```

  Then select the language as prompted, and select the DOS/Windows Client Installation option.

- If you are upgrading an existing workstation with older NetWare client software on it, map a drive to the network directory SYS:PUBLIC\CLIENT\DOSWIN and enter

  ```
  INSTALL
  ```

5 • Accept the default directory (C:\NWCLIENT).

6 • Allow the installation to modify the CONFIG.SYS and AUTOEXEC.BAT files.

7 • Specify whether or not to support Windows.

8 • Select the LAN driver that matches this workstation's network board. If you are installing from diskettes, insert the LAN driver diskette (Disk 5), and press Enter. If the driver you need isn't listed, press Esc, insert the manufacturer's diskette, and press Enter.

9 • When all the information on the screen is correct, press Enter.

10 • When the installation is complete, press Enter to quit the program.

11 • If installing from diskettes, insert Disk 1 when you are asked to "Insert the disk with batch file." The program is looking for the INSTALL file.

12 • If this workstation previously had NETX installed on it, edit AUTOEXEC.BAT and remove any commands that loaded IPX, IPXODI, LSL, and NETX. The NetWare DOS Requester places commands similar to these in the STARTNET.BAT file instead.

The following files are either copied to the workstation or modified during the NetWare DOS Requester installation. Some of these files can be edited later to add or change the workstation's functionality:

- CONFIG.SYS
- AUTOEXEC.BAT
- STARTNET.BAT
- VLMs
- LSL.COM
- LAN drivers
- Protocol drivers

- NET.CFG
- Unicode files
- Windows configuration files (SYSTEM.INI, WIN.INI, PROGMAN.INI)
- NetWare User Tools
- NetBIOS.EXE
- ROUTE.COM
- LANSUP.COM

In addition to the files listed here, the NetWare DOS Requester installs many support files, such as .DLL files, message files, and help files.

The client files are explained in the following sections.

CONFIG.SYS

CONFIG.SYS is a configuration file that, in most recent versions of DOS, is created at the root of the workstation's boot disk during DOS installation. It can also be created or edited with a text editor. CONFIG.SYS configures the workstation's DOS environment.

CONFIG.SYS is automatically modified by the NetWare DOS Requester installation, which adds following lines:

```
FILES=40

LASTDRIVE=Z
```

The following is an example of a CONFIG.SYS file:

```
DEVICE=C:\DOS\SETVER.EXE

DEVICE=C:\WINDOWS\HIMEM.SYS

DEVICE=C:\WINDOWS\EMM386.EXE NOEMS

DOS=HIGH,UMB

SHELL=C:\COMMAND.COM /P C:\ /E:4096

DEVICE=C:\DOS\POWER.EXE
```

```
FILES=40
LASTDRIVE=Z
DEVICE=C:\WINDOWS\SMARTDRV.EXE /DOUBLE_BUFFER
STACKS=9,256
```

AUTOEXEC.BAT

AUTOEXEC.BAT is a batch file created at the root of the disk during DOS installation for most recent versions of DOS. It can also be created or edited with a text editor. It automatically executes when the workstation boots to DOS. It can be used to load TSRs (Terminate and Stay Resident programs) that provide added funtionality for the workstation, such as CD-ROM support, DOS key buffering, network support, and so on. It can also be used to log the user into the network.

AUTOEXEC.BAT is automatically modified by the NetWare DOS Requester installation to add the following line that executes the STARTNET.BAT file:

```
@CALL C:\NWCLIENT\STARTNET
```

The installation program also adds a DOS search path in AUTOEXEC.BAT to the NWCLIENT directory.

After installation, you may want to add lines to set the user's variables for applications and automatically log the user into the network. The following is an example of an AUTOEXEC.BAT file:

```
PATH C:\NWCLIENT\;C:\WINDOWS;C:\DOS;C:\NOTEUT;C:\
C:\DOS\SHARE.EXE /L:500 /F:5100
C:\WINDOWS\SMARTDRV.EXE /L
PROMPT $P$G
SET TEMP=C:\DOS
SET NOTEUT=C:\NOTEUT
C:\DOS\DOSKEY
C:\NOTEUT\HK.COM
```

```
SET NWLANGUAGE=ENGLISH
SET EMAILUSER=LSNOW
SET WP=/U-LKS
ECHO ON
@CALL C:\NWCLIENT\STARTNET
F:
LOGIN .LSNOW.MKTG.WEST.OUTVIEW
```

STARTNET.BAT

STARTNET.BAT is a batch file created by the NetWare DOS Requester installation. It is located in the NWCLIENT directory. It can be edited with a text editor.

STARTNET.BAT specifies the workstation's language by setting the NWLANGUAGE environment variable, and then it loads the LSL, LAN driver, and protocol support files. It then executes VLM.EXE, which loads all necessary VLMs.

In older versions of NetWare client software, called NETX, the commands to load these files were located in the AUTOEXEC.BAT file (instead of in STARTNET.BAT), so if you upgrade a workstation from NETX, you'll need to edit the AUTOEXEC.BAT file to remove those lines.

The following is an example of a STARTNET.BAT file:

```
SET NWLANGUAGE=ENGLISH
C:\NWCLIENT\LSL.COM
C:\NWCLIENT\3C523.COM
C:\NWCLIENT\IPXODI.COM
C:\NWCLIENT\TCPIP.EXE
C:\NWCLIENT\VLM.EXE
```

VLMs

VLMs (Virtual Loadable Modules) are placed in the NWCLIENT directory by the NetWare DOS Requester installation. They control the workstation's communication and activities on the network.

After the NetWare DOS Requester has been installed on a workstation, the workstation's AUTOEXEC.BAT file contains a line that calls the STARTNET.BAT file from the NWCLIENT directory. STARTNET loads the LSL driver, the LAN driver, the protocol driver (such as IPXODI), and VLM.EXE.

VLM.EXE, by default, automatically loads twelve VLMs. Most of these VLMs are required, but a few are optional. In addition, there are eleven more VLMs that are not loaded by default, but which you can add.

Table 4.1 lists the twelve default VLMs in the order in which they execute:

TABLE 4.1

The Twelve Default VLMs

VLM	REQUIRED/OPTIONAL	FUNCTION
CONN.VLM	Required	Allows the workstation to connect to a specified number of servers.
IPXNCP.VLM	Required	Builds and transmits IPX packets using the IPX protocol.
TRAN.VLM	Required	Handles protocols and manages IPXNCP.VLM.
SECURITY.VLM	Optional	Helps provide security at the transport level.
NDS.VLM	Required	Allows the workstation to form an NDS-based connection with a NetWare 4.1 server.
BIND.VLM	Optional	Allows the workstation to form a bindery-based connection with a NetWare server. This provides backward compatibility for applications that are still using bindery-specific information to access the network.
NWP.VLM	Required	(NetWare Protocol Multiplexor) Allows other modules to log in and log out and to connect to network services.

TABLE 4.1

The Twelve Default VLMs (continued)

VLM	REQUIRED/OPTIONAL	FUNCTION
FIO.VLM	Required	Controls file input and output (I/O) and provides file-caching support, Large Internet Packet (LIP) support, and packet burst support.
GENERAL.VLM	Required	Provides general services to other VLMs, such as server and queue information and the handling of search drives.
REDIR.VLM	Required	(DOS Redirector) Redirects appropriate requests to the network.
PRINT.VLM	Optional	Provides printing redirection services using FIO.VLM.
NETX.VLM	Optional	Provides backward compatibility for applications that require APIs that were available in NETX.

Table 4.2 shows the additional VLMs that are also available but aren't loaded by default.

TABLE 4.2

The Eleven Additional VLMs

VLM	FUNCTION
AUTO.VLM	Tries automatically to reconnect the workstation if the connection to the server is temporarily broken.
MIB2IF.VLM	Provides support for MIB-II interface groups.
MIB2PROT.VLM	Provides MIB-II support for TCP/IP groups.
NMR.VLM	(NetWare Management Responder) Provides management information about the workstation to a network management program.
PNW.VLM	Implements NetWare protocol support for Personal NetWare.

(continued)

TABLE 4.2

The Eleven Additional VLMs (continued)

VLM	FUNCTION
RSA.VLM	Uses the RSA security encryption system to provide system-level background authentication for the workstation.
WSASN1.VLM	Provides SNMP ASN.1 translation.
WSDRVPRN.VLM	Gathers information about print mappings and captured printers.
WSREG.VLM	Provides SNMP MIB registration.
WSSNMP.VLM	Provides desktop SNMP support.
WSTRAP.VLM	Provides SNMP trap support.

To make one of these VLMs execute, you must add a command to the NET.CFG file under the NetWare DOS Requester heading, in the following format:

```
VLM=xxxx.VLM
```

For example, to load AUTO.VLM, the command would appear under the NetWare DOS Requester heading in a fashion similar to the following:

```
NETWARE DOS REQUESTER
FIRST NETWORK DRIVE = F
NETWARE PROTOCOL = NDS,BIND
VLM=AUTO.VLM
```

If you want to prevent one or more of the default VLMs from loading, you can add a new heading to NET.CFG, called USE DEFAULTS=OFF.

Then, under that heading, list all the default VLMs you want to load, excluding the unwanted ones from the list. For example, if you don't want to load BIND.VLM or NETX.VLM, this section of the NET.CFG file would look like this:

```
USE DEFAULTS=OFF
VLM=CONN.VLM
VLM=IPXNCP.VLM
VLM=TRAN.VLM
```

```
VLM=SECURITY.VLM
VLM=NDS.VLM
VLM=NWP.VLM
VLM=FIO.VLM
VLM=GENERAL.VLM
VLM=REDIR.VLM
VLM=PRINT.VLM
```

LSL.COM

LSL.COM is the Link Support Layer file, which enables the workstation to communicate with different protocols. It is placed in the NWCLIENT directory by the NetWare DOS Requester installation.

LAN Drivers

A *LAN driver* is the software module that allows the network board in a workstation (or server) to communicate with the network. You select and install the LAN driver during the NetWare DOS Requester installation. Novell ships several LAN drivers with NetWare 4.1, so the LAN driver you need may be on the client software diskettes. If the driver you need does not come with NetWare 4.1, you'll have to obtain it from the board manufacturer.

The NetWare DOS Requester automatically installs the LAN driver in the NWCLIENT directory.

Protocol Drivers

The *protocol driver* is placed in the NWCLIENT directory by the NetWare DOS Requester installation. It enables the LAN driver to communicate with a protocol, such as IPX or TCP/IP. *IPXODI.COM* is the protocol driver used to support the IPX protocol (the default protocol for most NetWare networks).

NET.CFG

NET.CFG is created by the NetWare DOS Requester installation. It is located in the NWCLIENT directory and can be edited with a text editor.

NET.CFG configures the NetWare DOS Requester and LAN driver for the workstation's needs. Because NET.CFG is used to configure a variety of different aspects of your workstation, NET.CFG can be quite simple or fairly involved.

The following is a sample NET.CFG file that was created automatically during installation to configure an NE2000 network board to use port 300, interrupt 3, and the Ethernet 802.2 frame type. Notice that the file is divided by headings. The Link Driver NE2000 heading contains indented lines that specify the information for that driver. The NetWare DOS Requester heading contains indented lines that specify general items for the Requester.

```
LINK DRIVER NE2000
PORT 300
INT 3
FRAME ETHERNET_802.2

NETWARE DOS REQUESTER
NETWARE PROTOCOL=NDS, BIND
FIRST NETWORK DRIVE=F
```

The following is a more complex NET.CFG file. In this file, there are two different boards loaded in the workstation, so there are two different Link Driver headings. Both boards are linked to more than one Ethernet frame type. Also, additional commands have been added beneath the NetWare DOS Requester heading to indicate a preferred Directory tree and a preferred server. Two of the optional VLMs are called out under this heading, also. Finally, because this workstation is using TCP/IP, a final section is added to the file to configure the TCP/IP support.

```
LINK DRIVER PE30DI
    FRAME ETHERNET_802.2
    FRAME ETHERNET_II
    PROTOCOL IPX E0 ETHERNET_802.2
```

```
LINK DRIVER 3C523
     FRAME ETHERNET_802.2
     FRAME ETHERNET_II
     INT 3
     PORT 300
     MEM C0000
     PROTOCOL IPX E0 ETHERNET_802.2
     PROTOCOL IP 800 ETHERNET_II
NETWARE DOS REQUESTER
     FIRST NETWORK DRIVE = F
     NETWARE PROTOCOL = NDS,BIND
     PREFERRED TREE = OUTVIEW_INC
     PREFERRED SERVER =PHOTO1
     NAME CONTEXT = "MKTG.WEST.OUTVIEW"
     NETWORK PRINTERS = 1
     PRINT HEADER =100
     PRINT TAIL = 100
     SHOW DOTS = ON
     AUTO RECONNECT = ON
     BIND RECONNECT = ON
     AUTO RETRY = 1
     VLM = AUTO.VLM
     VLM = RSA.VLM
     CONNECTIONS=10
```

```
LINK SUPPORT
     BUFFERS 8 1500
     MEMPOOL 4096
     MAX STACKS 8
PROTOCOL TCPIP
     PATH SCRIPT     C:\NET\SCRIPT
     PATH PROFILE      C:\NET\PROFILE
     PATH LWP_CFG      C:\NET\HSTACC
     PATH TCP_CFG      C:\NET\TCP
     IP_ADDRESS      135.26.101.26
     IP_ROUTER       135.26.101.254
     IP_NETMASK      254.254.254.0
     TCP_SOCKETS     8
     UDP_SOCKETS     8
     RAW_SOCKETS     1
     NB_SESSIONS     4
     NB_COMMANDS     8
     NB_ADAPTER      0
     NB_DOMAIN       DENVER.WEST.OUTVIEW.COM
```

There are numerous parameters that can be set in NET.CFG. Appendix A explains each of the commands you can enter in NET.CFG.

Unicode Files

Unicode files are used to help the NetWare client software run on machines that use different country-specific keyboards and language-specific versions of DOS. During the NetWare DOS Requester installation, the Unicode files specific to the country setting of your workstation are installed in the WINDOWS\NLS subdirectory.

For example, if you are using English on an American keyboard, the Unicode files with the extension .001 are copied to your WINDOWS\NLS subdirectory.

Windows Configuration Files

Windows configuration files are files that help define how Windows and Windows-based applications run. Some of the regular Windows configuration files — SYSTEM.INI, WIN.INI, and PROGMAN.INI — are modified during the NetWare DOS Requester installation to add support for the NetWare client software.

In the SYSTEM.INI file, the following lines are added or edited under the indicated headings (headings are always enclosed in brackets):

```
[boot]
network.drv=netware.drv
[boot.description]
network.drv=Novell NetWare (vx.x)
[386Enh]
network=*vnetbios;vipx.386;vnetware.386
TimerCriticalSection=1000
OverlappedIO=OFF
PSPIncrement=5
ReflectDOSInt2A=True
UniqueDOSPSP=True
```

In the WIN.INI file, the following line is edited under the [windows] heading:

```
[windows]
load=nwpopup.exe
```

In the PROGMAN.INI file, the following line is added under the [Groups] heading if NW.GRP does not exist, so that Windows will display the NetWare User Tools utility as an icon in the NetWare Tools program group when Windows is loaded:

```
[Groups]
Groupx=C:\WINDOWS\NW.GRP
```

Netware User Tools

NetWare User Tools is a Windows-based utility that is installed by the NetWare DOS Requester installation. It is part of the NETWARE.DRV driver. Users can use this utility to complete many network tasks instead of using utilities that are targeted toward the network administrator. With User Tools, users can easily map drives, capture printer ports, and so on.

NETBIOS.EXE

NETBIOS.EXE is an optional file. It is automatically placed in the NWCLIENT directory by the NetWare DOS Requester installation. You only need to use this file if you need NetBIOS emulation for applications designed to run peer-to-peer communications on the IBM PC Network and the IBM Token Ring Network.

The following is a checklist of the steps necessary to enable a workstation to access a NetBIOS application:

1 • Install the application on the server before you configure the workstations for the NetBIOS connection.

2 • Edit the STARTNET.BAT file (in the NWCLIENT directory) to add the following lines in this order (replace *LAN driver* with the name of the LAN driver your workstation uses):

```
CD C:\NWCLIENT
LSL
LAN driver
IPXODI
NETBIOS
VLM
```

3 • Edit NET.CFG (in the NWCLIENT directory) to specify any NetBIOS parameters you need. These parameters are explained in Appendix A.

4 • Reboot the workstation to make the changes take effect.

ROUTE.COM

ROUTE.COM is an optional file. It is automatically placed in the NWCLIENT directory by the NetWare DOS Requester installation. It is a source routing driver that allows the workstation to communicate across IBM Token Ring source routing bridges.

To use source routing, you must configure the workstation, plus you must also load ROUTE.NLM on the server. You can load ROUTE.NLM more than once, if you have more than one network board in the server that should support a Token Ring source routing network. You can either load ROUTE.NLM at the server console manually (with the LOAD ROUTE command) or you can put the LOAD ROUTE command in the AUTOEXEC.NCF file to ensure that it loads every time the server is rebooted.

The following is a checklist of the steps necessary to allow a workstation to communicate across Token Ring source routing bridges.

1 • At the server's console, load ROUTE.NLM on the server by entering

```
LOAD ROUTE
```

(You can also place this command in the AUTOEXEC.NCF file so that it loads automatically when the server is booted.)

2 • If you have two network boards in the server, load ROUTE.NLM again, specifying the appropriate board number. For example, to load ROUTE.NLM for the second network board, enter

```
LOAD ROUTE BOARD=02
```

(This command can also be placed in the AUTOEXEC.NCF file.)

3 • At the workstation, edit the workstation's STARTNET.BAT file (in the NWCLIENT directory) to add the following lines in this order (replace *LAN driver* with the name of the LAN driver your workstation uses, and replace *parameters* with any of the parameters explained in Table 4.3):

```
CD C:\NWCLIENT
LSL
LAN driver
```

```
ROUTE parameters

IPXODI

VLM
```

4 • Reboot the workstation to make the changes take effect.

The parameters shown in Table 4.3 can be used with the ROUTE command. To use more than one parameter in the command, separate each with a comma.

TABLE 4.3

ROUTE.COM Parameters

PARAMETER	DESCRIPTION
BOARD=*number*	Specifies the board number (determined by the order in which you load the LAN drivers in STARTNET.BAT).
CLEAR	Clears the source routing table and rebuilds it (used when an IBM bridge has gone down and an alternate route is available).
DEF	Forwards frame types with default (unknown) destination addresses as All Routes Broadcast frames instead of Single Route Broadcast frames.
GBR	Forwards all General Broadcast frames as All Routes Broadcast frames instead of Single Route Broadcast frames.
MBR	Forwards all Multicast Broadcast frames as All Routes Broadcast frames instead of Single Route Broadcast frames.
NODE=*number*	Specifies the number of table entries in the source routing table (*number* must be between 8 and 255, with a default of 16).
REMOVE=*number*	Deletes a node address from the workstation's source routing table (*number* must be a 12-digit hexadecimal number).
/U	Unloads ROUTE.COM from the workstation.
/?	Displays help for the ROUTE command.

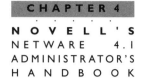

LANSUP.COM

LANSUP.COM is an optional file. It is automatically placed in the NWCLIENT directory by the NetWare DOS Requester installation. It is used to support the IBM LAN Support Extended Services and LAN Server programs.

The following is a checklist of the steps necessary to enable a workstation to use LANSUP.

1 • Install and load the Extended Services or LAN Server programs on the server before you configure the workstations.

2 • At the workstation, edit the workstation's STARTNET.BAT file (in the NWCLIENT directory) to add the following lines in this order:

```
CD C:\NWCLIENT
LSL
LANSUP
IPXODI
VLM
```

3 • Edit the workstation's NET.CFG file (in the NWCLIENT directory) to add the Link Driver LANSUP heading and specify the workstation board's frame type (either TOKEN-RING or TOKEN-RING_SNAP). For example, to load the TOKEN-RING_SNAP frame type, add the following lines to the top of the NET.CFG file:

```
LINK DRIVER LANSUP
        FRAME TOKEN-RING_SNAP
```

4 • Reboot the workstation to make the changes take effect.

Installing NetWare Client Software on an OS/2 Workstation

To make an OS/2 computer function as a workstation on a NetWare 4.1 network, you must install NetWare client software on the workstation. The NetWare client software for OS/2-based computers is called the NetWare Client for OS/2.

The NetWare Client for OS/2 consists of several files, which together regulate how the workstation communicates with the network and how tasks are accomplished.

Along with the NetWare Client for OS/2 files, the workstation also needs additional files to boot the machine and connect it with the network. Some of these files are regular OS/2 boot files that the workstation already has, but which need to be edited to provide NetWare support. Other files are provided by NetWare, such as the protocol drivers.

The NetWare Client for OS/2 installation program automatically copies all necessary NetWare files to the workstation, and edits any OS/2 files that require modifications. In addition, NetWare Tools (a NetWare utility that users can use to work with the network) is also installed on the workstation automatically.

PREPARING TO INSTALL THE NETWARE CLIENT FOR OS/2

Before you can install a new OS/2 workstation, you need to decide how you will install the client software. You have two choices: You can install the software from diskettes or from a network directory (only if you're upgrading the workstation).

To use diskettes, you must make client installation diskettes from the *NetWare 4.1 Operating System* CD-ROM. To make the diskettes, format six high-density diskettes (and label them Disk 1 through Disk 6). Then run INSTALL.NLM at the server and select the Create DOS/MS Windows/OS2 Client Install Diskettes option. Choose the set of diskettes you want to create (3.5-inch OS/2 Client Install) by making sure its check box is marked with an "X," and then press F10. This process then automatically copies the needed files to the diskettes, prompting you when to swap diskettes.

If the workstation already has an older version of NetWare client software installed on it and you are updating the workstation, you can run the client installation program from a network directory instead of from diskettes, if you selected the Set up a Network Directory for Client Install option during the installation of the NetWare 4.1 server.

INSTALLING THE NETWARE CLIENT FOR OS/2

The following is a checklist of the steps necessary to install the NetWare client software on an OS/2 workstation.

1 • Install a network board in the workstation according to the manufacturer's documentation. Be sure to record the board's configuration settings, such as its interrupt and port address. (You may want to use a worksheet such as the "Workstation Installation and Configuration" worksheet in Appendix D.)

2 • Cable the board to the network, using the correct cabling hardware, including terminators, hubs, or any other hardware required by your topology. See Chapter 1 and your hardware manufacturer's documentation for more information about limitations and guidelines for installing network hardware.

3 • Boot the workstation.

4 • Move to the appropriate directory from which you will install the client software and start INSTALL:

- If you are installing from diskettes, go to the OS/2 desktop, insert Disk 1 into the workstation's floppy disk drive, and select the Drive A icon. Then, from the Tree View window, select the drive A icon, and then select the INSTALL.EXE icon.

- If you are upgrading an existing workstation with older NetWare client software on it, map a drive to the network directory SYS:PUBLIC\CLIENT\OS2 and enter the following command:

```
INSTALL
```

5 • From the Installation menu, select Requester on Workstation.

6 • Accept the default directory (C:\NETWARE) and specify the source drive.

7 • Allow the installation to modify the CONFIG.SYS file and copy all files to the workstation.

8 • Select the LAN driver that matches this workstation's network board. If installing from diskettes, insert the LAN driver diskette (WSDRV_1) or a diskette from another manufacturer, and choose OK.

9 • Select the LAN driver you need, and choose Continue.

10 • Turn on IPX Support for DOS and Windows and Private NetWare Shell Support by clicking on their respective buttons, and then choose Continue.

11 • Accept the default settings for AUTOEXEC.BAT by choosing Save.

12 • Answer No when asked if you want to add files to another batch file.

13 • If asked if you want to change the DOS_LASTDRIVE setting, choose OK.

14 • Accept the default optional protocols by choosing Save.

15 • Save the CONFIG.SYS file by choosing OK.

16 • Choose the appropriate responses to let the installation program copy the ODI LAN driver files and requester files and finish the installation.

17 • From the Configuration menu, select This Workstation.

18 • Enter the path to your NET.CFG file (C:\NETWARE) and select Edit.

19 • Enter the NET.CFG commands this workstation needs by selecting the commands from the window on the left and editing them in the window on the right. The bottom window displays help for each command or parameter. (NET.CFG parameters are explained in Appendix A.)

20 • When you are finished, select Save and exit the installation program.

21 • Reboot the workstation to make the NetWare Client for OS/2 take effect.

Installing NetWare Client Software on a Windows NT Workstation

To make a Windows NT computer function as a workstation on a NetWare 4.1 network, you must install special NetWare software, called the NetWare Client for Windows NT, on it. This client software is not included in the NetWare 4.1 box, but is available on Novell's NetWire forums on CompuServe and on Novell's Internet site (http://www.novell.com). To make diskettes for the NetWare Client for Windows NT installation, download the necessary files from either online location onto your workstation's local hard disk, and then follow the readme instructions for creating the diskettes.

The NetWare Client for Windows NT consists of several files, which together regulate how the workstation communicates with the network and how tasks are accomplished.

Along with the NetWare Client for Windows NT files, the workstation also needs additional files to boot the machine and connect it with the network. Some of these files are regular NT boot files that the workstation already has, but which need to be edited to provide NetWare support. Other files are provided by NetWare.

The NetWare Client for Windows NT installation program automatically copies all necessary NetWare files to the workstation, and edits any NT files that require modifications. In addition, NetWare Tools (a NetWare utility that users can use to work with the network) is also installed on the workstation automatically.

If you plan to use the long file name formats that are allowed by NT, you must also load the OS/2 name space on the volume that will store the NT files. If you intend to use only DOS-type file names (eight character names with a three-character extension), you do not need to load the OS/2 name space. (The OS/2 name space simply allows long name spaces to be stored. It doesn't necessarily signify that you'll be storing OS/2 files on the volume.)

The following is a checklist of the steps necessary to install the NetWare client software on an NT workstation.

1 • Install a network board in the workstation according to the manufacturer's documentation. Be sure to record the board's configuration settings, such as its interrupt and port address. (You may want to use a worksheet such as the "Workstation Installation and Configuration" worksheet in Appendix D.)

2 • Cable the board to the network, using the correct cabling hardware, including terminators, hubs, or any other hardware required by your topology. See Chapter 1 and your hardware manufacturer's documentation for more information about limitations and guidelines for installing network hardware.

3 • Deactivate Microsoft's NetWare client program. You can't have both Microsoft's and Novell's NetWare clients active at the same time. To deactivate (or remove) the Microsoft client, choose the NT Control Panel, select Network, and then choose either Client Service for NetWare or Gateway Service for NetWare. Then select Remove to deactivate the client.

4 • Reboot the workstation to make the change take effect.

5 • Log in as an NT user who is a member of the Administrators group.

6 • From the NT Control Panel, select Network, choose Add Software, and then choose <Other>, and select Continue.

7 • Insert the NetWare Client Install diskette into drive A, and choose OK.

8 • Select Novell NetWare Client Services, and then choose OK.

9 • If the workstation already had a Microsoft NDIS driver installed to support a network board, you will be asked if you want to change it to an ODI driver, which is NetWare's format. The NetWare client will use either format, but the ODI driver will give you greater performance. Choose whichever type of driver you want. After you choose, the installation program installs the driver and client software on the workstation.

10 • If no driver was already installed, you will need to install an ODI driver. From the NT Control Panel, select Network, and then select Add Adapter. Then select the correct network board, insert the Drivers diskette (which you created when you made installation diskettes for the client software) into drive A and choose Continue. Select the board's settings and frame type, and then choose OK.

11 • Reboot the workstation to make the changes take effect.

CHAPTER 5

Managing NetWare Directory Services

Instant Access

Managing NDS Objects

- To create NDS objects, use the NetWare Administrator utility (which runs in Windows).
- To change a name context, use the CX command-line utility.

Managing Replicas and Partitions

- To manage replicas and partitions, use the NetWare Administrator utility or the PARTMGR menu utility (which runs in DOS).

Managing Bindery Services

- To set a bindery context, use SERVMAN.NLM to change the SET BINDERY CONTEXT parameter.
- To display the bindery context, use the CONFIG console utility.

Managing NetWare 3.1x Users

- To synchronize NetWare 3.1x servers' binderies with NDS, install NetSync. To install NetSync, load NETSYNC4.NLM on the NetWare 4.1 host server and load NETSYNC3.NLM and REMAPID.NLM on each NetWare 3.1x server.
- To manage users, use the NetWare Administrator utility.
- To manage merged print servers, use the NetWare Administrator utility or the PCONSOLE menu utility (which runs in DOS).

Merging NDS Trees

- To merge NDS trees, use DSMERGE.NLM.

Troubleshooting

- To monitor NDS messages, use SERVMAN.NLM to set the SET NDS TRACE parameter.

- To repair the NDS tree, use DSREPAIR.NLM.

NetWare Directory Services (NDS), in simplest terms, is a distributed database of network information. It contains information that defines every object on the network. *Objects* include network resources such as users, groups, printers, print queues, servers, and volumes.

In NetWare 3.1x and 2.x, this network information was stored in a database called the bindery. Each server had its own unique bindery. If you wanted a user to access more than one server, you had to create a separate account for that user on each server, because the different binderies couldn't talk to each other to see which users were valid across multiple servers.

With NetWare 4, NDS replaced the bindery. The NDS database is not confined to a single server, as binderies are. Instead, all the NetWare 4 servers on a network share a single, distributed database. This way, you only have to create a user or other object once on the network; each server will recognize that same object. You can allow that user to access different servers simply by granting him or her the appropriate rights to the necessary volumes on each server.

Another difference between binderies and NDS is how the network information can be organized. Binderies use a *flat database structure,* which means all network objects — users, groups, print queues, and so on — exist at the same level. NDS uses a *hierarchical database structure.* With this type of structure, you can group objects together under categories and subcategories. This makes it easier to find the object you're looking for. It also allows you to control objects as a group, such as when you're modifying those objects' security levels.

The NDS database is called the Directory tree, because it can be easily represented as an upside-down tree, with a root at the top and branches and subbranches fanning out below it. (See Figure 5.1.)

NDS Objects

For each type of network entity that will operate on the network, you will create an NDS object. This object will represent the real entity. Each NDS object contains several *properties,* which are the pieces of information that define the object. For example, a User object contains properties that can define the user's full name, his or her ID number, an e-mail address, group memberships, and so on. (Properties are also called *attributes.*) Each type of object, such as a server or printer object, may have different properties than another type of object.

Each type of object, such as a user, print queue, or server, is referred to as an *object class.*

FIGURE 5.1

A Directory Tree

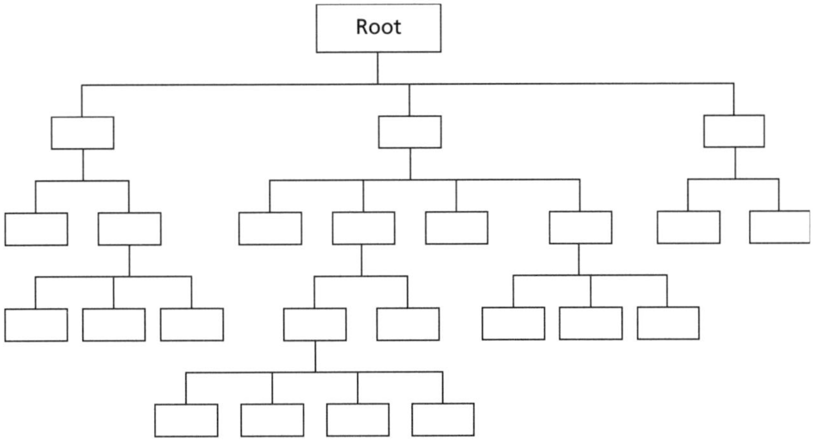

CATEGORIES OF OBJECT CLASSES

Object classes fall into three basic categories:

- *Root object.* The Root object is unique and is situated at the very top of the Directory tree.
- *Container objects.* These are objects that contain other objects. There are three available container object classes: Country, Organization, and Organizational Unit. You can have only one level of Country objects, which fall immediately below the Root object. Country objects are optional. You also can have only one level of Organization objects, which falls below the Country object if there is one, or the Root object if there isn't. You need at least one Organization object. Finally, you can have multiple levels of Organizational Unit objects, which fall below the Organization objects.
- *Leaf objects.* These objects represent the entities on the network. Leaf objects, such as users, servers, and volumes, cannot contain other objects.

Figure 5.2 shows how these three categories of object classes appear in the Directory tree.

FIGURE 5.2

Root, Container, and Leaf Objects in a Directory Tree

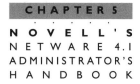

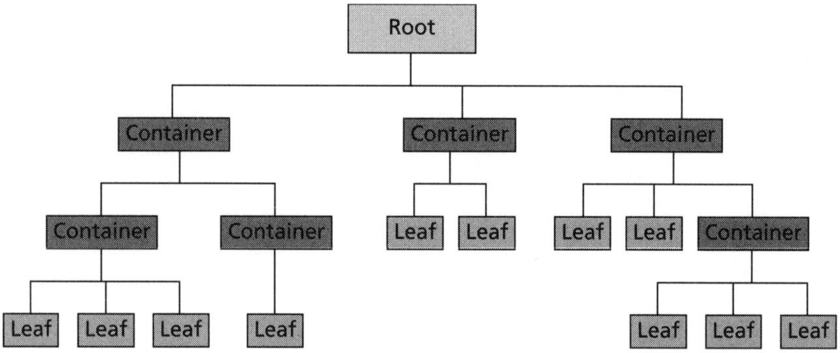

THE NDS SCHEMA

The types of NDS objects, their properties, and the rules that govern their creation and existence are called the *NDS schema*. The schema defines which objects and properties are allowed in the NDS database, and determines how those objects can inherit properties and trustee rights of other container objects above it. The schema also defines how the Directory tree is structured and how objects in it are named.

Software developers can expand or change the schema by identifying new classes of objects (say, for example, a database server) or adding additional properties to existing object classes.

NDS OBJECT CLASSES

In NetWare 4.1, a wide variety of object classes is available. Table 5.1 lists the object classes that are available.

TABLE 5.1

Object Classes Available by Default

OBJECT CLASS	DESCRIPTION
AFP Server	An AppleTalk File Protocol (AFP) server that is a node on the network
Alias	A representation of an object that is really located in another part of the Directory tree

TABLE 5.1

Object Classes Available by Default (continued)

OBJECT CLASS	DESCRIPTION
Bindery Object	An object that was upgraded from a bindery-based server, but which could not be converted into a corresponding NDS object
Computer	A computer
Country	An optional container object representing the country where a portion of your company is located
Directory Map	A representation of a directory path, which typically points to an application
External Entity	An object that stores information about non-NDS entities for other applications or services
Group	A list of users who have at least some identical characteristics, such as the need for access rights to the same application. Users listed as group members receive a security equivalence to the group.
List	A list of objects. Objects that are list members do not have a security equivalence to the List object.
Message Routing Group	A group of messaging servers that are connected directly to each other so that e-mail messages can be routed between them
Messaging Server	A server that receives and transfers e-mail messages
NetWare Server	A NetWare server
Organization	An organization's name (such as a company name)
Organizational Role	A position that various employees can occupy (allows you to assign rights to the position rather than to specific users)
Organizational Unit	A subdivision under the Organization, such as divisions, departments, project teams, or workgroups

(continued)

TABLE 5.1

Object Classes Available by Default (continued)

OBJECT CLASS	DESCRIPTION
Print Server	A NetWare print server, which provides print services
Printer	A printer attached to the network
Profile	An object whose sole function is to provide a login script that can be used by several users, all of whom do not need to be in the same container
Print Queue	A print queue
Root	The highest point (starting point) of the Directory tree (it contains no information)
User	A network user
Volume	A volume on a NetWare server

NDS OBJECT SECURITY

If you have used previous versions of NetWare, you know that NetWare uses a set of trustee rights that can be granted to and revoked from users to control what those users can do within specific files and directories.

NetWare 4 uses a similar set of trustee rights to control how NDS objects can work with other NDS objects. These NDS object rights are separate from the file system rights, but they operate in a similar fashion. Using NDS object rights, you can allow users to see and manipulate other NDS objects.

NDS object rights are explained in Chapter 7.

CREATING NDS OBJECTS

The primary tool for creating or modifying NDS objects is the Windows-based NetWare utility called *NetWare Administrator* (sometimes referred to as NWAdmin). There is a DOS-based utility, called *NETADMIN,* which can also be used to work with NDS objects. However, NetWare Administrator has more features than NETADMIN, and because of its graphical interface, NetWare Administrator can be easier to use in some situations. In addition, due to conventional memory limitations, NETADMIN may have difficulty working with NDS Directories that contain several thousand objects in a single context. Therefore, most people prefer to use the NetWare Administrator instead. For this reason, NETADMIN is not discussed in this book.

To use NetWare Administrator, you need to add its icon to a Windows program group. To do this, make sure a drive is mapped to SYS:PUBLIC, create a new program item called NWAdmin, and then select the file NWADMIN.EXE under SYS:PUBLIC. When the icon appears on your desktop, you can double-click it to start the NetWare Administrator.

To create a new NDS object, select Create from the Object menu, choose the class of object you want to create, and then fill in the appropriate information about the object in its property fields.

Planning the NDS Directory Tree

To plan your Directory tree, you can take advantage of the container objects to make the tree resemble your company's organization. For example, if your company is quite large, with many divisions and departments, you can use a single Organization object to represent the company's name, and multiple Organizational Unit objects to represent the various divisions and departments.

Individual users, printers, and so on can be placed inside the Organizational Unit that corresponds to their department. (These individual objects are all leaf objects.) Figure 5.3 shows how a large company, named RedHawk AeroSpace, Inc., might set up its Directory tree.

If your company is small, you may not need to break up your network into Organizational Units. You may want to just have a single Organization object, representing your company, and then place all leaf objects directly beneath that container. This is how the Simple Installation feature of the NetWare INSTALL utility works. Figure 5.4 shows how a tree for a small company, named Rise 'n Shine Clockworks, might look.

FIGURE 5.3

A Sample Directory Tree for a Large Company

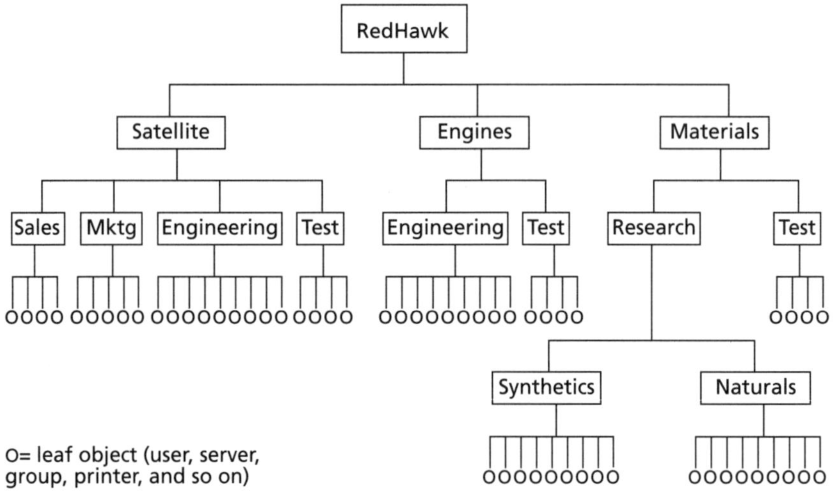

FIGURE 5.4

A Sample Directory Tree for a Small Company

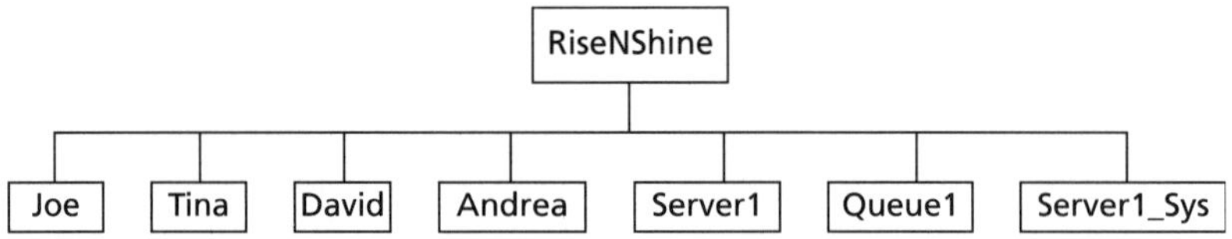

Name Context — Your Location in the Tree

Each object in the Directory tree exists in a specific location of the tree, which is called the object's *name context.* The name context is really a sort of "address" for that object's location, consisting of the names of any container objects over that object. An object's *full name* (or *distinguished name*) consists of the object's name, plus the list of container names, with the names separated by periods. The name of the object by itself (without the rest of the container names listed) is called its *common name* (CN).

Within any container, all object names must be unique. For example, you can have only one user with the common name Eric within the container called Mktg. However, there can be other users named Eric on the tree if they are within other containers. Say there's an Eric in Mktg, and another Eric in Sales, both of whom work in the Satellite division of RedHawk AeroSpace, Inc.

The Marketing Eric's full name would be Eric.Mktg.Satellite.RedHawk. Each container name is added to Eric's common name (separated by periods) to spell out his address in the Directory tree, clear back to the Organization's name. His name context, or location in the tree, is Mktg.Satellite.RedHawk.

The Sales Eric's full name would be Eric.Sales.Satellite.RedHawk. Because his full name is different from the other Eric's full name, NDS can keep them both straight.

Specifying objects in the Directory tree is very similar to specifying subdirectories in a DOS file system. In the file system, if you are at the root of the volume or disk or in a completely separate directory path, you have to specify a full directory path to get to the subdirectory you want. If you are at the root of the Directory tree or in a completely different branch of the tree, you have to specify an object's full name to find it.

However, if you are somewhere in the subdirectory's directory path already, you only need to specify the portion of the path that will get you to the desired subdirectory. You don't need to specify the subdirectory's full path. Similarly, if you are already within a container over an object's location, you only need to specify the portion of the Directory tree address that exists between you and the object. You don't need to specify the object's full name, back to the root. This is called specifying a *partial name* (or a *relative distinguished name*).

If you do want to specify an object's full name back to the root, place a period at the beginning of the object's name (in any commands you type) to indicate to the utility you're using that this is a full name and shouldn't be interpreted as a partial name. For example, you would type **.Eric.Mktg.Satellite.RedHawk** to indicate that this is Eric's full name.

To move around in the Directory tree's context, moving up and down through containers, you use a NetWare command-line utility called CX. This utility is similar to DOS's CD utility, which lets you move around in the file system's subdirectory structure.

NDS Replicas and Partitions

Because the NDS database is common to all servers on the network, if the database itself were stored on only one server (with all other servers accessing it from that server), the entire network would be disabled if that server went down.

To prevent this single point of failure, NetWare 4.1 can create *replicas* of the NDS database and store those replicas on different servers. Then, if one server goes down, all the other servers can still access the NDS database from another replica of the database.

If your NDS database is large enough, you may not want to store the entire database on multiple servers. In this case, you can create Directory *partitions,* which are portions of the database that can be replicated on different servers. A Directory partition is a branch of the Directory tree, beginning with any container object you choose. Partitions can also hold subpartitions beneath them (called *child partitions*). If you have a smaller NDS database, the whole database can reside in a single partition. Using partitions can improve network performance, especially if the network spans across a WAN (wide area network), and they can make it easier to manage portions of the tree separately.

TYPES OF NDS REPLICAS

There are four types of replicas that can be created and stored on servers:

- *Master replica.* The master replica is the only replica that can make changes to the Directory partition, such as adding, merging, or deleting replicas. There is only one master replica per partition.
- *Read-write replica.* Read-write replicas will accept requests to modify NDS objects. Any number of read-write replicas can exist on a network.
- *Read-only replica.* The information in a read-only replica can be read, but not modified. Any number of these replicas can exist on a network.
- *Subordinate reference replica.* A subordinate reference replica exists on a server if that server holds a replica of a parent partition, but does not hold a replica of the child partition. The subordinate reference replica basically provides pointers to the objects in the real child partition.

NetWare Directory Services handles the locations of any modifications to the NDS Directory in the background, so that you and other network administrators do not need to know which replica you need to use to make changes to the Directory. Whenever a change is made to a replica, the change is synchronized with all other replicas on the network. Critical changes are synchronized within four seconds. Less-important changes are queued for approximately ten seconds before being synchronized across the network.

To keep NDS performance optimal, you should have between three and six replicas of a partition. The more replicas you have of a partition, the more synchronization traffic occurs on the network, so you may not want to have more replicas than necessary.

When you install a new server into an existing NDS tree, the installation program determines how many replicas already exist of the partition into which you are installing the server. If there are three or more replicas, the installation program will not create a new replica on the new server by default.

WORKING WITH NDS PARTITIONS AND REPLICAS

To create, delete, or merge partitions, you can use the Windows-based NetWare utility called NetWare Administrator. There is also a DOS-based utility, called *PARTMGR*, which you can use to perform the same tasks, but because most administrators prefer the NetWare Administrator utility, PARTMGR is not discussed here. (For the most part, NetWare Administrator is easier to use because of its graphical interface, while the DOS-based menu utilities such as PARTMGR are less user-friendly.)

If problems occur with Directory partitions and replicas, you can use the DSREPAIR utility to analyze them and repair them if necessary. DSREPAIR is explained in the section "DSREPAIR.NLM" later in this chapter.

To use the NetWare Administrator utility to work with partitions, select Partition Manager from the Tools menu. The partitioning and replication tasks you can do with this utility are explained in Table 5.2.

TABLE 5.2

Partitioning and Replication

TASK	DESCRIPTION
Create a partition	You must create new partitions at the container level. Select the container you want to be the root of the partition, and then choose Create a New Partition.
Merge two partitions	You can merge a child partition into its parent partition. The end result is a single partition that includes all objects from both of the original partitions. To merge partitions, select the container that is the root of the child partition, and then choose Merge Partition. The merge is complete when the child partition's icon disappears. (You will have to refresh the screen by minimizing and then reopening it to verify that the icon has been deleted.)

(continued)

TABLE 5.2

Partitioning and Replication (continued)

TASK	DESCRIPTION
Move a partition	You can move a partition and its container object only if it does not have any child partitions. (If you want to move a partition that has a child partition, you can merge the two before you try to move the parent partition.) To move a partition, select the icon for the partition you want to move, and then choose Move Partition from the Object menu. Specify a destination by browsing through the directory and selecting a container. Then create an alias for the moved partition by selecting Create Alias in Place of Moved Container. By creating an alias, users will be able to find the partition in the location they're used to. Otherwise, you may have users unable to log in because their NET.CFG files specify the wrongname context. To update NET.CFG files with a new context, use the NCUPDATE utility. Finally, in the Move dialog box, choose OK, and the partition will be moved.
Stop a partition operation	If you need to stop a creation, deletion, or merge of a partition, you can do so as long as at least one of the replicas involved has not yet completed the operation (as indicated by the State box). To stop an operation, select the partition that is being affected and choose Abort Partition Operation, and then choose Abort, and select Yes.
Create a replica	To create a replica of a partition, select the partition you want to replicate, and then choose Replicas and Add Replica. Select the server you want to store the replica on, choose the type of replica you want this to be, and then click OK.
Delete a replica	To delete a replica, select the partition whose replica you want to delete, choose the server you want to delete the replica from, and then choose Delete Replica. Master replicas cannot be deleted. If you want to delete a master replica, you must first designate another replica as master, as explained under "Change a replica's type" later in this table. This will automatically change the original master to a read-write replica, so then you will be able to delete it.

TABLE 5.2
Partitioning and Replication (continued)

TASK	DESCRIPTION
Force replica synchronization	If you use DSREPAIR and discover that other replicas are out of synchronization with your master replica, you can force a manual update of those replicas. Select the partition whose replicas you want to update and choose Replicas. Then select the replica that has the correct information and choose Send Updates to Other Replicas.
Receive updates to a replica	If only one replica is out of sync, you can manually request an update from the master replica. Select the partition whose replicas you want to update, and choose Replicas. Select the replica you want to update, and choose Receive Updates.
Change a replica's type	To change a replica to a different type (read-write, master, or read-only), select the partition whose replica you want to change and choose Replicas. Then select the replica you want to change, select Change Type, and then choose the type you want.

Bindery Services

Some applications and network services do not take advantage of NDS's hierarchical database structure. Instead, those applications were designed to make requests to a version of NetWare that used a bindery.

To allow those applications to function with NDS, you can use a feature called *bindery services*. Bindery services makes the objects within a container appear as a bindery located on a particular server. That way, both bindery-based applications and NDS-aware applications can find the objects they need.

Bindery services also allows NetWare 3.x users to log in to a NetWare 4 server and use its resources.

SETTING UP A BINDERY CONTEXT

If you want to set up bindery services on a NetWare 4 server, you have to tell the server which *portion* of the tree you want to appear as its bindery. By default, the server installation process sets the container that the server was installed in as the bindery context for the server. This portion of the tree consists of any container you choose and its objects. You can specify up to 16 different containers to look like a single bindery on a server. To the bindery-based application, the objects in all 16 containers will look like objects in a single flat database. By specifying these containers, you are setting the server's *bindery context.*

To set a server's bindery context, you use the SET command. To set a server's bindery context to be a single container, for example Sales.Satellite.RedHawk, you would type the following command at the server's console:

```
SET BINDERY CONTEXT=Sales.Satellite.RedHawk
```

To set the bindery context to consist of two or more different containers, use the same command, and separate the name of each container by a semicolon, as follows:

```
SET BINDERY CONTEXT=Sales.Satellite.RedHawk;Mktg.Satellite.RedHawk
```

For a server to be able to use bindery services after you've set its bindery context to a container, you need to make sure the server has a read-write replica of the partition that holds that container. If the container specified in the bindery context is not in a replica on the given server, NetWare 4.1 still allows the container to be specified. However, the objects in that container will not be available for bindery services on that server until a replica of the container's partition is created on the server.

To view a server's current bindery context, type **SET BINDERY CONTEXT** at the server console. To set the bindery context to "nothing" (effectively preventing any objects from being available for bindery services on that server), type **SET BINDERY CONTEXT=**. (Don't put anything after the equal sign.)

NetSync: Managing NetWare 3.1x Servers from NetWare 4.1

If you are planning to manage both NetWare 4.1 servers and NetWare 3.1x servers on the same network, NetSync can help. *NetSync* is a tool that lets you manage NetWare 3.1x users and groups from the NetWare Administrator utility.

Without NetSync, you would have to log in to each NetWare 3.1x server individually and use NetWare 3.1x utilities, such as *SYSCON,* to change each user's account. In addition, if the user has an account on more than one server, you would have to change each account; you couldn't just change it once and have it affect all of the user's entities.

NetSync eliminates this extra work. With NetSync, you can synchronize all of the users and groups on up to 12 NetWare 3.1x servers with the Directory database on a single NetWare 4.1 server.

This feature is ideally suited to people who have to manage a mixed environment of NetWare 3.1x and 4.1 servers. However, if you have several people who are administrators of only the NetWare 3.1x servers, and you don't want to centralize management, you probably do not need to synchronize those servers.

HOW NETSYNC WORKS

To make NetSync work, you first load NETSYNC4.NLM on the host NetWare 4.1 server, and then you load NETSYNC3.NLM on each of the NetWare 3.1x servers. Then, all of the user and group information from the binderies on those servers is automatically uploaded into the NDS database on the NetWare 4.1 server. When the NetWare 4.1 server receives the information about the bindery-based users and groups, it converts them into NDS objects and places them all in a single bindery context, or container. Then, it downloads the new information about these users and groups to each of the NetWare 3.1x servers.

In essence, the 12 individual binderies have now been combined into what appears to be a single *super-bindery.* When this super-bindery is downloaded onto the NetWare 3.1x servers, each server ends up with an identical copy. Now, any user that existed on server A will also exist on server B, server C, and so on. The user will retain the same file system trustee rights as before, so that user will not suddenly have rights to files on servers that he or she didn't have before.

If you want to synchronize more than 12 NetWare 3.1x servers, you will need to install more than one NetWare 4.1 host server. If you set each NetWare 4.1 host server to the same bindery context, and then attach up to 12 NetWare 3.1x servers to each of those NetWare 4.1 servers, all of the 3.1x servers' bindery information will go into the same bindery context. In other words, if you have two NetWare 4.1 host servers and each has 12 NetWare 3.1x servers attached, the super-bindery will contain all 24 servers' bindery information. The only problem is that the increased number of objects in the super-bindery could overtax your servers' memory capabilities during uploads and downloads.

If a user had accounts on more than one NetWare 3.1x server, those accounts are merged together so that only one account exists for that user. (For this reason, be sure that you verify that all users have unique names on any servers that will be synchronized together. Otherwise you may accidentally merge two different users named Debbie, for example.)

Also during NetSync installation, your NetWare 3.1x printing services are upgraded to NetWare 4.1 printing services. All printing utilities are upgraded, and the PRINTCON and PRINTDEF databases are upgraded to the NetWare 4.1 format and duplicated in the NetWare 4.1 database.

You have the option of merging all of your NetWare 3.1x print servers into a single print server on the NetWare 4.1 host server. This also places your printers into the NDS tree so that you can manage them from a NetWare 4.1 print server.

LEAVING SYSCON BEHIND

Once the servers are all synchronized, you can use NetWare Administrator to make changes or add new users. Whenever you change or add a user from the NetWare Administrator, that change is automatically downloaded to all the NetWare 3.1x servers.

Note, however, that you cannot use SYSCON to make a change at the NetWare 3.1x level. After the initial installation, information is not uploaded from the NetWare 3.1x servers anymore. If you make a change using SYSCON, that change will affect only the single NetWare 3.1x server from which you executed SYSCON. The NDS database will not be updated, and the other servers will not receive that change, so this NetWare 3.1x server will be out of synchronization with the other servers. You can force a manual upload if this happens by reloading NETSYNC3. However, it's much easier to simply turn on NetSync once, let it run continuously, and make all your changes via the NetWare Administrator.

The only user change you can make at the NetWare 3.1x server using NetWare 3.1x utilities is a user's password. Password changes are synchronized both ways, from either the NetWare 4.1 or the NetWare 3.1x side.

HOW LOGIN SCRIPTS ARE SYNCHRONIZED

In NDS, server-specific system login scripts, such as those used in NetWare 3.1x, are not used. Instead, NDS container objects have login scripts, which apply drive mappings and other settings to all users in that container. This eliminates the need to have a different system login script on each server. Because of the difference between server-specific login scripts in NetWare 3.1x and container-specific login scripts in NetWare 4.1, system login scripts are not synchronized between the servers when NetSync is installed.

User login scripts, however, are synchronized between the NetWare 4.1 host server and the NetWare 3.1x server when you install NetSync. On the 3.1x server, the user login scripts are stored as files in the users' MAIL directories. On the NetWare 4.1 server, user login scripts are properties of the user object.

During NetSync synchronization, a user's NetWare 3.1x login script is automatically copied into two places:

- The login script property of the user's new NDS user object
- The user's MAIL directory on the NetWare 4.1 server

By putting a copy of the NetWare 3.1x login script file in the user's MAIL directory on the NetWare 4.1 server, the user will be able to log in to the NetWare 4.1 server using a bindery services connection.

After synchronization, you should make any login script changes to the user's NDS object property. Those changes will be automatically downloaded to both the NetWare 3.1x and the NetWare 4.1 MAIL directories. If you use SYSCON to change the user's login script file, the change is made only in the NetWare 3.1x MAIL directory. The changes will not be uploaded to the NetWare 4.1 MAIL directory or to the User object's login script property, and the login scripts will be out of sync.

The NetWare 3.1x system login script, which is a file on the NetWare 3.1x server, is not synchronized at all. It remains intact on the specific server for which it was created, so that when users log in to that server, they will get the drive mappings they need for that server alone.

For more information about login scripts, see Chapter 6.

INSTALLING NETSYNC

During the original NetWare 4.1 installation procedure, a NETSYNC directory is created beneath SYS:SYSTEM on the NetWare 4.1 server. This directory contains the NetSync files that will have to be copied to each NetWare 3.1x server. This directory will also contain the NetSync log file for this server. NETSYNC4.NLM appears directly in SYS:SYSTEM.

After you've set up the NetWare 4.1 server as usual, you can install NetSync.

The following is a checklist of the steps for installing NetSync on the NetWare 4.1 and NetWare 3.1x servers.

1 • On the NetWare 4.1 server, load NETSYNC4. (You must load NETSYNC4 before you can connect the NetWare 3.1x servers.)

2 • A blank list of authorized NetWare 3.1x servers appears. Press Enter and select Edit Server List. On a blank line, press Enter or Insert, and enter the name of the first NetWare 3.1x server you want to synchronize.

3 • Make up a password and enter it. Make a note of the password because you must enter this same password once at each NetWare 3.1x server, as you connect it to the NetSync network. After that, NetSync will automatically change the password to a randomly generated one for security. Even you won't know what it is. If you forget the password you just entered before you bring up the NetWare 3.1x server for the first time, you'll have to remove the server from this Authorized 3.1x Servers list and reauthorize it by giving it a brand-new password.

4 • Accept the default (Yes) to copy the NetSync files to the NetWare 3.1x server.

5 • To upload the bindery information from the NetWare 3.1x server to the NetWare 4.1 host server, accept the default (Yes).

6 • Press Esc, and then press Enter to save your responses.

7 • When asked for a NetWare 3.1x username, enter **SUPERVISOR** or the name of another user that has Read, Write, Modify, and Delete rights to the SYS:SYSTEM directory on the NetWare 3.1x server. Then enter that user's password.

8 • Press Enter, and the server will be added to the Authorized 3.1x Servers list.

9 • Allow the AUTOEXEC.NCF files on the NetWare 4.1 server and the 3.1x servers to be edited so that they load the appropriate NetSync files automatically.

10 • Now that the NetSync files have been copied to the NetWare 3.1x server, restart the server to load the newer NLMs. (Type **DOWN**, type **EXIT**, and then type **SERVER** to restart it.)

11 • Load NETSYNC3.NLM (which will automatically load other NLMs).

12 • Enter the name of the NetWare 4.1 host server and the NetSync password you entered earlier.

13 • If you have printers connected to workstations on the NetWare 3.1x network, replace the RPRINTER.EXE file on those workstations with the new NPRINTER.EXE file. NPRINTER.EXE was copied to your NetWare 3.1x server during NetSync installation.

14 • If you have printers connected directly to your NetWare 3.1x server, unload the PSERVER.NLM from the NetWare 3.1x server. Then load PSERVER.NLM on the NetWare 4.1 host server. Finally, load the new file NPRINTER.NLM on the NetWare 3.1x servers.

Now the servers are synchronized with each other. If you use NetWare Administrator to make changes to a user on the NetWare 4.1 server, those changes will be automatically and immediately downloaded to the NetWare 3.1x server.

MERGING PRINT SERVERS

After you have synchronized the servers, you may want to move your NetWare 3.1x print servers to the NetWare 4.1 host server. This step is optional. If you have only a few printers, you probably don't need to merge your printers. You will still be able to manage them as you have in the past, with the NetWare 3.1x utilities. The NetWare 3.1x print servers and printers will not be synchronized with each other.

However, if you wish to combine all print servers and merge them into a single print server on the NetWare 4.1 host server, you can do that with NetSync.

On a NetWare 4.1 server, only one PSERVER.NLM can be loaded, and it can support up to 255 printers. Therefore, if you have more than one print server on your NetWare 3.1x network, they will all have to be merged into a single print server on the NetWare 4.1 server or into different print servers on separate NetWare 4.1 servers.

Merging print servers and moving printers into the NDS tree will probably require some manual adjustments to printer configurations, such as changing printer numbers. The first print server you move to NetWare 4.1 will retain its configuration, including printer numbers. Any subsequent print servers you move will probably end up with printer number conflicts, so NetSync will automatically renumber those printers.

The following is a checklist of the steps required to move the print servers.

1 • Make sure NETSYNC3 and NETSYNC4 are already loaded on their respective servers.

2 • From the Options menu, select Move a Print Server.

3 • If more than one print server is available, select the one you want to move.

4 • At the prompt, enter a name for the print server you are moving. If you want to merge this print server into one that already exists on the NetWare 4.1 network, enter the NetWare 4.1 print server's name. If you give this print server a name that doesn't already exist on the NetWare 4.1 network, a new NetWare 4.1 print server object with that name will be created in the NDS database.

The print server is now moved to the NetWare 4.1 server.

Printers are moved into the NDS tree along with their print servers, and they will continue to service the same print queues they did before. New printer NDS objects are created for these printers.

Because printer numbers may have been changed if you merged more than one print server into the NDS tree, use PCONSOLE or NetWare Administrator to discover the new printer numbers. Then you may need to update the printer number at workstations that will load NPRINTER.EXE.

After the print servers are merged into NetWare 4.1, manage the NetWare 4.1 print server and queues using NetWare Administrator or the NetWare 4.1 PCONSOLE.

If you moved a print server to NetWare 4.1 and changed its name, a reference print server of that new name is created on the NetWare 3.1x server. The *reference print server* is a new bindery object located in the NetWare 3.1x bindery. The NetWare 4.1 print server will use it to attach to the NetWare 3.1x server so that it can service the NetWare 3.1x print queues. Therefore, do not delete the reference print servers.

AFTER THE INITIAL INSTALLATION OF NETSYNC

After the initial installation and synchronization of NetSync, you can just let the servers run. Any changes made on the NetWare 4.1 host server are automatically downloaded to the NetWare 3.1x server without intervention from you.

If a NetWare 3.1x server goes down and then comes back up, the NetWare 4.1 host will automatically download the super-bindery to it again, so that the NetWare 3.1x server will get any changes it might have missed.

If you want to unload NetSync from the NetWare 3.1x server to remove the server from the synchronizing cluster of servers, simply unload NETSYNC3. However, do not unload REMAPID.NLM. This NLM is automatically loaded by NETSYNC3. It controls how passwords are synchronized, so once it is loaded, you shouldn't unload it, or you will have to change every user's password on the server. (Make sure REMAPID.NLM is loaded by the AUTOEXEC.NCF file. This command should have been added to the file during NetSync installation.)

To see a log file of the NetSync messages that are generated during uploads and downloads, you can use the NETSYNC3 or NETSYNC4 NLMs. Choose View Active Log from the main NetSync window on the server whose log file you want to view. The file is named NETSYNC.LOG.

By default, the log file will grow to 0.5 MB in size. At that point, NetSync renames the file to NETSYNC.OLD and starts a new NETSYNC.LOG. Only two log files are retained at a time. Older log files are automatically deleted. You can change the default size of the log file by using the Log File Options item in NetSync's main window.

If you decide to upgrade a NetWare 3.1x server (which has been synchronized in the NetSync group of servers) to NetWare 4.1, simply unload NETSYNC3, and then remove the NetWare 3.1x server's name from the Authorized 3.1x Servers list. Then use the normal upgrade feature of NetWare 4.1's INSTALL.NLM (see Chapter 2) to upgrade the server to NetWare 4.1.

Merging Multiple NDS Trees into One Tree

If you have two or more NDS trees, you can merge them into a single tree by using DSMERGE.NLM. (Do not use this utility to try to merge Directory partitions. This utility should only be used for merging two Directory trees.) You can also use this utility to rename a tree.

DSMERGE merges both trees at their roots. The tree from which you are running DSMERGE is the *local source tree*. The tree you are merging your source tree into is called the *target tree*. The target tree's Root object will become the Root object for the new, merged tree, and the target tree's name is the new tree's name as well. Objects that were located immediately under the root of the source tree will be located immediately under the new tree's root.

Merging two trees doesn't change any contexts or NDS names. All containers in the original two trees are retained, along with their respective objects.

During the merge, all replicas of the source tree's root partition are removed from all servers. Then the server that contained the master replica of the source tree will receive a read-write replica of the new tree's root partition. In addition, DSMERGE will create new partitions for each container below the source tree's root.

The following is a checklist of the preliminary steps you must take to merge two trees.

1 • Remove any leaf objects or alias objects from the root of the source tree. Either move these objects to a container, or delete them for now and re-create them later.

2 • Make sure there are no similar names between the two trees. For example, if each tree has a container called Mktg immediately beneath the root, those two names will conflict. Rename one or the other before trying to merge them.

3 • Make sure all users are logged out of both trees, and close all connections.

4 • Verify that both trees are running the same version of NDS and are using the same NDS schema.

5 • Make sure all servers that have a replica of either tree's root partition are up and running.

6 • After the merge, only one Reference or Single Reference time server can exist. Therefore, before the merge, make sure only one of the trees has such a server. Convert the other tree's server to a Primary time server, if necessary. Ensure that all servers in both trees are synchronized to within two seconds of each other and that they are using only one time source. You can view the time synchronization information with DSMERGE before you begin the merge process.

7 • From a server on the source tree, load DSMERGE.NLM.

8 • If both trees have the same tree name, use the Rename this tree option to change the source tree's name. If the users on the source tree have PREFERRED TREE commands in their NET.CFG files, you will have to update those files to reflect the new name.

9 • Use the Check servers in this tree option to verify that each server's status is listed as Up.

10 • Use the Check time synchronization option to verify that the servers are synchronized and using the same time source.

11 • When satisfied that you can safely merge the trees, choose Merge Two trees.

12 • Enter the administrator's name and password for the source tree.

13 • Choose Target Tree and select the target tree from the list.

14 • Enter the administrator's name and password for the target tree.

15 • Press F10 to start the merge process.

16 • Evaluate the new partitions and replicas that exist. You may want to merge some or split others to make the partitions more useful in the new tree.

17 • If necessary, re-create any leaf or Alias objects you deleted from the source tree's root.

NDS Troubleshooting

There are two utilities you can use to diagnose and repair any suspected problems with your NDS database: the SET NDS TRACE console utility and DSREPAIR.NLM.

SET NDS TRACE

SET NDS TRACE is a set of server SET commands that lets you monitor NDS status and error messages. To turn on the NDS Trace screen, type the following command at the server console:

```
SET NDS TRACE TO SCREEN = ON
```

If you want to send the messages to a file so that they are saved for later reference, type:

```
SET NDS TRACE TO FILE = ON
```

The file that will receive these messages is called DSTRACE.DBG, and it is located in the SYS:SYSTEM directory.

If you see the following message:

```
All processed = YES
```

it means that all of the pending NDS activities have been successfully completed for the specified partition.

Messages with the numbers -601 through -699 and F966 through F9FE indicate NDS status or error messages. Not all messages will be errors. Many will simply indicate the current status of NDS. Therefore, you need to look up the messages in the System Messages manual (located online) to see if any of the messages require an action on your part.

To turn off the NDS tracing feature, type the following command:

```
SET NDS TRACE TO SCREEN = OFF
```

DSREPAIR.NLM

If you discover a problem with your NDS database, you may be able to fix it using DSREPAIR.NLM.

You use DSREPAIR.NLM to repair the NDS database on individual servers. You have to run it on each server that has a problem. Most DSREPAIR.NLM features are specific to the local server. DSREPAIR will also perform replica synchronization operations and allow you to see the current status of this server's view of the network or Directory. For example, DSREPAIR.NLM allows you to see a list of servers known to the given server. Not all DSREPAIR features are necessarily repair functions, but they can be used to help diagnose or verify the health of your NDS Directory.

With DSREPAIR.NLM, you can do tasks such as:

- Check the local Directory database records for consistency and repair them if necessary
- View the structure of the local NDS tree
- View file system trustees
- Update the NDS schema

- View the status of the Directory tree's replica synchronization and repair replicas
- Verify external references to objects in subordinate reference replicas
- View information about the network's time synchronization
- View NDS object and property information

DSREPAIR also lets you create a log file of DSREPAIR operations. If necessary, you can use DSREPAIR to create a *dump file* of a damaged NDS database for use in diagnosing a problem.

To use DSREPAIR, load the NLM on the server whose database you want to examine or repair. The options described in Table 5.3 are available for DSREPAIR:

TABLE 5.3

DSREPAIR.NLM Options

OPTION	DESCRIPTION
Unattended Full Repair	Repairs everything it can in the database without asking for user intervention.
Time Synchronization	Contacts all servers in this server's partition to display time synchronization information.
Replica Synchronization	Displays the status of each replica's synchronization.
View/Edit Repair Log File	Sends messages about DSREPAIR activities to a log file, and lets you view the file.
Advanced Options	Lets you manually perform repair options on the NDS tree (rather than choosing "Unattended Full Repair"). It can also display diagnostic information about the NDS database, let you configure the log file, create a database dump file, and so on.

CHAPTER 6

Managing Users and Groups

Instant Access

Creating Users and Groups

- To create User objects and Group objects, use the NetWare Administrator utility (which runs in Windows).
- To set up a template so all users you create receive a set of common characteristics, use the NetWare Administrator utility to create a User object and name it USER_TEMPLATE.

User Tasks

- To log in, users can use the LOGIN command-line utility, the NETUSER menu utility (which runs in DOS), or the NetWare User Tools utility (which runs in Windows).
- To log out, users can use the LOGOUT command-line utility, the NETUSER menu utility, or the NetWare User Tools utility.
- To specify a default name context (location in the NDS tree) for logging in, users can put the NAME CONTEXT command in their NET.CFG files.
- To change the name context after they are logged in, users can use the NetWare User Tools utility, the CX command-line utility, or the NETUSER menu utility.
- To control print jobs, users can use the NetWare User Tools utility or the NETUSER menu utility.
- To send brief messages to other network users, users can use the NetWare User Tools utility, the SEND command-line utility, or the NETUSER menu utility.
- To map drives to network directories, users can put MAP commands in their login scripts, or they can use the NetWare User Tools utility, the MAP command-line utility, or the NETUSER menu utility.

- To change their passwords, users can use the NetWare User Tools utility, the NETUSER menu utility, or the SETPASS command-line utility.

Managing Users' Work Environments

- To create login scripts, use the NetWare Administrator, select a container object, Profile object, or User object (depending on the type of login script you want to create), select Details from the Object menu, and then open the Login Script page.
- To create a menu program, use a text editor to create a source file, and then use the MENUMAKE command-line utility to compile it.
- To execute a menu program, use the NMENU command-line utility.
- To upgrade old menus from previous versions of NetWare, use the MENUCNVT command-line utility.

Once you've got the hardware and software set up, it's time to start managing the human elements of your network: users. After a brand-new installation, the only User objects that will exist in the tree are as follows:

- The Admin User object
- The Supervisor User object (which is used for bindery services only, and can only be accessed from NetWare 3.1x or 2.x utilities)

Before your users can begin using the network, you have to create user accounts for each of them. In addition, you may want to organize the users into groups to more easily manage security, printer assignments, and other issues that may affect many or all of the users in the same way.

To make the network easier to use for your users, you can also create login scripts and menus. Login scripts can automatically set up the users' workstation environments with necessary drive mappings and other types of useful environmental settings. Menus can shield the user from having to see or use commands at the DOS prompt. Menus can also be used to restrict the user to selecting common tasks from a menu that you design.

After the user has logged in to the network, there are a few common tasks that the user may want to perform, such as logging in and out, of course, redirecting the workstation's printer port to a network print queue, or mapping a drive to a directory. NetWare User Tools is a Windows-based NetWare utility that is geared toward end users. They can use this utility to perform most of these common tasks.

What Do Users Need?

Creating a user's account involves more than just creating a new object for the user in the NDS tree. Before a user can really work on the network, you need to set up many of the following tools or characteristics (some are optional, depending on your situation):

- The user's NDS account (which is an object for the user with its associated properties filled in, such as the user's last name, full name, telephone number, and so on)

- The user's group memberships
- A home directory for the user's individual files
- A login script that maps drives to the directories and applications to which the user will need access
- NDS trustee rights (to control how the user can see and use other NDS objects in the tree)
- File system trustee rights to the files and directories the user needs to work with (to regulate the user's access and activities in those files and directories)
- Account restrictions, if necessary, to control when the user logs in, how often the user must change passwords, and so on
- An e-mail account, if necessary
- Access to the network printers
- A menu program to prevent the user from having to use commands at the DOS prompt

The following section describes how to create user and group accounts on the network.

Creating Users and Groups

Users, of course, are the individual people who have accounts on the network. You can assign users to groups, so that you can manage things such as security and login script commands for many people simultaneously, rather than one-by-one. A *group* is really a Group object, which contains a list of users who are assigned to that group.

To create a new user or group on the network, you will use the NetWare Administrator utility from a workstation. The NetWare Administrator is a Windows-based NetWare utility, called NWADMIN.EXE, located in SYS:PUBLIC. To run NetWare Administrator, you need to add its program icon to the workstation's desktop.

SETTING UP THE NETWARE ADMINISTRATOR UTILITY

The following is a checklist of the steps to set up NetWare Administrator on a workstation.

1 • From a workstation, log in to the network as user Admin or as another user who has the Create right to the container object in which you will create this new user.

2 • Start Windows, and highlight the program group in which you want NetWare Administrator to appear. The NetWare Tools program group was already created during the workstation installation, so you can use that group.

3 • From the File menu, choose New, and that then select Program Item.

4 • For the Description, enter the name you want to use, such as NetWare Administrator or NWAdmin.

5 • Use the Browse button to specify the location of the NWADMIN.EXE file (SYS:\PUBLIC\NWADMIN.EXE) and the working directory (SYS:\PUBLIC).

6 • Click OK, and the NetWare Administrator icon will appear on the desktop.

Now you can use NetWare Administrator to create and manage all NDS objects, including users and groups.

CREATING A USER

To create a user, complete the steps in the following checklist.

1 • Create a directory for all users' home directories. For example, you might want to create a network directory called Users on volume VOL1.

2 • Start up NetWare Administrator.

3 • Select the container object that will hold the new user.

4 • From the Object menu, choose Create.

5 • From the New Object dialog box that appears, choose User, and then choose OK.

6 • In the Create User dialog box, enter the user's login name and last name. The login name is the name you want this user to type when he or she logs in.

7 • Create a home directory for this user.

a. Mark the check box next to Create Home Directory.

b. Click the Browse button.

c. From the Directory Contents panel on the right, double-click on the container and then the volume that will hold the user directories.

d. When the directory you created in step 1 appears in the left panel (under Files and Directories), select that directory and click OK. The path to that directory should now appear in the Create User dialog box.

8 • To specify additional, optional properties, mark the Define Additional Properties check box.

9 • Choose Create. The user's Identification page appears. The Identification page will appear every time you look at this object in the future. Along the right side of the screen are large rectangular buttons with turn-down corners. Each of these buttons represents a different page of information about the user. You can fill in some, none, or all of the information on these pages, depending on your needs. If you have entered new information in one of these pages that needs to be saved, the turn-down corner will appear black. Choose OK when finished.

10 • Mark the Create Another User check box, and then choose OK.

11 • Create another user by following the same steps.

USING A USER TEMPLATE

If you plan to assign all of your users some identical properties, you can use a user template. The template will automatically apply default properties to any new user you create. (It will not, however, apply those properties to any users that existed before you created the user template.)

A user template is actually a regular User object that you create and name USER_TEMPLATE. You can have a different template for each container. If you do not create a template for a child container, but there is a template in a parent container, you will be asked if you want to use the parent container's template when you create a new user in the child container.

To create a user template, complete the steps in the following checklist.

1 • Create a directory for all users' home directories. For example, you might want to create a directory called Users.

2 • Start up NetWare Administrator.

3 • Select the container object that will hold the new user template.

4 • From the Object menu, choose User Defaults.

5 • If there is a parent container above your current container that already has a template, specify whether or not you want the new template to inherit the parent's template. If you choose to inherit the template, the characteristics in the parent container's template will be copied to this new template you're creating. You can then change the characteristics, if you like, to customize it for this container.

6 • When the user template's Identification page appears, enter any information that you want to be identical for all users you create in this container. You can enter any information except for NDS rights or file system rights, which must be assigned separately, as discussed in Chapter 7.

7 • To save the template, choose OK.

8 • Next time you create a new user in this container, mark the Use User Template check box to use the information you just created in the user template.

CREATING GROUPS AND ASSIGNING GROUP MEMBERSHIP TO A USER

Creating a group is very similar to creating a user. The following is a checklist that outlines the steps to create a group and assign group membership to a user.

1. Start up NetWare Administrator.
2. Select the container object that will hold the new group.
3. From the Object menu, choose Create.
4. From the New Object dialog box that appears, choose Group, and then choose OK.
5. Enter the group's name.
6. Mark the check box next to Define Other Properties.
7. Choose Create. The group's Identification page appears. Enter any information you desire under the Identification page.
8. Choose the Members page.
9. Specify any existing users who should be members of this group. From the right panel, open the container that holds the user you want. From the left panel, select the user, and then choose OK. The user's name now appears as a member of the group.

If the group already exists, you can also assign a user to that group by selecting the user object, opening the user's Group Membership page, and selecting the group.

User Network Activities

Once users have been created, they can begin working on the network. In most cases, users on a network will notice very little difference from working on a stand-alone computer. They still use the applications they were used to before. They still open, save, and delete files the same way. They can still play the same games, if they can get away with it.

The primary differences for most users are that they have to enter a login name and password; they have more drives and directories available to them; there are some files that are restricted to them; and their print jobs go to the same printer as everyone else's. Whether or not you want them to be able to control most of these network activities themselves is up to you.

For most users, three NetWare utilities will take care of their networking tasks:

- LOGIN
- LOGOUT
- NetWare User Tools

LOGGING IN AND OUT

To log in to the network, the user uses the LOGIN utility at the DOS prompt and specifies a login name and a password.

Which login name the user enters depends on whether you've modified the user's NET.CFG file to specify the user's name context.

If you are using the default NET.CFG file that was created when you installed the workstation, the LOGIN utility doesn't know the context in which the user was created. It assumes the default context is at the root of the tree. If you've created the user in a container beneath the root, which is most likely the case, LOGIN won't find the user in the tree if the user enters only his or her common name and will deny the user access to the network.

There are two ways to make sure LOGIN finds the user's correct name context. The first way is for the user to specify a complete name, all the way back to the root of the tree. Obviously, this can be a little cumbersome for the user. For example, Eric would have to log in using the following command:

```
LOGIN .Eric.Mktg.Satellite.RedHawk
```

The period at the beginning of Eric's full name indicates that this name goes clear back to the root of the tree.

The other way to make sure LOGIN finds the user's context is to specify the context in the NET.CFG file under the NetWare DOS Requester heading. For example, to specify Eric's context, put the following command in the NET.CFG file:

```
NAME CONTEXT= "Mktg.Satellite.RedHawk"
```

Then, Eric can just log in using his common name, Eric, which is obviously going to be easier for him to remember.

To simplify the user's life even more, you may also want to put the LOGIN command in the user's AUTOEXEC.BAT file so that it executes every time the user boots the workstation.

To log out, the user simply enters the command:

```
LOGOUT
```

USING NETWARE USER TOOLS

NetWare 4.1 includes a special utility, called NetWare User Tools, that allows end users to perform their most common network tasks. There is both a DOS-based version and a Windows-based version of this utility. With this utility, users can do the following:

- Set up print queues and control how their print jobs are printed on the network
- Send short messages to other network users
- Map drive letters to network directories
- Change passwords
- Log in to and out of Directory trees and network servers (but without a login script executing)

- Change their own name context in the Directory tree
- Edit user login scripts (DOS version only)

NetWare User Tools for DOS

To execute the DOS-based version of NetWare User Tools, called NETUSER.EXE, simply enter the command

```
NETUSER
```

at the DOS prompt. NETUSER allows you to modify a user login script, so that you can make drive mappings and other aspects of the workstation environment "permanent" (which means they are in effect each time the user logs in to the network, until the user decides to change them). Use the F1 key to read help screens about the different tasks you can do with this utility.

NetWare User Tools for Windows

To use the Windows-based version of NetWare User Tools, double-click on the NetWare User Tools icon, which is automatically placed in the NetWare Tools program group when the NetWare client software is installed. The Windows-based version of this utility doesn't allow you to edit a login script. Instead, you can set up drive mappings and printer port redirection right in the utility, and click the Permanent button to make those assignments permanent. This has the same effect as placing the corresponding commands in a login script. Every time you log in, NetWare User Tools will automatically map the drives and capture printer ports the way you specified. Use the Help button to read about the tasks you can do with this utility.

Login Scripts

Login scripts are tools similar to batch files that you can use to automatically set up users' workstation environments. Each time a user logs in, the LOGIN utility executes the login scripts, which can set up frequently used drive mappings, capture the workstation's printer port to a network print queue, display connection information or messages on the screen, or do other types of tasks for the user.

In previous versions of NetWare (3.1x and 2.x), there were two types of login scripts: user login scripts and system login scripts. The system login script was a file on the server. It executed for every user who logged in to that server, so it was a good place to store drive mappings or other information that was common to all users. The user login script was a separate file for each user, stored in users' MAIL subdirectories. In the user login script, you could create drive mappings or other items that were specific to that user only.

In NetWare 4.1, there are three types of login scripts.

User Login Scripts User login scripts are the same in NetWare 4.1 as in previous versions, except that they are not stored as text files. Instead, they are actual properties of the User object. You still store user-specific drive mappings, and so on, in the user login script. If the user does not have a specific user login script, a default login script will execute instead, setting up the most basic drive mappings.

System Login Scripts Instead of belonging to a server, a system login script now belongs to a container object. Because users no longer log in to a server, and because all the users in a container may access different servers for files, keeping a server-specific login script seemed useless. However, a script that would apply to all users within a given container made much more sense. Therefore, the system login script (also called a container login script) is a property of a container object. It applies to every user in that container.

Profile Login Scripts Profile login scripts are new in NetWare 4.1. With a profile script, you can create a script that will apply to several users who don't necessarily have to be in the same container. It's kind of a group login script. The profile login script is a property of a Profile object, which defines a list of users who belong to the Profile. A user can have only one profile login script execute upon login.

These three types of login scripts work together to set up each user's environment upon login. They execute in the following order:

- System (container) login script
- Profile login script
- User login script (or default login script, if a user login script doesn't exist)

All three are optional. If you don't create one of them, LOGIN will skip to the next in the list.

Because up to three different login scripts can execute for a given user, conflicts between the login scripts could occur. If they do, the final login script to execute wins. Therefore, if the system login script maps a directory to drive letter G, and then the user script maps a different directory to drive letter G, the user script's mapping overwrites the system script's mapping.

System login scripts only apply to the users immediately within that container. They don't apply to users in a child container. If the container that holds user Andrea doesn't have a login script, no system login script will execute when Andrea logs in, even if a container higher up in the tree has a login script.

To simplify administration of login scripts, try to put as much common information as possible, such as drive mappings to application directories, in the container and profile login scripts. It's much easier to change a drive mapping in one script and have it apply to all your users than to make the same change dozens or hundreds of times for every user script.

If you upgrade a previous version of NetWare to NetWare 4.1, the user login scripts are automatically transferred into the Login Script property of each User object. Server-specific system login scripts, however, are not upgraded. You will need to re-create the system login script, if needed, as a property of a container object. (The server-specific system login script in previous versions of NetWare is a text file in the SYS:PUBLIC directory called NET$LOG.DAT. You can print out this file to refer to while creating a container system login script.)

TIP

If you want to log in to the network without executing a login script, add the /NS option to the login command. For example, user Lauren would type LOGINLAUREN/NS.

CREATING A LOGIN SCRIPT

You use the NetWare Administrator utility to create login scripts, just as you assign any other properties to NDS objects. Open the object's Details page, then click on the button for the Login Script page.

When you open up the Login Script property for a User, Profile, or container object, you are presented with a blank screen (or the previous login script, if one already exists).

In this screen, you type any commands you want the login script to hold: drive mappings, printer port captures, messages, environment settings, and so on.

To create or edit a login script, you must have the Write NDS right to the object that will contain the script.

When creating login scripts, keep the following conventions and rules in mind. (Login script commands mentioned here are explained in the next section.)

- Begin each command in the login script on its own line. (Commands that wrap automatically to another line are considered a single line. Commands are limited to 150 characters per line.)
- To make multiline WRITE commands display better and to avoid having a line misinterpreted by LOGIN, begin each line of the displayed message with the word WRITE.
- If you use the pound sign (#) to execute an external program, note that some programs may require that the user has drives mapped to particular directories. If so, make sure the MAP commands that map drives to those directories are placed in the login script ahead of the command that executes the external program.
- Enter commands in the general order you wish them to execute. If order isn't important, group similar commands together (such as MAP and CAPTURE commands) to make the login script easier to read.
- Remember that most commands are case-insensitive. The only exception is identifier variables enclosed in quotation marks and preceded by a percent sign (%); they must be uppercase.
- Use identifier variables to make generic commands useful to specific users. When a user logs in, his or her specific information is substituted for the identifier variable in the generic command. Identifier variables (explained later in the section "Using Identifier Variables") make it possible to put most necessary commands in the system or profile script, rather than in a user login script.

- Use blank lines to separate groups of commands in the script, if it makes it easier to read. Blank lines don't affect the execution of the login script.

- Use remarks in the login script to explain what commands in the script are doing, for future reference. Lines in the login script beginning with the word REM, an asterisk, or a semicolon are remarks, and they don't display when the login script executes.

- Copy portions of a login script by using the mouse to highlight the desired text and pressing Ctrl-Insert. To paste the text, either elsewhere in the script or in another object's script, press Shift-Insert.

ASSIGNING PROFILE LOGIN SCRIPTS TO USERS

To create a profile login script, you create a Profile object just as you create any other NDS object. Create its script in the Profile object's Login Script property. After you've created the script, you must assign it to individual users. To do this, complete the steps in the following checklist.

1 • Use the Browser to select a User object.

2 • Choose Details from the Object menu, then open the Login Script page.

3 • Enter the name of the Profile object in the Profile field beneath the login script text window.

4 • Save the information and return to the Browser.

5 • From the Browser, select the Profile object.

6 • From the Object menu, choose Trustees of This Object.

7 • Click the Add Trustee button and enter the name of the user who will use this profile login script.

8 • Make sure the Browse object right and Read property right are checked, and then choose OK to assign those rights to the user.

LOGIN SCRIPT COMMANDS

The many commands you can use in NetWare login scripts are explained in the following sections. Many of these commands are unique to NetWare login scripts. Some commands may work similarly to DOS commands or may actually execute DOS commands you might be familiar with, such as the SET and DOS BREAK ON commands. All of them are optional. You only need to use the commands that accomplish tasks you want performed for the user.

Command

This command executes an external command or program, such as a NetWare utility, from the login script. To execute the program, use the pound (#) symbol at the beginning of the command. When the program is finished executing, the login script will take over again and continue running.

When this command is used to execute another program, the LOGIN utility may be swapped out of conventional memory and into extended or expanded memory (if available) or onto the hard disk, to allow both LOGIN and the program to execute at the same time. If you do not want LOGIN to be moved out of conventional memory, use the NOSWAP login script command, covered later in this chapter.

The # command is commonly used with the CAPTURE utility (explained in Chapter 6). For example, to capture a user's LPT1 port to use a network print queue named LaserQ, you might put the following command in the login script:

```
#CAPTURE L=1 Q=.LaserQ.Sales.Satellite.RedHawk NB NT NFF TI=5
```

ATTACH Command

This command attaches the user to a NetWare 4.1 server using bindery services. It can also be used to attach the user to a NetWare 3.1x or 2.x server. ATTACH doesn't execute a login script for that server; it simply attaches you to the server so you can access its resources. Do not use ATTACH if you want to use NetWare Directory Services on a NetWare 4.1 server (there is no need to attach to a NetWare 4.1 server if you're already logged in to the NDS tree).

To use ATTACH, put the following command in the login script, replacing *server* with the server's name and *username* with the user's login name:

```
ATTACH server/username
```

BREAK ON Command

BREAK OFF is the default. This command lets you abort the login script while it is executing by pressing Ctrl-C or Ctrl-Break.

BREAK ON only lets you break out of the login script. To break out of programs other than the login script, use the DOS BREAK ON command, explained later in this chapter.

To use BREAK ON, put the following command in the login script:

```
BREAK ON
```

CLS Command

Use this command to clear the workstation's screen of any commands that have been displayed by the login script up to the point where this CLS command occurs.

To use CLS, put the following command in the login script:

```
CLS
```

COMSPEC Command

If you have set up your workstations to run DOS from a network directory instead of from a local disk, use this command. The COMSPEC command lets you tell the workstation that the DOS command processor (COMMAND.COM) is located on the network. If your workstations are running DOS locally, don't use this command.

OS/2 users who run virtual DOS sessions can't use this command in the login script. Instead, they must put it in the CONFIG.SYS file to indicate that DOS is on the local disk.

To use COMSPEC, put the following command in the login script:

```
COMSPEC=path COMMAND.COM
```

For example, if DOS is located in the directory SYS:PUBLIC\%MACHINE\%OS\%OS_VERSION, and you have mapped search drive S2 to that directory, you would enter the following command in the login script:

```
COMSPEC=S2:COMMAND.COM
```

CONTEXT Command

Use this command to set the user's name context. CONTEXT works in the login script similarly to how the CX workstation utility works when typed at the workstation's DOS prompt. This command will change the context the user sees after he or she logs in. To change the context before the user logs in, use the NET.CFG file instead of the login script.

To use CONTEXT, put the following command in the login script:

```
CONTEXT context
```

Replace *context* with the user's new name context, such as .Satellite.RedHawk.

DISPLAY Command

This command displays an ASCII text file on the workstation screen during login. If you want to display a word-processed file that has word-processing and printer codes embedded in it, use FDISPLAY instead. (FDISPLAY is covered later in this chapter.)

To use DISPLAY, put the following command in the login script, replacing *path\filename* with the directory path and name of the file you want to display:

```
DISPLAY path\filename
```

DOS BREAK ON Command

This command lets you abort a program (other than the login script) while it is executing, by pressing Ctrl-C or Ctrl-Break. DOS BREAK OFF is the default. (This command does not apply to OS/2 workstations.)

To break out of the login script, use the BREAK ON command instead (explained earlier in this chapter).

To use DOS BREAK ON, put the following command in the login script:

```
DOS BREAK ON
```

DOS VERIFY ON Command

Use this command to make DOS's COPY command verify that files can be read after they are copied. You do not need to use this command if you use only the NetWare NCOPY utility, because NCOPY verifies the copies automatically.

The default is DOS VERIFY OFF.

To use DOS VERIFY ON, put the following command in the login script:

```
DOS VERIFY ON
```

DRIVE Command

This command lets you change to a different default network drive while the login script is executing. Be sure to place this command in the login script after the MAP command that maps a drive to the desired directory.

For example, to map drive H to SYS:USERS\PAULINE\STATUS, and then make drive H the default drive, put the following commands in the login script:

```
MAP H:=SYS:USERS\PAULINE\STATUS
DRIVE H:
```

(On OS/2 workstations, DRIVE only changes the default directory while the login script is running. After the login script finishes, the default drive returns to the drive in effect when you executed the LOGIN utility.)

EXIT Command

Use this command at the end of a login script to stop the script and go immediately into another program, such as a menu program or an application, instead of returning to the DOS prompt.

This command does not apply to OS/2 workstations.

EXIT stops the current login script, which is why you must place it at the end of the script. In addition, it prevents any other login scripts from executing. If you put an EXIT command at the end of the container system login script, the profile and user scripts will not execute, so be sure you place the EXIT command at the end of any scripts you do want to execute.

To use EXIT, put the following command in the login script:

```
EXIT "program"
```

Inside the quotation marks, replace *program* with the command that executes the program you want the user to enter. The command inside the quotation marks can't exceed the number of the workstation's keyboard buffer length (typically 15) minus 1. (In other words, most workstations are limited to 14 characters inside the quotation marks.)

For example, to exit to a menu program called DATA, use the following command at the end of the login script:

```
EXIT "NMENU DATA"
```

If you have changed the workstation's long machine name in the NET.CFG file, you need to execute the PCCOMPATIBLE login script command before the EXIT command.

FDISPLAY Command

This command displays a word-processed file that has word-processing and printer codes embedded in it, on the workstation screen during login. It removes these embedded codes and displays just the text of the file. If you want to display an ASCII text file, you can use DISPLAY instead (covered earlier in this chapter).

To use FDISPLAY, put the following command in the login script, replacing *path\filename* with the directory path and name of the file you want to display:

```
FDISPLAY path\filename
```

FIRE PHASERS Command

This command makes the workstation emit a phaser sound. You can specify how many times (up to nine) the phaser sound occurs. You can use this command to draw attention to a displayed message during login.

To use FIRE PHASERS, put the following command in the login script:

```
FIRE PHASERS x TIMES
```

where *x* is a number from 1 to 9.

GOTO Command

Use this command to make the login script skip to another portion of the script:

```
GOTO label
```

To use this command, label the part of the login script you want to execute with a single word of your choice, and then put the following command in the login script, substituting the word you used in the script for *label*.

IF...THEN Command

Use this command to indicate that a command should execute only if certain conditions are met. For example, you could use IF...THEN to make a message display only on a particular day of the week.

The IF...THEN command uses this basic format:

```
IF something is true THEN
execute this command
ELSE execute this command
END
```

The ELSE portion of the command is optional. You only use it when you have two or more commands that you want to execute at different times, based on different circumstances.

For example, to display the message "Friday's here at last!" on Fridays, you would use the following commands:

```
IF DAY_OF_WEEK="Friday" THEN
WRITE "Friday's here at last!"
END
```

No message will appear on any other day of the week.

Suppose you want to make the same message appear on Fridays, and on all other days you want to display the message, "Customers are our first priority." To do this, use the same command, but add an ELSE portion:

```
IF DAY_OF_WEEK="Friday" THEN
WRITE "Friday's here at last!"
ELSE
WRITE "Customers are our first priority."
END
```

The first line of the IF...THEN command (IF *something is true*) is called a conditional statement, because this is the condition that makes the rest of the command execute. To use a conditional statement, you use a variable, and you indicate what value that variable has to have before it can execute the command.

These variables are called *identifier variables*. The identifier variables you can use in login scripts are explained later in this chapter, in the section "Using Identifier Variables."

For example, if you specify the DAY_OF_WEEK variable, you can also indicate the value you need the variable to have, such as "Friday." Then, whenever the day's value matches the one you indicated in the command, the command will execute. (In other words, on every Friday, the command will execute.)

In conditional statements, the value must be enclosed in quotation marks.

INCLUDE Command

This command lets you execute another text file or another object's login script as part of the login script currently executing. The other file or login script, called a *subscript*, must contain regular login script commands.

To call a subscript, put one of the following commands in the main login script at the point where you want the subscript to execute:

```
INCLUDE path\filename
```

or

```
INCLUDE object
```

Replace *path\filename* with the directory path and name of the text file that contains the login script commands, or replace *object* with the name of the object whose login script you want to execute.

LASTLOGINTIME Command

This command simply displays the time of the user's last login on the workstation screen.

To use LASTLOGINTIME, put the following command in the login script:

```
LASTLOGINTIME
```

MACHINE Command

Use this command to set the workstation's DOS machine name. The default is IBM_PC. Some programs, such as NetBIOS, may need this command if they were written to run under PC DOS, but in most cases, you shouldn't have to use this command. It does not apply to OS/2 workstations.

This command is different from the MACHINE indentifier variable. That variable, which can be used in MAP and WRITE login script commands, gets its value from the NET.CFG file.

The machine name can be up to 15 characters long.

To use MACHINE, put the following command in the login script, replacing *name* with the machine name:

```
MACHINE=name
```

MAP Command

Use this command to map drive letters to network directories. When you put a MAP command in a login script, that command will be executed every time the user logs in.

Use the MAP login script command just as you use the MAP utility at the DOS prompt, with the following command format:

```
MAP letter:=path
```

For example, to map drive L to VOL1:APPS\WP, the command would be as follows:

```
MAP L:=VOL1:APPS\WP
```

Because your users probably have home directories in which they store their individual files, you may want to map a drive to the user's home directory. You can do that generically in a system or profile script by using the LOGIN_NAME identifier variable. For example, if all your users have a subdirectory under the directory USERS, and you want the first available drive to be mapped to this subdirectory, you can put the following mapping in the system or profile login script:

```
MAP N=VOL1:USERS\%LOGIN_NAME
```

%LOGIN_NAME is the identifier variable. When user Tina logs in, her name will automatically be substituted for this variable, and the first available network drive will be mapped to VOL1:USERS\TINA.

For OS/2 workstations, map drive P to SYS:PUBLIC.

If users are running Windows from the network instead of from their own local hard disk, map drives to the user's directories that contain their individual files.

You can also use MAP to map search drives. Search drives are used to indicate directories that contain applications or utilities. Search drives let users execute an application without having to know where the application is; the network searches through the designated search drives for the application's executable file when the user types the program's execution command.

To map a search drive, you use the letter *S*, followed by a number, rather than designating a drive letter. The search drive will assign its own letters in reverse order, starting with the letter Z. (You can have up to 16 search drives mapped.) For example, to map the first search drive to the SYS:PUBLIC directory, enter the following line in the login script:

```
MAP S1:=SYS:PUBLIC
```

Search drive mappings are added to the workstation's DOS PATH environment variable. This means that if you specify that a search drive is S1, as in the preceding example, the mapping to SYS:PUBLIC will overwrite the first DOS path that had already been set. To avoid overwriting a path setting, use the INS option. By entering

```
MAP INS S1
```

instead of

```
MAP S1
```

the search drive mapping will be inserted at the beginning of the DOS path settings, moving the path setting that was previously first to the second position.

In login scripts, some drives should be mapped in a particular order. In the system login script, the following search drives should be mapped first:

```
MAP INS S1:=SYS:PUBLIC
MAP INS S2:=SYS:PUBLIC\%MACHINE\%OS\%OS_VERSION
```

The SYS:PUBLIC directory contains the NetWare utilities and other NetWare files that users need. The second mapping maps a search drive to the DOS directories. If you want your users to run DOS from the network instead of from their local disks, use this command, which points to the network directories that contain DOS. (This command uses identifier variables for some directory names. For example, the identifier variable %OS represents the workstation's operating system. Therefore, if a workstation requires MS-DOS version 5.0, the search drive would be mapped to SYS:PUBLIC\IBM_PC\MSDOS\50.)

After these two search drives, you can map additional search drives in any order you wish.

TIP

Instead of mapping search drives in order (S3, S4, S5, and so on), use MAP S16 for all subsequent mappings that don't require an exact position (as do the first two mappings, mentioned above). Each MAP S16 command will insert its drive mapping at the end of the list, pushing up the previous mappings. This just makes the list of search drives more flexible, so that if you delete one, the others will reorder themselves automatically. Also, you don't run the risk of overwriting a search drive that may have been specified in another login script.

There are several variations of the MAP command you can use to accomplish different tasks, as shown in Table 6.1.

TABLE 6.1

MAP Command Options

TASK	DESCRIPTION

Map drives in order, without your specifying drive letters	If you don't want to specify exact drive letters, you can map each available drive, in order. This is useful if you don't know what drive letters have already been mapped in a system or profile login script. To assign drive letters this way, use an asterisk, followed by a number. For example, to get the first and second available drives, you could use the following commands:
	`MAP *1:=VOL1:APPS\WP`
	`MAP *2:=VOL1:DATA\REPORTS`

Map the next available drive	To map the next available drive, use the letter *N* (without a colon), as in the following command: `MAP N=VOL1:APPS\WP`
Delete a drive mapping	To delete a mapping for drive G, for example, use the following command: `MAP DEL G:`
Turn off MAP's display	Whenever a MAP command is executed in the login script, it will display the new drive mapping on the workstation screen unless you specify otherwise. To turn off this display, use the following command: `MAP DISPLAY OFF`

Turn on MAP's display	At the end of the login script, you may want to turn MAP's display back on and show a listing of all the completed drive mappings. To do this, put the following commands at or near the end of the login script:
	`MAP DISPLAY ON`
	`MAP`

TABLE 6.1
Map Command Options (continued)

TASK	DESCRIPTION
Map a fake root	Some applications require that they be installed at the root of a volume or hard disk. If you would rather install the application in a subdirectory, you can do that, and then map a fake root to the application's subdirectory. You can map a fake root in a regular drive mapping or in a search drive mapping. To map drive H as a fake root to the `VOL1:APPS\CAD` subdirectory, use the following command: `MAP ROOT H:=VOL1:APPS\CAD`
Map a drive to a Directory Map object	You can create an NDS object, called a Directory Map object, that points to a particular directory. Then, you can map drives to that object instead of to the actual directory path. This way, if you later move the directory to another part of the file system, you can just change the Directory Map object's description instead of updating all the affected login scripts. Preferably, use Directory Map objects in the user's current context. If the Directory Map object is in another part of the NDS tree, create an Alias object for the Directory Map object in the user's current context. To map a search drive to a Directory Map object named Database, use the following command: `MAP S16:=DATABASE`

NO_DEFAULT Command

Use this command at the end of a system or profile login script if you do not want the default script to execute for a user who doesn't have a user login script.

To use NO_DEFAULT, put the following command in the login script:

```
NO_DEFAULT
```

NOSWAP Command

Use this command to keep LOGIN from being moved out of conventional memory into higher memory.

When the # command is used to execute another program, the LOGIN utility may be swapped out of conventional memory and into extended or expanded memory (if available) or onto the hard disk, to allow both LOGIN and the program to execute at the same time. This happens by default. If you do not want LOGIN to be moved out of conventional memory, use the NOSWAP login script command. If the workstation doesn't have enough memory to run both LOGIN and the external program, the external program will fail, but the rest of the login script will execute.

To use NOSWAP, put the following command in the login script:

```
NOSWAP
```

PAUSE Command

This command makes the login script pause in its execution. The message, "Strike any key when ready . . ." appears on the workstation's screen. When the user presses a key, the login script continues executing.

To use PAUSE, put the following command in a login script, wherever you want the pause to occur:

```
PAUSE
```

PCCOMPATIBLE Command

Use this command only if you are using the EXIT command and have changed the workstation's long machine name in the NET.CFG file to something other than IBM_PC.

This command doesn't apply to OS/2 workstations.

To use this command, place it before the EXIT command, as in the following example (which exits the login script and goes into a program called CAD):

```
PCCOMPATIBLE
EXIT "CAD"
```

PROFILE Command

Use this command in a system login script to set or override a user's assigned profile script. To use this command, replace *name* in the command shown here with the Profile object's name:

```
PROFILE name
```

REMARK Command

Use REMARK — or its equivalents REM, an asterisk (*), or a semicolon (;) — to indicate that the rest of the line in the login script is a comment and should not be displayed or executed. Use comments to describe commands in the login script so that you or others will recall why certain commands are there when you read the script later.

For example, the following line in the login script indicates that a map command follows it:

```
REM The next drive mapping is for students' temporary use.
Delete at end of quarter.
```

SCRIPT_SERVER Command

This command specifies a home server from which the workstation can read a bindery login script. This command does not apply to NetWare 4.1 servers.

To use SCRIPT_SERVER, put the following command in a login script, replacing *server* with the bindery server's name:

```
SCRIPT_SERVER server
```

SET Command

Use SET to set DOS and OS/2 environment variables. For OS/2 workstations, these variables are in effect only while the login script is running. For DOS workstations, the variables remain in effect after the login script is finished (unless you change them from the DOS command line at some point after login — but then the variables will be reset when the login script is executed again). You can use any of the regular DOS or OS/2 variables in this command.

Use the SET login script command just as you would use regular DOS SET variables, with one exception: For a login script command, you must enclose the value you are setting in quotation marks.

For example, to set the prompt to display the current directory, add the following command to the login script:

```
SET PROMPT= "$P$G"
```

If you use SET PATH, the path will overwrite any previous path settings established in AUTOEXEC.BAT or earlier in the login script.

To use a SET variable as an identifier variable in another login script command, enclose the variable in angle brackets, such as <path>. For example, the following MAP login script command uses the path variable:

```
MAP S16:=%<PATH>
```

If you want the variable to be set for a DOS workstation only while the login script is executing, and you want it to return to its original state after execution, add the word TEMP to the beginning of the SET command, as in the following example:

```
TEMP SET PROMPT= "$P$G"
```

SET_TIME OFF Command

By default, when a workstation logs in, it sets its time to the time of the first server it connects to. To prevent the workstation from adopting the server's time, use the command SET_TIME OFF. To allow the workstation to adopt its time from the server after all, use SET_TIME ON (the default).

To use SET_TIME OFF, put the following command in the login script:

```
SET_TIME OFF
```

SHIFT Command

This command changes the order in which variables entered at the LOGIN command line are interpreted. You can use special variables, called %*n* variables, as placeholders in a login script command. Then, when a user logs in, the values the user enters at the command line are substituted for the %*n* variable.

The SHIFT command lets you change the order in which the %*n* variables are executed. In the SHIFT command, specify a positive or negative number to indicate that you want to shift the variables one direction or the other. For example, the following command moves each %*n* variable one position to the right:

```
SHIFT +1
```

Using %*n* variables is described later in this chapter.

SWAP Command

Use this command to move LOGIN out of conventional memory into higher memory.

When the # command is used to execute another program, the LOGIN utility may be swapped out of conventional memory and into extended or expanded memory (if available) or onto the hard disk, to allow both LOGIN and the program to execute at the same time. This happens by default. However, if you do not want LOGIN to be moved out of conventional memory, you can use the NOSWAP login script command. If NOSWAP has been used earlier in the login script, you can use SWAP to again make LOGIN able to swap into higher memory.

To use SWAP, put the following command in the login script:

```
SWAP
```

WRITE Command

Use WRITE to display short messages on the workstation screen during login. To use WRITE, enter the command

```
WRITE
```

followed by quotation marks enclosing the text you want to appear on the user's screen. For example, to display the message "Have a nice day" enter the following command:

```
WRITE "Have a nice day"
```

To display a message that is too long for a single line, use the word WRITE at the beginning of each line. For example, suppose you want to display the following message:

```
Please attend today's weekly staff meeting in
Conference Room B.
Be prepared to discuss your client call status and
success stories.

Remember to bring your expense reports.
```

To get these sentences to appear correctly on five lines, you should enter the following commands:

```
WRITE "Please attend today's weekly staff meeting in"
WRITE "Conference Room B."
```

```
WRITE "Be prepared to discuss your client call status and
WRITE success stories."

WRITE "Remember to bring your expense reports."
```

For information about using identifier variables in WRITE commands, see the next section, "Using Identifier Variables."

There are a few special characters you can enter in a WRITE command to make the command appear as you want. These are shown in Table 6.2.

TABLE 6.2

Special Characters for the WRITE command

CHARACTER	DESCRIPTION
;	Links two WRITE commands together so they appear as a continuous sentence or paragraph. Can also be used to link text within quotation marks to an identifier variable that isn't included in the quotation marks.
\r	Causes a carriage return when used inside the text string.
\n	Begins a new line of text when used inside the text string.
\"	Makes a quotation mark display inside the text message when used inside the text string.
\7	Causes a beep sound to occur when used inside the text string.

USING IDENTIFIER VARIABLES

Using identifier variables in login scripts is effective for two reasons:

- It's an efficient way to make generic commands work for most users.
- It allows you to make different commands execute only at certain times or in particular situations.

An identifier variable is simply a placeholder for information that is substituted whenever a user logs in. An identifier variable might be replaced by specific user information, such as the user's login name or full name, or it might be replaced by information about the user's workstation, such as its address or machine type. It might also be replaced by general information that has nothing to do with the user, such as the day of the week, time, or network address.

You can use identifier variables in many different login script commands. You can use them in WRITE commands to display the value that is provided. For example, suppose you add the following command to the system login script:

```
WRITE "GOOD %GREETING_TIME, %LOGIN_NAME."
```

When user Eric logs in at 8:00 a.m., the following message displays on his screen:

```
Good MORNING, ERIC.
```

When user Maude logs in at 1:30 p.m., she receives this message:

```
Good AFTERNOON, MAUDE.
```

You can also use identifier variables in other types of commands, such as IF...THEN commands, to allow a particular command to execute only under certain conditions. For example, the following IF...THEN command will execute a WRITE command only on Wednesdays:

```
IF DAY_OF_WEEK="Wednesday" THEN

WRITE "Don't forget staff meeting today at 3:00."

END
```

For more about the IF...THEN command, see the section in the chapter called "IF...THEN Command."

Syntax for Using Identifier Variables

In the above examples, you may have noticed that sometimes a percent sign (%) is added the beginning of the variable, and sometimes it isn't. Ordinarily, in a WRITE command, everything inside the quotation marks is displayed. However, the percent sign indicates that the following word is not to be displayed as is; rather, it is an identifier variable, and the variable's value should be displayed instead.

In other commands, when the identifier variable is not enclosed in quotation marks, do not use the percent sign.

The basic syntax rules for identifier variables are as follows:

- Identifier variables should be typed in uppercase.
- If you want the variable's value to be displayed in a WRITE command, precede the variable with a percent sign and enclose it in quotation marks.
- To use a variable in any other command, do not use a percent sign.
- In an IF...THEN command, if you specify a desired value for the variable, enclose the value in quotation marks, such as IF DAY_OF_WEEK="Monday".

You can specify how an identifier variable matches a particular value in six different ways, as shown in Table 6.3.

TABLE 6.3

Operators for Assigning Values to Identifier Variables

OPERATOR	EXAMPLE
= (equals)	IF LOGIN_NAME = "David" means *If the user is David*
<> (doesn't equal)	IF LOGIN_NAME <> "Admin" means *If the user isn't Admin*
> (is greater than)	IF HOUR > "9" means *If the hour is 10:00 or later*
>= (is greater than or equal to)	IF HOUR >= "9:00" means *If the hour is 9:00 or later*
< (is less than)	IF HOUR < "5" means *If the hour is 4:00 or earlier*
<= (Is less than or equal to)	IF HOUR <= "5" means *If the hour is 5:00 or earlier*

Using the %*n* Identifier Variable

When users log in, they type a LOGIN command that usually includes at least two parameters: their login names, and either a tree name or a server name. If there is only one tree or server available, a user may only have to specify the login name parameter, but the other parameter is implied.

In addition, a user can add additional parameters to the LOGIN command, such as an application name or other keyword he or she wants to use. This can allow the user to have different login script commands execute depending on the parameter the user specifies in the LOGIN command.

In login scripts, you can insert a special type of identifier variable to use and display these LOGIN parameters. It is called the %*n* variable (where *n* is a number, such as 0, 1, and so on).

To use a %*n* variable, you insert it into a command just like any other identifier variable, except that it is always preceded by a percent sign and enclosed in quotation marks. Then, whenever a user logs in, the parameters he or she enters are substituted for the %*n* variable in the login script command.

The first two variables, %0 and %1, must always have the following values:

%0	The server or tree name, depending on how the user logs in
%1	The user's login name

Subsequent numbers, such as %2 and %3, can be fulfilled by whatever additional parameters the user enters with the LOGIN command.

The following is an example of how %*n* variables can be used in login script commands:

```
IF "%1"="Jessica" THEN

MAP *3:=VOL1:APPS\DB

IF "%2"="wp" THEN

MAP *4:=VOL1:APPS\WP

END
```

In this example, two %*n* variables are used: %1 and %2. Because %1 is always a user login name, the first line of the command is specifying that the following commands execute only if the login name is Jessica.

The second variable, %2, will be whatever variable user Jessica enters after her login name. If she enters

```
WP
```

after her login name, she will get an additional drive mapping to the WP subdirectory.

She would enter the following command when she logs in:

```
LOGIN JESSICA WP
```

In this command the first variable, %0, wasn't supplied but is implied to be the server to which she attaches, since %0 is always the server. The second variable, %1, is the user login name (Jessica in this case). The third variable, %2, is the WP parameter she entered after her login name. Whenever she uses this command to log in, Jessica will receive two drive mappings — one to the DB subdirectory, and one to the WP subdirectory.

If Jessica logs in using the following command

```
LOGIN JESSICA
```

she will receive only a drive mapping to the DB subdirectory.

If anyone other than Jessica logs in, they will not receive either drive mapping.

The SHIFT login command lets you actually shift the position of the parameters to the right or left, depending on whether you enter a positive or negative number. (See the description of the SHIFT login script command, earlier in this chapter.)

Identifier Variables

The identifier variables can be grouped into the following categories:

- User
- Workstation
- Network
- Date
- Time
- Miscellaneous

Table 6.4 lists each of the available user identifier variables.

TABLE 6.4

User Identifier Variables

IDENTIFIER VARIABLE	DESCRIPTION	EXAMPLE
%CN	Common name of the User object.	Eric
ALIAS_CONTEXT	Displays "Y" if the requester context is an alias.	
FULL_NAME	The user's full name, if defined in the User object's properties.	Eric V. McCloud
LAST_NAME	The user's last name in NDS (or full name on the bindery servers).	McCloud
LOGIN_CONTEXT	The user's name context in the NDS tree.	Mktg.Satellite.RedHawk
LOGIN_NAME	The user's login name (same as common name).	Eric
MEMBER OF "group"	The group a user might belong to. Can also use the word NOT with this variable.	`IF MEMBER OF "Design" THEN...` `IF NOT MEMBER OF "Design" THEN...`
PASSWORD_EXPIRES	Displays how many days before the user's password expires.	`WRITE "Your password expires in %PASSWORD_EXPIRES days."`
REQUESTER_CONTEXT	The context from which LOGIN was started. This may not necessarily be the same context the user will be in after login.	`IF REQUESTER_CONTEXT ="RedHawk" THEN...`
USER_ID	Unique number assigned to each user.	12345678

Table 6.5 lists each of the available workstation identifier variables.

TABLE 6.5

Workstation Identifier Variables

IDENTIFIER VARIABLE	DESCRIPTION	EXAMPLE
MACHINE	The workstation's computer type	IBM_PC (This is the default.)
NETWARE_ REQUESTER	Version of the NetWare client software for OS/2 or DOS and Windows	V1.20
OS	The workstation's type of operating system	MSDOS
OS_VERSION	The version of the workstation's operating system	V6.20
P_STATION	The workstation's node address	000106FFACDE (12-digit hexadecimal number)
SHELL_TYPE	The version of the workstation's DOS shell	V4.20A
SMACHINE	The workstation's short machine name	IBM (This is the default.)
STATION	The workstation's connection number	14

Table 6.6 lists each of the available network identifier variables.

TABLE 6.6

Network Identifier Variables

IDENTIFIER VARIABLE	DESCRIPTION	EXAMPLE
FILE_SERVER	The NetWare server name	Sales1
NETWORK_ADDRESS	The IPX external number of the cabling system attached to the server's network board	00120FED (eight-digit network hexadecimal number)

Table 6.7 lists each of the available date identifier variables.

TABLE 6.7

Date Identifier Variables

IDENTIFIER VARIABLE	DESCRIPTION	EXAMPLE OR VALUES
DAY	The day's date	Values: 01 through 31
DAY_OF_WEEK	The day's name	Example: Tuesday
MONTH	The month's number	Values: 01 through 12
MONTH_NAME	The month's name	Example: October
NDAY_OF_WEEK	The number of the day of the week	Values: 1 through 7 (1=Sunday)
SHORT_YEAR	The last two digits of the year	Example: 96
YEAR	All four digits of the year	Example: 1996

Table 6.8 lists each of the available time identifier variables.

TABLE 6.8

Time Identifier Variables

IDENTIFIER VARIABLE	DESCRIPTION	VALUES
AM_PM	Morning or afternoon	AM or PM
GREETING_TIME	General time of day	Morning, Afternoon, or Evening
HOUR	Hour on a 12-hour scale	1 through 12
HOUR24	Hour on a 24-hour scale	00 through 24 (00=Midnight)
MINUTE	Minute	00 through 59
SECOND	Second	00 through 59

Table 6.9 lists each of the miscellaneous identifier variables.

TABLE 6.9

Miscellaneous Identifier Variables

IDENTIFIER VARIABLE	DESCRIPTION	EXAMPLE OR VALUES
<DOS variable>	Any DOS variable, such as PATH, PROMPT, etc. Must be enclosed in angle brackets. If in a MAP command, must also be preceded by a percent sign (%).	Example: `MAP S16:=%<PATH>`
%n	Variable for LOGIN parameters, such as server name and user name.	Example: `IF %1="Joel" THEN...`
ACCESS_SERVER	Displays whether the access server is online.	Values: TRUE (functioning) or FALSE (not functioning)
ERROR_LEVEL	An error number.	Values: Any error number (0=No errors)

LOGIN SCRIPT EXAMPLE

The following is an example of a system (container) login script.

```
MAP DISPLAY OFF
IF "%1"="ADMIN" THEN
MAP *1:=SERVER1_SYS:SYSTEM
ELSE MAP *1:=SERVER1_VOL1:USERS\%LOGIN_NAME
END


MAP INS S1:=SERVER1_SYS:PUBLIC
MAP INS S2:=SERVER1_SYS:PUBLIC\%MACHINE\%OS\%OS_VERSION
COMSPEC=S2:COMMAND.COM
MAP S16:=VOL1:APPS\WORD
MAP S16:=VOL1:APPS\DATAB
```

```
IF MEMBER OF "Design" THEN
MAP ROOT S16:=VOL1:APPS\CAD
MAP *2:=VOL1:DESIGNS\PROJECTA
MAP *3:=VOL1:DESIGNS\PROJECTB
END
IF MEMBER OF "Field" THEN
MAP S16:=VOL1:APPS\CDBASE
MAP *4:=VOL1:REPORTS\CLIENTS\NEW
END


#CAPTURE L=1 Q=.LaserQ.Sales.Satellite.RedHawk NB NT NFF TI=5


MAP DISPLAY ON
MAP
WRITE "Good %GREETING_TIME, %LOGIN_NAME."


IF DAY_OF_WEEK="Monday" THEN
WRITE "Welcome back! It's a great week to design satellites!"
FIRE PHASERS 3 TIMES
END
```

The first line in the script

```
MAP DISPLAY OFF
```

turns off the display of any MAP commands as they're being executed during the login process. This simply keeps the screen from looking too busy and distracting or concerning the user.

The next group of four lines

```
IF "%1"="ADMIN" THEN
MAP *1:=SERVER1_SYS:SYSTEM
ELSE MAP *1:=SERVER1_VOL1:USERS\%LOGIN_NAME
END
```

maps the first network drive to a network directory. If the user who logs in is user Admin, then the first drive mapping is to the SYS:SYSTEM directory on server SERVER1. All other users who log in will get a drive mapped to their home directories on volume VOL1 instead.

The next line

```
MAP INS S1:=SERVER1_SYS:PUBLIC
```

maps the first search drive to the SYS:PUBLIC directory for all users. This is the directory where all NetWare utilities are stored, so it's important for users to have access to it.

The next two lines

```
MAP INS S2:=SERVER1_SYS:PUBLIC\%MACHINE\%OS\%OS_VERSION
COMSPEC=S2:COMMAND.COM
```

map a search drive to the directory that contains DOS, so that users can run DOS from the network instead of from the local hard disk. For every version of DOS your users will run on their machines, you should create a unique DOS directory, named with the workstation's machine type, DOS type, and DOS version, and load that version of DOS in the version subdirectory. For example, if your user is running an IBM compatible computer, with MS-DOS version 6.2 on it, the DOS directory would be

```
SYS:PUBLIC\IBM_PC\MSDOS\6.20
```

The login script command, which is using identifier variables in the directory path, will gather the workstation's particular information and map a drive to the correct directory.

The next two lines

```
MAP S16:=VOL1:APPS\WORD
MAP S16:=VOL1:APPS\DATAB
```

map search drives to two application directories so that users can access them.

The next five lines only execute if the user logging in is a member of the group called "Design." If so, then a fake root search drive is mapped to the CAD subdirectory, and regular network drives are mapped to two subdirectories: PROJECTA and PROJECTB.

```
IF MEMBER OF "Design" THEN
MAP ROOT S16:=VOL1:APPS\CAD
MAP *2:=VOL1:DESIGNS\PROJECTA
MAP *3:=VOL1:DESIGNS\PROJECTB
END
```

The next four lines

```
IF MEMBER OF "Field" THEN
MAP S16:=VOL1:APPS\CDBASE
MAP *4:=VOL1:REPORTS\CLIENTS\NEW
END
```

only execute if the user logging in is a member of the group called "Field." These users, who are field sales people, get a search drive mapped to their CDBASE application and a regular network drive mapped to the NEW subdirectory, where they log new clients.

The next line

```
#CAPTURE L=1 Q=.LaserQ.Sales.Satellite.RedHawk NB NT NFF TI=5
```

captures the workstation's LPT1 port to a network print queue named LaserQ. Its full NDS name is given in this case (`.LaserQ.Sales.Satellite.RedHawk`). The full name isn't necessary if the print queue is in the same context as the user logging in. The NB parameter means "No Banner," the NT parameter means "No Tabs," NFF means "No Form Feed," and TI=5 means that the capture will time out after five seconds, if necessary.

The next line turns MAP's display back on:

```
MAP DISPLAY ON
```

The next line displays a list of all the drive mappings that have been successfully mapped during the login process:

```
MAP
```

The next line displays a greeting to the user, such as "Good MORNING, ERIC."

```
WRITE "Good %GREETING_TIME, %LOGIN_NAME."
```

The final four lines

```
IF DAY_OF_WEEK="Monday" THEN
WRITE "Welcome back! It's a great week to design satellites!"
FIRE PHASERS 3 TIMES
END
```

only execute on Mondays. They display a supposedly inspirational message to the user and make the phaser sound three times as the login script ends.

Using Menus

Another way you can automate a user's working environment is to use a menu program. With a menu program, you can allow a user to choose items such as e-mail or word-processing programs from a menu. This way, the user does not ever have to see the DOS prompt or learn to execute commands.

NetWare allows you to create a simple menu program by using the NMENU utilities. NMENU is a pared-down version of Saber Software Corporation's Saber Menu System for DOS. If the menu programs you want to create are fairly simple, you can use the NMENU utilities. If you want to create more complex menu programs, you may want to get the complete Saber products or another third-party menu system.

You can use NMENU to create a new menu program for your users. In addition, if you are using a menu program you created with the older MENU utility included in NetWare 3.11 and earlier, NMENU can convert those old menu programs into the new NMENU format.

CREATING A NEW MENU PROGRAM

To create a new menu program, complete the steps in the following checklist:

1 • Create a program directory on the network to hold the menu program files. You can name it anything you like. If you create the directory under SYS:PUBLIC, users' search drives will be able to find the directory, which can help simplify matters.

2 • Create another directory that will hold the temporary files that the menu program will generate. This directory can be located either on the network or on each user's hard disk. It can be named anything you want.

3 • Use a text editor to create a text file containing the appropriate menu commands. (Menu commands are explained in the section, "NMENU Program Commands.") You must save the file with the file name extension .SRC.

4 • Use the MENUMAKE utility to compile the text file into a program file. If the file name of the text file is DESIGN.SRC, enter the following command (leave off the file's extension when you type its name):

```
MENUMAKE DESIGN
```

5 • If necessary, set up drive mappings in login scripts to the program and temporary directories so that users can access them. (See the section "MAP Command" earlier in this chapter for more information about mapping drives.)

6 • If the directory for the user's temporary files is in a network directory, add SET commands to the user or system login script to point to the directories and indicate the workstation's connection number. (You don't need to use SET login script commands if the files are on the local disk.) For example, if the directory is called MENUTEMP under SYS:PUBLIC, add the following commands to the login script:

```
SET S_FILEDIR="Z:\PUBLIC\MENUTEMP\"
SET S_FILE="%STATION"
```

7 • To execute the menu program from the DOS command line, use the NMENU utility. For example, to execute the DESIGN menu program, enter the command:

```
NMENU DESIGN
```

8 • If you want users to enter the menu program automatically when their login scripts finish executing, add the EXIT command to the end of the login script, as shown here (remember to enclose the execution command in quotation marks in the EXIT command):

```
EXIT "NMENU DESIGN"
```

UPGRADING AN OLD MENU PROGRAM

A different menu system was used in NetWare 3.11 and earlier versions. If you have a menu program you created using the older MENU utility (whose files have the extension .MNU), you can upgrade those programs to the new NMENU program.

To upgrade an older menu file, complete the steps in the following checklist:

1 • Create a program directory on the network to hold the menu program files. You can name it anything you like. If you create the directory under SYS:PUBLIC, users' search drives will be able to find the directory, which can help simplify matters. (If you already have a directory for your existing menu programs, you can use that directory.)

2 • Create another directory that will hold the temporary files that the menu program will generate. This directory can be located either on the network or on each user's hard disk. It can be named anything you want. (If you already have a directory for your existing menu programs, you can use that directory.)

3 • Use the MENUCNVT utility to convert the old menu file. The utility will create a new file with the file name extension .SRC and will leave the old .MNU file unchanged. To convert a menu file called ACCOUNT.MNU, for example, enter the following command (leave off the file's extension when you type its name):

```
MENUCNVT ACCOUNT
```

4 • If necessary, use a text editor to edit the new .SRC file to add any new commands or options.

5 • Use the MENUMAKE utility to compile the .SRC file into a program file. For example, enter the following command:

```
MENUMAKE ACCOUNT
```

6 • If necessary, set up drive mappings in login scripts to the program and temporary directories so that users can access them. (See the section "MAP Command" earlier in this chapter for more information about mapping drives.)

7 • If the directory for the user's temporary files is in a network directory, add SET commands to the user or system login script to point to the directories and indicate the workstation's connection number. (You don't need to use SET login script commands if the files are on the local disk.) For example, if the directory is called MENUTEMP under SYS:PUBLIC, add the following commands to the login script:

```
SET S_FILEDIR="Z:\PUBLIC\MENUTEMP\"

SET S_FILE="%STATION"
```

8 • To execute the menu program from the DOS command line, use the NMENU utility. For example, to execute the ACCOUNT menu program, enter the following command:

```
NMENU ACCOUNT
```

9 • If you want users to enter the menu program automatically when their login scripts finish executing, add the EXIT command to the end of the login script, as shown here (remember to enclose the execution command in quotation marks in the EXIT command):

```
EXIT "NMENU ACCOUNT"
```

NMENU PROGRAM COMMANDS

The following sections describe several different commands you can use to create menu program files for your users.

MENU Command

Command Format MENU *number*, *name*

Description Identifies the heading of a menu or submenu. The *number* is a unique number that is assigned to this menu or submenu so that other commands in the program file can reference it. The *name* is the title of the menu or submenu, and can be up to 40 characters long. Type it as you want it to display on the user's screen.

Example MENU 1,Design Group

ITEM Command

Command Format ITEM *name* {*option option ...*}

Description Names an option that will be displayed in the menu. The *name* is the text that will actually appear on this line of the menu. Type it as you want it to display on the user's screen. You can include one or more *options* inside a single pair of braces, separating each option with a space. The following options are available:

BATCH	Removes the menu program from the workstation's memory before executing the command or application called for by this option. BATCH automatically sets the CHDIR option. Do not use the EXEC DOS command with this option.
CHDIR	Changes the workstation back to the menu's original drive and directory after the command or application executed by the ITEM command is finished.
PAUSE	Pauses the executing command or application so that the user can read any messages displayed on the screen. The message "Press any key to continue" appears.
SHOW	Displays the name of the DOS command being executed by this ITEM command.

Example ITEM Spreadsheet {CHDIR}

EXEC Command

Command Format EXEC *command*

Description Executes the commands necessary to run the command or application being called by the ITEM option. For *command*, use the regular executable command that normally executes the application, command, or utility, such as "WP" for WordPerfect for DOS.

You can also use three EXEC commands that are specific to the menu program:

EXEC DOS	Temporarily takes users out of the menu program and sends them to the DOS prompt. When finished working in DOS, users type EXIT to return to the menu.
EXEC EXIT	Exits the menu program and sends the users to DOS.
EXEC LOGOUT	Logs the user out of the network.

Example EXEC wp

SHOW Command

Command Format SHOW *number*

Description Calls the submenu (identified by the *number*) to be displayed when the user chooses this option from the menu.

Example SHOW 2

LOAD Command

Command Format LOAD *filename*

Description Calls and displays a completely different menu program as a submenu. In the LOAD command, specify the *filename* of the NMENU file, and make sure that the menu program being called is located in the workstation's current directory or in a directory that has a search drive mapped to it. (The following example calls the ACCOUNT menu file to be displayed.)

Example LOAD ACCOUNT

GET*x* Command

Command Format GETx *text {prepend} length,default, {append}*

Description Requests input from the user before continuing the execution of a menu option. There are three different variations of this command:

GETR	Requests input that is required.
GETO	Requests input that is optional. Can also be used to allow the user to press any key to continue.
GETP	Requests input and assigns a variable to it so that the input can be reused.
	For *text*, insert the text you want displayed (up to 40 characters long), such as `Enter your password:`
	For *prepend* and *append*, insert any values that should be automatically added by the menu porgram to the beginning and ending of the user's input. If no values are needed, put a space in between the braces.
	For *length*, insert the maximum number number of characters that the user can input. Enter 0 if you want the user to press any key to continue.
	For *default*, insert any default response that will be displayed, which users can either select or replace with their own response. If you do not want to supply a default value, leave out the value, but still use the separating commas, as shown in the example below.

Example GETR Enter your password: { } 12,, { }

EXAMPLE OF AN NMENU MENU PROGRAM

Figure 6.1 shows a sample menu program that is executed whenever someone in the Design group logs in.

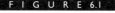

FIGURE 6.1

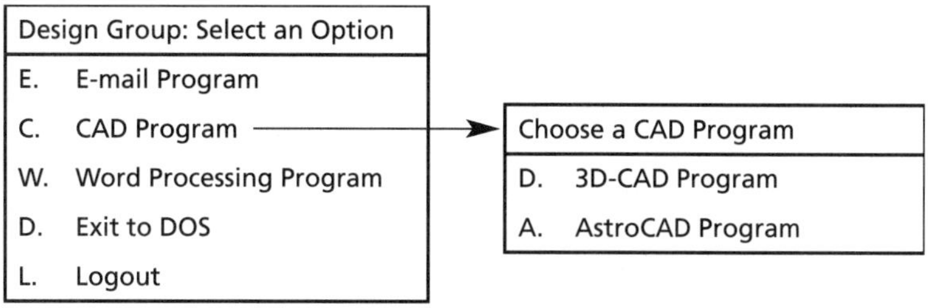

The source file to produce the menu program illustrated in Figure 6.1 would be as follows:

```
MENU 1, Design Group: Select an Option
         ITEM ^E-Email Program
                     GETR Enter your e-mail name: { } 8,, { }
                     EXEC mail
         ITEM ^CCAD Program
                     SHOW 2
         ITEM ^WWord Processing Program
                     EXEC WP
         ITEM ^DExit to DOS
                     EXEC DOS
         ITEM ^LLogout
                     EXEC LOGOUT

MENU 2, Choose a CAD Program
         ITEM ^D3D-CAD Program
                     EXEC 3dcad
         ITEM ^AAstroCAD Program
                     EXEC astro
```

In this menu source file, notice the formatting conventions:

- Each section of the file that pertains to a different menu or submenu is separated from the rest of the file by a blank line.
- Commands for each option in the menu are indented.
- Each ITEM command is followed by the EXEC command that executes that option. For example, for the imaginary CAD program called AstroCAD, the executable command is "astro," which is entered in the EXEC command.
- If you want users to be able to select an option by typing a single character (in addition to being able to use the up- and down-arrow keys to move to the option), add a caret (^) and the letter that should be typed to the beginning of the ITEM command. The caret will not appear on the screen.
- Under the E-mail Program option, the GETR command asks the user to enter an e-mail name. The text "Enter your e-mail name:" appears on the screen. Because there are no values you need to add automatically to either the beginning or the end of the user's e-mail name, both pairs of braces contain only a single space. The maximum length for an e-mail name in this e-mail system is eight characters, so **8** is entered in the length field. Finally, because you do not need to specify a default user name, you enter a comma instead of a default value.

CHAPTER 7

Network Security

Instant Access

Using Login Security

- To create account restrictions, use the NetWare Administrator utility (which runs in Windows).
- To create passwords, use the NetWare Administrator utility, LOGIN (a command-line utility), or SETPASS (a command-line utility).

Using NDS Security

- To view or change NDS rights, use the NetWare Administrator utility.

Using Directory and File Security

- To view or change file system rights, use the NetWare Administrator utility or RIGHTS (a command-line utility).
- To view or change directory and file attributes, use the NetWare Administrator utility or FLAG (a command-line utility).

Securing the Network from Intruders

- To use NCP Packet Signature, use both the SET command on the server and the NET.CFG file on the workstation.
- To set Intruder Detection, use the NetWare Administrator utility.
- To lock the server console, use MONITOR.NLM.
- To remove DOS and prevent NLMs from being loaded from insecure areas, use the SECURE CONSOLE console utility.

One of the aspects of NetWare that sets it apart from other networking operating systems is its high levels of security. How you implement this security is up to you. You can make your NetWare network as open as you need or as secure as Fort Knox.

NetWare uses several different types of security mechanisms to allow you to have control over your network's security. Those types of security are as follows:

- Login security, which ensures that only authorized users can log in to the network
- NDS security, which controls whether NDS objects, such as users, can see or manipulate other NDS objects and their properties
- File system security, which controls whether users can see and work with files and directories
- Intruder detection, which automatically detects someone trying to break into an account and locks them out
- NCP Packet Signature, which prevents fraudulent packets from being forged on a network
- Server protection, which includes ways to prevent unauthorized users from accessing the server

Each of these types of security is described in this chapter.

Login Security

Login security ensures that only authorized users can get into the network in the first place. Login security means that users are required to have valid user accounts and valid passwords. You can also use account restrictions to limit the times that users can log in, the workstations they can use, and such things as the length of their passwords and how frequently they must change their passwords.

ACCOUNT RESTRICTIONS

With account restrictions, you can put limits on how a user can log in to the network. Table 7.1 shows the four different types of account restrictions you can implement.

TABLE 7.1

Account Restrictions

RESTRICTION	DESCRIPTION
Login Restrictions	Control whether the account has an expiration date (which might be useful in situations such as schools, where the authorized users will change with each semester) and whether the user can be logged in from multiple workstations simultaneously.
Password Restrictions	Control whether passwords are required, how often they must be changed, whether they must be unique so that users can't reuse them, and how many grace logins a user can have before being locked out of the account.
Login Time Restrictions	Control the times of day by which users must be logged out of the network. By default, users can be logged in at any time; there are no restrictions.
Network Address Restrictions	Control which network addresses (workstations) a user can use to log in. By default, there are no restrictions on addresses.

You can set each of these types of account restrictions for individual users, or you can set them in a user template so that they apply to all users you create in a particular container. If you set them up in a user template, the restrictions will apply to any new users you create from that point on. They aren't retrofitted to users that already exist. Managing account restrictions for all new users in a user template can save you time if all your users need the same types of restrictions.

To set account restrictions, use the NetWare Administrator utility. (For instructions on setting up the NetWare Administrator utility on a workstation, see Chapter 6.)

To set account restrictions for a single user, use the NetWare Administrator utility and select the User object. Then select Details from the Object menu, open the appropriate information pages, and specify the restrictions you want. (Each type of account restriction has its own Information page.)

To set account restrictions for all users in a container, use the NetWare Administrator utility and select that container's User Template object. Then select Details from the Object menu, open the appropriate restriction pages, and specify the correct restrictions.

PASSWORDS

If passwords are to be a useful form of security, you should ensure that they are being used, that users are changing them frequently, and that users aren't choosing easily guessed passwords.

The following tips can help preserve password security:

- Require passwords to be at least five characters long (seven or eight are better). Five characters is the default minimum.
- Require that passwords be changed every 30 days or less.
- Require unique passwords so that users can't reuse a password they've used before.
- Do not allow unlimited grace logins. Limit the number of grace logins to three.
- Tell users to avoid choosing passwords that can be easily guessed, such as birthdays, favorite hobbies or sports, family member names, pet names, and so on.
- Remind users not to tell others their passwords or allow others to use their accounts.
- Tell users to mix words and numbers together to form words that can't be found in a dictionary, such as BRAVO42 or STAR2CLOUD.

To set password restrictions for a user or a user template, use the NetWare Administrator utility and select the User (or User Template) object. Then open the Details screen, select the Password Restrictions page, and enter the restrictions you want to apply to the user or the template.

Users can change their own passwords by entering the command

```
SETPASS
```

at the DOS prompt or by using the Password Restrictions page in the NetWare Administrator utility. More often, however, users will change their passwords when the LOGIN utility informs them that their passwords have expired and offers them the opportunity to type in new passwords.

NDS Security

Once you've created your NDS Directory tree, you've probably invested a fair amount of time in making sure that the objects you've created contain all the right information in their properties. Now you can decide who gets to see that information and who can change it.

To make the information about the objects in your tree secure, you can use NDS trustee rights to control how objects in the tree can work with other objects and their properties. *NDS trustee rights* are permissions that allow users or objects to perform tasks such as viewing other objects, changing their properties, deleting them, and so on.

When you assign a user enough NDS trustee rights to work with another object, you've made that user a *trustee* of the object. Each object contains a property called the Access Control List (ACL), which is a list of all the trustees of this particular object.

When the network is first installed, the user Admin has all NDS trustee rights to all objects in the tree. This means that when you log in as user Admin, Admin's NDS trustee rights let you create and delete other objects, see them, read and modify all their properties, and so on. Admin is the only user who has full NDS rights to everything in the network immediately after installation. However, while logged in as Admin, you can grant other users the same NDS rights, so that they can have the same privileges as Admin. By default, users are granted only a subset of NDS rights, so they have limited abilities to work with other objects. You can add to or remove these NDS rights to customize your users' abilities.

For security reasons, you should be frugal with NDS rights. NDS rights are a tool you use to protect your network objects from both accidental and intentional tampering. You may want to assign two users to have full NDS rights to the network, such as Admin and another user account that only you can use. This way, there is a backup account you can use if, for example, you forget the Admin's password.

There are two types of NDS trustee rights. *Object rights* control how the user works with the object but don't affect whether the user can see or work with the object's properties. These are listed in Table 7.2.

Property rights control whether the user can see and work with an object's properties. These are listed in Table 7.3.

To change object or property rights, see "Seeing and Changing an Object's NDS Rights," later in this chapter.

TABLE 7.2

NDS Object Rights

NDS OBJECT RIGHT	DESCRIPTION
Supervisor	Grants the trustee all NDS rights to the object and all of its properties. It can be blocked by the Inherited Rights Filter (explained in the next section).
Browse	Allows the trustee to see the object in the NDS tree.
Create	Allows the trustee to create a new object in this container. (This right only appears if you're looking at the trustee assignments for a container object.)
Delete	Allows the trustee to delete an object.
Rename	Allows the trustee to change the object's name.

TABLE 7.3

NDS Property Rights

NDS PROPERTY RIGHT	DESCRIPTION
Supervisor	Grants the trustee all NDS rights to the property. It can be blocked by the Inherited Rights Filter (explained in the next section).
Compare	Allows the trustee to compare the value of this property to a value the user specifies in a search. (For example, with the Compare right to the Department property, a user can search the tree for any object that has Marketing listed in its Department property.)
Read	Allows the trustee to see the value of this property. (The Read right automatically grants the Compare right, as well.)

(continued)

TABLE 7.3

NDS Property Rights (continued)

NDS PROPERTY RIGHT	DESCRIPTION
Write	Allows the trustee to add, modify, or delete the value of this property. (The Write right automatically grants the Add or Delete Self right, as well.)
Add or Delete Self	Allows trustees to add or remove themselves as a value of this property. This right only applies to properties that list User objects as values, such as group membership lists or the Access Control List.

INHERITING NDS RIGHTS

NDS object and property rights can be inherited. This means that if you have NDS rights to a parent container, you can inherit those rights and exercise them in an object within that container, too. Inheritance keeps you from having to grant users NDS rights at every level of the Directory tree.

However, it is sometimes desirable to block inheritance. For example, you may want to allow a user to delete objects in a parent container, but not let that user delete any objects in a particular subcontainer. Inheritance can be blocked in two ways:

- By granting a new set of NDS rights to an object within the container. Any new assignment will cause the inherited NDS rights from a parent container to be ignored. You can grant a new set of rights using the NetWare Administrator utility, as explained later in this chapter.
- By removing the right from an object's Inherited Rights Filter (IRF). Every object has an Inherited Rights Filter, which specifies which NDS rights can be inherited from a parent container. By default, an object's IRF allows all NDS rights to be inherited. You can change the IRF, however, to revoke one or more NDS rights. Any rights that are revoked from the IRF cannot be inherited.

You can only inherit an NDS right if you've been assigned that right at a higher level. If you don't have the Supervisor right in the parent container, for example, you can't inherit it and use it in another object even though that right is allowed in the IRF. The IRF doesn't grant NDS rights; it just allows you to inherit them if they've already been assigned to you.

When you assign a user property rights to an object's properties (by using the NetWare Administrator utility), you can click the All Properties button, which is a quick way to give the user the same property rights to all the properties of that object. Alternatively, you can choose Selected Properties and give the user different property rights to each individual property. If you select All Properties, those property rights can be inherited. Property rights assigned only to specific properties cannot be inherited.

NDS SECURITY EQUIVALENCE

You can assign one object to have the same NDS rights as another object by using the Security Equal To property. With security equivalence, you can make user Lila have the same NDS rights to the same NDS objects as user Erica, for example. (In fact, Lila will also receive the same file system rights as Erica, too. File system rights are explained later in this chapter.)

When you add a user to a Group object's membership list or to an Organizational Role object's list, the user really becomes security equivalent to that Group or Organizational Role object.

When you are given *security equivalence* to another user, you only receive the same NDS rights that the other user was explicitly granted. You do not get equivalences to that other user's equivalences. In other words, security equivalence doesn't travel. If Lila is equivalent to Erica, and Erica is equivalent to Jess, Lila doesn't end up being equivalent to Jess, too. Lila only receives whatever rights Erica received explicitly.

EFFECTIVE NDS RIGHTS

Because a user can be given NDS rights to an object and its properties through a variety of methods (explicit assignment, security equivalence, and inheritance), it can be confusing to determine exactly what NDS rights the user really has. A user's *effective NDS rights* are the NDS rights that the user can ultimately execute. The user's effective rights to an object are determined in one of two ways.

- The user's inherited NDS rights from a parent container, minus any rights blocked by the object's IRF.

- The sum of all NDS rights granted to the user for that object through direct trustee assignments and security equivalences to other objects. The IRF does not affect direct trustee assignments and security equivalences.

For example, suppose user Joanna has been given the Browse right to a container object. Joanna has also been given a security equivalence to user Eric, who has Create, Delete, and Rename rights to the same container. This means Joanna's effective NDS rights to this container are now Browse, Create, Delete, and Rename. Even if the container's IRF blocks the Delete right, Joanna still has that right. This is because the IRF only affects inherited rights, and inherited rights are completely ignored if the user has explicit trustee assignments to an object or a security equivalence that gives her NDS rights to that object.

SEEING AND CHANGING AN OBJECT'S NDS RIGHTS

To see the trustees of an object, use the NetWare Administrator utility (which runs in Windows). From the NetWare Administrator's Browser, select the object whose list of trustees you want to see, and then choose Trustees of This Object from the Object menu. (You can also click the right mouse button to bring up a menu that contains some of the more-frequently used tasks, and select Trustees of This Object from that menu.)

The Trustees of This Object screen appears, and you can see all the trustees of this object, as shown in Figure 7.1. If you click on each trustee, you can see the specific NDS object and property rights belonging to that trustee. You can also add or delete NDS rights from that trustee by marking the check boxes next to each right.

In addition, in this screen you can see the object's Inherited Rights Filter. By default, any object or property rights can be inherited from the parent object. If you want to block an NDS right from being inherited, click on the check box next to the right to clear its box.

If you want to see all the objects that a particular object has NDS rights to, use the NetWare Administrator's Browser, and select the object. Then, from the Object menu, choose Rights to Other Objects (or click the right mouse button and select the same option from the menu that appears). Specify the name context (location in the NDS tree) that you want to search for other objects. Then, the Rights to Other Objects screen appears, as shown in Figure 7.2.

FIGURE 7.1

The Trustees of This Object Screen

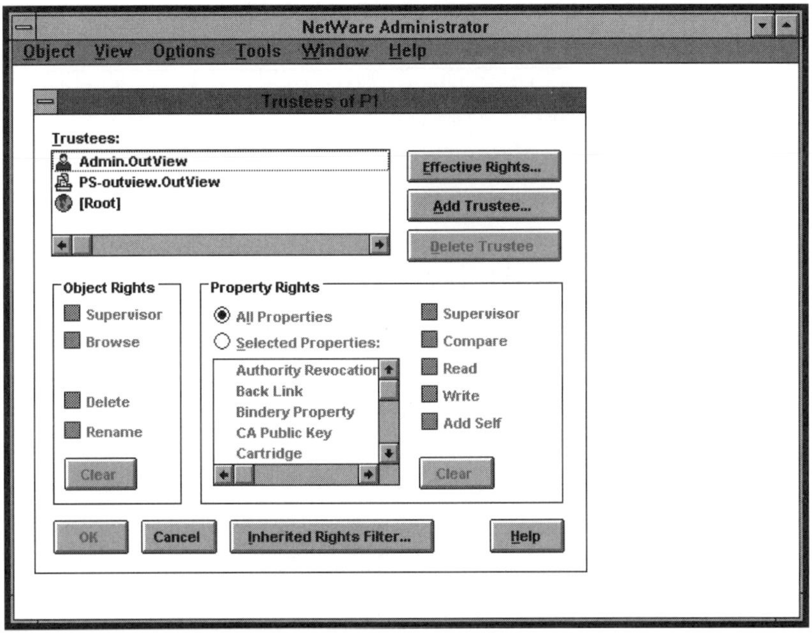

FIGURE 7.2

The Rights to Other Objects Screen

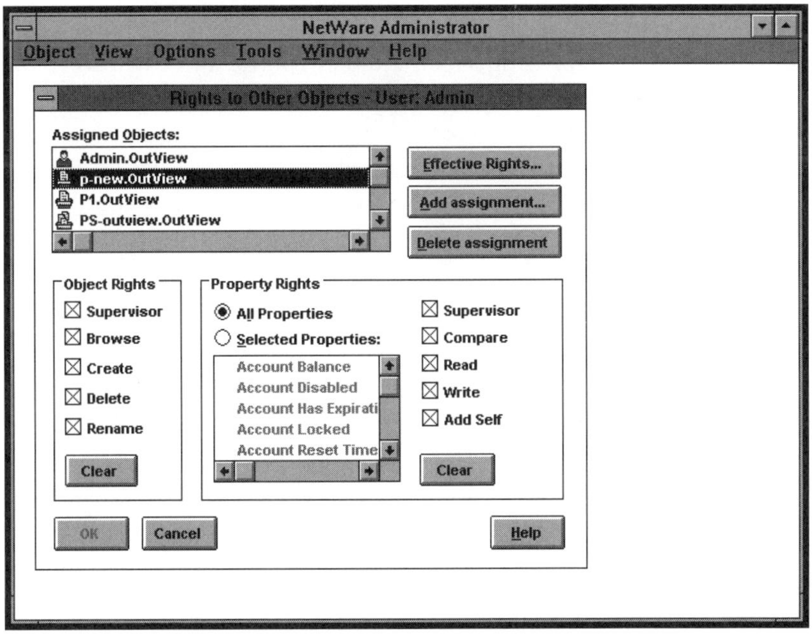

To see or change a user's security equivalence, use the NetWare Administrator's Browser and select the user. Then, from the Object menu, select Details, and then choose the Security Equal To page. There, you can add or delete other objects to which this user has a security equivalence.

File System Security

File system security ensures that users can only access and use the files and directories you want them to see and use. There are two different types of security tools that you can implement in the file system, either together or separately, to protect your files:

- File system trustee rights, which you assign to users and groups. Just as NDS object rights and NDS property rights control what users can do with other objects, file system trustee rights control what each user or group can do with the file or directory.
- Attributes, which you can assign directly to files and directories. Unlike file system rights, which are specific to different users and groups, attributes belong to the file or directory, and they control the activities of all users, regardless of those users' file trustee rights.

The next few sections explain file system trustee rights. File and directory attributes are explained later in this chapter, in the section "File and Directory Attributes."

FILE SYSTEM TRUSTEE RIGHTS

File system trustee rights allow users and groups to work with files and directories in specific ways. Each right determines whether a user can do things such as see, read, change, rename, or delete the file or directory. When a file system right is assigned to a file, the right affects the user's allowable actions in that file only. When a file system right is assigned to a directory, the right affects the user's allowable actions on that particular directory, as well as all the files within that directory.

Although file system rights are similar in nature to the NDS rights for objects and properties (described earlier in this chapter), they are not the same thing. File system rights are separate from NDS rights. They affect only how users work with files and directories. NDS rights affect how users work with other NDS objects.

The only place where NDS rights and file system rights overlap is at the NetWare Server object. If a user is granted the Supervisor object right to a Server object, that user is also granted the Supervisor file system right to any volumes attached to that server. Therefore, because user Admin has full NDS rights to all objects in the tree after the installation (although you can limit Admin's rights later), user Admin has the Supervisor file system right to the entire file system, too.

There are eight different file system trustee rights. You can assign any combination of those file system rights to a user or group, depending on how you want that user or group to work.

Table 7.4 lists the available file system rights and explains what each right means when assigned for a directory and for a file.

TABLE 7.4

File System Rights

FILE SYSTEM RIGHT	ABBREVIATION	DESCRIPTION
Read	R	Directory: Allows the trustee to open and read files in the directory. File: Allows the trustee to open and read the file.
Write	W	Directory: Allows the trustee to open and write to (change) files in the directory. File: Allows the trustee to open and write to the file.
Create	C	Directory: Allows the trustee to create subdirectories and files in the directory. File: Allows the trustee to salvage the file if it was deleted.

(continued)

TABLE 7.4

File System Rights (continued)

FILE SYSTEM RIGHT	ABBREVIATION	DESCRIPTION
Erase	E	Directory: Allows the trustee to delete the directory and its files and subdirectories. File: Allows the trustee to delete the file.
Modify	M	Directory: Allows the trustee to change the name, directory attributes, and file attributes of the directory and its files and subdirectories. File: Allows the trustee to change the file's name or file attributes.
File Scan	F	Directory: Allows the trustee to see the names of the files and subdirectories within the directory. File: Allows the trustee to see the name of the file.
Access Control	A	Directory: Allows the trustee to change the directory's IRF and trustee assignments. File: Allows the trustee to change the file's IRF and trustee assignments.
Supervisor	S	Directory: Grants the trustee all rights to the directory, its files, and its subdirectories. It cannot be blocked by an IRF. File: Grants the trustee all rights to the file. It cannot be blocked by an IRF.

Inheriting File System Rights

Just like NDS rights, file system rights can be inherited. This means that if you have file system rights to a parent directory, you can inherit those rights and exercise them in any file and subdirectory within that directory, too. Inheritance keeps you from having to grant users file system rights at every level of the file system.

Inheritance can be blocked by granting a new set of file system rights to a subdirectory or file within the parent directory. Any new assignment will cause the inherited rights from a parent directory to be ignored.

You can also block inheritance by removing the right from a file's or a subdirectory's Inherited Rights Filter. Every directory and file has an Inherited Rights Filter, which specifies which file system rights can be inherited from a parent directory. By default, a file's or directory's IRF allows all rights to be inherited. You can change the IRF, however, to revoke one or more rights. Any file system rights that are revoked from the IRF cannot be inherited.

You can only inherit a file system right if you've been assigned that right at a higher level. If you don't have the Supervisor right in the parent directory, for example, you can't inherit it and use it in another subdirectory even though that right is allowed in the IRF. The IRF doesn't grant rights; it just allows you to inherit file system rights if they've already been assigned to you at a higher level.

For instructions on assigning file system rights or changing the IRF, see "Seeing and Changing a User's File System Rights," later in this chapter.

File System Security Equivalence

Security equivalence for file system rights works the same way as security equivalence for NDS rights (explained earlier in this chapter). You can assign one user to have the same NDS rights and file system rights as another user by using the Security Equal To property. With security equivalence, you can make user Lila have the same rights to the same NDS objects, files, and directories as user Erica, for example.

When you add a user to a Group object's membership list or to an Organizational Role object's list, the user becomes security equivalent to that Group or Organizational Role object.

When you are given security equivalence to another user, you only receive the same rights that the other user was explicitly granted. You do not get equivalences to that user's other equivalences. Security equivalence doesn't travel. If Lila is equivalent to Erica, and Erica is equivalent to Jess, Lila doesn't end up being equivalent to Jess, too. Lila only receives whatever rights Erica received explicitly.

Effective File System Rights

Just as with NDS rights, determining which file system rights a user can actually exercise in a file or directory can be confusing at first. A user's *effective file system rights* are the file system rights that the user can ultimately execute in a given directory or file. The user's effective rights to a directory or file are determined in one of two ways.

- The user's inherited rights from a parent directory, minus any rights blocked by the subdirectory's (or file's) IRF.
- The sum of all rights granted to the user for that directory or file, through direct trustee assignment and security equivalences to other users.

A file's or directory's IRF does not affect direct trustee assignments and security equivalences. Therefore, if you have been given an explicit trustee assignment in a file or directory, any rights you might have inherited from a parent directory will be completely ignored. On the other hand, if you have not been given an explicit trustee assignment or security equivalence that specifically gives you rights in a file or directory, you will automatically inherit any rights you had in a parent directory, minus any rights blocked by the IRF.

Seeing and Changing a User's File System Rights

To see a user's file system rights, you can use either the NetWare Administrator utility (from Windows) or the RIGHTS command-line utility.

To use the NetWare Administrator utility, you can either select a user and see the user's trustee assignments (a list of the files and directories of which that user is a trustee), or you can select a file or directory and see a list of all its trustees.

To see or change a user's trustee assignments, complete the following checklist.

1. From the NetWare Administrator's Browser, select the user and choose Details from the Object menu.
2. Open the Rights to Files and Directories page.
3. To see the user's current file system rights, you must first select a volume that contains directories to which the user has rights. To do this, click on the Show button. Then, in the Directory Context panel on the right side,

navigate through the Directory tree to locate the desired volume. Select the volume from the Volumes panel on the left side, and then click OK.

4 • Now, under the Files and Directories panel, a list appears showing all of the files and directories of which the user is *currently* a trustee, as shown in Figure 7.3. To see the user's assigned file system rights to one of these directories or files, select the directory or file, and then look at the list of rights below. An "X" in the check box next to each right means that the user has rights to this file or directory. To change the user's rights, click on each desired check box to either mark it or clear it.

5 • To see the user's effective file system rights to this file or directory, click on the Effective Rights button.

6 • To assign the user file system rights to a *new* file or directory, click on the Add button. In the Directory Context panel on the right side, navigate through the Directory tree to locate the desired volume or directory. Then, select the volume, directory, or file from the left panel, and click OK. Now the newly selected file, directory, or volume appears under the Files and Directories panel. Make sure the new file, directory, or volume is selected, and then assign the appropriate file system rights by marking each desired check box.

7 • To see or change a user's security equivalence, open the user's Security Equal To page. There, you can add or delete other objects to which this user has a security equivalence. Remember that security equivalence affects both NDS and file system rights.

To use the NetWare Administrator utility to see all the trustees of a directory (or a file or volume), complete the following steps.

1 • From the NetWare Administrator's Browser, select the directory and choose Details from the Object menu.

2 • Open the Trustees of this Directory page. This page shows the containers and users that have trustee rights to this directory, as shown in Figure 7.4.

This page also shows the directory's IRF. By default, the IRF allows any file system rights to be inherited from the parent directory.

3 • To change the IRF to block a file system right from being inherited, click on the check box next to that right to clear its box.

4 • To see a particular trustee's effective file system rights to the directory, click the Effective Rights button, and then select the trustee. (You can either type in the trustee's name or click the Browse button next to the Trustee field to navigate the NDS tree and select the trustee that way.) That trustee's effective rights will appear in bold type.

5 • To add a trustee to the directory, click the Add Trustee button. Navigate through the Directory tree in the right panel, and then select the user you want from the Objects panel on the left side. That user now appears in the Trustees list. Select that user, and then mark the check boxes next to the file system rights you want the user to have.

FIGURE 7.3

Rights to Files and Directories

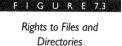

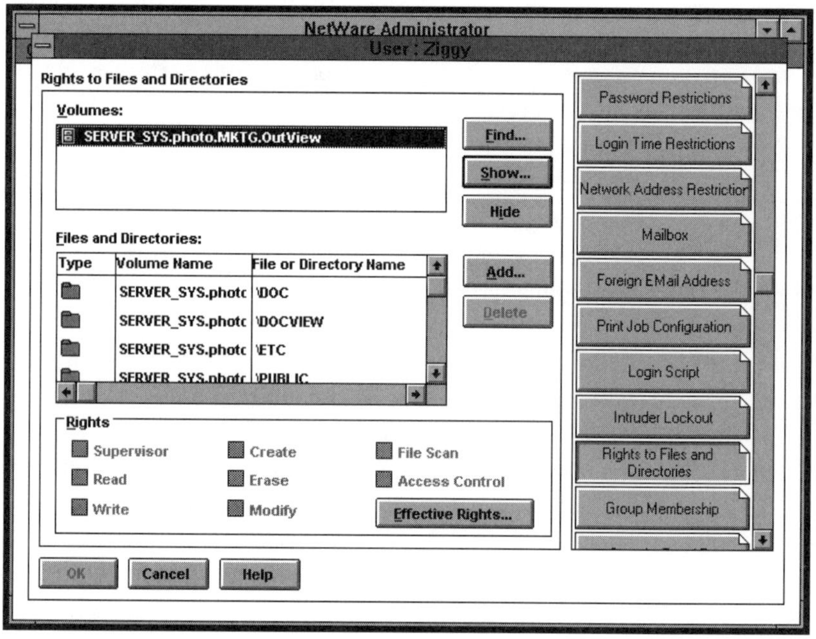

FIGURE 7.4

Trustees of this Directory

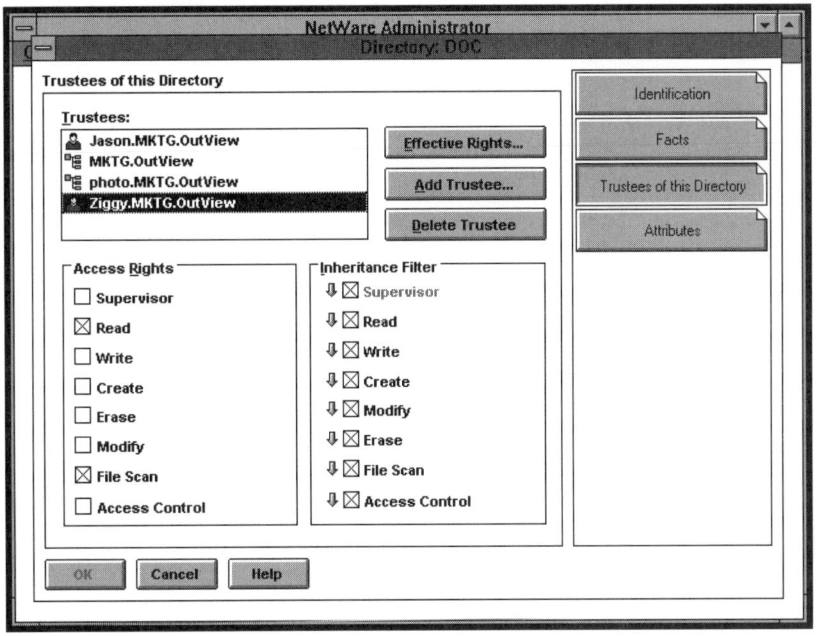

To use the RIGHTS command-line utility to see or change a user's current file system rights to a file or directory, use the following command at the workstation's DOS prompt:

```
RIGHTS path rights /option
```

For *path*, insert the path to the directory or file you want. To indicate the current directory, use a single period (.).

For *rights*, insert the list of rights you want to assign. (Use the rights' abbreviations, and separate each one with a space.) If you want to add some rights to the existing rights already assigned, you can use the plus (+) sign in front of the abbreviation. To delete a right, leaving the others intact, use a minus (-) sign. To replace all existing rights with the ones you specify, don't use either sign. If you want to assign all available rights, use the word *ALL* instead of specifying individual attributes. If you want to revoke all rights from the specified trustee, use the letter *N* (for No Rights) instead of specifying individual attributes. To completely remove the trustee from the file or directory, use the word *REM* (for Remove).

For *options*, insert the options you want. The available options are listed in Table 7.5.

TABLE 7.5
RIGHTS Options

RIGHTS OPTION	DESCRIPTION
/C	Scrolls continuously through the display.
/F	Displays the IRF.
/I	Displays where the inherited rights are coming from.
/NAME=*name*	Displays or changes the rights for the specified user or group. (If the user or group is in a different name context in the NDS tree than the volume is, you will have to specify the user's complete NDS name.)
/S	Displays or changes all subdirectories below the current directory.
/T	Displays the trustee assignments for a directory.
/VER	Displays the version number of the RIGHTS utility.
/?	Displays help screens for the RIGHTS utility.

For example, if you want to see the list of trustees for the SYS:PUBLIC directory, which is mapped to search drive Z, you could use the following command:

```
RIGHTS Z: /T
```

at the workstation's DOS prompt.

To assign user Paul all available rights to the directory that is currently mapped to drive G (assuming Paul is in the same name context in the NDS tree as the volume that contains this directory), use the following command:

```
RIGHTS G: ALL /NAME=PAUL
```

To grant user Teresa the Create, Erase, Modify, and File Scan rights to the REPORTS.2 file in the current directory, use the following command:

```
RIGHTS G:REPORTS.2 CEMF /NAME=.TERESA.MKTG.OUTVIEW
```

For more examples of how to use RIGHTS, display the help screens for the utility with the following command:

```
RIGHTS /? ALL
```

FILE AND DIRECTORY ATTRIBUTES

Another important NetWare security tool for securing files and directories is attributes. *Attributes* are properties of files and directories that control what can happen to those files or directories. Attributes, which are also called *flags*, are different from trustee rights in several ways:

- Attributes are assigned directly to files and directories, while rights are assigned to users.
- Attributes override rights. In other words, if that directory has the Delete Inhibit attribute, you can't delete the directory even if you've been granted the Erase right.
- Likewise, attributes don't grant rights. Just because a file has the Read-Write attribute doesn't mean you can write to it if you don't have the Write right.
- Attributes affect all users, including the Admin user.
- Attributes affect some aspects of the file that rights do not, such as determining whether or not the files in a directory can be purged immediately upon deletion.

Kinds of File and Directory Attributes

There are eight attributes that apply to either files or directories. There are an additional eight that apply only to files. These attributes are listed in Table 7.6. The table also shows the abbreviations used for each attribute (when using the FLAG command), and whether the attribute applies to both directories and files or only to files. The FLAG command is discussed in the next section ("Assigning File and Directory Attributes").

TABLE 7.6

File and Directory Attributes

ATTRIBUTE	ABBREVIATION	FILE	DIRECTORY	DESCRIPTION
Delete Inhibit	Di	X	X	Prevents users from deleting the file or directory.

(continued)

TABLE 7.6

File and Directory Attributes (continued)

ATTRIBUTE	ABBREVIATION	FILE	DIRECTORY	DESCRIPTION
Hidden	H	X	X	Hides the file or directory so it isn't listed by the DOS DIR command or in the Windows File Manager, and can't be copied or deleted.
Purge Immediate	P	X	X	Purges the file or directory immediately upon deletion. Purged files can't be salvaged.
Rename Inhibit	Ri	X	X	Prevents users from renaming the file or directory.
System	Sy	X	X	Indicates a system directory that may contain system files (such as DOS files). Prevents users from seeing, copying, or deleting the directory (however, does not assign the System attribute to the files in the directory.
Don't Migrate	Dm	X	X	Prevents a file or directory from being migrated to another storage device.
Immediate Compress	Ic	X	X	Compresses the file or directory immediately.
Don't Compress	Dc	X	X	Prevents the file or directory from being compressed.
Archive Needed	A	X		Indicates that the file has been changed since the last time it was backed up.

TABLE 7.6

File and Directory Attributes (continued)

ATTRIBUTE	ABBREVIATION	FILE	DIRECTORY	DESCRIPTION
Execute Only	X	X		Prevents an executable file from being copied, modified, or deleted. Use with caution! Once assigned, it cannot be removed, so assign it only if you have a backup copy of the file. You may prefer to assign the Read-Only attribute instead of the Executable Only attribute.
Read-Write	Rw	X		Allows the file to be opened and modified. Most files are set to Read-Write by default.
Read-Only	Ro	X		Allows the file to be opened and read, but not modified. All NetWare files in SYS:SYSTEM, SYS:PUBLIC, and SYS:LOGIN are Read-Only. Assigning the Read-Only attribute automatically assigns Delete Inhibit and Rename Inhibit.
Shareable	Sh	X		Allows the file to be used by more than one user simultaneously. Useful for utilities, commands, applications, and some database files. All NetWare files in SYS:SYSTEM, SYS:PUBLIC, and SYS:LOGIN are Shareable. Most data and work files should not be Shareable, so that users' changes do not conflict.

(continued)

TABLE 7.6

File and Directory Attributes (continued)

ATTRIBUTE	ABBREVIATION	FILE	DIRECTORY	DESCRIPTION
Transactional	T	X		When used on database files, allows NetWare's Transactional Tracking System (TTS) to protect the files from being corrupted if the transaction is interrupted.
Copy Inhibit	Ci	X		Prevents Macintosh files from being copied. (Does not apply to DOS files.)
Don't Suballocate	Ds	X		Prevents a file from being suballocated. Use on files, such as some database files, that may need to be enlarged or appended to frequently. (See Chapter 8 for information on block suballocation.)

Assigning File and Directory Attributes

To assign attributes to a file or directory, you can use either the NetWare Administrator utility (which runs in Windows) or the FLAG command-line utility.

To use NetWare Administrator, select the file or directory and choose Details from the Object menu. Then select the Attributes page. The marked check boxes show which attributes have been assigned to the file or directory. To change the attributes, click on the check boxes to mark or unmark them.

To use the FLAG utility, use the following command format at the workstation's DOS prompt:

```
FLAG path attributes /options
```

For *path*, indicate the path to the directory or file whose attributes you're changing.

For *attributes*, insert the list of attributes you want to assign. Use the attributes' abbreviations, and separate each one with a space. If you want to add an attribute to the existing attributes already assigned, you can use the plus (+) sign in front of the abbreviation. To delete an attribute from the file or directory, leaving the others intact, use a minus (-) sign. To replace all existing attributes with the ones you specify, don't use either sign. If you want to assign all available attributes, use the word *ALL* instead of specifying individual attributes. If you want to reset the attributes to the default settings, use the letter *N* (for Normal) instead of specifying individual attributes.

For *options*, insert the options you want. The available options are listed in Table 7.7.

TABLE 7.7

FLAG Options

FLAG OPTION	DESCRIPTION
/C	Scrolls continuously through the display.
/D	Displays details about the file or directory.
/DO	Displays or changes attributes for all subdirectories (no files) in the specified path.
/FO	Displays or changes attributes for all files (no subdirectories) in the specified path.
/M=*mode*	Changes the search mode for executable files. (Search modes are explained in Chapter 8.)
/NAME=*name*	Changes the owner of the file or directory.
/OWNER=*name*	Displays all files and directories owned by the specified user.
/S	Searches all subdirectories in the specified path.
/VER	Displays the version number of the FLAG utility.
/?	Displays help screens for the FLAG utility.

For example, to assign the Read-Only and Shareable attributes to the TEST.BAT file in the current directory, use the following command:

```
FLAG TEST.BAT RO SH
```

To add the Purge Immediate attribute to this same file, without removing the Read-Only and Shareable attributes, use the following command:

```
FLAG TEST.BAT +P
```

To reset the TEST.BAT file to its normal setting (the Read-Write attribute), use the following command:

```
FLAG TEST.BAT N
```

To see the attributes for the directory currently mapped to drive G, use the following command:

```
FLAG G: /DO
```

To see the help screens for FLAG (which contain more examples), use the following command:

```
FLAG /? ALL
```

Intruder Detection

NetWare can detect if an unauthorized user is trying to break into the network. You can set the network so that such unauthorized users are locked out after a given number of failed login attempts. This helps ensure that users don't try to break into the network by simply guessing at another user's password or by using programs that automatically generate passwords.

To set up intruder detection, you use the NetWare Administrator utility and assign intruder detection for a container. Then any user account within that container is subject to being locked if login attempts fail. To enable intruder detection, complete the following checklist.

1 • From the NetWare Administrator's Browser, select the container for which you want to set up intruder detection, and then choose Details from the Object menu.

2 • Open the Intruder Detection page (shown in Figure 7.5).

3 • To detect intruders, mark the Detect Intruders check box. Then specify the intruder detection limits. The Incorrect Login Attempts and Intruder Attempt Reset Interval allow you to specify how many incorrect login attempts will be allowed in a given time. If you mark the Detect Intruders check box, the default values that appear allow seven incorrect attempts within a 30-minute interval. You may want to reduce the number of attempts to four or five, depending on how likely your network is to have such an intruder.

4 • If you want the user's account to be locked after an intruder is detected, mark the Lock Account After Detection check box. Then specify how long you want the account to remain locked. The default locks the account for 15 minutes after the given number of failed login attempts. After 15 minutes, the account will be reopened automatically. You may want to increase this time if you are concerned about intruders.

FIGURE 7.5

Intruder Detection Page

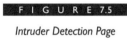

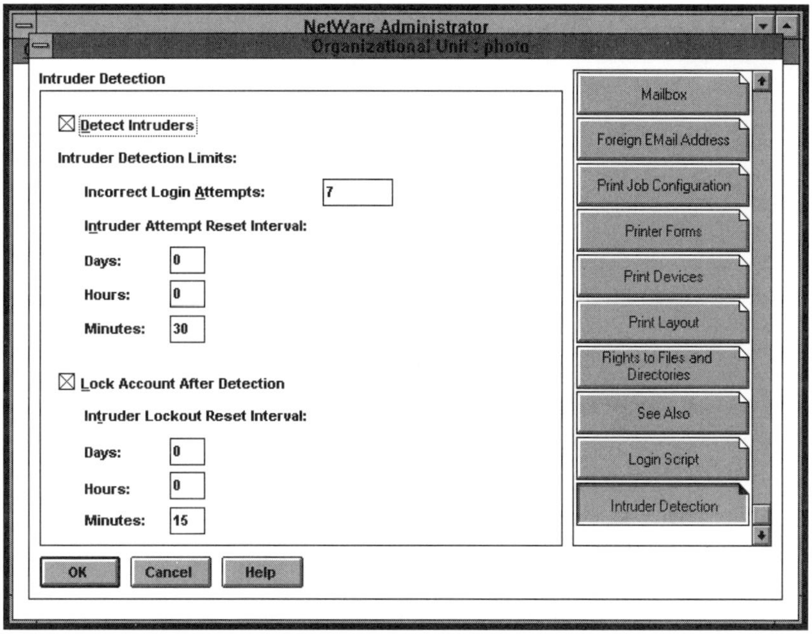

To see if a user's account has been locked, use the NetWare Administrator and select the user in question. Choose Details from the Object menu, and then open the user's Intruder Lockout page. This page shows whether the account is locked, as shown in Figure 7.6. If the Account Locked check box is marked, the account is locked. To unlock it, click the check box to clear it.

This page also shows the number of incorrect login attempts within the specified interval, when a user's account was locked, and the address of the workstation from which the failed login attempts were tried.

FIGURE 7.6

Intruder Lockout Page

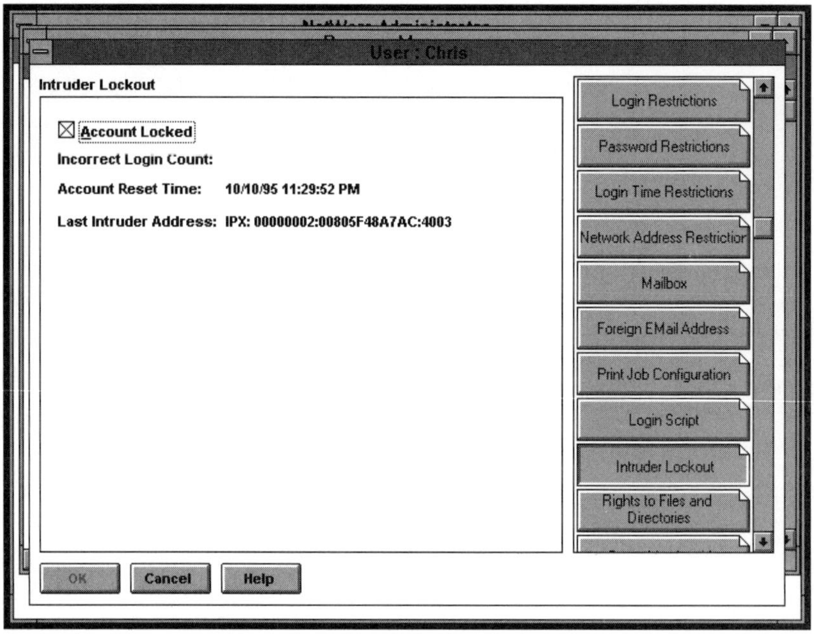

NCP Packet Signature

NCP Packet Signature is another feature designed to thwart intruders of a more persistent and knowledgeable type. NCP Packet Signature makes it impossible for someone to forge packets and access network resources through these forged packets. This feature requires workstations and servers to automatically "sign" each NCP packet with a signature and to change the signature for every packet.

NCP Packet Signature is an optional security feature. It can slow down network performance on busy networks, so you may prefer not to use packet signatures if your network is operating in a trusted environment with little threat of intruders stealing sensitive information.

There are four levels of NCP Packet Signature, which must be set on both workstations and servers. If the levels on the workstation and server don't form an allowable combination, the two computers will not be able to communicate with each other.

To set the signature level on a server, use SERVMAN.NLM to change the following SET command in the server's STARTUP.NCF or AUTOEXEC.NCF file.

```
SET NCP PACKET SIGNATURE OPTION=number
```

Replace *number* with the signature level (0 through 3) you want the server to use. After the server has been booted, you can execute the SET command at the server's console to increase the signature level. However, if you want to decrease the level, you have to add the SET command to the STARTUP.NCF or AUTOEXEC.NCF file (SERVMAN.NLM makes this easy to do) and reboot the server. Table 7.8 shows the NCP Packet Signature levels for servers.

TABLE 7.8

Server Levels for NCP Packet Signature

LEVEL	DESCRIPTION
0	Server does not sign packets.
1	Server signs packets only if workstation requests signature.
2	Server signs packets if the workstation can handle signatures (regardless of whether the workstation requests signatures).
3	Server and workstation must both sign packets.

To set the signature level on the workstation, add the following command to the NET.CFG file:

```
SIGNATURE LEVEL=number
```

Replace *number* with the signature level (0 through 3) you want the workstation to use. Table 7.9 shows the NCP Packet Signature levels for workstations.

TABLE 7.9

Workstation Levels for NCP Packet Signature

LEVEL	DESCRIPTION
0	Workstation does not sign packets.
1	Workstation signs packets only if server requests signature.
2	Workstation signs packets if the server can handle signatures (regardless of whether the server requests signatures).
3	Workstation and server must both sign packets.

Figure 7.7 shows how the signature levels on servers and workstations combine to either allow unsigned packets, force signed packets, or deny login.

FIGURE 7.7

NCP Packet Signature Levels Combine to Allow or Deny Login

Workstation Level

Server Level	0	1	2	3
0	Unsigned	Unsigned	Unsigned	Log in Denied
1	Unsigned	Unsigned	Signed	Signed
2	Unsigned	Signed	Signed	Signed
3	Log in Denied	Signed	Signed	Signed

Server Protection

An important aspect of network security is to make sure the server itself is secure from tampering. This is a simple task but is often overlooked, leaving the network vulnerable to either deliberate or accidental damage.

If the server is sitting in an area that is easily accessible and isn't protected with a keyboard lock or password, a malicious user can easily access the server and wreak havoc. Less dramatic, but potentially just as damaging, is the accidental tampering that could occur. A janitorial employee could unplug the server to plug in the vacuum cleaner; a helpful employee could try to load a virus-infected file directly on the server; another employee could try to "fix" a printing problem while you're not around and end up with a worse problem than the original one.

The following are some of the simple ways you can secure your server.

- Lock the server in a separate room. Just putting the server in a locked room can prevent much of the potential tampering that could occur.

- Lock the server's console with MONITOR.NLM. To do this, select Lock File Server Console from MONITOR's Available Options menu and type in a password to use to unlock the console (you'll have to type the password twice to verify it). Then, to unlock the console, you can either use the password you entered or the Admin user's password. (You may have to press any key to clear the screen saver first.) Use a different password each time you lock the console to ensure higher protection.

- Prevent loadable modules from being loaded from anywhere but SYS:SYSTEM by using the SECURE CONSOLE command at the server's console. Then make sure that only authorized users have rights to SYS:SYSTEM. Without SECURE CONSOLE enabled, an intruder could create an NLM that breaches security and load that NLM from the server's diskette drive or another directory where he or she has more rights than in SYS:SYSTEM. SECURE CONSOLE also prevents anyone from accessing the operating system's debugger and from changing the server's date and time. In addition, it unloads DOS from the server. To remove SECURE CONSOLE, you must down the server and reboot it.

- Use a secure password for the Remote Console feature. When you load REMOTE.NLM, you're asked to enter a password (it can be any password you make up at this time). To use Remote Console, then, you have to enter that same password. Make sure the REMOTE.NLM password is secure, and change the password periodically by reloading REMOTE.NLM.

- Protect the server from electrical problems by installing an *uninterruptible power supply* (UPS). Because the UPS allows the server to close all its files safely before shutting itself down in the event of a power problem, the UPS can prevent excessive damage to the server's files.

- Use disk mirroring or disk duplexing to protect the network data in case one disk fails.

- Use SFT III to mirror two entire servers, so that a hardware failure in one server won't stop the network from functioning.

- Keep a regular, up-to-date series of backups, so that all server and network files are archived and can be readily restored.
- Maintain updated virus protection software, and regularly scan for viruses.

Following these practices can help protect your server and, therefore, your entire network.

CHAPTER 8

File Management

Managing Disk Space

- To manage file compression, use SERVMAN.NLM to set file compression SET parameters.
- To manage data migration, install HCSS (see Chapter 3).
- To limit users' disk space, use the NetWare Administrator utility (which runs in Windows).

Managing Files

- To purge or salvage files that have been deleted, use the NetWare Administrator utility, FILER (a menu utility that runs in DOS), or PURGE (a command-line utility).
- To copy files, use NCOPY (a command-line utility).
- To display information about files and directories, use the NetWare Administrator utility, FILER, or NDIR (a command-line utility).
- To set the search mode for executable files, use FLAG (a command-line utility).
- To rename a directory, use RENDIR (a command-line utility).
- To extract a file from the *NetWare 4.1 Operating System* CD-ROM, use NWXTRACT (a command-line utility).

Creating a Fake Root

- To create a fake root for an application that needs to be installed at the root of the volume, use MAP (a command-line utility).

Backing Up and Restoring Files

- To back up and restore network files, use SBACKUP.NLM or a third-party backup solution.

Managing Volumes

- To create, delete, or enlarge a volume, use INSTALL.NLM, and select Volume Options.
- To mount a volume, use INSTALL.NLM or MOUNT (a console utility).
- To dismount a volume, use INSTALL.NLM or DISMOUNT (a console utility).
- To add name space support to a volume, load the name space module on the server, and then use the ADD NAME SPACE *module* TO *volume* command at the server console.

Protecting Database Transactions

- To manage the NetWare Transaction Tracking System (TTS), use SERVMAN.NLM to change the appropriate SET parameters.
- To set thresholds for TTS operation, use SETTTS (a command-line utility).
- To flag a file with the Transactional file attribute, use the NetWare Administrator utility, FILER, or FLAG.
- To reenable TTS after it's been disabled, use the ENABLE TTS console utility.

NetWare allows you to manage files in many different ways. How you manage your files can contribute significantly to how well users can find files, how well your disk space is conserved, and how easy it is to restore the network files when something goes wrong with them.

This chapter describes some of the techniques and features you can use to manage your file system.

Planning the File System

When you first set up your server, you will need to take into account how your file system will be structured. There are several factors that can affect how you organize your network files and applications. Careful planning can make it easier to back up and restore needed files, and it can make it easier to assign trustee rights to large numbers of users.

The following list indicates some tips that may help you plan an accessible, easy-to-manage file system. Note, however, that if you use the simple installation option for installing your server, your server will only have the SYS volume. This is acceptable, but having separate volumes can help save time in backup and restore processes, as explained in the following tips.

- You may want to reserve volume SYS for NetWare files and utilities. Try to avoid putting other types of files in SYS, such as applications or users' daily work files.

- Plan a separate volume for storing Macintosh files. To store Macintosh files on a volume, you have to load the Macintosh name space on that particular volume. The name space allows the Macintosh file's resource fork, long file name, and other characteristics to be preserved, but causes all files to take up twice as many directory entries as DOS files. The same principle holds true for OS/2 and NFS (Unix) name spaces, too. For more information about Macintosh and other name spaces, see the "Adding a Name Space to a Volume" section later in this chapter.

- To simplify backups, create a separate volume for applications and other non-NetWare utilities. That way, you only need to back up the volume containing applications occasionally, while you back up the volume with the users' daily work files more frequently. If an application and users' work files need to be stored in the same volume, this strategy won't work, of course. In this case, try to store the applications and the users' work files in separate branches of subdirectories in the same volume. For more information about backing up files, see the "Backing Up and Restoring Files" section later in this chapter.

- If different applications will be available to different groups of users, try to organize the applications' directory structures so that you can assign comprehensive rights in a parent directory. This may help prevent you from having to create multiple individual rights assignments at lower-level subdirectories. For more information about file system rights, see Chapter 7.

- If you want to use file compression to compress less-frequently used files, try to group those types of files into directories separate from other files that are used more often. That way, you can turn on compression for the less-used directories and leave it turned off for the frequently used directories. For more information about file compression, see the "File Compression" section later in this chapter.

- Determine if you want users to run DOS and Windows from their local drives or from a network directory. For more information about running DOS and Windows from the network, see the "DOS and Windows Directories" section later in this chapter.

- Decide where you want users' daily work files to reside: in personal directories, in project-specific directories, or in some other type of directory structure. Allow for ample network directory space for users to store their daily work files. Encourage your users to store their files on the network so that those files can be backed up regularly by the network backup process, and so that the files can be protected by NetWare security.

- Decide if you want users to have their own individual home directories. You can have home directories created automatically when you create a new user, as explained in Chapter 6.

DIRECTORIES THAT ARE CREATED AUTOMATICALLY

When you first install NetWare 4.1 on the server, some directories are created automatically in the SYS volume. These directories contain the files needed to run and manage NetWare 4.1. You can create additional directories and subdirectories in volume SYS or, if you created additional volumes during installation, you can create directories for your users in the other volumes.

The following directories are the ones that are created automatically on volume SYS:

- LOGIN contains a few files and utilities that will let users change their name context (location) in the NDS tree and log in to the network.

- SYSTEM contains NLMs that the network administrator can load.

- PUBLIC contains all of the NetWare utilities and related files. It also contains .PDF files (printer definition files). In addition, client subdirectories are located under PUBLIC. These client subdirectories contain the files required for installing NetWare client software on workstations.

- MAIL is empty when it is first created. It may be used by e-mail programs that are compatible with NetWare. In NetWare 3.1x and NetWare 2.x, the MAIL directory contained subdirectories for each individual user. Each of these subdirectories, named with the user's ID number, contained the user's login script file. If you upgrade a NetWare 3.1x or 2.x server to NetWare 4.1, those existing users will retain their MAIL subdirectories in NetWare 4.1, but the login scripts will become properties of their User objects instead.

- ETC contains files used for managing protocols and routers.

- DOCVIEW contains the DynaText viewers, which are used for reading the online documentation. (This directory is only created if you install the online documentation on the server.)

- DOC contains the actual online documentation. (This directory is only created if you install the online documentation on the server.)

Because these directories contain the files used for running and managing your NetWare network, do not rename or delete any of them without making absolutely sure they're unnecessary in your particular network's situation.

APPLICATION DIRECTORIES

You may find it makes assigning file system trustee rights easier for you if you group all applications on the network under a single volume or parent directory. By installing, for example, your word-processing, spreadsheet, and other programs into their own subdirectories under a parent directory named APPS, you can assign all of your users the minimum necessary rights to APPS, and then the users will inherit those rights in each individual application's subdirectory. For more information about file system rights, see Chapter 7.

If you install applications into subdirectories under a common parent directory, you can then usually designate that users' daily work files be stored in their own home directories elsewhere on the network.

When planning network subdirectories for your applications, you'll need to follow any special instructions from the manufacturer for installing the application on a network. Some applications can be run either from a local hard disk on the workstation or from a network directory. Be sure to follow the instructions supplied by the manufacturer.

In some cases, the instructions may indicate that the application has to be installed at the root of a volume. If your application requires this, you can still install it in a subdirectory under the APPS directory if you wish, and then map a "fake root" to the application's subdirectory. A fake root mapping makes a subdirectory appear to be a volume, so that the application runs correctly.

For example, suppose you want to install an application called ABC into a subdirectory under a directory called APPS on the volume called VOL1. However, the application's instructions say that ABC must be installed at the root of the volume. Create a subdirectory called ABC under VOL1:APPS, and install the application into ABC. Then, you can map a fake root to the ABC subdirectory and assign it to be a search drive at the same time by using the command

```
MAP ROOT S16:=VOL1:APPS\ABC
```

You can type this command at the workstation's DOS prompt if you only need the mapping to be in effect until the user logs out. If you want it to be in effect each time the user logs in, put the command in a login script. For more information about login scripts, see Chapter 6.

When you install an application, you may want to flag the application's executable files (usually files with the extension .COM or .EXE) with the Shareable and Read Only file attributes. This will allow users to simultaneously use the applications, but will prevent users from deleting or modifying them. You can use either the NetWare Administrator utility or the FLAG utility to assign file attributes. File and directory attributes are covered at length in Chapter 7.

DOS AND WINDOWS DIRECTORIES

Although most workstations run their own operating system from a local hard disk, it is possible to set up workstations so that they run DOS or Windows from a network directory instead of a local disk. (Macintosh workstations can't run System from the network. System must be run from the local hard disk.)

Setting up your workstations to run DOS and/or Windows from a network directory offers a few advantages:

- You can use diskless workstations on your network, which can help prevent virus infections and keep users from uploading or downloading their own files on the network.
- You can prevent users from accidentally deleting or modifying important DOS or Windows files.
- You can upgrade all workstations to a new version of DOS or Windows at the same time by updating the files in the network directory instead of having to change files on each individual workstation.

To allow workstations to run DOS or Windows from the network, you install DOS or Windows into network subdirectories under SYS:PUBLIC.

Planning DOS Network Directories

To install DOS onto the network, you will create a subdirectory under SYS:PUBLIC for each version of DOS and type of computer that you run, and then copy the DOS files into those subdirectories. If all of your workstations are running the same version of DOS and are the same type of computers (such as all IBM or all Compaq), you only need one DOS directory for the whole network.

However, if you have different brands of computers on your network, or if any of the computers are using different versions of DOS, you must create several DOS directories.

First, make a list of the types of computers on your network and the versions of DOS that each uses. For example, suppose you have the following workstations on your network:

- Twelve IBMs running DOS 5.1
- Twenty-seven Compaqs running DOS 5.1
- Four Compaqs running DOS 6.0
- Six AT&Ts running DOS 5.0

From this list, you can see that you need four different DOS directories on your network, to match the four different types of DOS running in various workstations.

Regardless of whether you need one DOS directory or several, you have to create a specific path to each one using the following format:

SYS:PUBLIC*machine name*\MSDOS*DOS version*

Replace *machine name* with the type of computer and replace *DOS version* with the DOS version number. For the workstations listed above, you would create four different DOS directories:

- SYS:PUBLIC\IBM_PC\MSDOS\5.1
- SYS:PUBLIC\COMPAQ\MSDOS\5.1
- SYS:PUBLIC\COMPAQ\MSDOS\6.0
- SYS:PUBLIC\ATT\MSDOS\5.0

After you create the appropriate DOS directories, complete the steps in the following checklist to set up workstations to run DOS from the network.

1 • Copy the DOS files into the subdirectory named with the appropriate version number, such as 5.1.

2 • Protect the DOS files by assigning them the Read Only and Shareable file attributes.

3 • In the system or profile login script, map a search drive (usually the second search drive) to the DOS directories. See Chapter 6 for more information on mapping search drives and using login scripts. If you use identifier variables in the MAP command, you can put a single command in the login script and it will locate the correct DOS directory for each workstation that logs in. Use the following command:

```
MAP INS S2:=SYS:PUBLIC\%MACHINE\%OS\%OS_VERSION
```

4 • Use the COMSPEC command in the login script to tell the workstation where to find the DOS command processor (COMMAND.COM). If you mapped the second search drive (S2) to the DOS directory, use the following COMSPEC command:

```
COMSPEC=S2:COMMAND.COM
```

5 • If the workstation's machine name is something other than IBM_PC (such as COMPAQ or ATT), put the machine name in the workstation's NET.CFG file. This way, the workstation will find its machine name in the NET.CFG file and know which DOS directory it should look for on the network. (IBM_PC is the default.)

Planning Windows Network Directories

In general, if you want to run Windows from the network, the most efficient way is to store the Windows program files in a common network directory that can be accessed by all users, and then copy the Windows user files into a separate directory for each individual user. However, you should still use a permanent swap file on each workstation's hard disk. (A *permanent swap file* is a file created by Windows that allows Windows to temporarily store programs and parts of Windows itself that are not currently in use. This file, in effect, acts like virtual memory for the workstation.)

If you prefer, you can store only the Windows program files in a network directory, and store both the users' files and the permanent swap file on each user's local disk. However, you may find that it's easier for you to manage the network if all the Windows files are in network directories.

Saving Disk Space

There are several features in NetWare 4.1 that will help you to conserve disk space:

- File compression, which compresses less-frequently used files, can conserve up to 63 percent of your hard disk space.
- Block suballocation allows several files to share a single block to avoid wasting space unnecessarily.
- Data migration lets you automatically move less-frequently used files to an alternate storage device, such as an optical jukebox system.
- Restricting users' disk space allows you to decide how much disk space users can fill up on a volume.
- Purging files lets you free up disk space by removing files that have been deleted but were still retained in a salvageable state. (You can also salvage deleted files, instead of purging them, but of course that doesn't free up any disk space.)

The following sections explain each of these features.

FILE COMPRESSION

File compression can save up to 63 percent of the server's hard disk space by compressing unused files. Compressed files are automatically decompressed when a user accesses them, so the user doesn't necessarily know that the files were compressed.

There are only two steps to make file compression occur on the server.

1. First, during installation, you choose whether to enable the volume for file compression, which simply means that the volume can handle file compression if needed. The default is to enable the volume, but you can choose not to enable it if you want to. (If you use the simple installation option of INSTALL, compression is automatically enabled.)

2. Second, you must decide whether you want file compression turned on of off. By default, file compression is turned on, so that any volumes enabled for compression will use file compression. However, you can easily turn off compression by changing the SET Enable File Compression parameter to Off. This SET parameter will affect file compression for all enabled volumes on the server.

Disabling and Reenabling Compression

By default, all NetWare volumes are enabled for file compression. Because you can easily turn on and off file compression using a SET parameter, there is really no reason to disable compression for a particular volume, especially because the only way to disable the volume is to delete and re-create it.

If the volume was disabled for compression, and you want to reenable it, use INSTALL.NLM. Load INSTALL, select Volume Options, choose the volume you want, go to the File Compression field, and press the Enter key, which will toggle the field from On to Off. Press the Esc key twice to save the new setting.

Managing Compression

By default, once the volume is enabled and compression is turned on, files and directories are compressed automatically after they've been untouched for seven days.

However, you can change several aspects of file compression, such as how long the files wait before being compressed, the time of day the compression activity occurs, and which files don't ever get compressed. To control file compression, you can use two file and directory attributes and several SET parameters.

The two file and directory attributes that affect compression are as follows:

- The Immediate Compress attribute compresses the file or directory immediately, without waiting for the standard duration of inactivity.
- The Don't Compress attribute prevents the file or directory from ever being compressed, even if compression is turned on for a parent directory.

To assign a file or directory one of these attributes, you can use the NetWare Administrator utility, the FLAG utility (covered in Chapter 7), or the FILER utility.

The SET parameters that affect file compression let you control characteristics such as when compression happens, how many files can be compressed at the same time, and so on. The easiest way to change these parameters is to use SERVMAN.NLM. If you change a SET parameter, the change will affect all files and directories in all volumes on the server that have been enabled for compression.

The SET parameters that affect compression are listed in Appendix B, under the "File System" section. To change the SET parameters, load SERVMAN and choose Server Parameters. Then, from the Select a Parameter Category menu, choose File System, and change the parameters you want. When you are finished, press Esc twice to get to the Update Options menu, and then update the STARTUP.NCF or AUTOEXEC.NCF files (or both) to save the new values. You do not need to reboot the server, because the values have already taken effect.

BLOCK SUBALLOCATION

A *block* is a unit that is allocated to store a file. A file may take up more space on the disk than its actual size because NetWare allocates the disk into uniformly sized blocks that are used to store pieces of files. The default block size depends on the volume's size, as shown in Table 8.1. In general, larger block sizes are better for large database records, because they can help speed up access. Smaller block sizes require more server memory, but help prevent disk space from being wasted.

TABLE 8.1 Default Block Sizes for Storing Files

VOLUME SIZE	BLOCK SIZE
0 to 31MB	4 or 8K
32 to 149MB	16K
150 to 499MB	32K
500MB or more	64K

If your block size is 32K, a 35K file will take two 32K blocks, using a total of 64K of disk space. In previous versions of NetWare, there wasn't anything you could do to prevent this inefficient use of disk space.

However, NetWare 4.1 includes a feature called *block suballocation*. Block suballocation lets the file system break a block into 512-byte suballocation blocks, so that several files (or pieces of files) can share a single block. With block suballocation turned on, the 35K file will use up one 32K block, and six 512-byte suballocation blocks, for a total of only 35K of disk space.

Block suballocation is turned on by default when NetWare 4.1 is installed. You do not need to do anything to use or manage block suballocation.

DATA MIGRATION

Data migration is a NetWare 4.1 feature that lets you extend the storage capabilities of your server to include optical disks. With data migration, less-frequently used files can be migrated seamlessly off of the server's hard disk onto an *optical storage system,* often called a *jukebox.*

Data migration is transparent to the user. The migrated files still appear to be available on the server's volume, just as they did before they were migrated. The user doesn't have to do anything different to access the file. When accessed the migrated file is quickly *de-migrated* back to the server's hard disk and opened as usual. The user may notice a delay of a second or two, however, as the file is being demigrated.

Data migration is managed by NetWare's High-Capacity Storage System (HCSS). For an explanation of how to set up and manage HCSS, see Chapter 3.

RESTRICTING USERS' DISK SPACE

You can restrict how much disk space a user can fill up on a particular volume. This can help prevent individual users from using an excessive amount of disk space. To limit the space individual users can use, use the NetWare Administrator and select a Volume object. Choose Details from the Object menu, and then choose the User Space Limits page.

On the User Space Limits page, you can see which users have restricted disk space allowances on this volume. You can see what their restrictions are, and how much space they still have available. You can also modify these limits or add other users and restrict their disk space, too.

PURGING AND SALVAGING FILES

In NetWare 4.1, when files are deleted, they are not actually removed from the server's hard disk. Instead, they are retained in a salvageable state.

Deleted files are usually stored in the same directory from which they were originally deleted. If, however, the directory itself was also deleted, the deleted files are stored in a special directory called DELETED.SAV at the volume's root.

Deleted files are stored in this salvageable state until one of three things happens:

- The file is salvaged, restoring it to its original form.
- The server runs out of free space on the disk and has to purge deleted files to make room. The oldest deleted files are purged first. When purged, a file is completely removed from the disk and cannot be recovered.
- The file is purged by the administrator or user. You can purge a file either manually, by using the NetWare Adminstrator utility, FILER (a DOS-based menu utility), or PURGE (a command-line utility), or you can use the Purge Immediate directory and file attributes to mark a file or directory to be purged immediately upon deletion.

Purging and Salvaging Files with NetWare Administrator

To use the NetWare Administrator utility to either purge or salvage a deleted file or directory, complete the steps in the following checklist.

1 • From the NetWare Administrator's Browser, select the directory containing the files or directories you want to salvage or purge.

2 • From the Tools menu, select Salvage. (This option will let you both salvage and purge files.)

3 • In the Include field of the Salvage dialog box that appears, indicate which files you want to see displayed. Specify a file name or use wildcards to indicate several files. A blank line or the wildcard symbols *.* will display all the deleted files in the selected directory.

4 • From the Sort Options drop box, specify how you want the displayed files to be sorted: by Deletion Date, Deletor, File Name, File Size, or File Type.

5 • From the Source drop box, choose whether you want to see deleted files in your current directory or in a deleted directory.

6 • Click the List button to display the files you've specified. Figure 8.1 shows an example of the Salvage dialog box with deleted files listed.

7 • From the displayed list, select the files you want to purge or salvage.

8 • Click either the Salvage button or the Purge button, depending on what you want to do. If you salvage files from an existing directory, the files are restored to that directory. If you salvage files from a deleted directory, the files are restored at the root directory.

9 • When finished, click the Close button.

FIGURE 8.1

Displaying Salvageable Files in NetWare Administrator

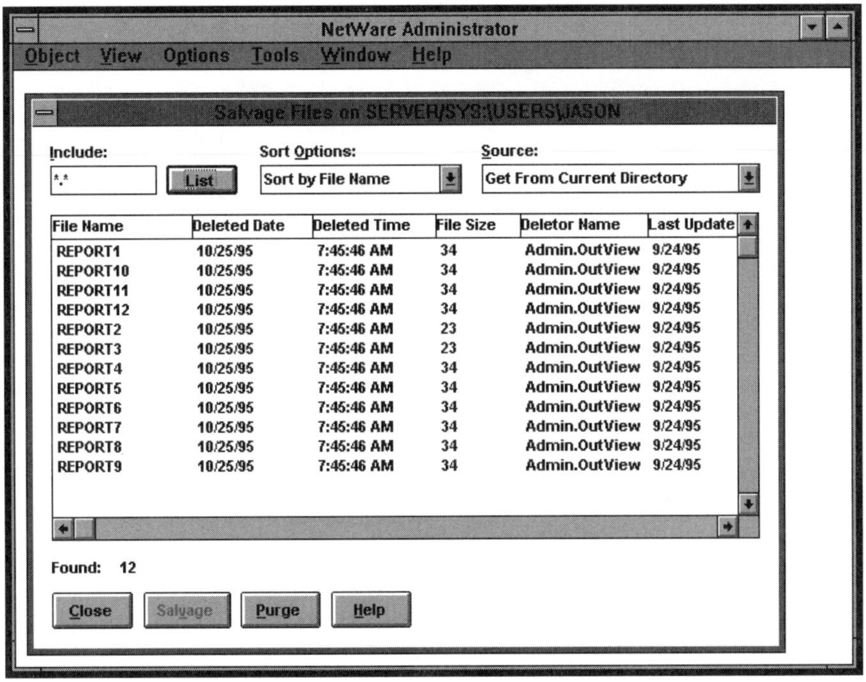

Purging and Salvaging Files with FILER

To use the DOS-based FILER utility to purge or salvage files or directories that have been deleted, complete the steps in the following checklist.

1 • At the DOS prompt, enter

```
FILER
```

to start the utility.

2 • If you are going to salvage or purge files from a current directory, choose Select Current Directory to make that directory current. To select a different directory, type in the name of the directory you want or press the Insert key to navigate through the file system.

3 • (This step is for salvaging only.) To salvage files, choose Salvage Deleted Files.

a. Choose View/recover deleted files if they are in an existing directory, or choose Salvage from deleted directories if the files are in a deleted directory.

b. Indicate which files you want to see displayed. Specify a file name or use wildcards (asterisks and question marks) to indicate several files. Use a single asterisk or *.* to display all the deleted files in the selected directory.

c. Specify how you want the displayed files to be sorted, by pressing F3 and choosing an option.

d. To salvage a single file, highlight the file and press Enter. To salvage multiple files, press the F5 key on each file to mark it, and then press Enter when you've selected all the files you want. If you salvage files from an existing directory, the files are restored to that directory. If you salvage files from a deleted directory, the files are restored at the root directory.

4 • (This step is for purging only.) To purge files, choose Purge Deleted Files.

a. Indicate which files you want to see displayed. Specify a file name or use wildcards (asterisks and question marks) to indicate several files. Use a single asterisk or *.* to display all the deleted files in the selected directory.

b. Choose whether you want to purge deleted files in the current directory only, or in the entire subdirectory structure of the current directory. As soon as you press Enter to select one of the options, the purging begins.

Purging Files with PURGE

To purge deleted files, you can also use the PURGE command-line utility. To purge files using PURGE, use the following command:

```
PURGE path\filename /option
```

Replace *path* with the path to the files you want to purge, and replace *filename* with a file name for the specific files. Wildcards are acceptable. The following options can be used with PURGE:

/A	Purges ALL files in the current directory and all of its subdirectories.
/VER	Displays the version number of PURGE.
/?	Displays help screens for PURGE.

For example, to purge all the deleted files with the extension .BAT in the current directory only, use the following command:

```
PURGE *.BAT
```

Backing Up and Restoring Files

Files can be lost or damaged in a variety of ways. They can be corrupted by viruses, accidentally deleted by users, overwritten by other applications, or destroyed when a hard disk fails. Despite all the best precautions, you can't always prevent files from being lost.

What you can do, however, is make sure that you always have current backup copies of your network data, so that you can restore files. If you have a carefully planned and executed backup strategy, you can minimize the amount of work that will be lost if you have to restore a file from your archives.

There are many different backup products available on the market. NetWare 4.1 includes a backup solution, called SBACKUP, that you can use, or you can purchase a third-party product that may provide additional features you need. Backup products can back up data onto a variety of storage media, such as tapes and optical disks.

Backing up network files involves more than just making a copy of the files. It's important to use a backup product, such as SBACKUP, that backs up not just the files themselves, but also the NetWare information associated with those files, such as trustee rights, Inherited Rights Filters, and file and directory attributes.

PLANNING A BACKUP STRATEGY

Planning an efficient backup strategy is one of the most beneficial tasks you can do as part of network management. With a good backup strategy, you can limit the time it takes to do backups, ensure that the least amount of working time is lost by your users, and avoid unnecessary headaches from searching for lost files.

Backup strategies can be different for every network. What works for someone else may not work well for you, and vice versa. First, consider the following questions:

- How long do you want to retain old copies of files? Do you want to keep backup files for one month only, and then copy over them? Or do you need to keep backups for twelve months or more?
- How many duplicate copies of the data do you want to keep?
- Where do you plan to store your backups? Noncritical data may be kept on-site (though when storing backups on-site, at least store them in a room separate from the server's room). If some of the data is mission critical, you may need to keep the backups in an off-site location in case of a physical disaster, such as a fire, flood, or earthquake. If the data is critical enough to store off-site, but you also want to have immediate access to it, consider making two backups, and storing one off-site and the other on-site.

Also take into account the following guidelines, which may help you plan a strategy that makes sense for your network needs:

- In general, don't back up files that change infrequently, such as application files and utilities, as often as files that change frequently.
- Whenever possible, avoid restoring the NDS tree from a backup tape. Instead, use partition replication to restore the NDS tree. See Chapter 5 for more information on partition replication.

- In determining how often to back up critical data that changes frequently, calculate how long you could afford to spend re-creating the information if it was lost. If you can't afford to lose more than a day's worth of work, you should perform daily backups of that information. If losing a week's worth of work is more of a nuisance than a devastating blow, perhaps you don't need to do daily backups.

- Encourage users to store files in network directories instead of on their local hard disks so that you can ensure they get backed up during your backup process. Relying on users to back up their own local files is seldom effective.

- Don't do a full backup of the complete network every night, even though your network data may be critical. Instead, plan a schedule that staggers complete backups with incremental backups, so that you still get full coverage without spending more time and money than necessary. For example, you can do a full backup of the network once a week. Then, once a day, do incremental backups of only those files that have changed. In the event of a total loss of files, you can restore all the files from the weekly backup, and then restore each of the daily tapes to update those files that changed during that week. In this way, you can cover all of your files while minimizing the time each backup session takes during the week.

- Plan a rotation schedule for backup tapes. If you have only one backup tape that you use every week, each time replacing the previous week's backup with the new one, you could unknowingly back up corrupted files onto your single tape, replacing your last good copy. To prevent this type of problem, plan to keep older backup tapes or disks on hand at all times. Many network administrators will use four or more tapes or disks for the same set of files, cycling through them one at a time. Each week, the most outdated tape or disk is used for the new backup. This way, three or more versions of backups are available at any given time. How many tape or disk sets you'll need depends on your rotation schedule. If you want to keep four weeks' worth of daily and weekly backups, you'll need at least 20 sets of tapes or disks — five for each week.

- Keep a backup log. A written record of all backups and your backup strategy can help someone else restore the files if you aren't there. See Appendix D for a worksheet you can use to help document your backups.

- Make sure the backups can be restored! A backup is only useful if the data in it can be successfully restored. Too many people discover a problem with their backups when they're in the middle of an important restoration process. Practice restoring files before you need to. By practicing, you may identify problems you didn't realize you had. Don't wait until it is too late.

USING SBACKUP

SBACKUP.NLM is the backup product that ships in NetWare 4.1. With SBACKUP, you can back up all the different types of files that can be stored on your server: DOS, Macintosh, OS/2, and Unix.

SBACKUP lets you select the type of backup you want to perform. There are four choices:

- *Full backup.* This option backs up all network files. It removes the Archive Needed file attribute from all files and directories. (This attribute is also called the *modify bit*. It is assigned to a file whenever the file is changed. When the file is backed up, most backup products can remove the attribute so that the next time the file is changed, the attribute is once again assigned.)

- *Differential backup.* This option backs up only files that were modified since the last full backup. It does not remove the Archive Needed attribute from these files.

- *Incremental backup.* This option backs up only files that were modified since the last full or incremental backup. It removes the Archive Needed attribute from these files.

- *Custom backup.* This option lets you specify particular directories to back up or restore. You can specify whether or not to remove the Archive Needed attribute from those files.

Backing Up Files with SBACKUP

To use SBACKUP.NLM to back up files, you load SBACKUP.NLM and device drivers for the backup device (tape or disk drive) on a server. This server is called the *host server.* Then you load Target Service Agents (TSAs), which also come in the NetWare 4.1 product, on any servers whose files you want to back up. These servers are called *targets.* (TSAs are NetWare Loadable Modules.)

To back up the host server, you load both SBACKUP and a TSA on that server. You can back up servers with TSAs on them (targets) from the host server. You do not need to run SBACKUP on the target servers.

Complete the steps in the following checklist to use SBACKUP to back up your network files.

1 • Attach the backup device (tape or disk drive) to the host server.

2 • Load the necessary backup device drivers on the host server. Then enter the command

```
SCAN FOR NEW DEVICES
```

at the console to register the device with the server. Check the manufacturer's documentation to find out which drivers you need. Place the commands that load the backup device drivers in the server's STARTUP.NCF file if you want them to load automatically when the server is rebooted.

3 • On each target server you want to back up, load the appropriate TSA. Don't forget to load a TSA on the host server that's running SBACKUP if you want to back up the host server itself. Use one of the following TSAs:

- For NetWare 4.1 target servers, load TSA410.NLM.
- For NetWare 4.0 target servers, load TSA400.NLM.
- For NetWare 3.12 target servers, load TSA312.NLM.
- For NetWare 3.11 target servers, load TSA311.NLM.

4 • Load SBACKUP on the host server.

5 • From SBACKUP's main menu, choose Backup.

6 • If multiple servers have TSAs loaded, choose the target server that you want to back up.

7 • When prompted, enter a user name and password for the target server. You may need to enter the Admin's full context name.

8 • If more than one storage device is available, select the backup device you want to use.

9 • Specify a location for both the session log and error files. The session log helps SBACKUP locate the backed up files for later restorations. The error files track any errors that may occur. Either press Enter to accept the default, or press Insert to navigate through the file system and select another location.

10 • Select the type of backup you want to do (full, differential, incremental, or custom).

11 • (This step is for custom backup only.) If you choose to do a custom backup, several screens appear that allow you to enter information about what you want to back up. You can select specific volumes, directories, and files to be either included or excluded from the backup. Use *exclude* options when you want to back up most of the file system while omitting only a small part. Everything that you don't specifically exclude is backed up. Use *include* options when you want to back up only a small portion of the file system. Everything you don't specifically include is excluded. (When specifying subsets to back up, two options allow you to exclude or include Major TSA resources. A *Major TSA resource* is simply a volume. You can choose to include or exclude volumes, directories, or files.)

12 • Enter a description for this backup session.

13 • If your backup device can append data to previous sessions on the same media, specify whether you want this session to be appended to the same media as another session or not. If you choose not to append, existing data on the media will be erased and replaced with the new backup session's data.

14 • Press F10 and choose whether to start the backup now or later. If you choose to start the backup later, enter the time and date you want it to begin.

Restoring Files with SBACKUP

To use SBACKUP.NLM to restore files, you load SBACKUP and device drivers for the backup device on the host server, just as you did when preparing to back up the files. Then you load TSAs on any target servers whose files you want to restore.

To restore files with SBACKUP, complete the steps in the following checklist.

1 • From SBACKUP's main menu, choose Restore.

2 • If multiple servers have TSAs loaded, choose the target server to which you want to restore files.

3 • When prompted, enter a user name and password for the target server. You may need to enter the Admin's full context name.

4 • If you are restoring files from a session (and you know where its session files are), select Choose a Session to Restore, and then enter the path to the session files and select the session you want.

5 • If the session files have been corrupted or deleted, and you want to restore the files directly from a backup media, choose Restore Without Session Files. Then specify a location for the new session log and error files for the restoration session.

6 • Select the type of backup device and media from which you want to restore.

7 • Choose whether you want to restore a single file or directory, an entire session, or do a custom restore. Then fill in any information about the files you want to restore.

Working with Volumes

A *volume* is the highest level in the file system hierarchy, and it contains directories and files. Each NetWare server has at least one volume, SYS, which contains all of the NetWare files and utilities. You can have additional volumes on a server if you want; in fact, a NetWare server can have up to 64 volumes.

Volumes are divided into volume segments. Each volume can have up to 32 volume segments, which can all be stored on the same hard disk or scattered across separate disks. Letting volume segments reside on different disks lets you increase the size of a volume by adding a new hard disk.

One hard disk can hold up to eight volume segments that belong to one or more volumes. By putting segments of the same volume on more than one hard disk, different parts of the volume can be accessed simultaneously, which increases disk input and output. If you spread volume segments across disks, it is important to mirror the disks so that a single disk's failure won't shut down the entire volume. (For more information about disk mirroring, see Chapter 3.)

When you create a physical volume using INSTALL.NLM, a Volume object is automatically created at the same time. The Volume object is placed in the NDS tree, in the same context as the server. By default, the Volume object is named with the server's name as a prefix. For example, if the server's name is Sales, the Volume object for volume SYS is named Sales_SYS.

CREATING AND MOUNTING VOLUMES

You create volumes as part of the installation process when you first install your NetWare 4.1 server. To create additional volumes after the initial installation, you use INSTALL.NLM. You can create a new volume out of any free space on the disk. The free space may be space that was never assigned to a volume before, or it may be free space on a new hard disk that's just been added.

After you've created a volume, you must mount it before it can be accessed by network users.

To create a volume, complete the steps in the following checklist.

1 • If you're installing a new hard disk, install the hard disk and use INSTALL.NLM to create a new NetWare partition for the disk, which will become the new volume.

2 • Load INSTALL.NLM and choose Volume Options.

3 • Press the Insert key to see a list of existing volume segments and free disk space.

4 • From the list, select any existing free space and press Enter.

5 • Enter a name for the new volume (up to 15 characters long). The name can be made up of letters or numbers.

6 • If you don't want the new volume to use all the available disk space, select the new volume, press Enter, and type in a new volume size in megabytes.

7 • Press F10 to save the new volume information.

8 • To mount the volume, choose Mount/Dismount an Existing Volume, and then choose Mount.

You can also mount a volume by using the MOUNT console command. For example, to mount the volume named VOL1, use the following command:

```
MOUNT VOL1
```

To mount all volumes on the server, use the following command:

```
MOUNT ALL
```

DELETING AND DISMOUNTING VOLUMES

Deleting a volume deletes all the files and directories on that volume as well, so be sure you only delete a volume if you don't need the files anymore, or if you have a reliable backup.

To delete a volume, complete the steps in the following checklist.

1 • Back up all files on the volume, if you want to keep them.

2 • If the volume you're going to delete contains HCSS directories, unload the HCSS media first.

3 • Dismount the volume you want to delete by typing the following console command (substitute the volume's name for *name*):

```
DISMOUNT name
```

4 • Load INSTALL.NLM and choose Volume Options.

5 • Select the volume you want to delete. (Do not delete volume SYS.)

6 • When prompted if you want to delete the volume, answer Yes.

You can also dismount a volume using INSTALL.NLM. To dismount the volume, Load INSTALL.NLM and select Volume Options. Then choose Mount/Dismount an Existing Volume, select the volume you want to dismount, and change its status to Dismounted.

INCREASING THE SIZE OF A VOLUME

To increase the size of a volume, you can add a volume segment to an existing volume. To do this, complete the steps in the following checklist.

1 • Load INSTALL and select Volume Options.

2 • Press Insert to see a list of existing volume segments.

3 • From the list, select a segment that has free space and no volume assignment, and press Enter.

4 • Choose Make This Segment Part of Another Volume, and press Enter.

5 • Choose the volume to which you want to add this segment, and press Enter.

6 • Press Esc, and then press F10 to save the new volume information.

ADDING A NAME SPACE TO A VOLUME

If you want a volume to store non-DOS files, such as Macintosh or Unix files, you need to add name space support to the volume. Name-space support is a feature that extends the volume's storage characteristics, allowing the volume to store the longer file names and additional information that non-DOS files may contain.

For example, Macintosh name-space support allows the volume to store a Macintosh file's resource fork and long file name.

The following name spaces are available for NetWare 4.1:

- MAC.NAM for Macintosh files
- OS2.NAM for OS/2 files (also provides long name support for NT files)
- FTAM.NAM (File Transfer, Access, and Management), which supports the FTAM protocol for remote file access (must be purchased separately).
- NFS.NAM (Network File System) for Unix files (must be purchased separately).

A volume with support for a non-DOS name space requires twice as much memory as a volume with DOS-only files, because the name spaces use twice as many directory entries that have to be cached.

To add name space support to a volume, complete the following checklist.

1 • Load the name space loadable module on the server. (For example, enter

```
LOAD MAC
```

to load the Macintosh name space, or

```
LOAD OS2
```

for the OS/2 name space.)

2 • Add the name space support to the desired volume by using the ADD NAME SPACE console command. To add the Macintosh name space to the volume VOL1, you would use the command:

```
ADD NAME SPACE MAC TO VOL1
```

Once you've added the name space support to a volume the only ways you can remove the name space support are to run VREPAIR.NLM or delete and re-create the volume.

To see a list of all the volumes on a server and their name spaces, use the VOLUMES console command.

REPAIRING A CORRUPTED VOLUME WITH VREPAIR

Occasionally, a server's hard disk problems may cause minor problems with one or more of the server's volumes. If a volume won't mount, the primary File Allocation Table (FAT) or Directory Entry Table (DET) may be corrupted. VREPAIR.NLM can usually repair these types of volume problems.

NetWare keeps two copies of the FAT and DET. VREPAIR compares the two tables for inconsistencies. If it finds one, it uses the most correct table entry as the corrected one. Then VREPAIR writes the corrected entry to both the primary and the secondary tables.

VREPAIR can also be used in the following circumstances:

- When a power failure corrupts the volume
- When a hardware problem causes a disk read error
- When bad blocks on the volume cause read or write errors, datamirror mismatch errors, multiple allocation errors, or fatal DIR errors
- When you want to remove a name space from a volume

If a volume doesn't mount when you boot the server, VREPAIR will run automatically and try to repair the volume. If the volume fails while the server is running, you can run VREPAIR manually. (A volume must be dismounted before you can run VREPAIR on it.)

Most volume problems that VREPAIR can fix are hardware related. Therefore, if you repeatedly have to repair the same volume, you should consider replacing the hard disk.

To use VREPAIR.NLM, load it at the server's console. If you are repairing a volume that has a non-DOS name space loaded (or if you're removing a name space from the volume), VREPAIR needs to load another NLM for that name space support. The VREPAIR name space modules are named V_*namespace*.NLM.

For example, for the MAC name space, VREPAIR looks for a module named V_MAC.NLM. If this module is located in SYS:SYSTEM (which is where it is installed by default), VREPAIR automatically loads it. If this module is in a different location, you'll have to load it manually before running VREPAIR.

You may want to copy VREPAIR and its name space support modules to the server's DOS partition, so that they will be available in case volume SYS has to be repaired.

To run VREPAIR, complete the steps in the following checklist.

1 • Make sure the volume you want to repair is dismounted.

2 • At the server's console, load VREPAIR. If you want VREPAIR to log any errors it finds in an error log file, add a filename to the end of the LOAD command, in the following format:

```
LOAD VREPAIR filename
```

3 • Choose Repair a Volume to begin trying to fix the volume. (If more than one volume is currently dismounted, you'll have to choose the volume you want to repair.)

4 • If you want to change how VREPAIR is displaying errors as it finds them, press F1. Then select option 1 if you don't want VREPAIR to pause after each error. Select 2 if you want the errors logged in a text file. Select 3 to stop the repair. Select 4 to resume the repair.

5 • When the repair is finished, choose Yes when asked if you want to write repairs to the disk.

6 • If VREPAIR found errors, run it again. Continue running VREPAIR repeatedly until it finds no more errors.

7 • After VREPAIR finds no more errors, remount the volume.

8 • If the volume still won't mount, delete the volume, re-create it, then restore all of its files from backups.

VREPAIR may have to delete some files during the repair operation. If it does, it stores those deleted files in new files named VR*nnnnnn*.FIL (where *n* is any number). These files are stored in the directories in which the original files were stored when they were found during VREPAIR's operation.

Files may be deleted if VREPAIR finds problems such as a file with a name that is invalid in DOS, or two files with the same file name.

Protecting Databases with TTS

Transaction Tracking System (TTS) is NetWare's feature for protecting database transactions. With TTS turned on, if a transaction is caught only half-completed when a problem such as a power outage occurs, the transaction is completely backed out so that the database isn't corrupted.

When a transaction is backed out, the database is restored to the original state it was in before the transaction began.

TTS protects data by making a copy of the original data before it is overwritten by new data. Then, if a failure of some component occurs in the middle of the transaction, TTS restores the data to its original condition and discards the incomplete transaction.

TTS protects the NDS database and the queuing database files from corruption. In addition, you can use it to protect your own database files. If your database application doesn't offer its own form of transaction tracking, NetWare's TTS can provide protection for it. If your database application does offer its own transaction tracking, NetWare's TTS still may benefit you by tracking the transactions in the server. By tracking the file writes in the server, less data is transferred across the network, and NetWare's disk caching system increases performance.

TTS can be used with any application that stores information in records and allocates record locks. It can't be used with applications such as word processors, which don't store data in discrete records.

Because TTS is used to protect the NDS database, TTS is enabled by default. You should not disable TTS. TTS may become disabled on its own if the SYS volume becomes full, because the SYS volume is the volume TTS uses for its backout data. In addition, TTS may become disabled if the server runs out of memory to run TTS. You can see if TTS has been disabled by checking the TTS$LOG.ERR file at the root of the volume.

If TTS has been disabled, you can use the ENABLE TTS console utility to reenable TTS after you correct the problem that caused it to become disabled.

Table 8.2 shows the tasks you can use to manage how TTS works.

TABLE 8.2

TTS Tasks

TASK	HOW TO DO IT
Make TTS track a file	Use FLAG, FILER, or NetWare Administrator to assign the file the Transactional file attribute.
Reenable TTS	Use the console command ENABLE TTS.
Make the server automatically back out incomplete transactions without prompting you for input	Load SERVMAN.NLM. Choose Server Parameters, and, then choose the Transaction Tracking category. Set theAuto TTS Backout Flag to On. Allow SERVMAN to save the command in the STARTUP.NCF file, and then reboot the server to make the change take effect.
Keep an error log for TTS data	Load SERVMAN.NLM. Choose Server Parameters, and then choose the Transaction Tracking category. Set the TTS Abort Dump Flag to On. Allow SERVMAN to save the command in the AUTOEXEC.NCF file.
Displayor change the levels of physical and logical record locks for TTS	Use the SETTTS workstation utility in the format: `SETTTS level` For *level*, insert the number of logical or physical locks you want TTS to ignore before tracking the transaction. Use the command: `SETTTS /?` to see help screens for SETTTS.

Managing Files and Directories

There are several NetWare utilities that you can use to work with files and directories. In addition, of course, you can use commands or features of your regular workstation operating system to work with files, such as DOS commands, the Macintosh Filer program, or the Windows File Manager.

Some of the NetWare utilities you can use are explained in the following sections.

FILER UTILITY

FILER is a DOS-based utility that lets you choose tasks from a menu. To execute FILER, enter the command

```
FILER
```

at the workstation's DOS prompt. Then select the tasks from the menus that appear. Press the F1 key for help with each screen. With FILER, you can see and work with the following types of file and directory information:

- List of subdirectories and files within a directory
- Trustees
- File system rights
- File owners
- Creation dates and times
- Available disk space and directory entries for a volume
- File and directory attributes
- Salvageable files

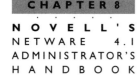

FLAG UTILITY

As explained in Chapter 7, the FLAG utility can be used to view and assign attributes to files and directories. In addition, it can also be used to assign search modes for executable files. To set a search mode for files, use the following command format:

```
FLAG path /M=number
```

For *path*, specify the path to the file or directory whose search mode you want to change. For *number*, insert the number of the search mode you want to be used for the executable files in this path. The search modes are explained in Table 8.3.

TABLE 8.3

FLAG Search Modes

SEARCH MODE NUMBER	DESCRIPTION
0	Looks for search instructions in the NET.CFG file. (Default mode.)
1	Searches the path specified in the file. If no path is found, searches the default directory, and then all search drives.
2	Searches the path specified in the file. If no path is found, searches only the default directory.
3	Searches the path specified in the file. If no path is found, searches the default directory. Then, if the open request is read-only, searches the search drives.
4	Not used.
5	Searches the path specified, and then searches all search drives. If no path is found, searches the default directory, and then all search drives.
6	Not used.
7	Searches the path specified. If the open request is read-only, searches the search drives. If no path is found, searches the default directory, and then all search drives.

NCOPY UTILITY

NCOPY is a command-line utility that lets you copy files and directories from one drive or disk to another. To use NCOPY, use the following command format:

```
NCOPY source_path/filename destination_path/filename /option
```

The options that can be used with the NCOPY utility are listed in Table 8.4.

TABLE 8.4

NCOPY Options

OPTION	DESCRIPTION
/A	(Archive Bit Only) Copies only those files that have the Archive Needed attribute (also called the archive bit). NCOPY does not, however, remove the attribute from the source file, so the file will still have the Archive Needed attribute.
/C	(Copy) Copies files, but does not preserve extended attributes or name space information.
/F	(Force Sparse Files) Forces the operating system to copy sparse files, which aren't normally copied.
/I	(Inform) Notifies the user when extended attributes or name space information can't be copied because the destination volume doesn't support those features.
/M	(Archive Bit Set) Copies files that have the Archive Needed attribute, and removes the attribute from the source file. This allows NCOPY to be used as a backup tool.
/R	(Retain Compression) Keeps compressed files compressed, rather than decompressing them during the copy process.
/R/U	(Retain Unsupported Compression) Keeps compressed files compressed even if they are copied to a destination volume that doesn't support compression.
/S	(Subdirectories) Copies all of the subdirectories (except empty subdirectories) as well as the files in the specified path.
/S/E	(Subdirectories, Empty) Copies all the subdirectories, including empty subdirectories, as well as files in the specified path.
/V	(Verify) Verifies that the original and the new files are identical. This option is useful for copies made on local DOS drives only.

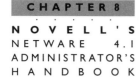

For example, to copy all the files from drive G to drive L, use the following command:

```
NCOPY G:*.* L:
```

To copy all of the files, plus the subdirectories (including empty ones) from drive G to drive L, use the following command:

```
NCOPY G:*.* L: /S/E
```

NDIR UTILITY

The NDIR command-line utility lets you list a directory's files, subdirectories, and related information. With it, you can see the following types of information about files and directories:

- List of subdirectories and files within a directory
- Inherited Rights Filters
- Effective file system rights
- File owners
- Creation dates and times
- File sizes
- File and directory attributes
- Archive information
- Volume information

With NDIR, you can sort the display of files so that they appear in different orders, such as from largest to smallest, newest to oldest, all those owned by a particular owner, and so on.

To use NDIR, use the following command format:

NDIR *path /option*

For example, to list all the files in the directory that is mapped to drive G, use the following command:

```
NDIR G:
```

To display the NDIR help screens, use the following command:

```
NDIR /?
```

The following are some of the most common options:

- To list any files in the directory's subdirectories, add the option /SUB.
- To list only the files in the directory, add the option /FO.
- To list only the subdirectories in the directory, add the option /DO.
- To list files in the order of their sizes, from smallest to largest, add the option /SORT SI.
- To list files in the order of their sizes, from largest to smallest, add the option /REV SORT SI.
- To list only the files owned by user Tina, add the option /OW EQ Tina.Sales.Satellite.RedHawk (EQ stands for "equals").
- To list only Macintosh files, add the option /MAC.

THE NETWARE ADMINISTRATOR UTILITY

With NetWare Administrator, you can use the Browser to select files and directories and view information about them, as explained in earlier sections of this chapter. Some of the types of information you can see about files and directories with the NetWare Administrator utility include the following:

- Name spaces
- Size restrictions of directories

- Creation dates and times
- Trustees
- Effective rights
- Inherited Rights Filters
- File and directory attributes
- File owners

NWXTRACT UTILITY

If you need to copy a single file or utility from the NetWare CD-ROM to your server, you can't just use NCOPY to copy it. The files are compressed on the CD-ROM, so you need to use a special utility, called NWXTRACT, to locate the file, decompress it, and copy it to the server.

To use NWSTRACT, use the following command format:

```
NWXTRACT path filename destination /option
```

To see specific help screens about NWXTRACT, use the following command:

```
NWXTRACT /?
```

RENDIR UTILITY

You can use the RENDIR command-line utility to rename a directory. To use this command, use the following format:

```
RENDIR oldname newname
```

For example, to rename the directory REPORTS to STATUS, use the following command:

```
RENDIR REPORTS STATUS
```

CHAPTER 9

Setting Up NetWare Print Services

Instant Access

Installing

- To install print services using default options (the quick and easy way), use the Quick Setup option of PCONSOLE, and then load PSERVER.NLM on the NetWare server.
- To install print services using custom settings, use PCONSOLE or the NetWare Administrator utility, and then load PSERVER.NLM on the NetWare server.
- To connect a network printer to a workstation, load NPRINTER.EXE on the workstation.
- To connect a network printer to a NetWare server, load NPRINTER.NLM on the NetWare server.

Defining Print Options

- To tell the printer how to print a job (type of paper, format, and so on), define print job configurations with PRINTCON.
- To define print forms (types of paper) for a printer, use PRINTDEF.
- To send print jobs to a print queue, redirect LPT1 to a print queue by putting a CAPTURE command in a login script, by using NetWare User Tools (which runs in Windows), or by configuring the application for network printing.
- To define print devices, use PRINTDEF.

Printing Jobs

- To print files from within an application, simply follow the application's normal printing procedures (make sure the application is configured to print to a network printer).

- To print text files or to print without using an application, use NPRINT.
- To cancel or move a print job that's already in a print queue, use PCONSOLE (select Print Queues, then select the queue, and then choose Print Jobs) or the NetWare Administrator utility (select the Print Queue object, choose Details from the Object menu, and then open the Job List page).

NetWare print services allow your network users to share printers that are connected to the network. With NetWare print services loaded, you can increase productivity and save on hardware expenses by allowing users to share a smaller number of printers than you would have to buy if each user had a stand-alone printer. (You may also be able to buy a single, more sophisticated printer instead of multiple lesser-quality printers.) In addition, users don't have to waste time waiting for printers to complete their print jobs before they can resume using an application, as they often do when printing to a directly connected stand-alone printer.

Another benefit is that users can send their print jobs to different printers for different purposes, without having to copy the file they want to print onto a diskette and then physically moving to a different workstation.

NetWare print services also let you prioritize print jobs, so that important print jobs are sent to the printer ahead of less-important print jobs.

How NetWare Printing Works

In stand-alone printing, a printer is connected directly to the parallel port (usually LPT1) on the workstation. When the user prints a file, the print job goes from the application to the print driver, which formats the job for the specific printer. (The print driver is software that converts the print job into a format that the printer can understand.) Next the print job goes to the LPT port, and then directly to the printer. Often, the application has to wait until the print job is finished before it can resume working.

With NetWare print services, the print job goes to the network instead of directly to the printer, though this process is transparent to users. Then the network takes care of sending the print job to the correct printer.

To accomplish this, NetWare print services employs two features, called print queues and print servers. The *print queue* is a special network directory, which stores print jobs temporarily before they are printed. Multiple network users can have their jobs stored in the same print queue. The print queue receives all incoming print jobs from various users, and stores them in a first-come, first-served order.

The *print server* is a software program, called PSERVER.NLM, which runs on the NetWare server. The print server controls how the print queues and printers work together. The print server takes the jobs from the print queue and forwards them on to the printer when the printer is available.

You can have more than one print queue on a network. Further, you can set up one print queue so that it services several printers (although this can be confusing because you never know which printer will print the job you send). You can also set up a single printer so that it services several print queues. However, it generally simplifies your administration tasks and reduces your users' confusion if you use a one-to-one correspondence between print queues and printers, so that each print queue sends jobs to its own printer.

When you set up NetWare print services, you assign a printer, a print server, and a print queue to each other. Then you redirect the workstation's parallel port to point to a network print queue instead of to a directly attached printer.

To redirect the workstation's LPT port, you can use the NetWare utility called CAPTURE (usually placing the CAPTURE command in a login script so that it is executed automatically). You can also use the NetWare User Tools utility (which runs under Windows) to assign LPT1 to a print queue.

Alternatively, most network-aware applications will let you set them up so that they redirect print jobs to a print queue themselves. In many cases, you can simply specify a printer in the application, and since the printer, print queue, and print server are all assigned to each other, the job will be sent automatically to the correct print queue.

NetWare print services allow printers to be attached directly to the server, attached to various workstations on the network, or attached directly to the network cabling (this last option is currently the most common).

If you attach printers directly to the NetWare server, the server must run an NLM called NPRINTER.NLM. This NLM is a port driver, which is software that routes jobs out of the print queue, through the proper port on the server, to the printer.

If you attach printers to workstations on the network, those workstations must also be running a port driver, called NPRINTER.EXE. The workstation's version of NPRINTER works the same way as the server's version, sending print jobs through the port on the workstation to the printer.

Workstations that have printers attached can still be used by workstation users to do regular, day-to-day work. The workstation simply acts as a connection to the network for that printer.

The workstation attached to the printer should still redirect its own LPT1 port to the network so that it uses network printing services like all the other workstations instead of printing directly to the printer. Even if there is a printer attached directly to the workstation, it is usually still more efficient to send the print job from the workstation to a network print queue, and then back to the printer. This also allows other workstations to use the printer.

Currently, the most common type of printing connection is to use printers that connect directly to the network cabling, rather than to a server or a workstation. These types of printers, often called *network-direct printers*, may run in either remote printer mode or queue server mode.

Remote printer mode lets the printer function as if it were running its own NPRINTER port driver. It doesn't need to be connected to a workstation; its internal NPRINTER-like software lets it be controlled by the NetWare print server and allows it to take advantage of NDS functionality.

Queue server mode is bindery-based, and used when the printer device has not been designed to work with NDS. This means that you must take care to install the printers, print queues, and the network-direct print devices in the same bindery context. In addition, there may be other restrictions that affect these devices. Be sure to read the manufacturer's documentation for more information about installing these devices.

With NetWare print services, the journey of a print job follows this path:

- The application works with the print driver to format the print job, just as it does in stand-alone mode.
- Instead of going through LPT1 directly to a printer, the print job is redirected to a print queue. If you specify that one print job goes to one printer and another job goes to a second printer, they will both be redirected from LPT1 to the correct print queues.
- When the printer is available, the print server takes the print job from the print queue and sends it to the port driver (such as NPRINTER.EXE or NPRINTER.NLM) running wherever the printer is connected.
- The port driver then sends the print job to the printer, and the job is printed.

Figure 9.1 illustrates the path a print job takes through the network. In this particular example, the printer is attached to a workstation that is running NPRINTER.EXE.

FIGURE 9.1

A Print Job's Path through the Network

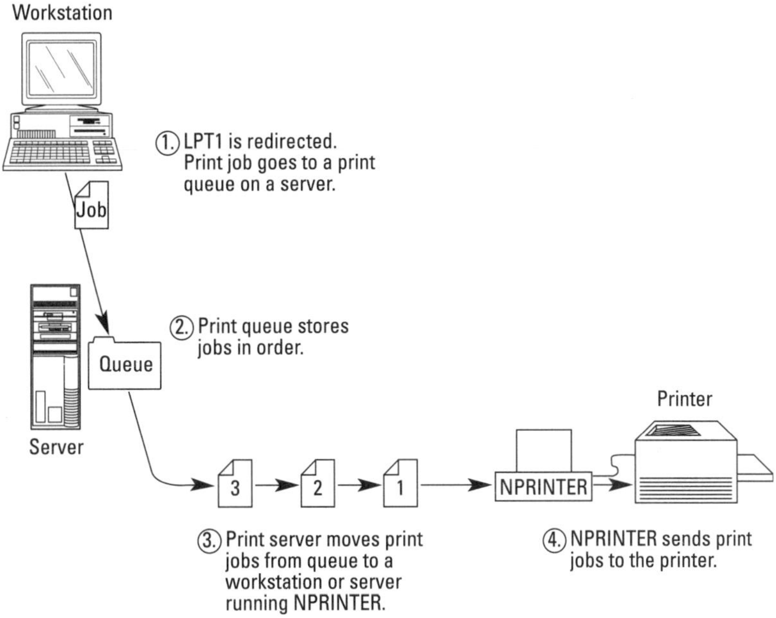

Planning NetWare Print Services

When you plan how to set up NetWare print services, keep the following guidelines and restrictions in mind:

- In general, PSERVER.NLM uses about 27K of server RAM for each configured printer.
- PSERVER.NLM can service DOS, UNIX, and Macintosh printers.
- A single print server can service up to 255 printers, although performance begins to degrade after about 60 printers or so.
- If you need more than one print server in your network, you can load PSERVER.NLM on additional NetWare servers, and those print servers can service more network printers.

- Printers, print queues, and print servers will all be created as NDS objects in the Directory tree.
- To set up and manage print services, you can use either the NetWare Administrator utility, which runs on Windows, or PCONSOLE (a menu utility that runs in DOS).
- When you use the CAPTURE utility to redirect an LPT port to a network print queue, you can also use CAPTURE to specify options such as whether or not to print a banner page, whether to use tabs, and so on.
- Instead of using CAPTURE, you may prefer to set up print job configurations. A print job configuration can simplify a user's task of selecting print options by predefining settings such as the designated printer, whether or not to print a banner page, and the type of paper to print on. To create a print job configuration, you can use either the NetWare Administrator utility or PRINTCON (a menu utility that runs in DOS).
- To define print devices and paper forms to be used in print job configurations, you can use either the NetWare Administrator utility or PRINTDEF (a menu utility that runs in DOS). (If the application you are using supports your printer, you do not need to define a print device with PRINTDEF.)
- To print a job from outside of an application (such as printing an ASCII file or a workstation screen), you can use a utility called NPRINT, a command-line utility that runs in DOS.

As you plan your printing setup, decide how many printers you need and where you want them to be located. If you are going to attach printers to workstations, you may want to choose workstations that are not used as heavily as others. In addition, it will be important for the users of those workstations to remember not to turn off the workstation when other users are using the network. Instead, those users should just log out of the network when they are finished using the workstation.

7 • If necessary, choose a different volume in which to store the print queue. Press Enter, and then either type in a new name or press Insert to navigate through the file system and select the volume that way. (If you need to use bindery services, select the default SYS volume.)

8 • Select the banner type for your printer. If your printer's default mode is PostScript, select PostScript. Otherwise, select Text.

9 • Choose the printer type you are using (parallel, serial, Unix, AppleTalk, other/unknown, XNP, or AIO).

10 • In the Printer Location field, press Enter and select either Auto Load (Local) or Manual Load.

a. Choose Auto Load (Local) if the printer will be attached directly to the server that is running PSERVER. This will make NPRINTER.NLM load automatically.

b. If the printer is attached to a server that is not running PSERVER, or if the printer is attached to a workstation, select Manual Load.

11 • Select the correct Interrupt mode. This mode determines whether NPRINTER uses *polled mode* and polls the printer port to see if the port is ready for data, or whether the port issues a specific interrupt to notify NPRINTER that it's ready for data. Specifying a specific interrupt can improve performance. However, polled mode is the default and causes fewer interrupt problems than specifying a particular IRQ, so you may be better off using polled mode.

12 • Select the port to which you've connected the printer (LPT1, LPT2, etc.).

13 • Press F10 to save all the information and return to PCONSOLE's main menu.

14 • To configure more printers, repeat steps 4 through 13, specifying the new information for the additional printers.

15 • From PCONSOLE's main menu, choose Printers.

16 • Select a printer from the list and write down its printer number. Then select any other printers and write down their numbers, too. You'll need these numbers to set up NPRINTER.

17 • Go to the network server that will run the print server (or use Remote Console to access that server's console) and load the print server software using the following command:

```
LOAD PSERVER
```

18 • Select the name of the print server you set up in PCONSOLE. Type in the print server's name or press Insert to navigate through the NDS tree. (Later, you can put the PSERVER command, along with the print server's name, in the NetWare server's AUTOEXEC.NCF file so it automatically loads when the server is rebooted.)

19 • If the printer is attached to a network server that is not running PSERVER, also load the NPRINTER.NLM, specifying the print server name and printer number in the NPRINTER command. (This command can also be placed in the NetWare server's AUTOEXEC.NCF file.) If you have more than one printer attached to this server, load NPRINTER multiple times, specifying a different printer number (and print server if necessary) for each printer. For example, to load NPRINTER for printer number 0, using print server PS-Tech, use the following command:

```
LOAD NPRINTER PS-Tech 0
```

20 • If the printer is attached to a workstation, run NPRINTER.EXE on that workstation. Specify the print server name and printer number in the command. (You can include this command in the workstation's AUTOEXEC.BAT file, after the login command.) For example, to load NPRINTER for printer number 0, using print server PS-Tech, use the following command:

```
NPRINTER PS-Tech 0
```

21 • Add a CAPTURE command to the system, profile, or user login script, so that users' LPT ports will be redirected to a network print queue. You may need to specify the queue's full name. For example, to redirect users' LPT1 ports to the queue named Q1, with no banner page, no tabs, no form feed, and a five-second timeout interval, add the following command to the system login script:

```
#CAPTURE L=1 Q=.Q1.Sales.Satellite.RedHawk NB NT NFF TI=5
```

22 • Configure your applications for printing, specifying queues, and so on. Follow the manufacturer's instructions for setting up the application for network printing.

23 • If your application isn't designed for network printing, use PRINTDEF or the NetWare Administrator utility to specify the brand of printer you are using and the types of paper (called forms) on which you want to print. This is helpful if you use applications that print on different types of paper, such as paychecks, invoices, and so on, and the printer doesn't reset correctly after each type of job.

24 • If your application isn't designed for network printing, use PRINTCON or the NetWare Administrator utility to set up print job configurations. Print job configurations tell the printer how the print job should be printed on the form you set up in PRINTDEF. Print job configurations can specify items such as whether or not a banner page will be printed, to which queue the job should be sent, and what paper form to use.

USING PCONSOLE TO SET UP CUSTOM PRINT SERVICES

If you want to set up a custom printing environment, such as designating multiple queues that will be serviced by a single printer or multiple printers that will service a single queue, you can use PCONSOLE or the NetWare Administrator utility. This section explains how to use PCONSOLE to set up this printing environment. (The next section explains how to use the NetWare Administrator utility.)

To set up custom printing services using PCONSOLE, complete the steps in the following checklist.

1 • Decide where you want your printers to be located, and attach them to the server, workstations, or network cabling.

2 • From any workstation, log in to the network as user Admin.

3 • Execute the PCONSOLE utility on the workstation by using the following command:

```
PCONSOLE
```

4 • From PCONSOLE's main menu, select Change Context and move to the name context (location in the NDS tree) in which you want the print server, printers, and print queues to reside. (You can either type in the context you want, or press Insert to navigate through the NDS tree and select the context that way.)

5 • From PCONSOLE's main menu, select the Print Queues option to create a new print queue.

a. Press Insert to create a new queue.

b. After you enter a name for the new queue and it appears in the queue list, highlight the queue in the list and press Enter.

c. From the menu that appears, select the various options to see information about the queue or to assign print queue users and operators. By default, the container in which this print queue resides is assigned as a user, so all objects within the container are also users of the queue. The user Admin is the default queue operator (a person assigned to manage the queue). When finished, press the Esc key to return to the main menu.

6 • Choose the Printers option to configure printers.

a. Press Insert to create a new printer.

b. After you enter a name for the new printer and it appears in the printers list, highlight the printer in the list and press Enter.

c. The form that appears shows default information about the printer. Because this printer is new, there is no print server or printer number assigned yet. Press the F1 key to read help on how to fill out the configuration information for this printer.

d. A print queue must be assigned to a printer before the printer can take print jobs from the network. Therefore, select the Print Queues Assigned field, press Enter, then press Insert to select a queue from the NDS tree. When finished, press the Esc key to return to the main menu.

7 • Choose the Printer Servers option to create a print server.

a. Press Insert to create a new print server.

b. After you enter a name for the new print server and it appears in the print servers list, select it from the list by pressing Enter.

c. From the menu that appears, select the various options to see information about the print server or to assign print server users and operators.

d. A printer must be assigned to a print server before the printing setup will work. Choose the Printers field, then press Insert to select a printer to service. When finished, press the Esc key to return to the main menu.

8 • Go to the network server that will run the print server (or use Remote Console to access that server's console) and load the print server software using the following command:

```
PSERVER.NLM
```

9 • Select the name of the print server you set up in PCONSOLE. (You can also put the PSERVER command, along with the print server's name, in the AUTOEXEC.NCF file.)

10 • If the printer is attached to a network server that is not running PSERVER, also load the NPRINTER.NLM, specifying the print server name and printer number in the NPRINTER command. (This command can also be placed in the AUTOEXEC.NCF file.) If you have more than one printer attached to this server, load NPRINTER multiple times, specifying a different printer number (and print server if necessary) for each printer.

11 • If the printer is attached to a workstation, run NPRINTER.EXE on that workstation. Specify the print server name and printer number in the command. (You can include this command in the workstation's AUTOEXEC.BAT file, after the login command.)

12 • Add a CAPTURE command to the system, profile, or user login script, so that users' LPT ports will be redirected to a network print queue. You may need to specify the queue's full name.

13 • Configure your applications for printing, specifying queues, and so on. Follow the manufacturer's instructions for setting up the application for network printing.

14 • If your application isn't designed for network printing, use PRINTDEF or the NetWare Administrator utility to specify the brand of printer you are using and the types of paper (called forms) on which you want to print.

15 • If your application isn't designed for network printing, use PRINTCON or the NetWare Administrator utility to set up print job configurations. Print job configurations tell the printer how the print job should be printed on the form you set up in PRINTDEF.

USING NETWARE ADMINISTRATOR TO SET UP CUSTOM PRINT SERVICES

If you want to set up a custom printing environment, such as designating multiple queues that will be serviced by a single printer or multiple printers that will service a single queue, you can use PCONSOLE or the NetWare Administrator utility. This section explains how to use the NetWare Administrator utility to set up this printing environment. (The previous section explained how to use PCONSOLE.)

The NetWare Administrator utility runs under Windows. For instructions on setting up the NetWare Administrator utility on a workstation, see Chapter 6.

To set up custom printing services using the NetWare Administrator utility, complete the steps in the following checklist.

1 • Decide where you want your printers to be located, and attach them to the server, workstations, or network cabling.

2 • From any workstation, log in to the network as user Admin.

3 • Run the NetWare Administrator utility on the workstation by double-clicking its icon.

4 • From NetWare Administrator's Browser, select the container object that you want to contain the printing objects.

5 • From the Object menu, choose Create.

6 • Select Print Queue. The screen that appears lets you specify information about the print queue you want to create. Choose Directory Service Queue, and then fill in a name for the queue and the volume that will store the queue.

7 • Click the Define Additional Properties option. Define any additional information for the queue at this time by opening pages and specifying the appropriate information. For example, you can assign users and queue operators to the queue. By default, the container in which this print queue resides is assigned as a user, so all objects within the container are also users of the queue. The user Admin is the default queue operator (a person assigned to manage the queue). When finished, click OK, and then click the Create button to actually create the queue, and you'll return to the Browser.

8 • Again, select the container you're creating the printing objects in, then choose Create from the Object menu.

9 • Select Printer. Enter a name for this printer.

10 • Click the Define Additional Properties option. A print queue must be assigned to a printer before the printer can take print jobs from the network. Assign this printer to a print queue by selecting the Assignments page. Click the Add button. Then navigate through the NDS tree using the Directory Context panel, and select the print queue you want from the Objects panel.

11 • Open additional pages to specify more information for the printer, such as configuration information. When finished, click OK, then click the Create button to actually create the printer, and you'll return to the Browser.

12 • Again, select the container you're creating the printing objects in, then choose Create from the Object menu.

13 • Select Print Server. Enter a name for this print server.

14 • Click the Define Additional Properties option. A printer must be assigned to a print server before network printing will work. Assign this print server to a printer by selecting the Assignments page. Click the Add button, then navigate through the NDS tree using the Directory Context panel, then select the printer you want from the Objects panel.

15 • Open additional pages to specify more information for the print server as necessary. When finished, click OK, then click the Create button to actually create the printer, and you'll return to the Browser.

16 • Go to the network server that will run the print server (or use Remote Console to access that server's console) and load PSERVER.NLM.

17 • Select the name of the print server you just set up with the NetWare Administrator utility. (You can also put the PSERVER command, along with the print server's name, in the NetWare server's AUTOEXEC.NCF file.)

18 • If the printer is attached to a network server that is not running PSERVER, also load NPRINTER.NLM, specifying the print server name and printer number in the NPRINTER command. (This command can also be placed in the NetWare server's AUTOEXEC.NCF file.) If you have more than one printer attached to this server, load NPRINTER multiple times, specifying a different printer number (and print server if necessary) for each printer.

19 • If the printer is attached to a workstation, run NPRINTER.EXE on that workstation. Specify the print server name and printer number in the command. (You can include this command in the workstation's AUTOEXEC.BAT file, after the login command.)

20 • Add a CAPTURE command to the system, profile, or user login script, so that users' LPT ports will be redirected to a network print queue. You may need to specify the queue's full name.

21 • Configure your applications for printing. In many cases, you may be able to simply configure the application to use a particular printer, since NetWare 4.1 will automatically associate the printer with a print queue. Follow the manufacturer's instructions for setting up the application for network printing.

22 • If your application isn't designed for network printing, use PRINTDEF or the NetWare Administrator utility to specify the brand of printer you are using and the types of paper (called forms) on which you want to print.

23 • If your application isn't designed for network printing, use PRINTCON or the NetWare Administrator utility to set up print job configurations. Print job configurations tell the printer how the print job should be printed on the form you set up in PRINTDEF.

Handling Print Jobs

After NetWare print services are set up on the network, users can send their jobs to network print queues as long as they have access to those printers.

A user has access to a queue if he or she is assigned as a print queue user. By default, the container in which a print queue resides is assigned as a user, so all objects within the container are also users of the queue. A print queue user can add jobs to a print queue, see the status of all jobs in the queue, and delete his or her own job from the queue. A queue user cannot delete other users' print jobs from the queue.

A print queue operator is a special type of print queue user who has the ability to manage the print queue. A queue operator can delete other users' print jobs, put them on hold, and so on. The user Admin is the default queue operator.

You can add or remove users and operators from the list of print queue users by using either the NetWare Administrator utility or PCONSOLE. You can also look at the current print jobs in the print queue using the same utilities.

To use the NetWare Administrator utility to change users and operators, select the Print Queue object, choose Details from the Object menu, then open the Users or Operator page. To see the current print jobs in the queue, open the Job List page. Here, users can delete their own print jobs or put them on hold. Queue operators can put on hold or delete any users' print jobs. Press the F1 key to read help on each of the available fields in the Job List screen.

To use PCONSOLE to change users and operators, execute PCONSOLE, select Print Queues, choose the queue you want from the list, then select either Users or Operators. To see the current print jobs in the queue, select Print Jobs. Press the F1 key to read help on the Print Jobs screen.

CHAPTER 10

Installing and Using NetWare for Macintosh

Instant Access

Installing NetWare for Macintosh

- To install NetWare for Macintosh NLMs on the server, use INSTALL.NLM, select Product Options, and select Install NetWare for Macintosh.
- To put the AppleTalk protocol stack on the server, load APPLETLK.NLM on the server.
- To set up and configure an AppleTalk router, use INETCFG.NLM.
- To load LAN drivers, bind protocols to LAN drivers, or configure the AppleTalk protocol stack, use INETCFG.NLM.

Setting Up a Macintosh Workstation

- If you want the Macintosh to log in to a NetWare 4.1 network and use NDS, install the NetWare MacNDS Client software.
- If you want the Macintosh to log in to a NetWare 4.1 in bindery services mode only, you do not need to install the MacNDS Client software. The Macintosh can log in to the server by using AppleShare instead, or using an older version of NetWare for Macintosh client software.

Setting Up NetWare for Macintosh Print Services

- To set up print services in a simple configuration, load ATPS.NLM, and then use ATPSCON.NLM to configure the print services.
- To set up print services using more complex features, such as print queue priorities, load ATRXP.NLM and PSERVER.NLM. You can then use PSERVER.NLM features to configure the print services.

Logging In to the Network

- To log in to the NDS network, pull down the menu beneath the NDS tree icon and select Login.
- To log in to a specific server (using either NDS or bindery services), use the Chooser.

Using HFS CD-ROMs

- To mount HFS CD-ROMs as network volumes, use HFSCD.NLM.

NetWare for Macintosh is a feature of NetWare 4.1 that allows you to attach Macintosh workstations to your NetWare network. With NetWare for Macintosh, Macintosh users can take advantage of NetWare's security systems, file and print sharing capabilities, and other powerful features. In addition, DOS-based users can access AppleTalk printers.

NetWare for Macintosh is not a stand-alone network product. NetWare for Macintosh is a set of NLMs that must be loaded onto a regular NetWare server. You cannot use a Macintosh computer as a NetWare server; the server must be a PC computer. Nor can you have a Macintosh-only NetWare network; you must have at least one PC workstation to set up your network.

To set up NetWare for Macintosh, you install and load a set of NLMs on the server. These NLMs create an AppleTalk router in the NetWare server and provide file and print services for Macintosh workstations. Then, on each Macintosh workstation, you can load the NetWare MacNDS Client software, which allows the Macintosh to communicate on the network and lets the user log in to the NDS tree.

If you want the Macintosh workstations to log in to the NetWare server using only bindery services, you do not have to load the MacNDS Client software. Instead, the Macintosh workstations can connect to the server using AppleShare or older versions of NetWare for Macintosh client software.

With NetWare for Macintosh loaded, Macintosh workstations have access to NetWare features without losing the Macintosh "look and feel." Macintosh users still open and work with files, launch applications, send print jobs to printers, and manage their desktops just as they always have. In most cases, the only differences users will notice is that now they can log into the NDS tree so that they can access files on network volumes and other NDS resources, and they can send their print jobs to network queues.

An additional benefit is that PC-based and Macintosh users can share files if they use a common application or an application that can convert files from another format.

NetWare for Macintosh NLMs

The main NLMs that make up NetWare for Macintosh are shown in Tables 10.1 through 10.5.

Table 10.1 lists each of the NLMs used for NetWare for Macintosh installation and configuration.

TABLE 10.1

NLMs for NetWare for Macintosh Installation and Configuration

NLM	DESCRIPTION
INSTALL.NLM	Lets you install NetWare for Macintosh NLMs on the server.
ATCONFIG.NLM	Lets you configure NetWare for Macintosh after installation. When you use INSTALL.NLM to install NetWare for Macintosh, this NLM is loaded automatically, allowing you to configure the newly installed product. You can also load ATCONFIG.NLM separately later to change the configuration.

Table 10.2 lists each of the NLMs used for AppleTalk routing and protocols.

TABLE 10.2

NLMs for AppleTalk Routing and Protocols

NLM	DESCRIPTION
APPLETLK.NLM	Loads the AppleTalk router and AppleTalk protocol stack on the server. The AppleTalk router connects an AppleTalk network with other AppleTalk networks or NetWare networks, so that all the nodes on each network can access services and nodes on any of the other networks. The AppleTalk protocol stack is a suite of AppleTalk protocols used to support AppleTalk applications, such as print and file services.
INETCFG.NLM	(Internetwork Configuration) Lets you configure the AppleTalk protocol stack. (Autoloaded by ATCONFIG.NLM.)
ATCON.NLM	(AppleTalk Console) Console utility for APPLETLK.NLM. Lets you configure the router. (Autoloaded by ATCONFIG.NLM.)
ADSP.NLM	(AppleTalk Data Stream Protocol) Protocol that allows applications to communicate over AppleTalk networks.
ATFLT.NLM	(AppleTalk Filter) AppleTalk filter support. Lets you restrict how routers see and communicate with each other.

(continued)

TABLE 10.2

NLMs for AppleTalk Routing and Protocols (continued)

NLM	DESCRIPTION
AURP.NLM	(AppleTalk Update-based Routing Protocol) Allows AppleTalk to be tunneled through IP, which lets AppleTalk networks connect to each other through an IP internetwork.
MACIPXGW.NLM	(MacIPX Gateway protocol) Allows IPX networks to communicate with Macintoshes running MacIPX applications on LocalTalk networks or Macintoshes that are using AppleTalk Remote Access (dial-up services).

Table 10.3 lists each of the NLMs used for AppleTalk file services.

TABLE 10.3

NLMs for AppleTalk File Services

NLM	DESCRIPTION
AFP.NLM	Provides NetWare for Macintosh file services on the server.
AFPCON.NLM	Console utility for AFP.NLM. Lets you manage the desktop database, manage access to the AFP server (a NetWare server that is running AFP.NLM), and control other file services. (Autoloaded by ATCONFIG.NLM.)

Table 10.4 lists each of the NLMs used for AppleTalk print services.

TABLE 10.4

NLMs for AppleTalk Print Services

NLM	DESCRIPTION
ATPS.NLM	(AppleTalk Print Services) Provides integrated AppleTalk print and print servicing, which lets both Macintosh and PC-based users send print jobs to network printers.
ATXRP.NLM	(AppleTalk Extended Remote Printer) Works with the NetWare print server to send a print job to an AppleTalk network printer from a NetWare print queue, taking advantage of PSERVER's benefits. It also allows AppleTalk printers to appear as objects in the NDS tree.
ATPSCON.NLM	(AppleTalk Print Services Console) Console utility for ATPS.NLM. Lets you configure ATPS.NLM. (Autoloaded by ATCONFIG.NLM.)

Table 10.5 lists each of the NLMs used to provide support for HFS-formatted CD-ROMs.

TABLE 10.5

NLMs that Provide Support for HFS-Formatted CD-ROMs

NLM	DESCRIPTION
HFSCD.NLM	(High-performance File System CD-ROM) Lets you manage the interaction between NetWare for Macintosh and a CD-ROM drive.
HFSCDCON.NLM	(HFS CD-ROM Console) Console utility for HFSCD.NLM. Lets you configure HFSCD.NLM. (Autoloaded by ATCONFIG.NLM.)

AppleTalk Networking Concepts

Before trying to install NetWare for Macintosh, it is important to understand some of the characteristics of AppleTalk networking.

To make NetWare for Macintosh work on a network, you have to load APPLETLK.NLM on the server. This NLM adds the AppleTalk protocol stack to the server so it can understand AppleTalk communications. In addition, you can use APPLETLK.NLM to create an AppleTalk router on the server.

The AppleTalk router allows AppleTalk traffic to be routed between two network boards in the NetWare server, connecting different networks together. The router also allows you to have more control over how resources are made available to users. With a router, you can specify the zones in which servers or print queues appear. If you have a relatively simple network, with only one network board in the server and you want all your resources to be in one zone, you probably do not need to set up the AppleTalk router.

INTERNAL AND EXTERNAL APPLETALK NETWORKS

If you choose to install the AppleTalk router, you will configure the router to have an internal network. An internal network doesn't actually involve any hardware. The *internal network* is simply a software feature of the AppleTalk router, which handles the communication between network boards installed in the server.

With an internal network configured, the AppleTalk router can allow devices on the server to be assigned to different zones (see the following section "Appletalk Zones"). In addition, it makes it easier to run applications (such as AFP.NLM) without having to assign those applications to a specific network board as an interface to the AppleTalk network.

Besides its own internal network, the AppleTalk router recognizes one or more external networks — the physical networks that contain the workstations.

The internal network and all external networks have to be configured with their own unique network numbers (or ranges of numbers for extended AppleTalk networks). You create these network numbers when you configure the AppleTalk router and when you bind the AppleTalk protocol to the LAN driver (as explained in the section "Installing NetWare for Macintosh on the Server" later in this chapter).

These network numbers don't exist before you configure the router and bind the AppleTalk protocol to a driver, so they can be any numbers you want. (However, if other AppleTalk routers already exist on the network, you must conform to their numbers for any physical networks they have in common with this router. You can't use conflicting numbers.)

At the same time you assign network numbers, you also specify to which zones you want the internal and external networks to belong.

APPLETALK ZONES

A *zone* is nothing more than a logical collection of devices, such as servers, workstations, and printers, on a network. These devices can be grouped into zones to make it easier for users to find them. A small network may have only a single zone with all devices contained within it. A larger network may have several zones. You may define a zone with respect to a location, such as "2nd Floor" or "Sales" if it will make it easier for users to locate devices in those areas.

Zones don't exist until you create them while configuring the AppleTalk router and binding the AppleTalk protocol to a LAN driver. You create zones at the same time you assign network numbers.

A zone name can be up to 32 characters long.

NONEXTENDED APPLETALK NETWORKS

Nonextended AppleTalk networks are also called Phase 1 networks because they support Phase 1 addressing. Nonextended AppleTalk networks can only support up to 254 nodes (workstations, printers, and so on) per network segment. All of those 254 nodes must be contained in a single zone.

LocalTalk, ARCnet, and EtherTalk 1.0 are all examples of Nonextended AppleTalk networks.

For a nonextended AppleTalk network, the network number can be any number you assign, between 1 and 65,279. (These are 16-bit numbers.) This number helps identify the AppleTalk network. Each AppleTalk network you have connected to a NetWare network must have its own unique network number.

Nodes on a nonextended AppleTalk network are each dynamically assigned unique 8-bit numbers when the nodes first boot up, which means their addresses can be between 1 and 254.

EXTENDED APPLETALK NETWORKS

Extended AppleTalk Networks are also called Phase 2 networks, because they support Phase 2 addressing. Phase 2 addressing lets you have far more nodes on a network than Phase 1 addressing.

Instead of limiting a network to only 254 node addresses, Phase 2 addressing adds the network's 16-bit number to the node's 8-bit number, which makes up a 24-bit number. This 24-bit number is then assigned as the node's full address. Theoretically, Phase 2 addressing allows more than 16 million addresses, as there are over 16 million 24-bit numbers available.

To allow an extended AppleTalk network to handle over 254 node addresses, you can assign the network a range of network numbers instead of a single network number, as is required in nonextended networks.

For example, if you assign a network a single network number (such as 25), that single network number, when combined with 254 8-bit addresses, still leaves only 254 possible combinations. However, if you assign the network a range of addresses (such as 26 – 30), that means there are five possible network address numbers (26, 27, 28, 29, and 30). Any of those five network numbers can be combined with the 254 node addresses. That makes for 1270 (5 × 254) possible combinations.

Although you can assign any numbers you like to the network range, it's a good idea not to make the range too much larger than you need it to be, for performance reasons.

In addition to allowing for a larger number of nodes, extended AppleTalk networks can also belong to up to 255 zones (the actual number may depend on other factors, such as other AppleTalk routers on the network).

SEED ROUTERS

When you bind the AppleTalk protocol to the LAN driver to form an external network, you will be asked if you want this router to learn its network numbers and zone names from the network. If you already have another AppleTalk router installed elsewhere on the network, you can set up other AppleTalk routers so that they "learn" their configuration from that first router, called a *seed router.*

The seed router has network numbers and zone names specifically configured for it.

Once a seed router is installed, other AppleTalk routers can be *non-seed routers,* or *learning routers.* Non-seed routers simply learn their network numbers and zone names from the seed router.

Each network needs at least one seed router per network segment. In other words, a learning router must be able to learn its configuration from a seed router firsthand. A learning router can't learn its configuration from a seed router if it has to first go through another intermediate learning router.

Installing NetWare for Macintosh on the Server

If you plan to install NetWare for Macintosh NLMs when you first install the NetWare server, you should probably plan to create a separate volume for Macintosh files. As explained in Chapter 8, in order for a volume to store Macintosh files, it must have the Macintosh name space module loaded. Having a separate volume for Macintosh files can help save server memory, and it may make backups and restores easier to manage.

Before installing NetWare for Macintosh, note that the default frame type that EtherTalk uses is Ethernet SNAP. Therefore, if you are using an Ethernet board in the server, be sure you configure the network board's LAN driver to use the Ethernet SNAP frame type. You can use INSTALL.NLM to reload the Ethernet LAN driver for the network board and specify the Ethernet SNAP frame type. (If you have transferred your LAN driver LOAD and BIND commands to the NETINFO.CFG file by using INETCFG.NLM, you must use INETCFG.NLM instead of INSTALL.NLM to add the Ethernet SNAP frame type.)

(You can load the same driver more than once for the same network board, assigning a different frame type to each instance of the LAN driver. Loading the same driver twice for a single board is sometimes referred to as loading the driver reentrantly.)

The steps for installing NetWare for Macintosh are outlined in the following checklist.

1 • If necessary, configure the server's Ethernet network board to use the Ethernet SNAP frame type.

2 • Load INSTALL.NLM, select Product Options, and then select Install NetWare for Macintosh. After you answer a few prompts, INSTALL.NLM copies the NetWare for Macintosh files to the server. Then choose the volumes to which you want to add the Macintosh name space. If you intend to install Macintosh client software on the SYS volume, be sure to add the Macintosh name space to SYS.

3 • After the files are copied, INSTALL.NLM automatically loads ATCONFIG.NLM, which is used to configure the various components of NetWare for Macintosh. The NetWare for Macintosh Configuration screen appears, which is the main menu for ATCONFIG.NLM.

4 • Choose Configure AppleTalk Router. This automatically loads INETCFG.NLM, which lets you configure protocols and bind them to LAN drivers.

a. When asked if you want to transfer LAN driver, protocol, and remote access commands from AUTOEXEC.NCF to NETINFO.NCF, you can answer Yes or No. You may find that INETCFG.NLM, with its menu interface, is easier to use than typing LOAD and BIND commands in AUTOEXEC.NCF.

b. To configure the AppleTalk protocol (and, optionally, the AppleTalk router), choose Protocols, and then choose AppleTalk. If you do not want to configure a router (you have a single network board and all your network resources can be in a single zone), make sure the AppleTalk Status field says Enabled, and then press Esc and save the changes. If you want to configure an AppleTalk router, complete the items in the following bullets:

- Change the AppleTalk Status and Packet Forwarding options to Enabled.
- Specify whether Packet Forwarding will use Phase 2 addressing or Transition mode (which lets the router send out Phase 1-compatible packets). Currently, in most AppleTalk networks, Phase 2 addressing is the norm.
- Change the Internal Network option to Enabled, specify a network number (any single number from 1 to 65,279) in the Network Number option, and specify one or more zones in the Zones option.
- When finished, press Esc to save the settings.

c. Choose Boards and press Insert to specify a new LAN driver and its associated board and configuration settings.

d. Choose Bindings and press Insert to bind the AppleTalk protocol to the LAN driver you specified in step 3c and configure the external network.

- Choose the AppleTalk protocol, and then select the board.
- (Router only) If this is a router, indicate whether this should be a non-seed or seed router.
- (Router only) If this is the seed router, specify the external network's network number (or range of numbers) and zones.

- (Router only) You only need to set the Provide Application Through this Interface option if you didn't create an internal network in the router.

- When finished, press Esc to save the settings.

e. If you wish, choose View Configuration to see how the settings you've chosen were converted to commands in the configuration files.

f. Press Esc twice to exit INETCFG.NLM.

5 • When you are back at ATCONFIG's NetWare for Macintosh Configuration menu, you can choose to configure other aspects of NetWare for Macintosh.

a. Choose Configure File Services to set whether to allow unencrypted passwords, guest logins, clear text passwords, and the like. This option automatically loads AFPCON.NLM. In most cases, the default responses in AFPCON.NLM should be adequate, and you won't need to use this option. (The defaults disable clear-text passwords, forcing passwords to be encrypted, which significantly improves security. Do not allow clear-text passwords on your network unless you need Mac workstations to connect to the server via Appleshare, in order to install the client software from the server.)

b. Choose Configure Print Services to set up print services using ATPS.NLM. This option executes ATPSCON.NLM. Configuring print services is explained later in this chapter.

c. Choose Configure CD-ROM Services if you want to set up Macintosh (HFS-formatted) CD-ROMs as network volumes. To speed up access to CD-ROM files, the files are moved to a NetWare volume whenever they are first opened. Then, after a period of nonuse, the files are migrated back to the CD-ROM. Use this option to manage this CD-ROM activity.

d. Choose Install Additional Language Support if you want to use additional languages.

e. Choose Install Macintosh Client Support to place the Macintosh client software on the server's SYS volume. (You must add the Macintosh name space to SYS before you can place the Macintosh client software on it.) This lets you access the client software on the server, rather than from the CD-ROM. See the next section for more information about installing client software.

f. Choose Add Macintosh Name Space if you want to add the name space to a volume.

g. When finished configuring NetWare for Macintosh, press Esc to return to INSTALL.NLM, and then press Esc again to exit INSTALL.NLM.

After you've installed and configured NetWare for Macintosh, you can set up Macintosh computers as network workstations.

Setting Up a Macintosh Client

If you want Macintosh users on your network to log in to the network using NDS, each of those users' Macintosh workstations must have the NetWare MacNDS Client software installed. The MacNDS Client software allows the workstation to communicate with the network, and lets the user log in to the NDS tree. It also allows you to force Macs to use encrypted passwords.

If the Macintosh users do not need to access the network via NDS, and can receive any services they need through bindery services instead, you do not need to install MacNDS on their workstations. Instead, they can use AppleShare (which is built in to the Macintoshes) to log in to a server that is running AFP.NLM.

A Macintosh workstation should meet the following system requirements to have NetWare client software installed:

- The Macintosh should be an SE or later, with at least 4MB of RAM installed.

- It should be running System 7 or better if you want to take advantage of NDS features. System 6 Macintoshes will still be able to work on the network, but they must connect to a server in bindery mode instead of connecting to a network using NDS, and thus cannot use all of the NDS features.

In addition, you should have selected the type of network cabling (*network connection type*) that your Macintosh portion of the network will use. Most Macintoshes currently have EtherTalk support built in. (Older Macintoshes may have LocalTalk support built in instead.) If your Macintosh has EtherTalk built in, you do not need to buy an additional network board for the computer. You can simply use Ethernet cabling to connect the Macintosh, as is, to the network.

Non-EtherTalk network connection types require that you install a network board in the Macintosh, just as you do with PCs. Generally, when you purchase a network board, you also receive from the manufacturer the software (called a *driver*) to run the board. You usually install the network connection driver in the Extensions folder, located in the System folder.

After you choose the network connection type you will use, open the Macintosh's Network Control Panel. Then select the corresponding AppleTalk network connection to activate the driver. (Even if you are using EtherTalk, check the Network Control Panel to make sure the EtherTalk network connection type is selected.)

There are five different network connection types available. They are listed in Table 10.6.

TABLE 10.6

Network Connection Types

NETWORK CONNECTION TYPES	
LocalTalk (Built-In)	The LocalTalk connection type used to be built into every Macintosh. If you have older Macintoshes that have LocalTalk, and want to use LocalTalk, you don't need to install a network board in the Macintosh. The Macintoshes can connect to each other with just LocalTalk cabling. If you want to access NDS over LocalTalk, you must install the AppleTalk interface for MacIPX, as explained in the section "Using the MacIPX Gateway" later in this chapter. (EtherTalk has replaced LocalTalk in more recent Macintoshes.)

(continued)

TABLE 10.6

Network Connection Types (continued)

NETWORK CONNECTION TYPES	
ARCnet	With ARCnet, you need to install an ARCnet network board in each workstation and a corresponding one in the server. ARCnet does not support IPX or the MacIPX gateway, however, so you can only connect to NetWare 4.1 servers in bindery services mode. Very few, if any, network board manufacturers still make ARCnet boards for Macs, so ARCnet is seldom used.
EtherTalk 1.0 and 2.0	The EtherTalk 2.0 connection type is currently built into every Macintosh. (It replaced LocalTalk as the built-in connection type.) EtherTalk is the Macintosh version of Ethernet. If EtherTalk is built into your Macintosh, you do not need to install a separate network board. If your Macintosh has LocalTalk built in, you must install an EtherTalk network board in the workstation. Make sure there is a corresponding Ethernet board in the server. In the Network Control Panel, the icon for EtherTalk 1.0, which is only used in a nonextended AppleTalk network, has single arrows pointing in opposite directions. The icon for EtherTalk 2.0, which supports extended AppleTalk networks, has double arrows pointing in opposite directions.
TokenTalk	With TokenTalk, you need to install a Token Ring network board in each workstation and a corresponding one in the server.

LOCATING THE MACNDS CLIENT SOFTWARE

The MacNDS Client software is located on the NetWare CD-ROM. Because the CD-ROM is formatted for PC machines, the Macintosh client files are packed into a self-extracting file on the CD-ROM. Before you can install the client software, you have to unpack this file. Unpacking the file places the actual Macintosh client files on the server volume.

To get the client software from the volume onto a Macintosh client, you have two choices:

- If you are upgrading at least one Macintosh that already had a previous version of NetWare client software on it, you can log in to the server using the older client software and install the files from the SYS volume.
- If you are installing Macintoshes onto your network for the first time (so you can't log in to the network using previous NetWare client software), you can log in to the server via AppleShare. You must first install NetWare for Macintosh on the server, configure the AppleTalk File Services (AFP.NLM) to allow clear text passwords, and then connect to the server running bindery services. Then you can access the files on the server's volume.

If you are upgrading an existing Macintosh workstation, complete the steps in the following checklist to unpack (extract) the client files.

1 • If you haven't already copied the Macintosh client software to the server using INSTALL.NLM, load INSTALL, select Product Options, and then choose View/Configure/Remove Installed Products, and, finally, NW-MAC. Then choose Install Macintosh Client Support and follow the prompts to install the files onto the SYS volume. (Be sure you've loaded the Macintosh name space on SYS volume before you install the client files on it.)

2 • From a Macintosh workstation, log in as user SUPERVISOR to a NetWare server that has bindery services enabled. (The SUPERVISOR's password is the same as the user Admin's password. The SUPERVISOR doesn't exist in NDS; it only exists for compatibility with bindery services.)

3 • From the Macintosh, mount the SYS volume so that you can access files in it.

4 • Open the MAC folder inside the PUBLIC folder. Then open the appropriate language folder (such as English).

5 • Locate the MacNDS.sea files and double-click on it to extract it. When prompted, select the default destination directory (MacNDS) for the extracted files. The extracted files are now ready to be installed on the Macintosh, as explained in the next section.

6 • If you want to create an installation diskette to use with this or other Macintoshes, format an 800K diskette in the Macintosh disk drive.

7 • Copy the files from the network directory where you sent the extracted files in step 5, to the diskette.

8 • Rename the diskette to MacNDS, the same name as the server directory containing the extracted files (chosen in step 5).

INSTALLING THE MACNDS CLIENT SOFTWARE

Once you've extracted the Macintosh client files from the CD-ROM, you can install the client software on a Macintosh. After the installation, you can use a Control Panel to set up NDS login features.

To install the client software, complete the steps in the following checklist.

1 • From the Macintosh, log in to the server, or insert the diskette containing the extracted files in the Macintosh's diskette drive, and open the folder that contains the extracted files.

2 • Double-click on the Installer icon. (There should be no other applications, including virus detectors, running on the Macintosh. The Installer will close any other running applications, including Finder, for you. You may prefer to close them yourself before you begin the installation.)

3 • From the Easy Install menu, select the disk on which you want to install the client software (generally the startup disk).

4 • Click the Install button to install all of the client software listed in the menu.

5 • When the installation is finished, click the Restart button to restart the Macintosh so that the MacNDS software will be activated.

6 • Open the MacNCP Control Panel. This Control Panel lets you set up your login procedure.

a. In the Directory Tree field, type in the name of the NDS Directory tree to which you want to log in. (You can use the Change Tree button to see a list of available trees.)

b. In the Directory Context field, type in the name context where your User object is located in the NDS tree.

c. In the Directory Services Login Name field, type in your user name.

d. Click the Verify Name button. This button makes sure the NDS tree, context, and user name you entered are all valid and exist where you said they did.

e. Only click the Revert button if you want to reset this information to the names that were specified when you first opened the Control Panel.

f. Click the Allow Incoming Messages check box to permit your workstation to receive messages sent from other users, including the administrator, and from AppleShare.

g. When finished, close the MacNCP Control Panel.

Now the Macintosh is ready to use as a workstation on the NetWare 4.1 network.

LOGGING IN TO THE NETWORK

After you've set up MacNCP using the MacNCP Control Panel, you can log in to the NDS Directory tree easily.

There are two ways to log in: You can use the NDS Tree menu or the Chooser.

Using the NDS Tree Menu to Log In

You can log in to the NDS network using the NDS Tree icon in the menu bar of a Macintosh workstation. Pull down the NDS Tree menu and select Login. Then just enter your login name and password, and click OK.

If the name context shown isn't your correct context, open the MacNCP Control Panel and change it there. To log in to a different tree, click the Change Tree button and locate the tree you want.

You can also log out of the network or change your password using the NDS Tree menu.

Using the Chooser to Log In

You can log in to a particular server using the Chooser. From the Apple menu, select the Chooser, and click the AppleShare icon in the Chooser's Services window. Select a zone, choose a server, and click the OK button.

If you are asked to select a login method, choose Encrypted NetWare Authentication.

When the Connect box appears, decide if you want to log in using bindery services or NDS.

If you want to log in using bindery services, make sure the Log In to NetWare Directory Services check box is clear. Then enter your name and password, and click OK.

If you want to log in using NDS, make sure the Log In to NetWare Directory Services check box is checked. If the name context shown isn't your correct context, open the MacNCP Control Panel and change it there. To log in to a different tree, click the Change Tree button and locate the tree you want. To finish logging in, enter your name and password, and click OK.

You can change your password by clicking the Set Password button.

You cannot log out of NDS using the Chooser. To log out of NDS, choose Logout from the NDS Tree menu instead.

Using the MacIPX Gateway

The MacIPX gateway is a NetWare for Macintosh feature that lets Macintosh workstations that are running MacIPX applications on LocalTalk networks (or dialing in using AppleTalk Remote Access) access NDS on a NetWare 4.1 network.

Most users will not have to use a MacIPX gateway.

LocalTalk and AppleTalk Remote Access use only AppleTalk protocols. They do not support IPX. MacIPX software provides support for IPX transport protocols. You don't need to use the MacIPX gateway if you've connected your Macintoshes directly to your NetWare network using Ethernet or Token Ring.

When a user logs in to an NDS network, the IPX protocol (NetWare's native network protocol) is used to authenticate the connection. After the authentication is complete, AppleTalk is used for other communications with NetWare for Macintosh.

If a user is logging in to an NDS network from a LocalTalk network or dialing up with AppleTalk Remote Access, where IPX is not supported, the user's workstation has to send IPX packets encapsulated in AppleTalk. The MacIPX gateway receives these encapsulated packets, strips off the AppleTalk data, and forwards the IPX packet to the appropriate node on the IPX network. The gateway also reverses the process, adding AppleTalk encapsulation to IPX packets, to send data from the IPX node to the MacIPX Macintosh workstation.

To set up the MacIPX gateway, you must use INETCFG.NLM to configure the gateway on the server, and then use the Macintosh Network Control Panel on each Macintosh workstation to provide MacIPX support.

Complete the steps in the following checklist to configure a MacIPX gateway and set up workstations for MacIPX support.

1 • On the server, load INETCFG.NLM.

2 • Choose Boards and press Insert.

3 • Select MACIPXGW and assign a board name to it. Press Esc to save the settings.

4 • Choose Bindings and press Insert.

5 • Choose the IPX protocol, and then select the board name you assigned to the MacIPX gateway driver.

6 • Specify the network number of the IPX network to which the gateway is attached.

7 • When finished, press Esc to save the settings.

8 • Use the REINITIALIZE SYSTEM console utility to make the gateway settings take effect.

9 • On a Macintosh workstation, open the MacIPX Control Panel. The panel displays icons for each available network interface.

10 • Select the appropriate interface and set the appropriate parameters. Choose the AppleTalk interface if the Macintosh is connected to a LocalTalk cable, or if you want to use AppleTalk Remote Access to dial into the IPX network.

11 • Select the zone in which the MacIPX gateway is located, so that the AppleTalk interface will automatically select the correct MacIPX gateway when the Macintosh is started.

12 • Close the Control Panel. The workstation is now prepared for MacIPX gateway support.

Setting Up Print Services for Macintoshes

With NetWare for Macintosh, AppleTalk and NetWare printing services are integrated so that Macintosh users can use NetWare print queues. In addition, both PC and Macintosh users can print to network printers.

When PC users send print jobs to be printed, the print job goes directly from the workstation to a print queue on the server. Then, the print server takes the print job from the queue and sends it to the printer in the correct order. This works efficiently for PC workstations, because their parallel ports have been redirected to send jobs directly to a print queue.

Macintosh workstations, however, can't recognize print queues. They want to print directly to the printer. To accommodate this, NetWare for Macintosh provides an additional step, called an AppleTalk *print spooler.* To the Macintosh, the spooler appears to be a regular Apple printer, so the workstation will send the print job to it. The print spooler then sends the job to the NetWare print queue, where it waits in line to be processed by a print server. When users look for printers in the Chooser, they will see the spooler names instead.

If the job is going to be printed on a printer across the IPX portion of the network, the regular NetWare print server (PSERVER.NLM) takes the job from the queue to the printer.

However, if the job is going to be printed on a printer that is on the AppleTalk network, there are two options. You can use PSERVER with another module, named ATXRP.NLM, which lets PSERVER send a job over an AppleTalk network. If you prefer, you can use a special NetWare for Macintosh AppleTalk print server to manage the job. The NetWare for Macintosh print server is created by ATPS.NLM.

ATXRP.NLM allows you to integrate AppleTalk printers into NDS, so that the printers have objects you can manage in the NDS tree. It also works with PSERVER so that you can use PSERVER features to manage forms, assign priorities to queues, create notification lists (lists of users to notify in the event of printing problems), and print to remote printers. This setup also allows you to manage both AppleTalk and non-AppleTalk printers from the same utility. You may want to use ATXRP.NLM if your printing setup requires you to use some of these advanced features of PSERVER.NLM.

If your printing setup is fairly straightforward (you don't need to assign priorities to queues, define special print forms, and so on), ATPS.NLM lets you install printing services quickly and easily. It allows you to set up accounting services to monitor and limit printer use, and you can use the ATPS console utility, ATPSCON.NLM, to manage the AppleTalk print server.

USING ATXRP AND PSERVER TO SET UP PRINTING

To use ATXRP and PSERVER to set up print services for both PC and Macintosh users, complete the steps in the following checklist.

1 • Connect the printers to the network.

2 • Make sure each Macintosh workstation has the correct Apple printer driver software installed.

3 • Use PRINTDEF from a PC workstation to import Apple printer definition files (.PDF files) into the NetWare print devices database.

4 • From a PC workstation, run PCONSOLE. Just as you do for a PC-based printer, create a print queue, Printer object, and print server (if necessary), then associate them with each other, as explained in Chapter 9. Then exit PCONSOLE.

5 • Load PSERVER.NLM at the server, which should automatically load ATXRP.NLM if you created an AppleTalk printer in step 1 and associated it with this print server.

6 • Load ATPSCON.NLM at the server to configure the AppleTalk print spooler.

a. Select Change Context and change to the NDS context containing the print queue you will associate with the spooler.

b. Choose Configure Printer Servers to configure a print server as a query source from which the spooler can receive information about the printer, such as available fonts, memory, and so on. Press Insert to select a printer, accept the settings (don't select a queue), and press Esc to save the settings. You'll be warned that no queue was selected. Choose Configure Printer Anyway.

c. From the main Configuration Options menu, choose the Configure Spoolers option. To configure a new spooler, press Insert and specify the spooler settings. Press Esc to save the settings.

d. When finished, exit ATPSCON.

7 • To allow PC users to print to AppleTalk printers that support PostScript, create a print job configuration for the PC users.

a. Use PRINTDEF to assign a print form called Normal that defines 8½ by 11-inch sheets of paper.

b. Use PRINTCON to create print job configurations and assign them to users. For PostScript printers, set Form Feed to No and set Device to show the correct type of AppleTalk printer. Then, set the correct Mode. For a LaserWriter, the mode must be PostScript, PostScript (Binary Graphics), Diablo 630 with a CPI (characters per inch) specification, or PostText with a CPI specification. For an ImageWriter, the mode must be a CPI specification.

USING ATPS TO SET UP PRINTING

ATPS.NLM lets you set up an AppleTalk printer so that both PC and Macintosh users can send print jobs to it. ATPS.NLM lets you set up printing services in two ways:

- The Quick Configuration option lets you quickly set up a spooler, print queue, and a printer server for submitting jobs to an AppleTalk printer.
- The customize setup allows you to choose the individual options Configure Printer Servers and Configure Spoolers.

To use ATPS.NLM to set up print services for both PC and Macintosh users, complete the steps in the following checklist.

1 • Connect the printers to the network.

2 • Make sure each Macintosh workstation has the correct Apple printer driver software installed.

3 • Load ATPSCON.NLM at the server.

4 • Select Change Context and change to the NDS name context containing the print queue you will associate with the spooler.

5 • Choose whether you want to use the Quick Configuration or set up a customized environment. Select Quick Configuration to quickly set up a spooler, print queue, and a printer server. If you want to customize, do both of the following:

  - Choose Configure Printer Servers to configure a print server as a query source for the spooler to receive information about the printer, such as available fonts, memory, and so on. Press Insert to select a printer, accept the settings (don't select a queue), and press Esc to save the settings. You'll be warned that no queue was selected. Choose Configure Printer Anyway.
  - Choose Configure Spoolers. To configure a new spooler, press Insert and specify the spooler settings. Press Esc to save the settings.

6 • When finished, exit ATPSCON.

7 • To allow PC users to print to AppleTalk printers that support PostScript, create a print job configuration for the PC users.

a. Use PRINTDEF to assign a print form called Normal that defines $8^1/_2$ by 11-inch sheets of paper.

b. Use PRINTCON to create print job configurations and assign them to users. For PostScript printers, set Form Feed to No and set Device to show the correct type of AppleTalk printer. Then, set the correct Mode. For a LaserWriter, the mode must be PostScript, PostScript (Binary Graphics), Diablo 630 with a CPI (characters per inch) specification, or PostText with a CPI specification. For an ImageWriter, the mode must be a CPI specification.

PRINTING FROM A MACINTOSH WORKSTATION

Printing to a network printer is really no different, as far as the user is concerned, from printing to a directly attached printer.

The AppleTalk spooler appears in the Chooser. When users want to print jobs, they open the Chooser, select the spooler name, and close the Chooser.

Sending print jobs to the spooler, which then sends them to the NetWare print queue, is usually more efficient that trying to print directly to a printer. This is because it leaves the workstation free for other tasks. In addition, if other users are sending print jobs to the same printer, the print queue manages the printing traffic and ensures that the jobs are printed in the correct order.

PRINTING FROM A PC WORKSTATION

Likewise, sending print jobs from a PC workstation to an AppleTalk printer is really no different from printing to a PC-based printer. The users simply select the print queue to which they want to send their print jobs. (In most cases, however, in order to send print jobs to an AppleTalk printer, PC workstations must use a PostScript print driver.)

If an application supports network printing, you can select the print queue from within the application. If the application doesn't support network printing, you can specify the print queue by using the CAPTURE and NPRINT utilities, as explained in Chapter 9.

Sharing Macintosh and DOS Files

With NetWare for Macintosh installed on a NetWare server, Macintosh and PC users can see the names of each other's files displayed in file listings or folders, access the same directories, and take advantage of the same NetWare features. (Of course, which files and directories they access depends upon the trustee rights they've been granted. See Chapter 7 for more information about trustee rights.)

However, just because a Macintosh user can see a DOS file doesn't necessarily mean the Macintosh user can open the file. This is because Macintosh and DOS files have completely different formats. NetWare can store both formats (if the Macintosh name space is loaded), but it can't control how applications create files.

With the Macintosh file format, files have two parts:

- The *data fork* portion of the file contains the actual text of the file. This fork corresponds somewhat to a DOS-based file.
- The *resource fork* portion of the file contains information about the file, such as the application used to create the file (which lets you auto-launch a file by double-clicking its icon). In addition, the resource fork includes information about the type of icon that should be displayed for the file, and so on. DOS and OS/2 files don't have resource forks.

Another difference between DOS and Macintosh files is the rules that govern file names:

- Macintosh names can be up to 31 characters long and can contain spaces and punctuation.

- DOS file names can only consist of 11 characters (an 8-character name, followed by a period, followed by a 3-character extension). In addition, you cannot use spaces or punctuation marks, except for the underscore character (_).

When Macintosh file names are displayed on a PC, those names are shortened to appear in the DOS file name format. The names are shortened for display purposes only and are not actually changed. When you look at the file from a Macintosh, the name still appears in its original format.

These differences, however, do not mean that PC and Macintosh users can never share files. That depends entirely upon the applications that the users are using. Many applications have been created with both a Macintosh and a DOS or Windows version. Most of these applications can take a file from one format and convert it into the other format so that either user can open it.

Note: A common mistake new users make is to think that Mac users can actually execute PC-based applications or games from a Mac. This is not true. Applications can't run on both PCs and Mac workstations because of the same differences in file format mentioned earlier. However, many applications do have two versions (or more) — one that works on PCs and one that works on Mac workstations.

Another option, if the users don't have common applications, is to convert the files into a format that is supported by applications the users do have. For example, if a Macintosh application allows you to save a file in an ASCII format, you can then open the file from a DOS or Windows application that also supports ASCII. However, this process converts only the text in a file; any graphic or formatting elements will be lost.

This means that if your users need to share files, you should make sure that they have applications that can convert files between the two formats. Also, you may want to recommend that Macintosh users use DOS-style file names so the names are comprehensible to PC users.

CHAPTER 11

Managing Protocols

Instant Access

Configuring Protocols

- To configure IPX, TCP/IP, or AppleTalk, use INETCFG.NLM.

Monitoring Protocols

- To monitor IPX, use IPXCON.NLM.
- To monitor AppleTalk, use ATCON.NLM.
- To monitor TCP/IP, use TCPCON.NLM.
- To test the TCP/IP connection between a workstation and a server, use PING at the workstation and IPXPING.NLM on the server.
- To capture server messages to a screen so you can read them for diagnostic purposes, use CONLOG.NLM.

A *protocol* is a set of defined rules that controls how processes or machines communicate. A protocol regulates how the processes perform activities such as establishing communication, transferring packets of data, and terminating communication.

There are many different types of protocols that have been developed by various organizations to control how information is exchanged across a network. NetWare 4.1 supports many of these protocols.

Discussions about protocols can become very confusing because there are so many different types of protocols, as well as protocols that layer on top of each other. Protocols are associated with several types of properties, such as:

- The network architecture they support, such as bus- or ring-oriented architectures. Protocols designed for a bus architecture behave differently than protocols designed for a ring architecture.

- Whether they support synchronous or asynchronous transmissions. *Synchronous protocols* use timing to identify transmission of data, and are better suited for transmissions that occur at a relatively constant rate. Most mainframe and terminal-handling protocols are synchronous. *Asynchronous protocols* allow data to be transmitted in bursts. These protocols use start and stop bits to mark the individual transmission elements so that the data doesn't have to arrive in its original order. Most network protocols are asynchronous.

- Whether they support connection-oriented or connectionless transmission. A *connection-oriented protocol* establishes a connection between the source and destination. It terminates the connection when the transmission is finished. With such a connection, the data packets only need a destination address. A *connectionless protocol* transmits data across any available path. Packets may take different routes to the destination. Therefore, the packets need both a source and a destination address, and they must be labeled so that they can be reassembled in the correct order when they all arrive at the destination.

- Whether they support character-oriented or bit-oriented transmission. *Character-oriented* (or *byte-oriented*) *protocols* use characters (or bytes) to manage timing and the communication link. These protocols have generally been replaced with more efficient *bit-oriented protocols.*

- The OSI layer at which they function. The OSI Reference Model is described in the next section.

The OSI Reference Model

The International Standards Organization (ISO) has defined a model for allowing any combination of devices to communicate with each other. This model, called the OSI (Open Systems Interconnection) Reference Model, defines seven layers of communication that can occur between devices.

At each layer of the OSI Reference Model, different types of functions must be provided, although the model doesn't dictate *how* those functions must happen. When manufacturers and other organizations implement those functions, they get to determine *how* they are implemented. The protocol is essentially the manufacturer's or organization's definition of how the communication functions required at that level occur.

Figure 11.1 illustrates the seven layers of the OSI Reference Model.

FIGURE 11.1

The Seven Layers of the OSI Reference Model

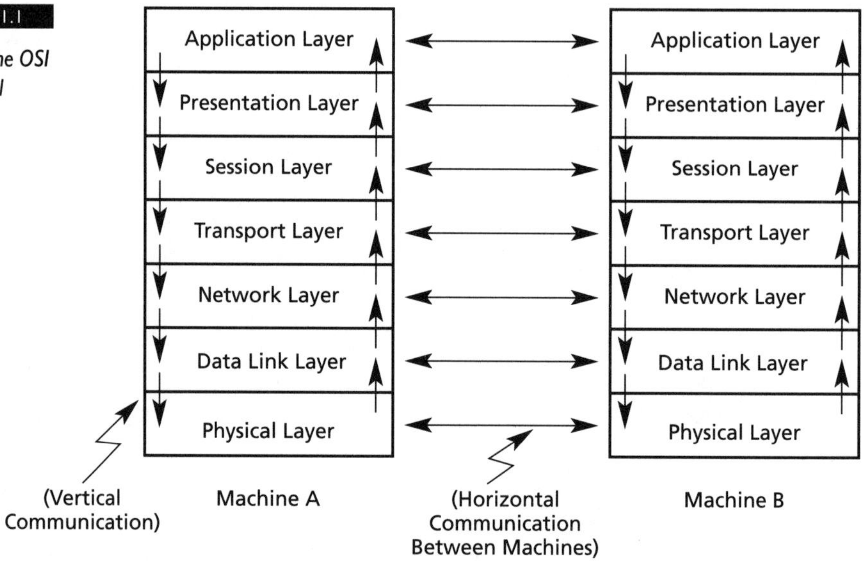

In the OSI Reference Model, a single machine minds its own internal communication by transferring information, such as data packets or service calls, between all seven layers. This is sometimes referred to as vertical communication in the OSI layers.

Two or more machines that want to communicate with each other work horizontally across the OSI layers. They use protocols to let a layer on one machine communicate with the same layer on another machine. The protocol for a particular layer translates the communication between the two machines, whether they are using the same program or different programs to send the communications to each other.

The top three layers are sometimes referred to as the *application-* and *service-oriented layers.* These layers control how applications communicate between machines, how connection sessions on the network are managed, and how data packets are encoded for transmission.

The bottom three layers are called the *subnet layers,* or the *communication-* and *network-oriented layers.* These layers control the physical communication between the hardware components, determine hardware and network addresses, find and manage a route between the components, and create packets that fit the network architecture. Relay devices, such as routers or bridges, only use these three layers, because they only relay data to other devices.

The middle layer, the *transport layer,* forms the link between the upper three layers and the lower three layers. The transport layer provides the delivery and verification services that allow a session to be maintained.

Some protocols contain functions that actually span more than one layer.

The seven layers are described in the following sections.

APPLICATION LAYER

The *application layer* gives applications access to the network. It controls functions such as e-mail services, file transfer, and network management. Application programs are found at this layer.

Some portions of the NetWare Core Protocol (NCP) operate at the application layer. (NCP operates across all of the top three layers.) The NetWare server uses NCP to handle workstation requests. In addition, some activities of the NetWare client software operate at this layer to enable the workstation to join the network.

Other examples of application layer protocols include File Transfer Protocol (FTP), X.400 (which specifies protocols for message handling and e-mail services), and Telnet (which provides terminal emulation and remote login support). AppleTalk Filing Protocol (AFP) operates at both the application layer and the next layer down — the presentation layer.

PRESENTATION LAYER

The *presentation layer* works closely with the application layer above, and the session layer below, to present data in a form that can be handled by applications or users. This layer can provide services such as data encryption, data conversion between character sets, and data compression.

AFP operates at this layer and the application layer. Various TCP/IP protocols, such as File Transfer Protocol (FTP) and Simple Mail Transfer Protocol (SMTP) also have functions that operate at this layer.

SESSION LAYER

The *session layer* maintains a network connection (called a session) during data transmission. Functions at this layer synchronize and sequence the communication and packets being transferred over a network connection, as well as ensure that appropriate security is maintained during the session.

AppleTalk Data Stream Protocol (ADSP), which lets two AppleTalk nodes create a reliable connection for transferring data, is an example of a session layer protocol. NetBIOS and NetBEUI also provide session layer capabilities.

TRANSPORT LAYER

The transport layer ensures that packets are transmitted at an acceptable, predefined level of reliability. It assigns numbers to outgoing packets and tracks them at the receiving end to make sure the packets arrived, and that they are placed in the correct order for the recipient.

NetWare's Sequenced Packet Exchange (SPX) protocol is a transport layer protocol. SPX provides a connection-oriented link between nodes.

Other examples include TCP and UDP, which are used in most Unix-based networks, and some of the protocols in the AppleTalk protocol suite: AEP, ATP, NCP, and RTMP.

NETWORK LAYER

Sometimes known as the *packet layer*, the *network layer* determines hardware and network addresses. Once those addresses are determined, protocols at this layer find and establish routes between sources and destinations.

Protocols at the network layer allow applications to communicate over different network links, regardless of differences in frame type, data link protocols, or hardware specifications.

NetWare 4.1 supports the three most commonly used network layer protocols:

- NetWare's Internetwork Packet Exchange (IPX) and the routing protocols it uses: Router Information Protocol (RIP) and Service Advertising Protocol (SAP). IPX is responsible for addressing and routing packets to nodes on the same network or on other networks.

- Internet Protocol (IP), a network layer protocol for the TCP/IP protocol suite. IP uses RIP and OSPF (Open Shortest Path First) for routing.

- Datagram Delivery Protocol (DDP), which provides connectionless service in AppleTalk networks. DDP uses RTMP (Routing Table Maintenance Protocol) and AURP (AppleTalk Update Routing Protocol) for routing.

DATA LINK LAYER

The *data link layer* creates, transmits, and receives data packets in a form that is appropriate for the network architecture (the form of these packets is often called a *frame* at this layer). These packets are passed down to the next layer, the physical layer, from which the data is transmitted to the physical layer on the destination machine.

The data link layer has been divided into two sublayers. The *logical-link control sublayer* (LLC), which provides an interface for the network layer protocols, is at the top. The *media-access control layer* (MAC), which provides access to a particular physical encoding and transport scheme, is at the bottom.

Network protocols, such as Ethernet, ARCnet, Token Ring, LocalTalk, and FDDI, cover both the data link layer and the physical layer. These are the most common protocols at this layer, and NetWare 4.1 supports them all. AppleTalk protocols used at this layer include EtherTalk Link Access Protocol (ELAP), LocalTalk Link Access Protocol (LLAP), and TokenTalk Link Access Protocol (TLAP).

Serial Line Interface Protocol (SLIP), which can be used to access the Internet over serial lines, and Point-to-Point Protocol (PPP), which provides direct medium-speed communication over serial lines between two machines, are other examples of data link layer protocols.

PHYSICAL LAYER

The *physical layer* defines the mechanical and electrical properties of the network hardware. For example, specifications at this layer define connector pin assignments for cables and connectors, the encoding scheme for electrical 0 and 1 signals in a digital transmission, and the physical connections and signaling methods used by the network hardware.

Protocols Supported by NetWare

By default, NetWare 4.1 supports IPX/SPX when it is installed. However, NetWare 4.1 also supports both IP and AppleTalk. If you need to connect your network to TCP/IP systems, you can configure the NetWare server to support IP. If you need to connect Macintoshes to your NetWare network, you can configure the server to support AppleTalk (specifically, AppleTalk's Datagram Delivery Protocol, also called DDP, which defines packet delivery between AppleTalk nodes).

For a workstation to communicate on the network, it must use the same protocol that is being used on the network. Fortunately, workstations can be configured to use multiple protocols.

Configuring Protocols on a NetWare Network

When you configure your NetWare network, you will configure primarily two types of protocols:

- Data link protocols (Ethernet, Token Ring, LocalTalk, ARCnet, or FDDI). Configuring these protocols essentially means that you are loading a LAN driver for a network board and specifying a few parameters for the board.

- Network protocols (IPX, IP, or AppleTalk). To add IP or AppleTalk to your NetWare network, you load the appropriate protocol NLM, specify necessary options, such as an address or whether the server should be a router for that protocol, then bind the protocol to a LAN driver.

During server installation, the IPX protocol is automatically configured and bound to the network boards you select. After the initial installation, you can either modify the configuration or add protocols to the network.

To configure both data link and network protocols, you can use an NLM called INETCFG. INETCFG is a menu-driven utility that makes it relatively easy to configure the protocols. You can also use the LOAD and BIND console commands (either typing them at the console or adding them to AUTOEXEC.NCF), but you may find INETCFG easier to work with.

To configure any of the protocols, complete the steps in the following checklist.

1 • At the server console, load INETCFG.NLM. You may be asked if you want to transfer your LAN driver, protocol, and remote access commands. What this really means is that you will move the LOAD and BIND commands from the AUTOEXEC.NCF file to INETCFG's startup files. If you want to manage all your LAN drivers and protocols from INETCFG, choose Yes.

2 • From the main menu, select Boards.

3 • If you're modifying the configuration for an existing network board, select the board and press Enter. To add a new network board, press Insert and select the appropriate LAN driver for the board.

4 • Specify or change any necessary parameters for the network board.

5 • Press Esc to save your changes. (You have now configured the data link protocols.)

6 • Next, if necessary, select Protocols to configure the network protocol you want this network board and LAN driver to work with.

- If you are using IPX, you can select IPX to review the configuration settings. By default, IPX is enabled, so chances are good you won't need to change any of its parameters.
- If you want to enable AppleTalk on the network, select AppleTalk. Configure the AppleTalk protocol as described in Chapter 10.
- To enable IP on the network, select TCP/IP. Change the TCP/IP Status field to Enabled. Leave the IP Packet Forwarding option set to Disabled if you want this server to act as an end-node, or change it to Enabled if you want this server to act as a router.

7 • Now select Bindings to bind the protocol you configured in step 7 to the LAN driver you configured in steps 4 and 5.

8 • Press Insert, select the protocol you want, and press Enter.

9 • From the list, choose the network board to which you want this protocol assigned, and press Enter. Depending on the protocol you've chosen, you will be asked for configuration information, such as an IPX network number, a frame type, or an IP address. Enter this information and press Esc when finished to save your changes.

10 • Exit INETCFG.

11 • To make the new binding take effect, enter the command

```
REINITIALIZE SYSTEM
```

at the console, or restart the server.

Utilities for Monitoring the Protocols

There are several utilities you can use to test and monitor the protocols you've configured:

- IPXCON.NLM lets you monitor information about IPX. With this utility, you can configure SNMP parameters, display IPX statistics and error counts, display information about NLSP, RIP, and SAP on the server, and list information such as known services and destination networks. When using IPXCON, press the F1 key to read help for each option.

- ATCON.NLM lets you monitor information about AppleTalk. ATCON lets you see the status of the AppleTalk Update-based Router Protocol, which lets AppleTalk be tunneled through IP. ATCON also lets you see information about network interfaces, manage the error log files, do a Name Binding Protocol (NBP) look-up of network entities, see statistics about AppleTalk packets, display the configuration of the AppleTalk router, and so on. When using ATCON, press the F1 key to read help for each option.

- TCPCON.NLM lets you monitor information about the TCP/IP protocol suite loaded on the server. You can view information about the protocols in the TCP/IP suite, SNMP configuration information, usage statistics, and so on.

- CONLOG.NLM lets you create a file, called CONSOLE.LOG, that captures all the messages that display on the server's screen. You can read this file to see any messages that may have scrolled off the screen before you were able to read them.

- IPXPING.NLM lets you send test messages (pings) to another node on the network to see if it is communicating with this server via TCP/IP.

- PING, a workstation utility, lets you test that a workstation and server are communicating via TCP/IP.

CHAPTER 12

Installing and Using Online Documentation

Instant Access

Installing

- To install documentation files on the server, use INSTALL.NLM.
- To install a DynaText viewer on a Windows workstation, use the Windows Program Manager, and run the DTEXTRW.EXE file.
- To install a DynaText viewer on a Macintosh workstation, decompress the DYNATEXT.HQX file and edit the workstation's DYNATEXT.CFG file to point to the documentation files.

Using

- To use the DynaText viewer, double-click on the DynaText icon.

In an effort to save trees, book-shelf space, and the administrator's time, most of the documentation for NetWare 4.1 is online, located on a CD-ROM. The only printed documentation that is included in the NetWare 4.1 package is the documentation you'll need to get your server up and running. The rest of the documentation is located on the CD-ROM.

Having the documentation online allows you to access the documentation from anywhere on the network. Obviously, this is more handy than having to tote two dozen manuals with you to a user's office. In addition, the online documentation's search features can help you locate the information you need quickly.

To allow network users to access the online documentation, you can store the documentation files on the server in a network directory, or you can mount the online documentation CD-ROM as a NetWare volume and access the documentation directly from the CD-ROM. To read the online documentation, you must then install a DynaText viewer on each machine that may be used to access the documentation.

NetWare 4.1 includes DynaText viewers for both Windows (or OS/2) and Macintosh workstations. The following sections describe how to install the online documentation files onto the server and how to install and use the DynaText viewers.

A full set of printed documentation, which you can purchase separately, is also available. To order the printed documentation, you can send in the order form that came in your NetWare box or call 800-336-3892 (in the United States) or 512-834-6905.

Installing the Online Documentation on the Server

Use INSTALL.NLM to copy the online documentation files onto a network directory so that network users can access them. After you install the documentation files, you have to install a DynaText viewer on each workstation that you want to be able to access the documentation.

The following is a checklist of the steps to install the online documentation.

1 • Insert the *NetWare 4.1 Online Documentation* CD-ROM into the server's CD-ROM drive and make sure that it is mounted as either a DOS device or a NetWare volume.

2 • At the server console, load INSTALL.NLM.

3 • Select Product Options, and then choose Install Online Documentation and Viewers.

4 • Press F3 and specify the path to the documentation CD-ROM (either the CD-ROM drive's letter or the CD-ROM's volume name).

5 • Select the documentation files you want to install. Select the NetWare 4.1 Documentation database, which is the set of actual documentation files, and the viewer your workstations will need (Macintosh, Windows, or both).

6 • Accept the default destination for the documentation files, and they will begin copying.

7 • When prompted for the user Admin's password, enter the password.

8 • Install the viewers on the workstations as explained in the following section.

Setting Up the DynaText Viewer on a Workstation

When you set up the DynaText viewer on a workstation, you can use it to read multiple collections of documentation. A *collection* is a set of documentation. For example, all of the manuals that are shipped with NetWare 4.1 are contained in a single collection. If you purchase additional NetWare products, those products may have their own collections of documentation. You can add these collections so that you can access all of them from the same viewer session.

You can also install documentation in more than one language, if you choose.

The following sections tell how to set up the viewer on Windows, OS/2, and Macintosh workstations.

WINDOWS AND OS/2 WORKSTATIONS

The following is a checklist that explains how to set up a DynaText viewer on a Windows or OS/2 (running WIN-OS/2) workstation. Once the viewer is set up, you can use this workstation to view the online documentation, whether the documentation is installed on a network directory or on a CD-ROM mounted as a NetWare volume. (Windows-based workstations should support VGA or SVGA, be running Windows 3.1 or better, and have at least 4MB of memory — although 8MB is preferred.)

1 • Make sure the workstation's AUTOEXEC.BAT file contains the command to specify the correct language, such as:

```
SET NWLANGUAGE=ENGLISH
```

2 • Start Windows or WIN-OS/2.

3 • Select File, and then select New to specify a new program item.

4 • Type in a description for the program, such as **Documentation**.

5 • For the Command Line field, press the Browse button to select the file DTEXTRW.EXE in the directory SYS:DOCVIEW\DTAPPWIN (or type it in).

6 • Set the working directory to the same directory (SYS:DOCVIEW\DTAPPWIN).

7 • Choose OK. When the DynaText icon appears, the viewer is ready to use.

8 • If you will be accessing the documentation files directly from the CD-ROM mounted as a NetWare volume on the server, edit the DYNATEXT.INI file on the workstation (located in the DOCVIEW\DTAPPWIN directory). Change the SYSCONFIG line to show the location of the SYSDOC.CFG file (\PUBLIC on the CD-ROM's volume).

9 • If you need to install multiple collections, multiple languages, or place the documentation files in a different directory (other than the default directory), use a text editor to edit the appropriate lines in the DYNATEXT.INI file. (The file contains editing instructions within it.)

MACINTOSH WORKSTATIONS

To set up a Macintosh workstation to use the DynaText viewer, you need a utility that can decompress "BinHexed" StuffIt archives. You can use a StuffIt program from Aladdin Systems, or you can use a freeware utility called StuffIt Expander, which can be obtained from Macintosh bulletin boards and Internet sites. (Whenever you download software from external sources such as bulletin boards, be sure to scan the software for viruses before installing it on your network.)

To set up the viewer, complete the steps in the following checklist.

1 • Insert the *NetWare 4.1 Online Documentation* CD-ROM into the server's CD-ROM drive and make sure that it is mounted as either a DOS device or a NetWare volume.

2 • Copy the DYNATEXT.HQX file from the CD-ROM's DOCVIEW:DTAPPMAC:ENGLISH folder (or select another language folder) to your Macintosh.

3 • Launch the program that will decompress StuffIt archives.

4 • Open and decompress the DynaText archive. This will create a folder called DYNATEXT Folder. Install it at the root of the workstation for easier configuration.

5 • If you want to access the files from the server or from the CD-ROM, skip to step 6. If you want the documentation database files to be stored locally on this Macintosh, copy the documentation database from the CD-ROM's DOC:ENGLISH folder to a folder of the same name on the Macintosh's hard disk.

6 • Edit the DYNATEXT.CFG file, located in the DYNATEXT Folder: DTAPPMAC:ENGLISH folder, to specify where the documentation database files are located. This file contains editing instructions within it.

7 • If you need to install multiple collections or multiple languages, edit the appropriate lines in the DYNATEXT.INI file.

8 • Set up an alias to the DynaText viewer by browsing to the DynaText program's installation location and clicking on its icon. Then choose Make Alias from the File menu, and drag the DynaText alias icon to a convenient location.

Using the DynaText Viewer

After the viewers and the documentation database are installed, you can access the online documentation. To do this, double-click on the DynaText icon to start up the viewer.

Select the NetWare 4.1 collection to see all of the manuals that are included in the collection. To open a manual, simply select it. The manual will appear on the workstation screen, with part of the screen showing the book's text and another part of the screen showing the Table of Contents.

Once you've opened the book, you can scroll through the text page by page, using the up- and down-arrow keys or the scroll bar. You can also move quickly to different sections of the book by clicking on a heading in the Table of Contents. If a plus sign appears next to a heading in the Table of Contents, you can click on the plus sign to display the subheadings beneath that topic. In addition, you can search for specific words or phrases in a book by using the Find field.

As you read through the manual's text, you will see references to related information. These references will appear in a different color and underlined. If you click on those references, they will take you instantly to the location of the related information, which may be in another section of the manual, or in a completely different manual. If you want to return to a previous section you were reading, choose Go Back from the Book menu.

The Master Index is an index to all of the manuals in the collection. You can look up a topic, then click on the topic's index marker to move directly to the correct location in any of the manuals.

CHAPTER 13

Disaster Planning and Recovery

Planning for Disasters

- Write an emergency plan, including emergency contacts and procedures.
- Keep good records of your network, including hardware settings, inventory, and so on.
- When troubleshooting a problem, isolate the problem and try solutions one at a time.

Disasters come in many guises. A disaster that affects your network could be anything from a crashed hard disk on your server, to a security breach, to a fire that destroys your building. When it comes to computers, a malfunctioning water sprinkler system can cause as much damage as a hurricane.

The best way to recover from a disaster, regardless of what type of disaster it is, is to have planned for one ahead of time. Armed with a disaster plan, good backups, and accurate records of your network, the task of reestablishing your network will not seem nearly as daunting.

Planning Ahead

If you haven't already created a disaster plan, do it today. It doesn't need to be that difficult, and it could save you a tremendous amount of wasted time, frustrated users, lost revenue, and sleepless nights. An earthquake or electrical fire isn't going to wait for a convenient time in your schedule to occur, so the sooner you plan for it, the better.

Be sure to document the plan. Write it down, get it approved by your organization's heads, and then make copies and store them in several locations so that you'll be able to find at least one of them if disaster should strike.

It's important to have a documented plan because having the plan in your head only works if you happen to be around, of course. More importantl, if you've gotten the CEO to approve your plan to restore the production department's network before the administration department's, you won't have to deal with politics and egos while you're trying to restring cables.

What should be in a disaster plan? Everyone's disaster plan will be different, but there are a few key points to consider when planning yours:

- Decide where you will store your emergency plan. It needs to be in a location where you or others can get to it easily. Ideally, there should be multiple copies of the plan, perhaps assigned to different individuals. Just storing the emergency plan in your office will not be adequate if the building burns down, so you may consider storing a copy off-site, too, such as in a safety deposit box or even at your home.

- Plan whom to call in case of an emergency and include their names, home phone numbers, pager numbers, and cellular phone numbers in your emergency plan. List key network personnel, such as any network administrators for various branches of the NDS tree, personnel who perform the weekly and daily backups, and so on. You may want to include names of security personnel who should be notified in case of a potential security breach.

- Plan the order in which you will restore service to your company. Who needs to be back online first? Is there a critical department that should be restored before any other? Are there key individuals who need to be reconnected first?

- Once you've identified the key people who need to be reconnected, determine if there is an order to the files or services they'll need. Which servers need to be restored first? What applications must those users have immediately? Which files will they need?

- Document the location of your network records. Where do you keep your hardware inventory, purchase requisitions, backup logs, and so forth?

- Document the location of your network backup tapes or disks. Don't forget to document instructions for restoring files, or indicate the location of the backup system's documentation, in case the backup operator is unavailable. Record your backup rotation schedule so that other people can figure out how to restore files efficiently.

- Include a drawing of the network layout, showing the exact location of cables, servers, workstations, and other computers. Highlight the critical components, so that anyone else reading your plan will know at a glance where to find the priority servers.

In addition to writing a disaster plan, there are other ways you can plan ahead to avert — or at least diminish — disaster. Some of these preparatory measures include:

- Keeping a faithful schedule of backups, so that files can be restored quickly.

- Implementing disk mirroring (or duplexing), so that a simple hard disk failure in the server won't cause users to lose working time and files because the server is down and they can't do their work.

- Implementing SFT III (mirrored servers) on your mission-critical servers. If you can't afford to have the server go down at all, SFT III can be your best fail-safe.

- If you're using database applications, use NetWare's TTS (Transaction Tracking System). TTS ensures that any transactions that are in progress when the server dies or the power goes out are backed out completely, so that the database isn't corrupted.

- Periodically reviewing your network's security, so that you can make sure there are no potential security leaks. Investigate security measures such as NCP Packet Signature, access rights, and password security to make sure that your network is as secure as you need it to be.

Keeping Good Records of Your Network

Another line in your defense against disaster is to maintain up-to-date records about your network. When something goes wrong with your network, it will be much easier to spot the problem if you have accurate documentation.

Good network documentation isn't just helpful in an emergency. Paperwork is always a distasteful task, but you'll be thankful you've done it the next time you have to add new hardware to the network, resolve an interrupt conflict, justify your hardware budget to management, get a workstation repaired under warranty, or train a new assistant.

How you track your network information is up to you. You may want to keep a three-ring binder with printed information about the network, or you may prefer to keep the information online in databases or spreadsheets.

However you document your network, be sure you keep the information in more than one location. If a disaster occurs, you don't want to lose your only copy of the information that can help you restore the network quickly. Try to keep copies of your network information in separate buildings, if possible, so that you won't lose everything if you can't access one building.

What types of network information should you record? Again, networks vary, so your documentation needs will vary, too. The worksheets in Appendix D can help you get started. You can photocopy and use those worksheets, or you can design your own worksheets or databases to keep track of the information you need.

Some recommendations for information you should maintain include:

- An inventory of existing and new hardware and software purchases. Record the product's version number, serial number, vendor, purchase date, length of warranty, and so on. This can help you when management asks for current capital assets or budget-planning information. It can also help you with insurance reports and replacements, should a loss occur.

- A record of configuration settings for servers, workstations, printers, and other hardware. This information can help save you hours that you would otherwise spend locating and resolving interrupt conflicts.

- A history of hardware repairs. You may want to file all paperwork associated with repairs along with the worksheet that documents your original purchase of the item.

- A drawing of the network layout. If you store this with your disaster plan, you (and others) will be able to locate critical components quickly. On the drawing, show how all the workstations, servers, printers, and other equipment are connected. The drawing doesn't have to be to scale, but it should show each machine in its approximate location. Label each workstation with its make and model, its location, and its user. Show the cables that connect the hardware, and show what types of cable they are.

- Batch files and workstation boot files. Using a text editor or other program, print out these files and keep them with the worksheets that document the workstation. You may also want to store copies of the files on diskette. If the workstation needs to be reinstalled, you can re-create the user's environment quickly if you have these files archived.

- SET parameters. SERVMAN.NLM allows you to save a server's SET parameters to a file. If you've changed the default SET parameters, print out this file, and store the printout and a diskette copy with your network records. This will make it much easier to reinstall the server to the configuration you originally had, should the need arise.

- Backup information. It is very important to record your backup rotation schedule, the location of backup tapes or disks, the names of any backup operators, the labeling system you use on your backup tapes or disks, and any other information someone may need if you're not around to restore the system.

Troubleshooting Tips

Unfortunately, despite the best possible planning, something may still go wrong with your network. The majority of network problems are related to hardware issues — interrupt conflicts, faulty components, incompatible hardware, and so on. However, software creates its own set of problems, such as application incompatibility, Windows bugs and incompatibility, and installation errors.

There are endless combinations of servers, workstations, cabling, networking hardware, operating systems, and applications. This makes it impossible to predict and document every possible problem. The closest anyone can do is approach the problem with a methodical system for isolating the problem, and then fix it.

The following troubleshooting guidelines can help you isolate the problem and find solutions.

NARROW DOWN THE LIST OF SUSPECTS

First, of course, you need to try to narrow your search to suspicious areas.

- Were there any error messages? If so, look up their explanations in the *NetWare 4.1 System Messages* online manual.
- How many machines did the problem affect?
- Can you identify a particular cabling segment or branch of the Directory tree that is having the problem?

- Does the problem occur only when a user is accessing a particular application, or does it perhaps occur only when the user executes applications in a particular order?
- If the problem occurred when you installed new workstations or servers on the network, have you checked their network addresses and hardware settings for conflicts with other boards or with machines that already exist on the network? Also double-check the installation documentation to make sure you didn't misspell a command or accidentally skip a step.
- Are the servers and workstations using the same frame type to communicate? If a server is using Ethernet 802.2 and a workstation is using Ethernet 802.3, they won't see each other.
- Are the servers and workstations using compatible NCP Packet Signature levels to communicate?
- If a user is having trouble working with files or applications, have you checked the security features? Does the user have appropriate rights in the necessary directories? Are the files already opened by someone else? Do the files or directories have attributes assigned that are restricting the user from some actions?
- Are some of a user's DOS path commands gone? Look in the login scripts for search drive mappings that were mapped without using the INS keyword (which inserts the mapping into the DOS path instead of overwriting existing paths).
- For printing problems, have you checked that the printer, print server, and print queue are all correctly assigned to each other? You can use the NetWare Administrator utility to check on your printing setup. Select the print server from the Browser, choose Details from the object menu, then open the Print Layout page to see whether the print server, printer, and queue are all assigned together correctly.
- Do you have a volume that won't mount? If so, you may need to run

VREPAIR.NLM to fix it. VREPAIR is explained in Chapter 8.

- Have you verified that applications are using the correct print drivers for your printers?

CHECK THE HARDWARE

Hardware problems can be relatively common in networks. Network cables are notorious for developing problems, partially because of the abuse they get from being coiled up, walked on, bent around corners, and so on. A network analyzer, such as NetWare LANalyzer, can be a useful tool for diagnosing cable problems. As you diagnose hardware problems, keep the following tips in mind:

- Cables have an annoying tendency to work loose from their connectors, so check all connections between cables and boards first.
- Test suspicious cables by replacing them with cables you know work, and see if the problem persists.
- Make sure cables are terminated correctly, don't exceed length limits, and don't form endless loops in topologies that don't allow that.
- If the problem is with a computer or printer, try disconnecting it from the network and running it in stand-alone mode. If the problem still shows up in stand-alone mode, it's probably not a problem with the network connection. You can then eliminate the network components and concentrate on the configuration of the machine itself.
- If the problem occurred when you installed a new workstation or server, or added a board to an existing computer, check hardware settings for conflicts with other boards or with machines that already exist on the network.

REFER TO THE DOCUMENTATION

Forget the jokes about only reading the manual as a last resort. The NetWare online manuals contain explanations of error messages that may occur. In addition, they include troubleshooting tips, configuration instructions, and so on.

In addition, check the manufacturer's documentation for any network hardware or applications you're using. Some applications have special instructions for installing on a network.

LOOK FOR PATCHES OR WORKAROUNDS

When Novell engineers find a problem with NetWare, they usually either solve the problem with a patch (a piece of software that loads as an NLM on your server and repairs it) or a recommended workaround.

Novell distributes these patches and workarounds on NetWire (on CompuServe and the Internet) and in the *Novell Support Encyclopedia Professional Volume* (NSEPro). See Appendix C for more information about these resources.

TRY EACH SOLUTION BY ITSELF

After you've isolated the problem to a suspicious area, try implementing the solutions you've found, but implement them one at a time. The tendency is to try several possible fixes simultaneously to save time.

Start with the easiest, cheapest solution, and work up from there.

Trying solutions simultaneously may save time in the short run, but it could cost you extra money for unnecessary repairs or replacements. In addition, you won't know for sure what fixed the problem, so you'll have to start from scratch again should the problem reappear on another machine or at another time.

CALL FOR TECHNICAL SUPPORT

There is a wide variety of places you can go to get help, advice, tips, and fixes for your NetWare problems or issues. Appendix C lists several of the resources you should know about. These resources range from Internet user groups, to classes, to publications that deal with NetWare support issues. If you're looking for more formal technical support, try these ideas:

- You can often find the technical help you need online, through the Internet Usenet groups that focus on NetWare or through the NetWire forums on the Internet and CompuServe. These forums are moderated by knowledgeable sysops (system operators) and populated by knowledgeable users.
- Try calling your reseller or consultant for help.
- Novell's technical support is available by calling 1-800-NETWARE. However, Novell's technical support is not free. You'll be charged a fee for each incident, so have your credit card handy. (An incident may involve more than one phone call, if necessary.)
- Before you call, be sure you've tried your other resources first — especially the documentation. It's embarrassing and expensive to have technical support tell you that the answer to your question is on page 25 of the *NetWare 4. 1 Installation* manual.

DOCUMENT THE SOLUTION

When you find a solution, write it down and store it with your network documentation. This may prevent you or someone else from duplicating efforts and wasting time going through the same troubleshooting process to fix a similar problem later.

APPENDIX A

NET.CFG Parameters

The NET.CFG file on a workstation configures the NetWare DOS Requester and LAN driver for the workstation's needs. Because NET.CFG is used to configure a variety of different aspects of your workstation, it can be quite simple or fairly involved.

NET.CFG is created by the NetWare DOS Requester installation. It is located in the NWCLIENT directory and can be edited with a text editor.

NET.CFG must be formatted with headings for various categories of configuration parameters. Each heading must be flush with the left margin; commands beneath that heading are indented once. (The only exception to these formatting conventions is NETBIOS commands. They are all flush with the left margin.) It doesn't matter if you use uppercase or lowercase in the commands in NET.CFG. (The examples in this chapter use mixed case for readability.)

The following is a sample NET.CFG file that was created to configure an NE2000 network board to use port 300, interrupt 3, and the 802.2 Ethernet frame type. Notice that the file is divided by headings. The Link Driver NE2000 heading contains indented lines that specify the information for that driver. The NetWare DOS Requester heading contains indented lines that specify general items for the Requester. Each heading is preceded by a blank line, which makes it easier to read the file. The NET.CFG file that will be created when you first install the NetWare DOS Requester will vary from this sample, depending on your configuration.

```
LINK DRIVER NE2000
        Port 300
        Int 3
        Frame Ethernet_802.2


NETWARE DOS REQUESTER
      NetWare Protocol=NDS, BIND
      First Network Drive=F
```

There are fifteen categories of NET.CFG parameters:

- Desktop SNMP
- Link Driver
- Link Support
- Named Pipes
- NetBIOS
- NetWare DOS Requester
- NetWare DOS TSA
- Protocol IPX
- Protocol ODINSUP
- Protocol RFCNBIOS
- Protocol RPL
- Protocol SPX
- Protocol TCPIP
- TBMI2
- Transport Provider IPX (or UDP)

The following sections explain the available parameters for each of these categories.

Desktop SNMP Parameters

Desktop SNMP parameters configure the desktop SNMP option. To use these parameters, add the Desktop SNMP heading to the NET.CFG file, and then place each parameter command beneath the heading, indented as shown.

```
DESKTOP SNMP
        parameter
```

The following parameters can be used with this heading:

- **Asynchronous timeout *number*** Sets the timeout (in ticks) for asynchronous connections. When an SNMP manager requests data from a managed object, the desktop SNMP waits the specified amount of time before trying to cancel a request. Default: 20 ticks (about 1.2 seconds).

- **Control community "*name*"** Specifies the control community, which is the read-write community that is allowed to do SET operations. Enclose the *name* in quotation marks. Default: Public. Values: Public, Private, or other name.

- **Enable control community *status*** Specifies which control communities can be used to gain access. Default: Specified. Values: Specified, Any, Off, Omitted.

  - **Specified** Only the community in the Control Community command is allowed.

  - **Any** Any community is allowed.

  - **Off** Access for this community type is disabled.

  - **Omitted** If "Omitted" is used, Desktop SNMP defaults to "Specified" and looks for a specified community. If none is found, the default community becomes the Public community.

- **Enable monitor community *status*** Specifies which monitor communities can be used to gain access. Default: Specified. Values: Specified, Any, Off, Omitted.

  - **Specified** Only the community in the Monitor Community command is allowed.

  - **Any** Any community is allowed.

  - **Off** Access for this community type is disabled.

  - **Omitted** If "Omitted" is used, Desktop SNMP defaults to "Specified" and looks for a specified community. If none is found, the default community becomes the Public community.

- **Enable trap community *status*** Specifies which trap communities can be used to gain access. Default: Specified. Values: Specified, Off, Omitted. ("Any" is not a possible value for this parameter.)

  - **Specified** Only the community in the Trap Community command is allowed.

  - **Off** Access for this community type is disabled.

  - **Omitted** If "Omitted" is used, Desktop SNMP defaults to "Specified" and looks for a specified community. If none is found, the default community becomes the Public community.

- **Monitor community *"name"*** Specifies the monitor community, which is the read-only community that is allowed to do GET and GET NEXT operations. Enclose the *name* in quotation marks. Default: Public. Values: Public, Private, or other name.

- **Snmpenableauthentrap *on/off*** When set to On, tells the Desktop SNMP to send a trap message if an unauthorized user tries to use SNMP to get or change data that SNMP manages. Default: Off.

- **Syscontact "*name*"** Specifies the name of the person who should be notified if the workstation needs maintenance. Enclose the *name* in quotation marks. You can enter a name and phone number, or other information, such as "Ray Snow ext. 3354."

- **Syslocation "*location*"** Specifies the physical location of the workstation. Enclose the *location* in quotation marks. Enter any location, such as "West wing 2nd floor."

- **Sysname "*name*"** Specifies the user's login name or TCP/IP host name, if available, such as "lksmith." Enclose the *name* in quotation marks.

- **Trap community "*name*"** Specifies the trap community. Enclose the *name* in quotation marks. Default: Public. Values: Public, Private, or other name.

Link Driver Parameters

Link Driver parameters configure hardware and software options for the workstation's LAN driver. They also allow you to specify frame types and protocols for the LAN driver.

To use these parameters, add the Link Driver heading to the NET.CFG file, and then place each parameter command beneath the heading, indented as shown here. Substitute the name of your LAN driver, such as NE2000 or 3C523, for *driver* in the heading.

```
LINK DRIVER driver
          parameter
```

The following parameters can be used with this heading:

- **Accm *address*** Sets whether the PPP protocol should use ACCM (asynchronous control character map). Replace *address* with the correct address for the remote host. Default: FFFFFFFF.

- **Accom *yes/no*** When set to Yes, tells the PPP protocol whether to compress the address and control field of the PPP header. Default: No.

- **Alternate** Specifies an alternate network board.

- **Authen pap *username password*** Tells the PPP protocol to use authentication (based on the Password Authentication Protocol — PAP). PPP uses the username and password to identify the local system to the peer host.

- **Baud *rate*** Specifies the baud rate for the SLIP_PPP driver. Default: 2400. Values: 300, 1200, 2400, 4800, 9600, 14400, 19200, 38400.

- **Bus ID *name number*** Specifies the bus into which the network board is inserted. Used with LAN drivers that support multiple bus types. Replace *name* with the name of the LAN driver, such as NE2000. The default value for *number* (-1 0FFh) makes the LAN driver search each bus for a supported network board and then initialize the first board found. Default: -1 0FFh. Example values are as follows:

ISA	0
MCA	1
EISA	2
PCMCIA	3
PCI	4
VL (VESA Local)	5

- **Counter *protocol timeout config# term# nak#*** Specifies a *protocol,* which can be LCP (Link Control Protocol), IPCP (Internet Protocol Control Protocol), or PAP (Password Authentication Protocol). Sets the protocol's timeout value (in seconds) for retransmitting request packets (*timeout*), the maximum number of retries for sending a configuration request (*config#*), the maximum number of retries for sending a terminate request (*term#*), and the maximum number of retries for sending a configuration NAK (*nak#*).

- **Dial *number*** Specifies the phone number for the SLIP_PPP driver to call when it is loaded. Used only when the Direct parameter is set to No. Values: Any dial modifiers supported by your modem, up to 30 characters.

- **Direct** ***yes/no*** Specifies whether the SLIP or PPP link is direct. Set to No only if you use the Dial or Listen parameters. Default: Yes.

- **Dma [#1 or #2]** ***number*** Configures the network board's DMA channels. Select #1 or #2 to specify which of the configurable DMA channels you're configuring, and then specify the DMA channel you want it to use. For example, to set the first configurable channel to use DMA channel 3, type **dma #1 3**.

- **Frame** ***frametype*** **[*mode*]** Sets the frame type the LAN driver will use. Can also set the address mode to either LSB (canonical addressing mode) or MSB (noncanonical addressing mode) for LAN drivers that support this. Default frame types:

  - For Ethernet drivers: Ethernet_802.2

  - For Token Ring drivers: Token-Ring

  - For TCP/IP SLIP_PPP drivers: SLIP

- **Ipaddr** ***address*** Specifies the IP addresses for PPP, in dotted decimal notation, such as 129.46.01.5. If the remote host did not specify an address in its configuration request, the specified address in this parameter is used. Default: none.

- **Irq [#1 or #2]** ***number*** Sets the interrupt (IRQ) that the network board will use. Use #1 or #2 to specify the network board you're configuring, and then replace *number* with the interrupt number you want to assign. Recommended values: 3, 5, or 7 for most network boards, to avoid conflicting with other hardware. See the manufacturer's documentation for more information.

- **Link stations** ***number*** Specifies the number of link stations needed for the LANSUP driver. Used with the IBM LAN Support Program. Default: 1.

- **Listen** Indicates the passive end of a modem connection for the SLIP or PPP protocol.

- **Magic** ***number*** Specifies a number used by the SLIP_PPP driver as a seed number to generate a unique number for process recognition. This parameter enables you to detect looped-back links and other problems. Default: Disabled.

- **Max frame size** ***number*** Specifies the maximum frame size, in bytes, that the NTR2000 and LANSUP LAN drivers can send out onto the network.

  - Default for NTR2000: 4222 bytes, or 2174 if the network board has 8K or shared RAM available.

  - Default for LANSUP: 1150 bytes, or 1496 if you're using the IBM LAN Support Program with an Ethernet LAN driver.

  Values: Between 638 and 17,954 for a line speed of 16 Mbps. Between 638 and 4464 for a line speed of 4 Mbps. Value includes number of bytes in a data packet, plus bytes in the largest possible header (currently 126 bytes — 52 bytes for LAN driver header plus 74 bytes for protocol header).

- **Mem [#1 or #2]** ***address length*** Sets the memory range that the network board can use. Specify the board by typing either **#1** or **#2**. Replace *address* with the hex starting address of the memory used by the network board. If necessary, replace *length* with the number of hex paragraphs (16 bytes each) of the memory address range.

- **Mru** ***number*** **m** Specifies the maximum receive and transmit units (MRU) for the SLIP or PPP protocol. Add the optional "m" to the command if the SLIP_PPP driver should assume a worst-case scenario for character mapping, in which data bytes in a packet are mapped into 2 bytes each. Default for PPP: 1500. Default for SLIP: 1006. Values: 76 to 1500.

- **Node address** ***address*** **[*mode*]** Sets the hex address number for the network board, which overrides the hard-coded address. Can also set the address mode to either LSB (canonical addressing mode) or MSB (noncanonical addressing mode) for LAN drivers that support this.

- **Open** Allows the LANSUP file to increase the frame size for a Token Ring driver for networks using the IBM LAN Support Program.

- **Open *mode*** Specifies the active or passive open mode for LCP (Link Control Protocol) and IPCP (Internet Protocol Control Protocol) for networks using the PPP protocol. Default: Active. Values: Active or Passive.

- **Pcomp *yes/no*** When set to Yes, tells the PPP protocol to compress the protocol field of the PPP header. Default: No.

- **Port [#1 or #2] *address* [*number*]** Sets the hex address for the starting I/O port and, if necessary, the number of ports in the range. Use #1 or #2 to specify the appropriate network board.

- **Protocol *name ID type*** Adds additional protocols to the LAN driver. *Name* is the new protocol's name. *ID* is the protocol's hex ID number. *Type* is the protocol's frame type. See Table A.1 for a list of protocols with their frame types and ID numbers.

- **Saps *number*** Sets the number of Service Access Points needed by the LANSUP driver. Used with the IBM LAN Support Program. Default: 1.

- **Slot *number*** Specifies the board's slot number so the driver doesn't have to scan the slots to find the board.

- **Tcpipcomp [vj or no] *slots number*** Uses VJ (Van Jacobson) header compression for the SLIP or PPP protocols. If you do not want VJ compression, set this parameter to No. If you want VJ compression, enter VJ, and specify the conversation slot you want and whether to compress the slot ID (when *number* is 0, do not compress slot ID; when *number* is 1, compress slot ID). Default: No compression. If you set compression to VJ, defaults: slots = 16, number = 0. If you set compression to VJ, values: slots = 1 to 16, number = 0 or 1.

TABLE A.1

Protocols with Their Frame Types and ID Numbers

FRAME ID	FRAME TYPE	PROTOCOL	PROTOCOL ID NUMBER	DESCRIPTION
0	VIRTUAL_LAN	IPX/SPX	0	Use where no Frame ID/MAC envelope is necessary.
1	LOCALTALK	AppleTalk	0	Apple LocalTalk frame
2	ETHERNET_II	IPX/SPX	8137h	Ethernet using a DEC Ethernet II envelope
2	ETHERNET_II	XNS	600h	Ethernet using a DEC Ethernet II envelope
2	ETHERNET_II	AARP	80F3h	Ethernet using a DEC Ethernet II envelope
2	ETHERNET_II	AppleTalk	809Bh	Ethernet using a DEC Ethernet II envelope
2	ETHERNET_II	ARP	806h	Ethernet using a DEC Ethernet II envelope
2	ETHERNET_II	RARP	8035h	Ethernet using a DEC Ethernet II envelope
2	ETHERNET_II	IP	800h	Ethernet using a DEC Ethernet II envelope
3	ETHERNET_ 802.2	IPX/SPX	E0h	Ethernet (802.3) using an 802.2 envelope
3	ETHERNET_ 802.2	RPL	FCh	Ethernet (802.3) using an 802.2 envelope
3	ETHERNET_ 802.2	SNA	04h	Ethernet (802.3) using an 802.2 envelope

(continued)

(Table reprinted from NetWare Client for DOS and MS Windows Technical Reference *manual, 1994, Novell, Inc. All rights reserved. Used with permission.)*

TABLE A.1

Protocols with their Frame Types and ID Numbers (continued)

FRAME ID	FRAME TYPE	PROTOCOL	PROTOCOL ID NUMBER	DESCRIPTION
3	ETHERNET_ 802.2	NetBIOS	F0h	Ethernet (802.3) using an 802.2 envelope
4	Token-Ring	IPX/SPX	E0h	Token ring (802.5) using an 802.2 envelope
4	Token-Ring	RPL	FCh	Token ring (802.5) using an 802.2 envelope
4	Token-Ring	SNA	04h	Token ring (802.5) using an 802.2 envelope
4	Token-Ring	NetBIOS	F0h	Token ring (802.5) using an 802.2 envelope
5	ETHERNET_ 802.3	IPX/SPX	00h	IPX 802.3 raw encapsulation
6	802.4	IPX/SPX	N/A	Token-passing bus envelope
7	RESERVED			Reserved for future use.
8	GNET	IPX/SPX	E0h	Gateway G/Net frame envelope
9	PRONET-10	IPX/SPX	N/A	Proteon ProNET I/O frame envelope
10	ETHERNET_ SNAP	IPX/SPX	8137h	Ethernet (802.3) using an 802.2 envelope with SNAP
10	ETHERNET_ SNAP	XNS	600h	Ethernet (802.3) using an 802.2 envelope with SNAP
10	ETHERNET_ SNAP	AARP	80F3h	Ethernet (802.3) using an 802.2 envelope with SNAP

TABLE A.1

Protocols with their Frame Types and ID Numbers (continued)

FRAME ID	FRAME TYPE	PROTOCOL	PROTOCOL ID NUMBER	DESCRIPTION
10	ETHERNET_SNAP	AppleTalk 8000	7809Bh	Ethernet (802.3) using an 802.2 envelope with SNAP
10	ETHERNET_SNAP	ARP	806h	Ethernet (802.3) using an 802.2 envelope with SNAP
10	ETHERNET_SNAP	RARP	8035h	Ethernet (802.3) using an 802.2 envelope with SNAP
10	ETHERNET_SNAP	IP	800h	Ethernet (802.3) using an 802.2 envelope with SNAP
11	Token-Ring_SNAP	IPX/SPX	8137h	Token ring (802.5) using an 802.2 envelope with SNAP
12	LANPAC_II	IPX/SPX	N/A	Racore frame envelope
13	ISDN	IPX/SPX	N/A	Integrated Services Digital Network (not available)
14	NOVELL_RX-NET	IPX/SPX	FAh	Novell RX-Net envelope
17	OMNINET/4	IPX/SPX	N/A	Corvus frame envelope
18	3270_COAXA	IPX/SPX	N/A	Harris Adacom frame envelope
19	IP	IPX/SPX	N/A	IP Tunnel frame envelope
20	FDDI_802.2	IPX/SPX	E0h	FDDI using an 802.2 envelope
20	FDDI_802.2	RPL	FCh	FDDI using an 802.2 envelope

(continued)

TABLE A.1

Protocols with their Frame Types and ID Numbers (continued)

FRAME ID	FRAME TYPE	PROTOCOL	PROTOCOL ID NUMBER	DESCRIPTION
20	FDDI_802.2	SNA	04h	FDDI using an 802.2 envelope
21	IVDLAN_802.9	IPX/SPX	N/A	Commtex, Inc. frame envelope
22	DATACO_OSI	IPX/SPX	N/A	Dataco frame envelope
23	FDDI_SNAP	IPX/SPX	8137h	FDDI using 802.2 with a SNAP envelope
23	FDDI_SNAP	XNS	600h	FDDI using 802.2 with a SNAP envelope
23	FDDI_SNAP	AARP	80F3h	FDDI using 802.2 with a SNAP envelope
23	FDDI_SNAP	AppleTalk 80007	809Bh	FDDI using 802.2 with a SNAP envelope
23	FDDI_SNAP	ARP	806h	FDDI using 802.2 with a SNAP envelope
23	FDDI_SNAP	RARP	8035h	FDDI using 802.2 with a SNAP envelope
23	FDDI_SNAP	IP	800h	FDDI using 802.2 with a SNAP envelope
24	IBM_SDLC	Unknown		Novell frame type
25	PCO_FDDITP	Unknown		PC Office frame type
26	WAIDNET	Unknown		Hyper communications frame type
27	SLIP	Unknown		Novell frame type

TABLE A.1
Protocols with their Frame Types and ID Numbers (continued)

FRAME ID	FRAME TYPE	PROTOCOL	PROTOCOL ID NUMBER	DESCRIPTION
28	PPP	Unknown		Novell frame type
29	RANGELAN	Unknown		Proxim frame type
30	X.25	Unknown		Novell frame type
31	Frame_Relay	Unknown		Novell frame type
32	IWI_BUS-NET_ SNAP	Unknown		Integrated Workstations frame type
33	SNA_LINKS	Unknown		Novell frame type
34	WAN_Client_ LAN	Unknown		Novell frame type

Link Support Parameters

Link Support parameters configure options for the Link Support Layer (LSL.COM), such as the size of packet receive buffers, the size of memory pool buffers, and so on.

To use these parameters, add the Link Support heading to the NET.CFG file, and then place each parameter command beneath the heading, indented as shown here.

```
LINK SUPPORT
        parameter
```

The following parameters can be used with this heading:

- **Buffers *number* [*size*]** Sets the number of communication buffers (if applicable) and the size (in bytes) of receive buffers that LSL.COM can handle. The buffer size should be the same size as the largest packet size that your workstation receives over the network.
    - For IPX Default *number*: 0 (IPX uses its own buffers and does not need the LSL to provide buffers for it.) Default *size*: 1500.
    - For TCP/IP Default *number*: 8. Default *size*: 1500.
    - For LSL Default *number*: none. Default *size*: 1514.

- **Max boards *number*** Sets the maximum number of logical boards LSL.COM can maintain. Default: 4. Values: 1 to 16.
- **Max stacks *number*** Sets the maximum number of logical protocol stack IDs that LSL.COM can support. Default: 4. Values: 1 to 16.
- **Mempool *number* [K]** Configures the size of the memory pool buffers (in bytes) for some protocols (not used with IPXODI). Include the K option to indicate the value is in kilobytes.

Named Pipes Parameters

Named Pipes parameters regulate how a workstation interacts with a Named Pipes server.

To use these parameters, add the Named Pipes heading to the NET.CFG file, and then place each parameter command beneath the heading, indented as shown here.

```
NAMED PIPES
          parameter
```

The following parameters can be used with this heading:

- **Np max comm buffers *number*** Indicates the maximum number of communication buffers that the extender can use when communicating with the Named Pipes server. Default: 6. Values: 4 to 40.
- **Np max machine names *number*** Sets the DOSNP software for peer mode and specifies how many Named Pipes servers the extender can communicate with. Sets the maximum number of Named Pipes servers that the DOSNP software can maintain in a local name table. Default: 10. Values: 4 to 50.
- **Np max open named pipes *number*** Sets the maximum number of Named Pipes that the workstation can have open simultaneously. Default: 4. Values: 4 to 128.

- **Np max sessions *number*** Sets the maximum number of Named Pipes servers that the extender can communicate with in default mode. Not used in peer mode. Default: 10. Values: 4 to 50.

NetBIOS Parameters

NetBIOS parameters let you configure NetBIOS sessions, buffers, and broadcasts.

To use these parameters, you don't need to add a NetBIOS heading to the NET.CFG file. Each NetBIOS command can be entered flush with the left margin.

```
NETBIOS parameter
NETBIOS parameter
```

The following NetBIOS parameters can be used:

- **Netbios abort timeout *number*** Sets the time NetBIOS waits for a response before ending a session. Default: 540 ticks (30 seconds).

- **Netbios broadcast count *number*** Sets how many queries or claims NetBIOS broadcasts for the name being used by the application. When multiplied by NetBIOS Broadcast Delay number, sets the time required to broadcast a name resolution packet across the network. With NetBIOS Internet On, default: 4. With NetBIOS Internet Off, default: 2. Values: 2 to 65,535.

- **Netbios broadcast delay *number*** Sets how many ticks NetBIOS waits between query or claim broadcasts. When multiplied by NetBIOS Broadcast Count number, sets the time required to broadcast a name resolution packet across the network. With NetBIOS Internet On, default: 36. With NetBIOS Internet Off, default: 18. Values: 18 to 65,535.

- **Netbios commands *number*** Specifies the number of NetBIOS commands that can be buffered in the NetBIOS driver at a time. Default: 12. Values: 4 to 250.

- **Netbios internet *on/off*** Speeds up packets when set to Off if you are using NetBIOS applications on a single network. If using multiple networks through bridges, leave On. Default: On.

- **Netbios listen timeout *number*** Sets the time NetBIOS waits before requesting another packet to make sure the connection is still valid. Default: 108 ticks (6 seconds). Values: 1 to 65,535 ticks.

- **Netbios receive buffers *number*** Sets the number of IPX receive buffers that NetBIOS uses. Default: 6. Values: 4 to 20.

- **Netbios retry count *number*** Specifies how many times NetBIOS resends a packet to establish a NetBIOS session with a remote partner. With NetBIOS Internet On, default: 20. With NetBIOS Internet Off, default: 10. Values: 4 to 20.

- **Netbios retry delay *number*** Specifies how long NetBIOS waits between sending packets to establish a session. Default: 10 ticks (0.5 seconds). Values: 10 to 65,535 ticks.

- **Netbios send buffers *number*** Sets the number of IPX send buffers that NetBIOS uses. Default: 6. Values: 4 to 250.

- **Netbios session *number*** Specifies the maximum number of simultaneous NetBIOS sessions. Default: 32. Values: 4 to 250.

- **Netbios verify timeout *number*** Sets the interval between packets sent to keep a connection open. Default: 54 ticks (3 seconds). Values: 4 to 65,535 ticks.

- **Npatch *offset*, *value*** Patches any location in the NETBIOS.EXE data segment with the specified value. *Offset* is the number of the data segment you want patched. *Value* is the number of the data segment with which you want to patch it.

NetWare DOS Requester Parameters

NetWare DOS Requester parameters configure the NetWare DOS Requester and VLM files.

To use these parameters, add the NetWare DOS Requester heading to the NET.CFG file, and then place each parameter command beneath the heading, indented as shown here.

```
NETWARE DOS REQUESTER
          parameter
```

The following parameters can be used with this heading:

- **Auto large table=*on/off*** When set to On, creates a connection table of 178 bytes per connection for bindery reconnects. When set to Off, creates a small table of 34 bytes. Default: Off.
- **Auto reconnect=*on/off*** When set to On, AUTO.VLM reconnects the workstation after a connection has been broken. Default: On. (You must also load AUTO.VLM and RSA.VLM. Bind Reconnect = On must also be set for bindery reconnections.)
- **Auto retry=*number*** Sets the time AUTO.VLM waits before retrying. Default: 0. Values: 0 (no retries) to 3640.
- **Average name length=*number*** Sets the average length of server names, which is used to create a table to store those names. Default: 48 characters. Values: 2 to 48 characters.
- **Bind reconnect=*on/off*** Rebuilds bindery connections after a connection has been broken. (You must also load AUTO.VLM, and Auto Reconnect = On must be set to make autoreconnection work.)
- **Broadcast retries=*number*** Specifies how many times the NetWare DOS Requester broadcasts a request. Default: 3. Values: 1 to 255.
- **Broadcast send delay=*number*** Specifies how long (in ticks) the NetWare DOS Requester waits before performing the next function. Default: 0 ticks. Values: 0 to 255 ticks.

- **Broadcast timeout=*number*** Specifies how long (in ticks) the NetWare DOS Requester waits between broadcast retries. Default: 2 ticks. Values: 1 to 255 ticks.

- **Cache buffers=*number*** Specifies the number of cache buffers used for local caching. Default: 5. Values: 0 to 64.

- **Cache buffers size=*number*** Sets the size of cache buffers used by FIO.VLM. Default: Media maximum minus 64 bytes. Values: 64 to 4096 bytes. See manufacturer's documentation for your media type's cache buffer size.

- **Cache writes=*on/off*** Specifies whether writes are cached. Default: On.

- **Checksum=*number*** Sets level at which NCP packets are validated. Default: 1. Values: 0 = disabled; 1 = enabled but not preferred; 2 = enabled and preferred; 3 = required.

- **Confirm critical error action=*on/off*** Specifies how network-critical error messages, intended for the NetWare DOS Requester, are handled by Windows. Default: On. Values: On = message displays the server that has lost the connection, and you are prompted to cancel or retry before Windows responds; Off = Windows may intercept critical errors and automatically respond to error messages intended for the NetWare DOS Requester.

- **Connections=*number*** Sets the maximum number of connections. Default: 8. Values: 2 to 50.

- **Dos name="*name*"** Specifies the name of DOS on the workstation. Enclose the *name* in quotation marks. Default: MSDOS.

- **Eoj=*on/off*** Determines whether files, locks, semaphores, and so on are automatically closed at the end of a job. Default: On.

- **Exclude vlm=*path\vlm*** Specifies a VLM file that should not load. Replace *path\vlm* with the path to and the name of the VLM you don't want to load.

- **First network drive=*letter*** Specifies which drive letter will be the first network drive. Default: First available. Values: A to Z.

- **Force first network drive=*on/off*** If set to On, ensures that, after the user logs out, the SYS:LOGIN directory is mapped to the same drive letter specified in the First Network Drive command. If set to Off, this command maps SYS:LOGIN to the drive letter from which the user logged out. Default: Off.

- **Handle net errors=*on/off*** Sets how network errors are handled. Default: On. Values: On = interrupt 24 handles errors; Off = NET_RECV_ERROR is returned.

- **Large internet packets=*on/off*** Allows maximum packet size to be used. Default: On.

- **Lip start size *number*** Sets the packet size used when starting LIP negotiations. Default: 0 (0 = Off). Values: 576 to 655535 bytes.

- **Load conn table low=*on/off*** Specifies whether the connection table is loaded in high or conventional memory. Set to On *only* if you are using the initial release of NetWare 4.0 utilities. Default: Off.

- **Load low conn=*on/off*** If set to Off, makes CONN.VLM load in upper memory, which saves memory but decreases performance. Default: On.

- **Load low ipxncp=*on/off*** If set to Off, makes IPXNCP.VLM load in upper memory, which saves memory but decreases performance. Default: On.

- **Load low redir=*on/off*** If set to Off, makes REDIR.VLM load in conventional memory, which increases performance but sacrifices memory. Default: Off.

- **Local printers=*number*** Tells the workstation how many local printers are attached. Default: 3. Values: 0 to 9. Set to 0 to prevent Shift-Print Screen from hanging the workstation if CAPTURE isn't in effect.

- **Lock delay=*number*** Specifies how long (in ticks) the NetWare DOS Requester waits before trying to get a lock. Default: 1 tick. Value: 0 to 255 ticks.

- **Lock retries=*number*** Specifies how many times the NetWare DOS Requester tries to get a lock on the network. Default: 1 tick. Values: 0 to 255 ticks.

- **Long machine type="*name*"** Specifies the type of computer being used. Enclose the *name* in quotation marks. Used by the %MACHINE variable in login script drive mappings. Default: IBM_PC.

- **Max tasks=*number*** Sets the maximum number of simultaneously active tasks. Default: 31. Values: 5 to 254.

- **Message level=*number*** Sets which messages are displayed during load. Default: 1. Values: 0 = copyright and critical errors; 1 = warning messages; 2 = load information for VLMs; 3 = configuration information; 4 = diagnostic information. (Each message level also displays the previous level's messages.)

- **Message timeout=*number*** Sets how long broadcast messages remain on the screen before being cleared. Default: 0 ticks. Values: 0 (wait for user intervention) to 10,000 ticks (9 minutes).

- **Minimum time to net=*number*** Overrides the time-to-net value defined by the local router during connections. Used on bridged WAN or satellite links with time-to-net values set too low for workstations to make a connection. Default: 0 milliseconds. Values: 1 to 65,535 milliseconds.

- **Name context="*context*"** Sets the user's current location, or context, in the NDS tree. Enclose the *context* in quotation marks. Default: The root of the NDS tree.

- **Netware protocol=*list*** Sets the order in which NetWare protocols (NDS, BIND, and PNW) are used. Lets you prioritize protocols for login or load order. Separate protocols by a comma or space. Default order: NDS BIND PNW.

- **Network printers=*number*** Specifies how many LPT ports can be captured. Default: 3. Values: 0 to 9. (If set to 0, PRINT.VLM will not load.)

- **Pb buffers=*number*** Turns Packet Burst on and off. Default: 3. Values: 0 (0 = Off) to 10.

- **Pburst read windows size=*number*** Specifies the read buffer size for Windows. Default: 16 bytes. Values: 3 to 128 bytes.

- **Pburst write windows size=*number*** Specifies the write buffer size for Windows. Default: 10 bytes. Values: 3 to 128 bytes.

- **Preferred server="*server*"** Specifies which server to attach to first. Enclose the *server* in quotation marks. Default: none.

- **Preferred tree="*tree*"** Specifies which Directory tree to attach to first. Enclose the *tree* in quotation marks. Default: none.

- **Preferred workgroup="*workgroup*"** Specifies which Personal NetWare workgroup to attach to first. Used only with Personal NetWare. Enclose the *workgroup* in quotation marks. Default: none.

- **Print buffer size=*number*** Sets the size for the print buffer. Default: 64 bytes. Values: 0 to 256 bytes.

- **Print header=*number*** Specifies the size of the buffer to hold initialization information for each print job. Default: 64 bytes. Values: 0 to 1024 bytes.

- **Print tail=*number*** Specifies the size of the buffer to hold reset information after a print job. Default: 16 bytes. Values: 0 to 1024 bytes.

- **Read only compatibility=*on/off*** If set to On, allows a read-only file to be opened with a read-write access call. Default: Off.

- **Responder=*on/off*** If set to Off, makes the workstation ignore broadcasts and diagnostic communication, which reduce the NetWare DOS Requester's use of conventional memory. Default: On.

- **Search mode=*number*** Sets the search mode for finding files in directories. Default: 1. Values: 0 to 7.

- **Set station time=*on/off*** If set to On, the workstation's time is synchronized to the time of the server to which it first attaches. Default: On.

- **Short machine type="*name*"** Sets the computer name to determine which overlay files to use. Enclose the *name* in quotation marks. Default: IBM.

- **Show dots=*on/off*** If set to On, displays dots (. and ..) for parent directories in Windows 3.x. Default: Off.

- **Signature level=*number*** Sets the level of NCP Packet Signature security. Default: 1. Values: 0 = no signing; 1 = signs if server requests; 2 = signs if server can sign; 3 = required.

- **True commit=*on/off*** Specifies whether the commit NCP is sent on DOS commit requests. Default: Off.

- **Use defaults=*on/off*** When set to Off, lets you override default loading of VLMs and specify exact files to load. Default: On.

- **Vlm=*path\vlm*** Loads a VLM file. Replace *path\vlm* with the path to and the name of the VLM you want to load.

- **Workgroup net=*address*** Specifies an address for a workgroup that resides on a network segment outside your local network. Used only with Personal NetWare. Change this parameter only with Personal NetWare utilities.

NetWare DOS TSA Parameters

NetWare DOS TSA parameters let you configure the DOS TSA (Target Service Agent) software. The DOS TSA lets you back up a DOS-based workstation using SBACKUP.NLM.

To use these parameters, add the NetWare DOS TSA heading to the NET.CFG file, and then place each parameter command beneath the heading, indented as shown here.

```
NETWARE DOS TSA
          parameter
```

The following parameters can be used with this heading:

- **Disk buffers *number*** Specifies the size of disk buffers. Default: 1 byte. Values: 1 to 30 bytes.
- **Drives *letter*** Specifies which hard disk drives are being managed by the TSA. Separate multiple drive letters with a space. Default: C.
- **Password *name*** Sets a unique password for the workstation. Default: none.
- **Stack size *number*** Sets the stack size for the TSA. Use only if the available RAM on the workstation is extremely limited. Default: 2048 bytes. Values: 512 to 4096 bytes.
- **Tsa server name *server*** Specifies the network server to which this workstation should attach.
- **Workstation name *name*** Identifies this workstation's unique name.

Protocol IPX Parameters

Protocol IPX parameters configure the IPX protocol.

To use these parameters, add the Protocol IPX heading to the NET.CFG file, and then place each parameter command beneath the heading, indented as shown here.

```
PROTOCOL IPX
         parameter
```

The following parameters can be used with this heading:

- **Bind *driver*** Binds the protocol to a LAN driver. *Driver* is the LAN driver name or logical board number.
- **Int64 *on/off*** If set to Off, allows an application to use interrupt 64h. Default: On.

- **Int7a *on/off*** If set to Off, allows an application to use interrupt 7Ah. Default: On.

- **Ipatch *offset, value*** Allows an address in IPXODI.COM to be patched with the specified byte offset value.

- **Ipx packet size limit *number*** Sets the maximum size of packets to reduce wasted memory. Default: 4160 bytes or the size specified by the LAN driver, if smaller. Values: 576 to 6500 bytes.

- **Ipx retry count *number*** Specifies the number of times a workstation resends a packet that failed. Default: 20.

- **Ipx sockets *number*** Sets the maximum number of sockets that IPX can have open. Default: 20.

Protocol ODINSUP Parameter

The Protocol ODINSUP parameter allows the NDIS protocol stack (used with Extended Services and LAN Services) to communicate using ODI Token Ring or Ethernet drivers.

To use this parameter, add the Protocol ODINSUP heading to the NET.CFG file, and then place the parameter command beneath the heading, indented as shown here.

```
PROTOCOL ODINSUP
          parameter
```

The following parameter can be used with this heading:

- **Bind *driver*** Binds the ODINSUP protocol to an ODI LAN driver. *Driver* is the Token Ring or Ethernet LAN driver name or logical board number.

Protocol RFCNBIOS Parameter

The Protocol RFCNBIOS parameter lets you configure RFCNBIOS, which implements the NetVIOS B-node protocols as defined in RFC 1001 and 1002.

To use this parameter, add the Protocol RFCNBIOS heading to the NET.CFG file, and then place the parameter command beneath the heading, indented as shown here.

```
PROTOCOL RFCNBIOS
          parameter
```

The following parameter can be used with this heading:

- **Remotename *number ip_address*** Specifies an IP address on a different broadcast network. This address is preloaded in the NetBIOS name cache. Replace *number* with the number of addresses that should be reloaded in the NetBIOS name cache. Replace *ip_address* with the IP (Internet Protocol) address assigned to this workstation.

Protocol RPL Parameters

Protocol RPL parameters configure the RPL protocol stack.

To use these parameters, add the Protocol RPL heading to the NET.CFG file, and then place each parameter command beneath the heading, indented as shown here.

```
PROTOCOL RPL
          parameter
```

The following parameters can be used with this heading:

- **Bind *driver*** Binds the protocol to an ODI LAN driver that uses the IEEE 802.2 frame type. Use only when running RPL on enhanced Remote Boot PROMs. *Driver* is the LAN driver name or logical board number. Default: RPL binds to the first Ethernet or Token Ring LAN driver it finds.

- **Buffers *number*** Sets the number of receive buffers to configure. Default: 5 buffers. Values: 4 to 40 buffers.

- **Cache size *number*** Specifies the maximum amount of memory to use for loading the BOOTCONF.SYS file. Default: none.

Protocol SPX Parameters

Protocol SPX parameters configure the SPX protocol.

To use these parameters, add the Protocol SPX heading to the NET.CFG file, and then place each parameter command beneath the heading, indented as shown here.

```
PROTOCOL SPX
          parameter
```

The following parameters can be used with this heading:

- **Minimum spx retries *number*** Sets the minimum number of unacknowledged transmit requests that occur before assuming the connection has failed. Default: 20. Values: 0 to 255.

- **Spx abort timeout *number*** Sets the time that SPX waits for a response before terminating a connection. Default: 540 ticks (30 seconds).

- **Spx connections *number*** Sets the maximum number of simultaneous SPX connections a workstation can have. Default: 15.

- **Spx listen timeout *number*** Sets the time that SPX waits for a packet before requesting another packet to make sure the connection is still valid. Default: 108 ticks (6 seconds).

- **Spx verify timeout *number*** Sets the interval between packets that SPX sends to verify a connection is working. Default: 54 ticks (3 seconds).

Protocol TCPIP Parameters

Protocol TCPIP parameters configure the TCP/IP protocol.

To use these parameters, add the Protocol TCPIP heading to the NET.CFG file, and then place each parameter command beneath the heading, indented as shown here.

```
PROTOCOL TCPIP
          parameter
```

The following parameters can be used with this heading:

- **Bind** ***driver*** **[*number frametype network*]** Binds the TCP/IP protocol to a LAN driver. *Driver* is the LAN driver name. *Number* is the board number when you have two boards with the same name. *Frametype* is the frame type for your network connection. *Network* is a descriptive name for this network connection.

- **Ip_address** ***address*** **[*name*]** Specifies this workstation's IP address. *Name* is a descriptive name for this network connection.

- **Ip_netmask** ***address*** **[*name*]** Specifies this workstation's default subnetwork mask if subnetworks are being used. *Name* is a descriptive name for this network connection.

- **Ip_router** ***address*** **[*name*]** Specifies the default router address for all packets being sent to remote networks. *Name* is a descriptive name for this network connection.

- **Nb_adapter [0 or 1]** Sets the network board to use when binding NetBIOS to the TCP/IP protocol stack. Default: 0. Values: 0 = first network board; 1 = second network board.

- **Nb_brdcast [0 or 1]** Sets the format of IP broadcasts sent by the RFCNBIOS.EXE program. Default: 1. Values: 0 = broadcast address uses zeros for the host portions of the IP address; 1 = broadcast address uses 255 for the host portions of the IP address.

- **Nb_commands *number*** Sets the maximum number of asynchronous NetBIOS commands. Default: 8. Values: 0 to 80.

- **Nb_domain *name*** Sets the name of the logical domain for a NetBIOS workstation.

- **Nb_sessions *number*** Specifies the maximum number of simultaneous NetBIOS sessions. Default: 4. Values: 0 to 64.

- **No_bootp** Forces the workstation to bypass any network BOOTP server (which provides TCP/IP configuration data) and use RARP (Reverse Address Resolution Protocol) to identify the workstation's IP address.

- **Path tcp_cfg *path*** Indicates the directories that contain the database configuration files HOSTS, NETWORKS, SERVICES, and RESOLV.CFG. This command works with the same syntax as the DOS PATH command. Default path: C:\NET\TCP.

- **Raw_sockets *number*** Sets the maximum number of raw IP sockets (connections). Default: 1.

- **Tcp_sockets *number*** Sets the maximum number of concurrent TCP (Transmission Control Protocol) sockets (connections). Default: 8. Values: 0 to 64.

- **Udp_sockets *number*** Sets the maximum number of UDP (User Datagram Protocol) sockets (connections). Default: 8. Values: 0 to 32.

TBMI2 Parameters

TBMI2 parameters configure the workstation's task-switching environment.

To use these parameters, add the TBMI2 heading to the NET.CFG file, and then place each parameter command beneath the heading, indented as shown here.

```
TBMI2
        parameter
```

The following parameters can be used with this heading:

- **Data ecb count *number*** Sets the number of data ECBs (event control blocks) allocated by DOS programs needing virtualization. Default: 60. Values: 10 to 89.
- **Ecb count *number*** Sets the number of nondata ECBs allocated by DOS programs needing virtualization. Default: 20. Values: 10 to 255.
- **Int64 *on/off*** If set to Off, allows an application to use interrupt 64h. Default: On.
- **Int7a *on/off*** If set to Off, allows an application to use interrupt 7Ah. Default: On.
- **Use max packets** Lets TBMI2 use the maximum IPX packet size.
- **Using windows 3.0** Lets TBMI2 use TASKID, which identifies tasks in each DOS BOX as separate tasks.

Transport Provider IPX (or UDP) Parameter

The Transport Provider parameter lets you specify the trap target address for SNMP desktops. The two Desktop SNMP transport providers, STPUDP.COM and STPIPX.COM, read the configuration file to find trap targets on the network.

To use this parameter, add either the Transport Provider IPX or Transport Provider UDP heading to the NET.CFG file, and then place the parameter command beneath the heading, indented as shown here. (The example shows the Transport Provider IPX heading.)

```
TRANSPORT PROVIDER IPX
          parameter
```

The following parameter can be used with this heading:

- **Trap target *address*** Specifies the management workstation address so that the workstation can receive traps sent by Desktop SNMP. Replace *address* with either the IPX address (for the IPX transport) or the IP address (for the UDP/IP transport) of the management workstation.

APPENDIX B

SET Parameters

When you first install NetWare 4.1, the operating system is tuned by default so that its performance is optimized for most systems. Occasionally, you may find that your system could benefit by a modification in some aspect of the server's operation.

For this reason, there are numerous parameters with which you can change the way the server handles things such as memory or file locks. These parameters, called SET parameters, can be set in three different ways:

- At the server console, using the SET console command. Parameters set this way are only in effect until the server is rebooted.
- In the server startup files, using STARTUP.NCF and AUTOEXEC.NCF. Parameters set in these files remain in effect when the server is rebooted.
- In SERVMAN.NLM, which allows you to select the parameters you want from menus instead of typing in complete SET commands at the console. SERVMAN.NLM can also automatically update the STARTUP.NCF and AUTOEXEC.NCF files.

In most cases, you probably will not need to change any SET parameters. However, should you need to change them, each SET parameter is explained in this appendix.

The thirteen categories of SET parameters are as follows:

- Communication
- Directory Caching
- Directory Services
- Disk
- Error Handling
- File Caching
- File System
- Locks

- Memory
- Miscellaneous
- NCP
- Time
- Transaction Tracking

The following sections explain the available SET parameters for each of these categories.

Communication Parameters

Communication parameters configure the way the operating system handles communication buffers. The following communication parameters are available:

- **Maximum packet receive buffers=*number*** Sets the maximum number of packet receive buffers the server can allocate. Default: 159. Values: 50 to 4000.

  Can be set in STARTUP.NCF, AUTOEXEC.NCF, or at the console.

- **Minimum packet receive buffers=*number*** Sets the minimum number of packet receive buffers that the server can allocate. This number is allocated automatically when the server is booted. Default: 50. Values: 10 to 2000.

  Can be set in STARTUP.NCF only.

- **Maximum physical receive packet size=*number*** Sets the largest size of packets that can be transmitted. Default size is acceptable for Ethernet and Token Ring boards. If some boards on the network can transmit more than 512 bytes of data per packet, use the largest packet size. Default: 4202 bytes. Values: 618 to 24682 bytes.

  Can be set in STARTUP.NCF only.

- **IPX netbios replication option=*number*** Sets how replicated NetBIOS broadcasts are handled by the IPX router. Default: 2. Values: 0 = no replication of broadcasts; 1 = replicate broadcasts (causes duplicate broadcasts when there are redundant routes); 2 = replicate broadcasts, but suppress duplicate broadcasts.

  Can be set in AUTOEXEC.NCF or at the console.

- **Maximum interrupt events=*number*** Sets the maximum number of interrupt time events (such as IPX routing) that occurs before a thread switch is guaranteed to have occurred. Default: 10. Values: 1 to 100000.

  Can be set in AUTOEXEC.NCF or at the console.

- **Reply to get nearest server=*on/off*** When set to On, this server will respond to workstations that request a connection to their nearest server. Default: On.

  Can be set in STARTUP.NCF, AUTOEXEC.NCF, or at the console.

- **Number of watchdog packets=*number*** Sets the number of watchdog packets the server sends to an unresponsive workstation before clearing the workstation's connection. Default: 10. Values: 5 to 100.

  Can be set in AUTOEXEC.NCF or at the console.

- **Delay between watchdog packets=*time*** Sets the time the server waits before sending each watchdog packet. Default: 59.3 seconds. Values: 9.9 seconds to 10 minutes, 26.2 seconds.

  Can be set in AUTOEXEC.NCF or at the console.

- **Delay before first watchdog packet=*time*** Sets the time the server waits before sending the first watchdog packet to an unresponsive workstation. Default: 4 minutes, 56.6 seconds. Values: 15.7 seconds to 14 days.

  Can be set in AUTOEXEC.NCF or at the console.

- **New packet receive buffer wait time=*seconds*** Sets the time the operating system waits after allocating the minimum number of buffers before granting the next packet receive buffer. Default: 0.1 second. Values: 0.1 to 20 seconds.

  Can be set in AUTOEXEC.NCF or at the console.

- **Console display watchdog logouts=*on/off*** When set to On, a console message is displayed when a workstation's connection is cleared by the watchdog. Default: Off.

  Can be set in AUTOEXEC.NCF or at the console.

Directory Caching Parameters

Directory Caching parameters allow you to configure how directory cache buffers are used to optimize access to frequently used directories. A *directory cache buffer* is a portion of server memory that holds a directory entry that is being accessed frequently. A directory entry held in memory is accessed faster than a directory entry stored on the hard disk. The following Directory Caching parameters are available:

- **Dirty directory cache delay time=*seconds*** Specifies how long a directory table write request is kept in memory before it is written to disk. Default: 0.5 seconds. Values: 0 to 10 seconds.

  Can be set in AUTOEXEC.NCF or at the console.

- **Maximum concurrent directory cache writes=*number*** Sets the maximum number of write requests that can be stored before the disk head begins a sweep across the disk. Default: 10. Values: 5 to 50.

  Can be set in AUTOEXEC.NCF or at the console.

- **Directory cache allocation wait time=*time*** Specifies how long the server waits after allocating one directory cache buffer before allocating another one. Default: 2.2 seconds. Values: 0.5 seconds to 2 minutes.

  Can be set in AUTOEXEC.NCF or at the console.

- **Directory cache buffer nonreferenced delay=*time*** Sets how long a directory entry is held in cache before it is overwritten. Default: 5.5 seconds. Values: 1 second to 5 minutes.

  Can be set in AUTOEXEC.NCF or at the console.

- **Maximum directory cache buffers=*number*** Sets the maximum number of directory cache buffers that the server can allocate. Prevents the server from allocating so many directory cache buffers that other server processes run out. Default: 500. Values: 20 to 4000.

  Can be set in AUTOEXEC.NCF or at the console.

- **Minimum directory cache buffers=*number*** Sets the minimum number of directory cache buffers to be allocated by the server before the server uses the Directory Cache Allocation Wait Time to determine if another directory cache buffer should be allocated. Allocating buffers too quickly will cause the server to eat up memory resources during peak loads. Waiting too long may cause a delay in file searches. This wait time creates a leveling factor between peak and low access times. Default: 20. Values: 10 to 2000.

  Can be set in AUTOEXEC.NCF or at the console.

- **Maximum number of internal directory handles=*number*** Sets the maximum number of directory handles that are available to internal NLMs that use connection 0. A directory handle is allocated each time an NLM accesses a file or directory. Allocating directory handles decreases the time required to gain access rights. Default: 100. Values: 40 to 1000.

  Can be set in STARTUP.NCF or at the console.

- **Maximum number of directory handles=*number*** Sets the maximum number of directory handles that each connection can obtain. Default: 20. Values: 20 to 1000.

  Can be set in STARTUP.NCF or at the console.

Directory Services Parameters

Directory Services parameters allow you to configure NDS maintenance characteristics. The following NDS parameters are available:

- **NDS trace to screen=*on/off*** When set to On, the NDS trace screen, which displays information about NDS events, is turned on. Default: Off.

  Can be set in AUTOEXEC.NCF or at the console.

- **NDS trace to file=*on/off*** When set to On, the NDS trace information is sent to a file in the SYS:SYSTEM directory, named DSTRACE.DBG by default. Default: Off.

  Can be set in AUTOEXEC.NCF or at the console.

- **NDS trace filename=*path\filename*** Specifies a different path or file name for the NDS trace file.

  Can be set in AUTOEXEC.NCF or at the console.

- **NDS client NCP retries=*number*** Sets the number of NCP retries that are sent before the NDS client is disconnected from a connection. Default: 3. Values: 1 to 20.

  Can be set in AUTOEXEC.NCF or at the console.

- **NDS external reference life span=*hours*** Sets the number of hours that unused external references (local IDs assigned to users when they access other servers) can exist before they are removed. Default: 192 hours. Values: 1 to 384 hours.

  Can be set in AUTOEXEC.NCF or at the console.

- **NDS inactivity synchronization interval=*minutes*** Sets how much time can elapse between exhaustive synchronization checks. Set high (up to 240 minutes) if replicas have to synchronize across WAN connections to reduce network traffic. Default: 30 minutes. Values: 2 to 1440 minutes.

  Can be set in AUTOEXEC.NCF or at the console.

- **NDS synchronization restrictions=*on/off*, *versions*** When set to Off, the server synchronizes with all versions of NDS that are available on the network. When this parameter is turned On, the server synchronizes only with the versions of NDS specified. Default: On.

  Can be set in AUTOEXEC.NCF or at the console.

- **NDS servers status=*up/down*** Sets the status of all Server objects in the local NDS database as either up or down, so that you can force the network to recognize that a particular server is up when the network thinks it is down. Default: none.

  Can be set in AUTOEXEC.NCF or at the console.

- **NDS janitor interval=*minutes*** Specifies how often the janitor process runs. The janitor process cleans up unused records, reclaims disk space, and purges deleted objects. Default: 60 minutes. Values: 1 to 10080 minutes.

  Can be set in AUTOEXEC.NCF or at the console.

- **NDS backlink interval=*minutes*** Specifies how often backlink consistency is checked. Backlinks indicate that an object in a replica has an ID on a server where the replica does not exist. Default: 780 minutes. Values: 2 to 10080 minutes.

  Can be set in AUTOEXEC.NCF or at the console.

- **NDS trace file length to zero=*on/off*** When set to On, the server deletes the contents of the NDS trace file (but does not delete the trace file itself). To delete the file contents, also set the NDS Trace to File parameter to On, so that the file will be open for the deletion process. Default: Off.

  Can be set in AUTOEXEC.NCF or at the console.

- **Bindery context=*context;context;...*** Specifies which containers and their objects will be used as the server's "bindery" when the server provides bindery services. You can include up to 16 containers as part of this server's bindery context. Separate each context with a semicolon. Default: The bindery context set for this server during installation, if one was set.

  Can be set in STARTUP.NCF or at the console.

Disk Parameters

Disk parameters allow you to control Hot Fix redirection, which helps protect data on the server from hard disk failures. The following Disk parameters are available:

- **Enable disk read after write verify=*on/off*** Specifies whether data written to disk is compared with the data in memory to verify its accuracy. If set to On, this parameter tells the driver to perform the highest level of read-after-write verification that it can. If set to Off, this parameter turns off any form of read-after-write verification that the driver may do. The disk controller may have a built-in function that performs read-after-write verification. If so, set this parameter to Off. Default: On.

  Can be set in STARTUP.NCF, AUTOEXEC.NCF, or at the console.

- **Remirror block size=*number*** Specifies the remirror block size in multiples of 4K. Default: 1 (4K). Values: 1 to 8 (1 = 4K, 2 = 8K, 3 = 12K, and so on).

  Can be set in AUTOEXEC.NCF or at the console.

- **Concurrent remirror requests=*number*** Specifies how many simultaneous remirror requests can occur per logical disk partition. Default: 4. Values: 2 to 32.

  Can be set in STARTUP.NCF only.

- **Mirrored devices are out of sync message frequency=*minutes*** Specifies how often devices are checked for out-of-sync status. Default: 30 minutes. Values: 5 to 9999 minutes.

  Can be set in STARTUP.NCF, AUTOEXEC.NCF, or at the console.

Error Handling Parameters

Error Handling parameters let you manage the server, volume, and TTS error log files. The server log file is named SYS$LOG.ERR. The volume log file is named VOL$LOG.ERR. The TTS log file is named TTS$LOG.ERR. The following parameters are available:

- **Server log file state=*number*** Specifies what action to take when the log file reaches its maximum size. Default: 1. Values: 0 = take no action; 1 = delete the log file; 2 = rename the log file.

  Can be set in STARTUP.NCF, AUTOEXEC.NCF, or at the console.

- **Volume log file state=*number*** Specifies what action to take when the log file reaches its maximum size. Default: 1. Values: 0 = take no action; 1 = delete the log file; 2 = rename the log file.

  Can be set in STARTUP.NCF, AUTOEXEC.NCF, or at the console.

- **Volume TTS log file state=*number*** Specifies what action to take when the log file reaches its maximum size. Default: 1. Values: 0 = take no action; 1 = delete the log file; 2 = rename the log file.

  Can be set in STARTUP.NCF, AUTOEXEC.NCF, or at the console.

- **Server log file overflow size=*number*** Specifies the maximum size of the log file. Default: 4194304 bytes. Values: 65536 to 4294967295 bytes.

  Can be set in STARTUP.NCF, AUTOEXEC.NCF, or at the console.

- **Volume log file overflow size=*number*** Specifies the maximum size of the log file. Default: 4194304 bytes. Values: 65536 to 4294967295 bytes.

  Can be set in STARTUP.NCF, AUTOEXEC.NCF, or at the console.

- **Volume TTS log file overflow size=*number*** Specifies the maximum size of the log file. Default: 4194304 bytes. Values: 65536 to 4294967295 bytes.

  Can be set in STARTUP.NCF, AUTOEXEC.NCF, or at the console.

File Caching Parameters

File Caching parameters allow you to configure how file cache buffers are used to optimize access to frequently used files. A *file cache buffer* is a portion of server memory that holds a file or portion of a file that is being accessed frequently. A file in memory is accessed faster than a file on the hard disk. The following File Caching parameters are available:

- **Read ahead enabled=*on/off*** When set to On, background reads are allowed to be done during sequential file access so that blocks are placed into the cache before they are requested. Default: On.

  Can be set in AUTOEXEC.NCF or at the console.

- **Read ahead LRU sitting time threshold=*time*** Sets the time the server will wait before doing a read ahead. (LRU means Least Recently Used.) Default: 10 seconds. Values: 0 seconds to 1 hour.

  Can be set in AUTOEXEC.NCF or at the console.

- **Minimum file cache buffers=*number*** Sets the minimum number of cache buffers that must be reserved for file caching. Default: 20. Values: 20 to 1000.

  Can be set in AUTOEXEC.NCF or at the console.

- **Maximum concurrent disk cache writes=*number*** Sets the maximum number of write requests that can be stored before the disk head begins a sweep across the disk. Default: 50. Values: 10 to 4000.

  Can be set in AUTOEXEC.NCF or at the console.

- **Dirty disk cache delay time=*seconds*** Sets how long the server will keep a write request in memory before writing it to the disk. Default: 3.3 seconds. Values: 0.1 to 10 seconds.

  Can be set in AUTOEXEC.NCF or at the console.

- **Minimum file cache report threshold=*number*** Sets how close to the minimum number of allowed buffers the system can drop before a warning message is sent. Default: 20. Values: 0 to 1000.

  Can be set in AUTOEXEC.NCF or at the console.

File System Parameters

File System parameters allow you to configure aspects of the file system, such as volume disk space warnings, file purging, and file compression. The following parameters are available:

- **Minimum file delete wait time=*time*** Specifies how long a deleted file must be stored before it can be purged. Default: 1 minute, 5.9 seconds. Values: 0 seconds to 7 days.

  Can be set in AUTOEXEC.NCF or at the console.

- **File delete wait time=*time*** Sets the maximum amount of time a deleted file must be stored in a salvageable state. After this time has elapsed, the file can be purged if the space is needed. Default: 5 minutes, 29.6 seconds. Values: 0 seconds to 7 days.

  Can be set in AUTOEXEC.NCF or at the console.

- **Allow deletion of active directories=*on/off*** When set to On, a directory can be deleted even if a user has a drive mapped to it. Default: On.

  Can be set in AUTOEXEC.NCF or at the console.

- **Maximum percent of volume space allowed for extended attributes=*number*** Limits the amount of disk space that can be used to store extended attributes. Default: 10 percent. Values: 5 to 50 percent.

  Can be set in STARTUP.NCF, AUTOEXEC.NCF, or at the console.

- **Maximum extended attributes per file or path=*number*** Specifies the maximum number of extended attributes that can be assigned to a file or a subdirectory (path) on any of the server's volumes. Default: 16. Values: 4 to 512.

  Can be set in AUTOEXEC.NCF or at the console.

- **Maximum percent of volume used by directory=*number*** Limits the amount of disk space that can be used as directory space. Default: 13 percent. Values: 5 to 50 percent.

  Can be set in AUTOEXEC.NCF or at the console.

- **Immediate purge of deleted files=*on/off*** Specifies whether files are purged immediately when they are deleted or stored in a salvageable state. If turned On, this parameter purges deleted files immediately, and they cannot be salvaged. Default: Off.

  Can be set in AUTOEXEC.NCF or at the console.

- **Maximum subdirectory tree depth=*number*** Sets the maximum level of subdirectories the server can support. Default: 25. Values: 10 to 100.

  Can be set in STARTUP.NCF only.

- **Volume low warn all users=*on/off*** When set to On, all users are notified when the free space on a volume reaches a minimum level. Default: On.

  Can be set in AUTOEXEC.NCF or at the console.

- **Volume low warning reset threshold=*number*** Specifies the number of disk blocks above the Volume Low Warning Threshold value that must be freed up to reset the low volume warning. This parameter controls how often you receive the low volume warning if your free space is fluctuating around the threshold. Default: 256 blocks. Values: 0 to 100000 blocks.

  Can be set in AUTOEXEC.NCF or at the console.

- **Volume low warning threshold=*number*** Sets the minimum amount of free space (in blocks) that a volume can have before it issues a warning that it is low on space. Default: 256 blocks. Values: 0 to 1000000 blocks.

  Can be set in AUTOEXEC.NCF or at the console.

- **Turbo FAT re-use wait time=*time*** Sets how long a turbo FAT (File Allocation Table) buffer stays in memory after an indexed file is closed. Default: 5 minutes, 29.6 seconds. Values: 0.3 seconds to 1 hour, 5 minutes, 54.6 seconds.

  Can be set in AUTOEXEC.NCF or at the console.

- **Compression daily check stop hour=*hour*** Specifies the hour when the file compressor stops searching volumes for files that need to be compressed. If this value is the same as the Compression Daily Check Starting Hour value, then the search starts at the specified starting hour and goes until all compressable files have been found. Default: 6 (6:00 a.m.). Values: 0 (midnight) to 23 (11:00 p.m.).

  Can be set in STARTUP.NCF, AUTOEXEC.NCF, or at the console.

- **Compression daily check starting hour=*hour*** Specifies the hour when the file compressor begins searching volumes for files that need to be compressed. Default: 0 (midnight). Values: 0 to 23 (11:00 p.m.).

  Can be set in STARTUP.NCF, AUTOEXEC.NCF, or at the console.

- **Minimum compression percentage gain=*number*** Specifies the minimum percentage that a file must be able to be compressed in order to remain compressed. Default: 2 percent. Values: 0 to 50 percent.

  Can be set in STARTUP.NCF, AUTOEXEC.NCF, or at the console.

- **Enable file compression=*on/off*** When set to On, file compression is allowed to occur on volumes that are enabled for compression. Default: On.

  Can be set in STARTUP.NCF, AUTOEXEC.NCF, or at the console.

- **Maximum concurrent compressions=*number*** Specifies how many volumes can be compressing files at the same time. Increasing this value may slow down server performance during compression times. Default: 2. Values: 1 to 8.

  Can be set in STARTUP.NCF, AUTOEXEC.NCF, or at the console.

- **Convert compressed to uncompressed option=*number*** Specifies how a compressed file is stored after it has been accessed. Default: 1. Values: 0 = always leave the file compressed; 1 = leave the file compressed after the first access. Leave the file uncompressed after the second access. 2 = leave the file uncompressed after the first access.

  Can be set in STARTUP.NCF, AUTOEXEC.NCF, or at the console.

- **Decompress percent disk space free to allow commit=*number*** Specifies the percentage of free disk space that is required on a volume before committing an uncompressed file to disk. This helps you avoid running out of disk space by uncompressing files. Default: 10 percent. Values: 0 to 100 percent.

  Can be set in STARTUP.NCF, AUTOEXEC.NCF, or at the console.

- **Decompress free space warning interval=*time*** Specifies the interval between warnings when the volume doesn't have enough disk space for uncompressed files. Default: 31 minutes, 18.5 seconds. Values: 0 seconds (which turns off warnings) to 29 days, 15 hours, 50 minutes, 3.8 seconds.

  Can be set in STARTUP.NCF, AUTOEXEC.NCF, or at the console.

- **Deleted files compression option=*number*** Specifies how the server handles deleted files. Default: 1. Values: 0 = don't compress deleted files; 1 = compress deleted files during the next day's search; 2 = compress deleted files immediately.

  Can be set in STARTUP.NCF, AUTOEXEC.NCF, or at the console.

- **Days untouched before compression=*days*** Specifies how many days a file or directory must remain untouched before being compressed. Default: 7. Values: 0 to 100000.

  Can be set in STARTUP.NCF, AUTOEXEC.NCF, or at the console.

- **Allow unowned files to be extended=*on/off*** When set to On, files can be changed even if their owner has been deleted. Default: On.

  Can be set in STARTUP.NCF, AUTOEXEC.NCF, or at the console.

Locks Parameters

Locks parameters allow you to configure how workstations and the server work with file and record locks. The following parameters are available:

- **Maximum record locks per connection=*number*** Sets the number of record locks a workstation can use simultaneously. Default: 500. Values: 10 to 100000.

  Can be set in AUTOEXEC.NCF or at the console.

- **Maximum file locks per connection=*number*** Sets the number of opened and locked files a workstation can use simultaneously. Default: 250. Values: 10 to 1000.

  Can be set in AUTOEXEC.NCF or at the console.

- **Maximum record locks=*number*** Sets the number of record locks the server can support simultaneously. Default: 20000. Values: 100 to 400000.

  Can be set in AUTOEXEC.NCF or at the console.

- **Maximum file locks=*number*** Sets how many opened and locked files the server can support simultaneously. Default: 10000. Values: 100 to 100000.

  Can be set in AUTOEXEC.NCF or at the console.

Memory Parameters

Memory parameters allow you to configure how the server's memory is managed. The following parameters are available:

- **Allow invalid pointers=*on/off*** When set to On, invalid pointers are allowed to map in a nonexistent page with only one notification. Default: Off.

  Can be set in STARTUP.NCF, AUTOEXEC.NCF, or at the console.

- **Read fault notification=*on/off*** When set to On, the console and error log file are notified of emulated read page faults. Default: On.

  Can be set in STARTUP.NCF, AUTOEXEC.NCF, or at the console.

- **Read fault emulation=*on/off*** When set to On, specifies that a read that occurs from a nonpresent page should be emulated. Default: Off.

  Can be set in STARTUP.NCF, AUTOEXEC.NCF, or at the console.

- **Write fault notification=*on/off*** When set to On, the console and error log file are notified of emulated write page faults. Default: On.

  Can be set in STARTUP.NCF, AUTOEXEC.NCF, or at the console.

- **Write fault emulation=*on/off*** When set to On, specifies that a write that occurs from a nonpresent page should be emulated. Default: Off.

  Can be set in STARTUP.NCF, AUTOEXEC.NCF, or at the console.

- **Garbage collection interval=*time*** Sets the maximum time between garbage collections. Default: 15 minutes. Values: 1 minute to 1 hour.

  Can be set in STARTUP.NCF, AUTOEXEC.NCF, or at the console.

- **Number of frees for garbage collection=*number*** Sets the minimum number of times memory must be freed up before a garbage collection can occur. Default: 5000. Values: 100 to 100000.

Can be set in STARTUP.NCF, AUTOEXEC.NCF, or at the console.

- **Minimum free memory for garbage collection=*number*** Sets the fewest number of free allocation bytes required for garbage collection. Default: 8000 bytes. Values: 1000 to 1000000 bytes.

  Can be set in STARTUP.NCF, AUTOEXEC.NCF, or at the console.

- **Alloc memory check flag=*on/off*** When set to On, the server is set to do corruption checking in the alloc memory nodes. Default: Off.

  Can be set in STARTUP.NCF, AUTOEXEC.NCF, or at the console.

- **Auto register memory above 16 megabytes=*on/off*** When set to On, the server automatically adds memory above 16MB that can be detected on EISA-bus computers. This parameter should be set to Off if you are using a network board or disk controller board that uses an online DMS or AT bus. Default: On.

  Can be set in STARTUP.NCF only.

- **Reserved buffers below 16 meg=*number*** Sets a number of cache buffers in lower memory for device drivers that cannot access memory above 16MB. Default: 16. Values: 8 to 300.

  Can be set in STARTUP.NCF only.

Miscellaneous Parameters

The Miscellaneous parameters set a variety of server options. The following parameters are available:

- **Sound bell for alerts=*on/off*** When set to On, a sound emits whenever an alert message appears on the server's console screen. Default: On.

  Can be set in AUTOEXEC.NCF or at the console.

- **Replace console prompt with server name=*on/off*** When set to On, the server's name is displayed on the server's screen instead of the normal console prompt (:). Default: On.

  Can be set in STARTUP.NCF, AUTOEXEC.NCF, or at the console.

- **Alert message nodes=*number*** Determines how many alert message nodes are preallocated. Default: 20. Values: 10 to 256.

  Can be set in STARTUP.NCF, AUTOEXEC.NCF, or at the console.

- **Worker thread execute in a row count=*number*** Determines how many times in a row the scheduler dispatches new work before allowing other threads to execute. Default: 10. Values: 1 to 20.

  Can be set in AUTOEXEC.NCF or at the console.

- **Halt system on invalid parameters=*on/off*** When set to On, the system stops whenever invalid parameters or conditions are detected. When this parameter is set to Off, the system displays an alert message but continues running if an invalid parameter is detected. Default: Off.

  Can be set in STARTUP.NCF, AUTOEXEC.NCF, or at the console.

- **Upgrade low priority threads=*on/off*** When set to On, low-priority threads are scheduled at regular priority. Some modules can freeze low-priority threads, which may cause problems such as shutting down file compression. Default: Off.

  Can be set in AUTOEXEC.NCF or at the console.

- **Display relinquish control alerts=*on/off*** When set to On, messages are displayed when an NLM uses the server's processor for more than 0.4 seconds without giving up control to other processes. This command is useful if you are writing your own NLMs and want to see if your NLM is using the CPU correctly. Default: Off.

  Can be set in STARTUP.NCF, AUTOEXEC.NCF, or at the console.

- **Display incomplete IPX packet alerts=*on/off*** When set to On, alert messages are displayed when IPX receives incomplete packets. Default: On.

  Can be set in STARTUP.NCF, AUTOEXEC.NCF, or at the console.

- **Display old API names=*on/off*** When set to On, messages are displayed when old NetWare 3.0 API calls are used by an NLM. If you receive these messages, you may want to contact the NLM's manufacturer for an upgrade that uses the faster, newer APIs. Default: Off.

  Can be set in STARTUP.NCF, AUTOEXEC.NCF, or at the console.

- **Developer option=*on/off*** When set to On, options that are associated with a developer environment are enabled. Default: Off.

  Can be set in STARTUP.NCF, AUTOEXEC.NCF, or at the console.

- **Display spurious interrupt alerts=*on/off*** When set to On, error messages are displayed when the server hardware creates an interrupt that has been reserved for another device's interface board. If you receive this error, remove all add-on boards and run SERVER.EXE (the NetWare operating system). If the message doesn't appear, add the boards one at a time, until you locate the board that is generating the message. Then contact the board's vendor or manufacturer for assistance. Default: On.

  Can be set in STARTUP.NCF, AUTOEXEC.NCF, or at the console.

- **Display lost interrupt alerts=*on/off*** When set to On, error messages are displayed when a driver or board makes an interrupt call but drops the request before it's filled. To identify the problem driver, unload all drivers, and then reload them one at a time. When you locate the driver that is generating the message, contact the driver's manufacturer. Default: On.

  Can be set in STARTUP.NCF, AUTOEXEC.NCF, or at the console.

- **Pseudo preemption count=*number*** Sets how many times threads can make file read or write system calls before they are forced to relinquish control. Default: 10. Values: 1 to 4294967295.

  Can be set in AUTOEXEC.NCF or at the console.

- **Global pseudo preemption=*on/off*** When set to On, all threads are forced to use pseudo preemption. Default: Off.

  Can be set in AUTOEXEC.NCF or at the console.

- **Maximum service processes=*number*** Sets the maximum number of service processes the server can create. Increase this parameter if the number of service processes (as shown in MONITOR.NLM) is at the maximum. Default: 40. Values: 5 to 100.

  Can be set in AUTOEXEC.NCF or at the console.

- **New service process wait time=*seconds*** Determines how long the server waits to allocate another service process after receiving an NCP request. If a service process is freed up during this time, a new one will not be allocated. Default: 2.2 seconds. Values: 0.3 to 20 seconds.

  Can be set in AUTOEXEC.NCF or at the console.

- **Automatically repair bad volumes=*on/off*** When set to On, VREPAIR will run automatically on a volume that fails to mount. Default: On.

  Can be set in STARTUP.NCF, AUTOEXEC.NCF, or at the console.

- **Allow unencrypted passwords=*on/off*** When set to On, the server will accept unencrypted passwords. Only turn on this parameter if your network includes servers running NetWare 2.11 or earlier versions of NetWare. If you have servers running NetWare 2.12 or 2.2, copy the NetWare 3.1x utilities to those servers and leave this parameter off, so that passwords will be encrypted. Default: Off.

  Can be set in AUTOEXEC.NCF or at the console.

NCP Parameters

NCP (NetWare Core Protocol) parameters allow you to configure NCP packets, control boundary checking, and change NCP Packet Signature security levels on the server. The following parameters are available:

- **NCP file commit=*on/off*** When set to On, an application is allowed to issue a File Commit NCP and flush the file immediately from cache to disk. Default: On.

  Can be set in AUTOEXEC.NCF or at the console.

- **Display NCP bad component warnings=*on/off*** When set to On, NCP bad component alert messages are displayed. Default: Off.

  Can be set in STARTUP.NCF, AUTOEXEC.NCF, or at the console.

- **Reject NCP packets with bad component=*on/off*** When set to On, the server rejects NCP packets that fail component checking. Default: Off.

  Can be set in STARTUP.NCF, AUTOEXEC.NCF, or at the console.

- **Display NCP bad length warnings=*on/off*** When set to On, NCP bad-length alert messages are displayed. Default: Off.

  Can be set in STARTUP.NCF, AUTOEXEC.NCF, or at the console.

- **Reject NCP packets with bad lengths=*on/off*** When set to On, the server rejects NCP packets that fail boundary checking. Default: Off.

  Can be set in STARTUP.NCF, AUTOEXEC.NCF, or at the console.

- **Maximum outstanding NCP searches=*number*** Determines the maximum number of NCP directory searches that can be performed at the same time. Default: 51. Values: 10 to 1000.

  Can be set in AUTOEXEC.NCF or at the console.

- **NCP packet signature option=*number*** Sets the server's NCP Packet Signature security level. See Chapter 7 for more information about NCP Packet Signature levels. Default: 1. Values: 0 to 3.

  Can be set in STARTUP.NCF, AUTOEXEC.NCF, or at the console.

- **Enable IPX checksums=*number*** Sets the IPX checksum level. Default: 1. Values: 0 = no checksums; 1 = checksums performed if enabled on the client; 2 = checksums required.

  Can be set in STARTUP.NCF, AUTOEXEC.NCF, or at the console.

- **Allow change to client rights=*on/off*** When set to On, a job server is allowed to assume a client's rights for NCP Packet Signature. If you are concerned that a job or print server may forge packets, turn this parameter to Off. Default: On.

  Can be set in STARTUP.NCF, AUTOEXEC.NCF, or at the console.

- **Allow LIP=*on/off*** When set to On, support for Large Internet Packets is enabled. Default: On.

  Can be set in STARTUP.NCF, AUTOEXEC.NCF, or at the console.

Time Parameters

Initially, you set up time services on the server during installation. Time services are controlled by TIMESYNC.NLM, which is loaded automatically when the server is started up. To modify time synchronization after installation, you can use the Time and Time Synchronization SET parameters.

Depending on which time-related SET parameters you are modifying, you may need to add them to either AUTOEXEC.NCF or to the time synchronization file, TIMESYNC.CFG, if you want them to be in effect when the server is rebooted.

All SET parameters that start with the word "TIMESYNC" must be added to the TIMESYNC.CFG file. The others can be added to AUTOEXEC.NCF. With most of the parameters, you can modify the appropriate file using SERVMAN.NLM, but a few of the parameters must be added directly to TIMESYNC.CFG using EDIT.NLM instead of SERVMAN. This information is indicated in the list shown here.

The following parameters are available:

- **Timesync add time source=*server*** Specifies which server should be used as a time source.

  Can be set in TIMESYNC.CFG only, using either SERVMAN or EDIT.

- **Timesync configuration file=*path\filename*** Specifies the directory and file name of the time synchronization configuration file, if it is not SYS:SYSTEM\TIMESYNC.CFG.

  Can be set in TIMESYNC.CFG only, using either SERVMAN or EDIT.

- **Timesync configured sources=*on/off*** When set to On, the server ignores SAP (Service Advertising Protocol) time sources and instead accepts time sources configured with the TIMESYNC Time Source parameter. When this parameter is turned Off, it causes the server to listen to any advertising time source. Default: Off.

  Can be set in TIMESYNC.CFG only, using either SERVMAN or EDIT.

- **Timesync directory tree mode=*on/off*** When set to On, time synchronization ignores SAP (Service Advertising Protocol) packets that don't originate from within the server's Directory tree. When this parameter is set to Off, the server accepts SAP packets from any time source on the network, regardless of the tree from which it originates. If SAP is turned on, this parameter should also be set to On. Default: On.

  Can be set in TIMESYNC.CFG only, using either SERVMAN or EDIT.

- **Timesync hardware clock=*on/off*** When set to On, Primary and Secondary time servers set the hardware clock, and Single Reference and Reference servers set their time from the hardware clock at the start of each polling interval. Only set this parameter to Off if this server uses an external time source such as a radio clock. Default: On.

  Can be set in TIMESYNC.CFG only, using either SERVMAN or EDIT.

- **Timesync polling count=*number*** Determines the number of time packets to exchange while polling. Increasing this number may increase unnecessary traffic on the network. Default: 3. Values: 1 to 1000.

  Can be set in TIMESYNC.CFG only, using either SERVMAN or EDIT.

- **Timesync polling interval=*time*** Determines the polling interval, in seconds. All servers in the tree must use the same polling interval. Default: 600 seconds. Values: 10 to 2678400 seconds (31 days).

  Can be set in TIMESYNC.CFG only, using either SERVMAN or EDIT.

- **Timesync remove time source=*server*** Removes a server from the time source list, thus preventing it from being a time source.

  Can be set in TIMESYNC.CFG only, using EDIT.NLM only.

- **Timesync reset=*on/off*** When set to On, all servers are removed from the time source list, and time synchronization is reset. The parameter automatically resets itself to Off. Default: Off.

  Can be set in TIMESYNC.CFG only, using EDIT.NLM only.

- **Timesync restart flag=*on/off*** When set to On, you can reload TIMESYNC.NLM without rebooting the server. Default: Off.

  Can be set in TIMESYNC.CFG only, using either SERVMAN or EDIT.

- **Timesync service advertising=*on/off*** When set to On, SAP (Service Advertising Protocol) is turned on, meaning Single Reference, Reference, and Primary time sources advertise using SAP. Only set this parameter to Off if you are configuring a custom list of time sources. Default: On.

  Can be set in TIMESYNC.CFG only, using either SERVMAN or EDIT.

- **Timesync synchronization radius=*time*** Determines the maximum time (in milliseconds) that a server is allowed to vary from the synchronized time while still being considered synchronized. Do not set this parameter for under 2 seconds (2000 milliseconds) unless you have an application that uses synchronized time stamps that will not tolerate a 2-second deviation between time sources. Default: 2000 milliseconds. Values: 0 to 2147483647 milliseconds.

  Can be set in TIMESYNC.CFG only, using either SERVMAN or EDIT.

- **Timesync time adjustment=*+or- hour:minute:second* [*at month/day/year hour:minute:second*]** Determines when a time adjustment will take place. This parameter does not apply to Secondary time servers. Use sparingly to correct networkwide time errors. Overuse can corrupt time synchronization. The default date and time is six polling intervals or one hour (whichever is longer) from the current time. Default: None scheduled.

  Can be set in TIMESYNC.CFG only, using either SERVMAN or EDIT.

- **Timesync time source=*server*** Specifies a server as a time source. If used at the console, and no server name is entered, the parameter displays the list of configured servers.

  Can be set in TIMESYNC.CFG only, using either SERVMAN or EDIT.

- **Timesync type=*type*** Specifies the type (Reference, Primary, etc.) of the default time source. Default: Single (for Single Reference). Values: Single, Reference, Primary, Secondary.

  Can be set in TIMESYNC.CFG only, using either SERVMAN or EDIT.

- **Timesync write parameters=*on/off*** When set to On, parameters specified by the TIMESYNC Write Value parameter are written to the TIMESYNC.CFG file. Default: Off.

  Can be set in TIMESYNC.CFG only, using either SERVMAN or EDIT.

- **Timesync write value=*number*** Specifies which parameters are written by the TIMESYNC Write Parameters parameter to the TIMESYNC.CFG file. Default: 3. Values: 1 = write internal parameters only; 2 = write configured time sources only; 3 = write both parameters and configured time sources.

  Can be set in TIMESYNC.CFG only, using either SERVMAN or EDIT.

- **Time zone=*zone*** Specifies the abbreviation for this server's time zone, its offset from UTC (Universal Coordinated Time, which used to be called Greenwich Mean Time), and the abbreviation for this server's time zone that is used when daylight saving time is in effect. Example: *zone* is MST7MDT for Mountain Standard Time in the U.S.A. Mountain Standard Time is offset 7 hours from UTC, and the abbreviation used when daylight savings time is in effect is MDT.

  Can be set in STARTUP.NCF, AUTOEXEC.NCF, or at the console.

- **Default time server type=*type*** Specifies the type of time server for this server. Values: Single (for Single Reference), Reference, Primary, or Secondary.

  Can be set in STARTUP.NCF, AUTOEXEC.NCF, or at the console.

- **Start of daylight savings time=*date time*** Indicates the day that daylight saving time begins locally. (You must also set the ending date with the End of Daylight Savings Time parameter.) To specify the beginning of daylight saving time so that it recurs every year, enclose the date and time in parentheses, and use the following format: (April Sunday First 2:00:00 a.m.).If you do not enclose the date in parentheses, the change will occur only in the current year. "April Sunday First" indicates that the change occurs on the first Sunday in April. Default: (April Sunday First 2:00:00 a.m.).

  Can be set in AUTOEXEC.NCF or at the console.

- **End of daylight savings time=*date time*** Indicates the day that daylight saving time ends locally. (You must also set the starting date with the Start of Daylight Savings Time parameter.) To specify the end of daylight saving time so that it recurs every year, enclose the date and time in parentheses, and use the following format: (October Sunday Last 2:00:00 a.m.).If you do not enclose the date in parentheses, the change will occur only in the current year. "October Sunday Last" indicates that the change occurs on the last Sunday in October. Default: (October Sunday Last 2:00:00 a.m.).

  Can be set in AUTOEXEC.NCF or at the console.

- **Daylight savings time offset=*+or- hour:minute:second*** Specifies the offset applied to time calculations when daylight saving time is in effect, causing UTC time to be recalculated from local time. Default: +1:00:00.

  Can be set in STARTUP.NCF, AUTOEXEC.NCF, or at the console.

- **Daylight savings time status=*on/off*** When set to On, this parameter indicates that daylight saving time is currently in effect. If this parameter is set to On, also set the Daylight Savings Time Offset parameter. Changing this parameter does not change the local time on the server. Default: Off.

  Can be set in STARTUP.NCF, AUTOEXEC.NCF, or at the console.

- **New time with daylight savings time status=*on/off*** When set to On, the local time on the server is adjusted by adding or subtracting the time indicated in the Daylight Savings Time Offset parameter. Default: Off.

  Can be set in AUTOEXEC.NCF or at the console.

Transaction Tracking Parameters

Transaction Tracking parameters allow you to configure NetWare's Transaction Tracking System. The following parameters are available:

- **Auto TTS backout flag=*on/off*** When set to On, incomplete transactions can be backed out automatically when a downed server is rebooted. Default: On.

  Can be set in STARTUP.NCF only.

- **TTS abort dump flag=*on/off*** When set to On, the TTS$LOG.ERR file is created to record backout data in the event of a failure. Default: Off.

  Can be set in AUTOEXEC.NCF or at the console.

- **Maximum transactions=*number*** Specifies how many transactions can occur simultaneously across all connections. Default: 10000. Values: 100 to 10000.

  Can be set in AUTOEXEC.NCF or at the console.

- **TTS unwritten cache wait time=*time*** Sets the time that a block of transactional data can be held in memory. Default: 1 minute, 5.9 seconds. Values: 11 seconds to 10 minutes, 59.1 seconds.

  Can be set in AUTOEXEC.NCF or at the console.

- **TTS backout file truncation wait time=*time*** Sets the minimum amount of time that allocated blocks remain available for the TTS backout file. Default 59 minutes, 19.2 seconds. Values: 1 minute, 5.9 seconds to 1 day, 2 hours, 21 minutes, 51.3 seconds.

  Can be set in AUTOEXEC.NCF or at the console.

APPENDIX C

Sources of More Information and Help

Whenever a product becomes as popular and as widely used as NetWare, an entire support industry crops up around it. If you are looking for more information about NetWare, you're in luck. There is a variety of places you can go for help.

NetWare information is as local as your bookstore or local user group, and as international as the Internet forums that focus on NetWare. It can be as informal as articles in a magazine, or as structured as a college course. This appendix describes the following ways you can get more information or technical support for NetWare:

- General Novell product information
- Novell on the Internet
- Novell technical support
- The *Novell Support Encyclopedia*
- DeveloperNet, Novell's developer support
- *Novell Application Notes*
- Novell Education classes and CNE certification
- NetWare Users International (NUI)
- Network Professional Association (NPA)

General Novell Product Information

The main Novell information number, 1-800-NETWARE, is your inroad to all types of information about Novell or its products.

By calling this number, you can obtain information about Novell products, the locations of your nearest resellers, pricing information, technical support (see the section "Novell Technical Support" later in this chapter), and so on.

To order the printed manuals for NetWare 4.1, you can use the order form that came in your NetWare 4.1 box, or call 800-336-3892 (in the United States) or 512-834-6905.

Novell on the Internet

There is a tremendous amount of information about Novell and NetWare products, both official and unofficial, on the Internet. Officially, you can obtain the latest information about Novell from NetWire, a collection of forums on CompuServe and on the Internet. Unofficially, there are several active user forums that deal specifically with NetWare or generally with computers. (NetWire will also be on the AT&T NetWare Connect Services when it becomes available.)

The NetWire forums offer users access to a wide variety of information and files dealing with NetWare and other Novell products, such as GroupWise. You can receive information such as technical advice from sysops (system operators) and other users, updated files and drivers, and the latest patches and workarounds for known problems in Novell products.

NetWire also provides a database of technical information from the Novell Technical Support division, as well as information about programs such as Novell Education classes and NetWare Users International (NUI). There is also marketing and sales information about the various products that Novell produces.

NetWire is managed by Novell employees and by sysops who have extensive knowledge about NetWare. Public forums can be quite active, with many knowledgeable users offering advice to those with problems.

To get technical help with a problem, post a message and address the message to the NetWire sysops. (But don't send the sysops a personal e-mail message asking for help — the public forums are the approved avenue for help.)

To access NetWire on CompuServe, you need a CompuServe account. There is no additional monthly fee for using NetWire, although you are charged the connection fee (on an hourly rate) for accessing the service.

If you have a connection to the Internet, you can access NetWire through one of the following communication options:

- World Wide Web: http://www.novell.com/
- Gopher: gopher.novell.com
- File Transfer Protocol (FTP): anonymous FTP to ftp.novell.com

(Users in Europe should replace .com with .de.)

Novell Technical Support

If you encounter a problem with your network that you can't solve on your own, there are several places you can go for help:

- Try calling your reseller or consultant.
- Go online, and see if anyone in the online forums or Usenet forums knows about the problem or can offer a solution. The knowledge of people in those forums is broad and deep. Don't hesitate to take advantage of it, and don't forget to return the favor if you know some tidbit that might help others.
- Call Novell technical support. You may want to reserve this as a last resort, simply because Novell technical support charges a fee for each incident (an incident may involve more than one phone call, if necessary). The fee depends on the product for which you're requesting support.

When you call technical support, make sure you have all the necessary information ready, such as the versions of NetWare and any utility or application you're using, the type of hardware you're using, network or node addresses and hardware settings for any workstations or other machines being affected, and so on. You'll also need a major credit card.

To get in touch with Novell's technical support, call 1-800-NETWARE.

The *Novell Support Encyclopedia*

A subscription to the *Novell Support Encyclopedia Professional Volume* (*NSEPro*) can update you every month with the latest technical information about Novell products. The *NSEPro* is a CD-ROM containing technical information such as:

- Novell Technical Information Documents
- Novell Labs hardware and software test bulletins

- Online product manuals
- *Novell Application Notes*
- *Bullets*, a monthly technical journal for developers
- All available NetWare patches, fixes, and drivers
- The *Novell Buyer's Guide*
- Novell corporate information such as event calendars and press releases

The *NSEPro* includes Folio information-retrieval software that allows you to access and search easily through the NSEPro information from your workstation using DOS, Macintosh, or Microsoft Windows.

To subscribe to the *NSEPro*, contact your Novell Authorized Reseller or Novell directly at 1-800-377-4136 (in the United States and Canada) or 303-297-1601.

DeveloperNet: Novell's Developer Support

Developers who create applications designed to run on NetWare may qualify to join Novell's program for professional developers, called DeveloperNet. Subscription fees for joining DeveloperNet vary, depending on the subscription level and options you choose. If you are a developer, some of the benefits you can receive by joining DeveloperNet include:

- The *Novell SDK* (Software Development Kit) CD-ROM, which contains development tools you can use to create and test your application
- The *DeveloperNet Handbook*
- Special technical support geared specifically toward developers

- *Novell Developer Notes*, a bimonthly publication from the Novell Research department, that covers software development topics for NetWare products
- Discounts on various events, products, and Novell Press books

For more information, to apply for membership, or to order an SDK, call 800-REDWORD or 801-429-5281, or contact the program administrator via e-mail at devprog@novell.com. More information is available online on CompuServe (GO NETWIRE) or on the World Wide Web at http://developer.novell.com.

Novell Application Notes

Novell's Research Department produces a monthly publication called *Novell Application Notes*. Each issue of *Novell Application Notes* contains research reports and articles on a wide range of topics. The articles delve into topics such as network design, implementation, administration, and integration.

A year's subscription costs $95 ($135 outside the United States), which includes access to the *Novell Application Notes* in its electronic form on CompuServe. An electronic-only subscription costs $35 (plus access charges).

To order a subscription, call 800-377-4136 or 303-297-2725. You can also fax an order to 303-294-0930.

Novell Education Classes and CNE Certification

Are you looking for a way to learn about NetWare in a classroom setting, with hands-on labs and knowledgeable instructors? Novell offers a variety of classes on various aspects of running NetWare networks.

NetWare classes are taught at over a 1,000 Novell Authorized Education Centers (NAECs) throughout the world. They are also taught at more than 100 NAEPs (Novell Authorized Education Partners), which are universities and colleges that teach these courses.

These classes often offer the best way to get some direct, hands-on training in just a few days. Some of the classes are also available in Computer-Based Training (CBT) form, in case you'd rather work through the material at your own pace, on your own workstation, than attend a class.

These classes also help prepare you if you want to become a Certified Novell Engineer (CNE).

The Novell CNE program provides a way to ensure that networking professionals meet the necessary criteria to adequately install and manage NetWare networks. To achieve CNE status, you take a series of exams on different aspects of NetWare. In many cases, you may want to take the classes Novell offers through its NAECs to prepare for the exams, but the classes aren't required.

The classes and exams you take depend somewhat on the level of certification you want to achieve. Although there are certain core exams that are required for all levels, you may also take additional "electives" to achieve the certification and specialization you want.

The following levels of certification are available:

- CNA (Certified Novell Administrator) This certification is the most basic level. It prepares you to manage your own NetWare network. It does not delve into the more complex and technical aspects of NetWare. If you are relatively new to NetWare, the classes offered for this certification are highly recommended.

- CNE (Certified Novell Engineer) This certification level ensures that you can adequately install and manage NetWare networks. While pursuing your CNE certification, you "declare a major," meaning that you choose to specialize in a particular Novell product family. For example, you may become a NetWare 4 CNE or a GroupWise CNE.

- Master CNE This certification level allows you to go beyond CNE certification. To get a Master CNE, you declare a "graduate major." These areas of specialization delve deeper into the integration- and solution-oriented aspects of running a network than the CNE level.

- CNI (Certified Novell Instructor) CNIs are authorized to teach NetWare classes through NAECs. The tests and classes specific to this level ensure that the individual taking them will be able to adequately teach others how to install and manage NetWare.

The ECNE (Enterprise Certified Novell Engineer) level is being phased out. The ECNE level's series of tests emphasized aspects of networking encountered in larger, enterprisewide networks, such as routing, gateways, NetWare Directory Services, and so on.

The Master CNE program is replacing the ECNE level because it adds more flexibility to the type of specialization the candidate can pursue. If you've already achieved ECNE status, you will retain the title, and Novell will still recognize it. However, Novell stopped certifying new ECNEs on September 30, 1995.

CNEs and ECNEs qualify for membership in the Network Professional Association (NPA), which is explained later in this Appendix.

For more information about Novell Education classes or to find the nearest NAEC near you, call 1-800-233-3382.

To purchase a CBT version of a class, contact your nearest NAEC.

There are also numerous organizations that provide classes and seminars on NetWare products. Some of these unauthorized classes are quite good. Others are probably of lower quality, because Novell does not have any control over their course content or instructor qualifications. If you choose an unauthorized provider for your NetWare classes, try to talk to others who've taken a class from the provider before, so you'll have a better idea of how good the class will be.

NetWare Users International (NUI)

NetWare Users International (NUI) is a nonprofit association for networking professionals. With more than 250 affiliated groups worldwide, NUI provides a forum for networking professionals to meet face to face, to learn from each other, to trade recommendations, or just to share war stories.

By joining the NetWare user group in your area, you can take advantage of the following benefits:

- Local user groups that hold regularly scheduled meetings
- A discount on Novell Press books through *NetWare Connection* magazine and also at NUI shows
- *NetWare Connection,* a bimonthly magazine that provides feature articles on new technologies, network management tips, product reviews, NUI news, and other helpful information
- NUInet, NUI's home page on the World Wide Web at http://www.nuinet.com, which provides NetWare 3 and NetWare 4 technical information, a calendar of NUI events, and links to local user group home pages
- Regional NUI conferences, held in different major cities throughout the year (with a 15 percent discount for members)

The best news is, there's usually no fee or only a very low fee for joining an NUI user group.

For more information or to join an NUI user group, call 800-228-4NUI or send a fax to 801-228-4577.

For a free subscription to *NetWare Connection,* fax your name, address, and request for a subscription to 801-228-4576. You can also mail NUI a request at:

NetWare Connection
P.O. Box 1928
Orem, UT 84059-1928
USA

Network Professional Association (NPA)

If you've achieved, or are working toward, your CNE certification, you may want to join the Network Professional Association (NPA), formerly called CNEPA. The NPA is an organization for network computing professionals. Its goal is to keep its members current with the latest technology and information in the industry.

If you're a certified CNE, you can join the NPA as a full member. If you've started the certification process, but aren't finished yet, you can join as an associate member.

When you join the NPA, you can enjoy the following benefits:

- Local NPA chapters (more than 100 worldwide) that hold regularly scheduled meetings that include presentations and hands-on demonstrations of the latest technology

- *Network News,* a monthly publication that offers technical tips for working with NetWare networks, NPA news, classified ads for positions, and articles aimed at helping CNEs make the most of their careers

- Discounts on NPA Satellite Labs (satellite broadcasts of presentations)

- Product discounts from vendors

- Hands-On Technology Labs (educational forums at major trade shows and other locations as sponsored by local NPA chapters)

- Discount or free admission to major trade shows and conferences

Membership in NPA costs $150 per year. For more information or to join NPA, call 801-379-0330.

APPENDIX D

Worksheets

Keeping accurate and up-to-date documentation about the various aspects of your network can save you a tremendous amount of time and energy if something goes wrong. You can photocopy and use the worksheets in this section to begin documenting your network. If you prefer, you can design your own forms or databases for tracking important information such as hardware and software inventory, NDS information, and your backup schedules.

Worksheet A: Server Installation and Configuration

Server name: ______________________________

Make and model: ______________________________

Current location: ______________________________

Serial number: ______________________________

Memory: ______________________________

Server's internal IPX network number: ______________________________

Directory tree name: ______________________________

Type of time sync server: ______________________________

Server's time zone: ______________________________

Server's name context in the Directory tree: ______________________________

Protocols

PX/SPX (required): Yes __ No __

TCP/IP: Yes __ No __

AppleTalk: Yes __ No __

Network Board

Type: ______________ Node address: ______________

LAN driver: ______________ Frame type: ______________

Settings: ______________________________

IP address (for TCP/IP only): ______________________________

Subnet mask (for TCP/IP only): ______________________________

Network Board

Type: ______________ Node address: ______________

LAN driver: ______________ Frame type: ______________

Settings: ______________________________

IP address (for TCP/IP only): ______________________________

Subnet mask (for TCP/IP only): ______________________________

Network Board
Type: ______________________________ Frame type: ____________________
LAN driver: ________________________ Node address: __________________
Settings: ____
IP address (for TCP/IP only): ____
Subnet mask (for TCP/IP only): _______________________________________

Network Board
Type: ______________________________ Frame type: ____________________
LAN driver: ________________________ Node address: __________________
Settings: ____
IP address (for TCP/IP only): ____
Subnet mask (for TCP/IP only): _______________________________________

Hard disk size: ____
DOS partition size: ____
Disk mirrored? Yes __ No __
Disk duplexed? Yes __ No __
SFT III installed? Yes __ No __
CD-ROM drive? Yes __ No __

Disk Controller Board
Name: ____
Disk drive name: ____
Settings: ____

Other Boards
Name: ____
Settings: ____
Name: ____
Settings: ____
Name: ____
Settings: ____
Name: ____
Settings: ____

Comments: ____
____
____
____

Worksheet B: Volumes

Server name: ______________________________

SYS Volume

Size: ______________________________

Name spaces: ______________________________

File compression on? Yes __ No __

Block suballocation on? Yes __ No __

Data migration on? Yes __ No __

Other volume (name): ______________________________

Size: ______________________________

Name spaces: ______________________________

File compression on? Yes __ No __

Block suballocation on? Yes __ No __

Data migration on? Yes __ No __

Other volume (name): ______________________________

Size: ______________________________

Name spaces: ______________________________

File compression on? Yes __ No __

Block suballocation on? Yes __ No __

Data migration on? Yes __ No __

Other volume (name): ______________________________

Size: ______________________________

Name spaces: ______________________________

File compression on? Yes __ No __

Block suballocation on? Yes __ No __

Data migration on? Yes __ No __

Comments: ______________________________

____

____

____

____

____

Worksheet C: Hardware and Software Purchases

Product: ______________________________

Serial number: ______________________________

Version number: ______________________________

Vendor name: ______________________________

Address: ______________________________

____

Phone: ______________________________

Fax: ______________________________

Manufacturer name: ______________________________

Address: ______________________________

____

Phone: ______________________________

Fax: ______________________________

Purchase date: ______________________________

Purchase order number: ______________________________

Purchase price: ______________________________

Warranty card sent in? Yes __ No __ Not applicable __

Length of warranty: ______________________________

Current location of product: ______________________________

Comments: ______________________________

____

____

____

____

____

Worksheet D: Hardware Maintenance

Product: ____

Serial number: ____

Repair date: ____

Purchase order number: _________________________________

Repair vendor name: ____________________________________

Address: ____

____

Phone: ____

Fax: ____

Repair cost: ____

Repaired under warranty? Yes __ No __

New warranty granted? Yes __ No __

Warranty expiration date: _______________________________

Comments: ____

____

____

____

____

____

Worksheet E: Time Synchronization Servers

NDS Directory tree: ______________________________

Single reference server: ______________________________

Reference server: ______________________________

Primary servers: ______________________________

____

____

____

____

____

____

____

____

Comments: ______________________________

____

____

____

____

____

Worksheet F: Hot Fix Bad Block Tracking

Server: ______________________________

Disk: ______________________________

Total redirection area: ______________________________

Date: ____________ Redirection blocks used: ____________

Date: ____________ Redirection blocks used: ____________

Date: ____________ Redirection blocks used: ____________

Date: ____________ Redirection blocks used: ____________

Date: ____________ Redirection blocks used: ____________

Date: ____________ Redirection blocks used: ____________

Date: ____________ Redirection blocks used: ____________

Date: ____________ Redirection blocks used: ____________

Date: ____________ Redirection blocks used: ____________

Date: ____________ Redirection blocks used: ____________

Date: ____________ Redirection blocks used: ____________

Comments: ______________________________

Worksheet G: Workstation Installation and Configuration

Workstation's user and/or location: ______________________________

Make and model: ______________________________

Serial number: ______________________________

Memory: ______________________________

Size of floppy disk drives: A:__________ B:__________

Size of hard disk: C:__________ D:__________

CD-ROM drive? Yes __ No __

PC

DOS version: __________

Windows version: ______

OS/2 version: __________

NT version: __________

Macintosh

System version: __________

Filer version: __________

NetWare client software version: ______________________________

Network Board

Type: ____________________ Node address: ______________

LAN driver: ________________ Frame type: ______________

Settings: ______________________________

Network Board

Type: ____________________ Node address: ______________

LAN driver: ________________ Frame type: ______________

Settings: ______________________________

Other Boards

Name: ______________________________

Settings: ______________________________

Name: ______________________________

Settings: ______________________________

Name: ______________________________

Settings: ______________________________

Name: ______________________________

Settings: ______________________________

Comments: ______________________________

____

____

Worksheet H: Backup Schedule

Server name (of server backed up): ______________________

Server location: ______________________

Backup system used (hardware and software): ______________________

____

____

Location of backup media: ______________________

____

____

Backup schedule:

Full backup: ______________________

Incremental backup: ______________________

Differential backup: ______________________

Custom backup: ______________________

If custom backups are done, describe: ______________________

____

____

____

Media rotation schedule: ______________________

____

____

Media labeling instructions: ______________________

____

____

Primary backup administrator name: ______________________

Phone numbers: ______________________

____

____

Secondary backup administrator name: ______________________

Phone numbers: ______________________

____

Comments: ______________________

____

____

____

Worksheet I: Printer Installation and Configuration

Printer object's full name: ____________________

Make and model: ____________________

Current location: ____________________

Serial number: ____________________

Directory tree name: ____________________

Printer number: ____________________

Print queues assigned: ____________________

____

____

____

Print server assigned: ____________________

How is the printer attached: To server __ To workstation __ Direct __

Print queue operators: ____________________

Print server operators: ____________________

Printer type (parallel, serial, AppleTalk, etc.): ____________________

Interrupt mode (polled or specific IRQ): ____________________

Parallel printer configuration

Port (LPT1, LPT2, or LPT3): ____________________

Poll: ____________________

Interrupt (LPT1=7, LPT2=8): ____________________

Serial Printer Configuration

Port (COM1 or COM2): ____________________

Baud rate: ____________________

Word size: ____________________

Stop bits: ____________________

Parity: ____________________

XON/XOFF: ____________________

Poll: ____________________

Interrupt (COM1=4, COM2=3): ____________________

Comments: ____________________

____

____

____

____

APPENDIX E

Glossary

Abend (Abnormal End) A serious error encountered in the server, which stops the server from operating.

Access Control List *See* ACL.

Access rights *See* Rights, file system; Rights, object; and Rights, property.

Account restrictions Restrictions you can impose that limit how the user can log in to the network. There are four different types of account restrictions you can implement if you wish (all are optional): login restrictions, password restrictions, login time restrictions, and network address restrictions.

Accounting services A NetWare feature that lets you charge users for using a server's resources. You can charge them for the time they are connected to your server, for the number of blocks they write to or read, and so on.

ACL (Access Control List) The property of an object that lists all the trustees of that object.

AFP (AppleTalk Filing Protocol) The AppleTalk protocol that allows servers and workstations on an AppleShare network to communicate and exchange data.

Alias object An object in the NDS tree that points to a real object located in a different part of the tree. With an alias in your name context in the tree, you can access the real object easily, without having to navigate through the rest of the tree to locate the real object.

AppleShare The networking software from Apple Computer that allows a Macintosh to function as a file server and other Macintosh workstations to attach to that server.

AppleTalk The networking protocol suite developed by Apple Computer. It provides peer-to-peer networking capabilities between all Macintoshes and Apple hardware. AppleTalk capability is automatically built into every Macintosh.

AppleTalk extended network An AppleTalk network that can support more than 254 nodes and multiple zones (up to 255) on an AppleTalk network. These are also called Phase 2 networks, because they support Phase 2 addressing. Phase 2 addressing lets you have far more nodes on a network than Phase 1 addressing. Theoretically, Phase 2 addressing allows more than 16 million addresses.

AppleTalk Filing Protocol *See* AFP.

AppleTalk nonextended network An AppleTalk network that can only support up to 254 nodes (workstations, printers, and so on), all of which must be contained in a single zone. These are also called Phase 1 networks because they support Phase 1 addressing. LocalTalk, ARCnet, and EtherTalk 1.0 are all nonextended AppleTalk networks.

AppleTalk print spooler *See* Print spooler, AppleTalk.

AppleTalk router A NetWare 4.1 feature that allows AppleTalk traffic to be routed between two network boards in the NetWare server. The AppleTalk router also communicates with any other AppleTalk routers on the network. If an AppleTalk router exists in a NetWare server, the Macintosh workstations can communicate with the server, as well as with other Macintoshes or AppleTalk printers on the other side of the server.

AppleTalk zone A logical grouping of devices, such as servers, workstations, and printers, on an AppleTalk network. These devices can be grouped into zones to make it easier for users to find them. A small network may have only a single zone, with all devices contained within it. A larger network may have several zones.

ARCnet A relatively simple and inexpensive cabling architecture that has been used for many years. Because its performance is not generally as fast as other network architectures (its transmission rate is only 2.5 Mbps, or megabytes per second), it is typically used in smaller networks. ARCnet Plus is a newer version of ARCnet; its transmission rate is 20 Mbps. ARCnet can use either a star or a bus topology, but the star topology usually provides better performance.

Attribute, file and directory Assigned directly to files and directories. Unlike rights, which are specific to different users and groups, these attributes belong to the file or directory itself. They control the activities of all users, regardless of those users' trustee rights.

Attribute, NDS object *See* Property.

Authentication Verification that the user or process requesting services from the NetWare 4.1 network is authorized to do so.

AUTOEXEC.BAT A batch file created at the root of the disk during DOS installation for most recent versions of DOS. It can also be created or edited with a text editor. It executes when the computer is booted, automatically loading files. It also can be used to log the user into the network.

AUTOEXEC.NCF A server boot file that loads the server's LAN drivers, specifies the server name and internal network number, mounts volumes, loads any NLMs you want automatically loaded (such as MONITOR), and executes some SET parameters.

Backup An archived copy of files that you can restore if something goes wrong with the original files on the network. Backing up network files involves more than just making a copy of the files. It's important to use a backup product, such as NetWare's SBACKUP.NLM, that backs up not just the files themselves, but also the NetWare information associated with those files, such as trustee rights, Inherited Rights Filters, and file and directory attributes.

Bind To assign a protocol (IPX, AppleTalk, or IP) to a LAN driver so that the LAN driver can use that protocol to communicate with the rest of the network.

Bindery The flat-structured database of network information used in NetWare 3.12 and earlier versions of NetWare. Each server had an individual and unique bindery, so if a user needed access to multiple servers, that user would need a separate user account on each of those servers. In NetWare 4.0 and later versions, the bindery was replaced with the NDS database, which is shared by all servers on the network. *See also* NetWare Directory Services.

Bindery context The portion of the NDS tree that a server considers to be its bindery if it has been set up to support bindery services. The portion of the tree that becomes a server's bindery context consists of any container you choose and its objects. You can specify up to 16 different containers to look like a single bindery on a server. To the bindery-based application, the objects in all sixteen containers will look like objects in a single flat database. *See also* Bindery services.

Bindery emulation *See* Bindery services.

Bindery object An object that was upgraded from a bindery-based server and placed in the NDS tree, but which could not be converted into a corresponding NDS object.

Bindery Queue object A Queue object that was upgraded from a bindery-based server and placed in the NDS tree, but which could not be converted into a corresponding NDS object.

Bindery services A NetWare 4.1 feature that takes a container object and its portion of the Directory tree and makes it appear to be flat and located on a particular server. That way, both bindery-based applications and NDS-aware applications can find the objects they need. Bindery services also allow NetWare 3.x users to log in to a NetWare 4.1 server and use its resources. (Also referred to as bindery emulation.) *See also* Bindery context.

Block A unit of disk space allocated to store a file. Block sizes range from 4K to 64K, depending on the size and needs of the network.

Block suballocation A NetWare 4.1 feature that breaks a block into 512-byte suballocation blocks so that several smaller files can share a single block. By default, block suballocation is turned on during server installation.

Bridge A device that relays data from one segment of a network to another but does not determine routes. *See also* Router.

Browser A feature of the NetWare Administrator utility that allows you to navigate through the NDS tree and see the available objects (provided you have the NDS Browse right to those objects). You can open the Browser by choosing Browse from the NetWare Administrator utility's Tools menu or by clicking the Browse button next to fields that require you to enter the name of an object.

Cabling architecture The cabling scheme that connects the nodes together into a network. The most common cabling architectures are Ethernet, ARCnet, Token Ring, and AppleTalk. High-speed architectures, such as Fiber Distributed Data Interface (FDDI), Thomas Conrad Network System (TCNS), Fast Ethernet, and ARCnet Plus, are becoming more and more prevalent.

Cache buffer A block of memory that temporarily stores files that are being frequently used. Accessing files from the cache is faster than accessing files from the disk.

Capture To redirect a workstation's LPT (parallel) port to point to a network print queue instead of directly to a locally attached printer.

Channel *See* Controller channel.

Client A computer, program, or process that requests services from a server. Generally, in NetWare documentation, a client is a workstation.

CNA (Certified Novell Administrator) A certification level received by taking exams offered by the Novell Education division. This certification is the most basic of the certification levels. It prepares you to manage your own NetWare network. It does not delve into the more complex and technical aspects of NetWare, covered in the CNE and Master CNE exams. *See also* CNE; CNI; Master CNE.

CNE (Certified Novell Engineer) A certification level received by taking exams offered by the Novell Education division. A CNE certification helps ensure that you can adequately install and manage NetWare networks. *See also* CNA; CNI; Master CNE.

CNI (Certified Novell Instructor) A certification level received by taking exams offered by the Novell Education division. CNIs are authorized to teach NetWare classes through NAECs (Novell Authorized Education Centers). The tests and classes specific to this level ensure that the individual taking them will be able to adequately teach others how to install and manage NetWare. *See also* CNA; CNE; Master CNE.

Code page A table DOS uses to determine which letters, numerals, and symbols are supported by the version of DOS running on the computer. Since DOS versions and computer hardware can vary depending on the country they are being used in, different countries may use different code pages.

Compile To convert a file into an executable file. For example, the MENUMAKE utility compiles a text file containing menu-formatting commands into a data file with a .DAT extension. The NMENU program then uses this compiled file to display the menu on the workstation screen.

Compression *See* File compression.

Computer object An NDS object that represents a computer.

Concentrator Similar to an active hub but used with different topologies. The cables attached to workstations feed into the concentrator which boosts the signals before sending them on to the main network cable. *See also* Hub.

CONFIG.SYS A DOS boot file created at the root of the disk during DOS installation for most recent versions of DOS. It can also be created or edited with a text editor. It configures the workstation's DOS environment.

Console utilities Commands you type at the server's console (keyboard and monitor) to change some aspect of the server or view information about it. To read online help for console utilities, type HELP at the server console.

Container login script *See* System login script.

Container object An NDS object that contains other objects. There are three available container object classes: Country, Organization, and Organizational Unit. Container objects can contain other container objects or leaf objects (or both). *See also* Leaf object.

Context *See* Name context.

Controller board A circuit board installed in a computer that allows the computer to communicate with a device, such as a hard disk.

Controller channel The path data travels between a storage device, such as a hard disk, and the computer. The channel can include the controller board, any cables, and so on.

Country object An optional container object in the NDS tree representing the country where this portion of the tree is located. The Country object exists just below the Root object and above the Organization object.

Data fork The portion of a Macintosh file that contains the actual text of the file. This fork corresponds somewhat to a DOS-based file. *See also* Resource fork.

Data migration A NetWare 4.1 feature that lets less frequently used files be migrated off the server's hard disk onto an external storage device, such as a tape, a different hard disk, or optical disk. These files are automatically "demigrated" back onto the server's hard disk when a user accesses them. This process is usually transparent to the users.

Data packet A unit of data that is transferred across the network. The format of a data packet varies depending on the type of protocol, but it usually consists of the actual information that's being transferred, plus administrative information that helps get the actual information where it needs to go.

Directory attribute *See* Attribute, file and directory.

Directory cache A block of memory that stores the server's directory entries so that the server can locate files more quickly than if it were searching through the directory entries on the disk.

Directory entry An item in the server's Directory Entry Table (DET), which points to the first of the disk blocks used to store a file or directory. The directory entry also provides information about the file or directory, such as the name, creation date and time, size, and so on. Each directory, DOS file, and trustee list on the network uses up one directory entry. Each Macintosh file or directory takes up two directory entries. If you run out of directory entries on your disk, no one will be able to create a new file or directory.

Directory Map object An NDS object that represents a directory path to an application. You can map a drive to a Directory Map object in login scripts. That way, if the location of the application changes, you can update the Directory Map object without having to modify any of the login scripts. The login scripts still point to the Directory Map object.

Directory partition *See* Partition, directory.

Directory replica *See* Replica.

Directory tree *See* NDS tree.

Disk driver A software program that enables the operating system to communicate with a disk controller board installed in the file server.

Disk duplexing Attaching mirrored disks to separate disk controller boards. Disk duplexing provides more security than disk mirroring because it duplicates not just the disk but also the controller channel (which includes the controller board and cables) as well. *See also* Disk mirroring.

Disk mirroring Using two or more disks in the server that are updated simultaneously with network data so that both disks contain identical copies of all network files. This ensures that data is safe and accessible even if one disk goes down. If one disk fails, the other continues to operate normally. If the mirrored disks are using the same disk controller board, it's called disk mirroring. If mirrored disks are using separate disk controller boards, it's called disk duplexing. Disk duplexing provides more security than disk mirroring because it duplicates not just the disk but also the controller channel (which includes the controller board and cables) as well. *See also* Disk duplexing.

Disk partition *See* Partition, disk.

Disk redirection area A separate area on the server's hard disk where data is stored if the Hot Fix feature detects that the original destination for the data contained bad blocks. *See also* Hot Fix.

Domain An area of server memory where NLMs can execute. To test an unknown NLM or an NLM you are developing, run it in the protected memory domain (called OS_PROTECTED), where it cannot corrupt the operating system memory. When you are satisfied that the NLM is using memory correctly, you can run it in the regular domain (called OS).

Drive mapping The drive letter assigned to a network directory. With a drive letter mapped to a directory, you can type the drive letter (such as F: or L:) instead of typing the entire directory path in a command.

Driver A software program that allows software and hardware to communicate with each other. For example, print drivers allow your applications to communicate with your printers, tape drivers allow tape backup systems to receive network data from the backup program, and LAN drivers allow the network board to transfer data onto the network.

Drop cable A cable used to connect a node (such as a workstation) to the trunk cable in a thick Ethernet network.

Duplexing *See* Disk duplexing.

DynaText The online version of the NetWare documentation. The DynaText viewer is used to actually display the documentation on a workstation screen.

ECNE (Enterprise Certified Novell Engineer) A certification level that is being phased out of the Novell Education program. The ECNE level's series of tests emphasized aspects of networking encountered in larger, enterprisewide networks, such as routing, gateways, NetWare Directory Services, and so on. The Master CNE program is replacing the ECNE level because it adds more flexibility to the type of specialization the candidate can pursue. *See also* CNE; Master CNE.

Ethernet The most commonly used network architecture. Ethernet cabling is relatively easy to install at a moderate cost. Because it has been so widely used for many years, its technology has been well tested. Ethernet networks can use either bus or star topologies.

EtherTalk Apple Computer's implementation of Ethernet. EtherTalk Phase 1 was based on the Ethernet 2.0 version of Ethernet. EtherTalk Phase 2 is based on the Ethernet 802.3 version. EtherTalk Phase 2 has replaced LocalTalk as the built-in networking architecture in most newer Macintoshes.

External Entity object An NDS object that stores information about non-NDS entities for other applications or services.

Fake root A drive mapping that makes a subdirectory appear to be a root directory. This is useful for some applications, which require that they be installed at the root of a drive.

FDDI (Fiber Distributed Data Interface) A network architecture for using fiber-optic cables at very high speeds. It supports speeds of up to 100 Mbps, and it uses a dual-ring topology in which data can travel in opposite directions.

FDDITalk Apple Computer's implementation of the 100 Mbps FDDI architecture.

File attribute *See* Attribute, file and directory.

File compression A NetWare 4.1 feature that compresses unused files on the server, thus saving up to 63 percent of the server's hard disk space. Compressed files are automatically decompressed when a user accesses them, so the user doesn't even know that the files were compressed.

Flag To assign a file or directory attribute to a file or directory. Also used to refer to the actual attribute itself. *See also* Attribute, file and directory.

Frame type Variations in the data packet formats used by a topology, such as Ethernet. In most cases, a given network will support only one Ethernet frame type. However, NetWare allows you to support more than one frame type by configuring the LAN driver for the server's network board to recognize two or more types.

Grace login An allowance that lets the user log in using an expired password. You can limit the number of grace logins that a user has on your network.

Group object An NDS object that contains a list of users that have at least some identical characteristics, such as the need for access rights to the same application. Users listed as group members receive a security equivalence to the group.

HCSS (High-Capacity Storage System) A NetWare feature that lets you integrate an optical storage disk (jukebox) into the NetWare file system. With HCSS, lesser-used files are migrated off the server's hard disks onto the optical disks. When accessed, the files on the optical disk are "demigrated" back onto the hard disks.

Home directory A network directory that can be created automatically for each user as he or she is added to the network. A home directory is generally named with the user's login name and can be used to store that user's own work files.

Hot Fix A NetWare feature that monitors the blocks that are being written to on a disk. When a bad block is encountered, the data that was being written to that block is redirected to a separate area on the disk, called the disk redirection area, and the bad block is listed in a bad block table. *See also* Disk redirection area.

Hub A device used for relaying, and possibly enhancing cable signals. Some cabling architectures require that the cables attached to workstations all feed into a separate piece of hardware before being connected to the main network cable. Passive hubs simply gather the signals and relay them. Active hubs actually boost the signals before sending them on their way. *See also* Concentrator.

Identifier variable A variable used in login script commands. An identifier variable is a placeholder for information that is substituted whenever a user logs in. An identifier variable may adopt specific user information, such as the user's login name or full name, or it might adopt information about the user's workstation, such as its address or machine type. It might also adopt general information that has nothing to do with the user, such as the day of the week, time, or network address.

Inheritance NDS rights and file system rights can be inherited. This means that if you have rights to a parent container (or directory), you can inherit those rights and exercise them in an object within that container (or a file or subdirectory within that directory), too. Inheritance keeps you from having to grant users' rights at every level of the Directory or file system tree. Inheritance can be blocked by granting a new set of rights to an object within the container or by removing the right from an object's Inherited Rights Filter (IRF).

Inherited Rights Filter *See* IRF.

Intruder detection A NetWare feature that can detect if an unauthorized user is trying to break into the network. You can set the network so that such unauthorized users are locked out after a given number of failed login attempts. This helps ensure that users don't try to break into the network by simply guessing at another user's password or by using programs that automatically generate passwords.

IOAUTO.NCF An SFT III server boot file that loads LAN drivers and binds protocols to them, and loads NLMs that must run in the IOEngine but require the MSEngine to be running (such as backup and print services).

IOEngine The I/O engine. This portion of the SFT III NetWare operating system handles the hardware input and output for this particular server computer. The I/O engine is not mirrored. *See also* MSEngine.

IOSTART.NCF An SFT III server boot file that specifies the IOEngine's name and IPX internal network number, loads the disk drivers and MSL board drivers, executes IOEngine SET parameters, and loads NLMs that run in the IOEngine and don't need the MSEngine running.

IP (Internet Protocol) The network protocol used on the Internet, and by many Unix-based networks.

IPX (Internetwork Packet Exchange) NetWare's native network protocol, which is responsible for addressing and routing packets to nodes on the same network or on other networks.

IPX external network number A network number that is assigned to the portion of the network that is attached to a network board in the server. When a protocol is bound to a LAN driver/board combination, that combination is assigned an IPX external network number. Every node on that cabling segment of the network uses that same network number. Since a server can have more than one board/driver combination installed, the server may support more than one IPX external network number. This is different from the IPX internal network number.

IPX internal network number A network number that identifies each individual server on the network. Each server on the network must have a unique internal IPX network number, which is assigned during installation. This is different from the IPX external network number.

IRF A filter assigned to each NDS object, file, or directory that specifies which rights can be inherited from a parent container or directory. By default, the IRF for an object, file, or directory allows all rights to be inherited. You can change the IRF, however, to revoke one or more rights. Any rights that are revoked from the IRF cannot be inherited. The IRF does not affect any explicitly granted rights for that object, file, or directory, however. The IRF affects only inherited rights.

LAN driver A software program that enables the operating system to communicate with a network board installed in the file server or workstation.

Leaf object An NDS object that represents an entity on the network. Leaf objects, such as users, servers, and volumes, cannot contain other objects. *See also* Container object.

List object An NDS object that contains a list of objects but doesn't imply that those objects have a security equivalence to anything (unlike a Group object, which actually grants security equivalence).

LocalTalk Apple's built-in network architecture in most older Macintoshes. Using LocalTalk cabling, you can connect Macintoshes together in a network without having to install a separate network board and driver in each Macintosh. (If you don't want to use LocalTalk, you can install a board and driver for another type of architecture, such as EtherTalk, and buy the appropriate cabling.) LocalTalk has been replaced by EtherTalk as the built-in network architecture in most newer Macintoshes.

Login script A property of a User object or container object, which you can use to automatically set up users' workstation environments. A login script works similarly to a batch file. Each time a user logs in, the login scripts will execute, setting up frequently used drive mappings, capturing the workstation's printer port to a network print queue, displaying connection information or messages on the screen, or doing other types of tasks for the user. System login scripts (also called container login scripts), which are properties of containers, execute for all users in that container. Profile login scripts are properties of Profile objects, which contain a list of any users for which you want to have this particular login script run. Profile login scripts, which are optional, execute after the system login script. User login scripts are properties of individual users, and they execute after the profile and system login scripts.

LSL.COM The Link Support Layer file. It is placed in the NWCLIENT directory by the NetWare DOS Requester installation. It enables the workstation to communicate with different protocols.

MacIPX gateway A NetWare for Macintosh feature that lets Macintosh workstations on LocalTalk networks, or Macintoshes that are dialing in using Apple Remote Access, exchange data with IPX networks.

Map To assign a drive letter to a network directory. With a drive letter mapped to a directory, you can type the drive letter (such as F: or L:) instead of typing the entire directory path in a command.

Master CNE (Certified Novell Engineer) A certification level received by taking exams offered by the Novell Education division. This certification level allows you to go beyond CNE certification. To get a Master CNE, you declare a "graduate major." These areas of specialization delve deeper into the integration- and solution-oriented aspects of running a network than the CNE level does. *See also* CNA; CNE; CNI.

MAU (Multistation Access Unit) A wiring concentrator for Token Ring networks. Nodes connect to these MAUs, which in turn are connected to other MAUs to form the ring. The wiring inside the MAU forms a ring of the attached nodes.

Menu program A program you create that allows a user to choose a program, such as e-mail or word processing, from a menu. This way, the user can be prevented from even seeing the DOS prompt or executing commands.

Message Routing Group object An NDS object that contains a list of messaging servers that are connected directly to each other so that e-mail messages can be routed between them.

Messaging Server object An NDS object that represents a server that receives and transfers e-mail messages.

Migration *See* Data migration.

Mirrored server engine *See* MSEngine.

Mirroring *See* Disk mirroring.

MSAUTO.NCF An SFT III server boot file that executes commands after the servers are mirrored and volume SYS is mounted, loads most NLMs, loads NetWare Directory Services, initializes time synchronization, and so on.

MSEngine The mirrored server engine. This portion of the SFT III NetWare operating system mirrors all the network data and operations. *See also* IOEngine.

MSL (mirrored server link) boards Network boards that form a special high-speed network link between two SFT III mirrored servers to ensure that all data is instantly duplicated between the two servers. *See also* SFT III.

MSSTART.NCF An SFT III server boot file that executes commands and SET parameters that affect the MSEngine.

Multistation Access Unit *See* MAU.

Name context The specific location in the Directory tree where an object resides. The address of that location consists of the names of any container objects over that object, separated by periods.

Name space module A NetWare Loadable Module (NLM) that enables volumes on a server to store non-DOS files (such as Macintosh, OS/2, and NFS files), preserving their longer file names and different file formats.

NCP Packet Signature A NetWare security feature designed to make it impossible for someone to forge packets and access network resources through these forged packets. This feature requires workstations and servers to "sign" each NCP packet with a signature and to change the signature for every packet. You set levels of NCP Packet Signature security on the server and on each workstation, and those levels must combine correctly for login to occur.

NDS (NetWare Directory Services) The NetWare 4.1 database of network information. It defines every object on the network, such as users, groups, printers, print queues, servers, and volumes. All NetWare 4.1 servers on a network share a single NDS database. This way, you only have to create a user or other object once on the network; each server will recognize that same object. You can then allow that user to access different servers simply by granting him or her the appropriate rights to the necessary volumes on each server. The user doesn't have to log in to each server separately.

NDS object An item in the NDS database that represents a real entity on the network, such as a user, group, printer, or server. Each network entity on the network must have an NDS object. An NDS object contains several properties, which are the pieces of information that define the object, such as a full name, ID number, phone number, e-mail address, or access rights to other objects. Each type of object, such as a user, print queue, or server, is referred to as an object class. *See also* Property.

NDS schema The set of allowable types of NDS objects and their properties that can exist on a network. The schema defines which objects and properties are allowed in the NDS database, and it determines how those objects can inherit properties and trustee rights of other container objects above it. The schema also defines how the Directory tree is structured and how objects in it are named.

NDS tree The logical representation of the objects in the NDS database. Using container objects, you can organize the objects in the database so that they are grouped into separate branches of the tree.

NET.CFG A workstation configuration file that configures the NetWare DOS Requester and LAN driver for the workstation's needs. NET.CFG is created by the NetWare DOS Requester installation. It is located in the NWCLIENT directory and can be edited with a text editor.

NetSync A NetWare 4.1 feature that allows you to merge the binderies of NetWare 3.1x servers and synchronize them with a NetWare 4.1 NDS database. NetSync allows you to manage those NetWare 3.1x users from a NetWare 4.1 host server, using the NetWare Administrator utility.

NetWare Directory Services *See* NDS.

NetWare DOS Requester The NetWare client software that is installed on DOS- and Windows-based workstations on a NetWare 4.1 network. The NetWare DOS

Requester includes Virtual Loadable Modules (VLMs), which control how the workstation connects to and communicates with the workstation's local operating system and with the network. The NetWare DOS Requester replaces earlier NetWare shell software (NETX, EMSNETX, and XMSNETX).

NetWare Loadable Module *See* NLM.

NetWare Server object An NDS object that represents a NetWare server.

NetWare User Tools A NetWare 4.1 utility (which runs under Windows) that users can use to complete many network tasks instead of using the other utilities that are targeted toward the network administrator. With NetWare User Tools, users can easily map drives, capture printer ports, and so on. It is installed by the NetWare DOS Requester installation, and it is part of the NETWARE.DRV driver.

NetWire Novell's online forums that offer users access to a wide variety of information and files dealing with NetWare and other Novell products, such as WordPerfect, Quattro Pro, and GroupWise. NetWire, which is located on CompuServe and on the Internet, provides information such as technical advice and support, updated files and drivers, the latest patches and workarounds, information about programs such as Novell Education classes and NetWare Users International (NUI), and marketing and sales information about the various products that Novell produces.

Network adapter *See* Network board.

Network board A special circuit board, installed in each workstation or server, that connects the computer to the network cables. Also called network interface board (or card) and network adapter.

Network interface board *See* Network board.

NLM (NetWare Loadable Module) A software module that you load into the server's operating system to add or change functionality. There are four different types of NetWare Loadable Modules that you can use: NLM utilities, name space modules, LAN drivers, and disk drivers. Many software manufacturers create NLMs to work on NetWare 4.1.

Node address The physical address of the network board installed in a node, such as a workstation, on the network. Each computer on the network must have a unique node address.

Object *See* NDS object.

Organization object An NDS object that represents an organization, such as a company.

Organizational Role object An NDS object that represents a position that various employees can occupy. Using an Organizational Role object allows you to assign rights to the position rather than to specific users, which is especially useful if there are multiple workers in this position or a high turnover rate of workers.

Organizational Unit object An NDS object that represents a subdivision under the Organization object, such as a division, department, project team, or workgroup.

OSI Reference Model A model established by the International Standards Organization (ISO) that defines functions for allowing any combination of devices to communicate with each other. The OSI model defines seven layers of communication that can occur between devices: Application, Presentation, Session, Transport, Network, Data Link, and Physical.

Packet signature *See* NCP Packet Signature.

Partition, directory A portion of the NDS database that can be replicated on different servers. A Directory partition is a branch of the Directory tree, beginning with any container object you choose. Partitions can also hold subpartitions beneath them (known as child partitions). If you have a smaller NDS database, the whole database can reside in a single partition. Partitions can increase network performance, especially if the network spans across a WAN (wide area network). They also can make it easier to manage portions of the tree separately. *See also* Replica.

Partition, disk A logical (not physical) portion of a hard disk that can be assigned to be part of a volume. On a server, the DOS partition can be used to store regular DOS boot files and other files that run under DOS. The server's NetWare partitions are assigned to NetWare volumes, which store all of the NetWare files and the NetWare operating system. Users access the server's NetWare volumes from workstations.

Patch A software module that can be applied to your NetWare server to repair a bug or add an enhancement.

Patch cable A cable used to connect two hubs in a network cabling system.

Path (directory) The location of a file or subdirectory in the file system. A file's directory path is a list of all the parent directories above that file to the root of the disk or volume.

Path (DOS) Pointers that tell DOS which directories to search through when looking for executable files that are not found in the current directory. (You can display a workstation's current paths by typing the DOS command PATH.) NetWare search drives are added to the workstation's path environment variables.

Phase I network *See* AppleTalk nonextended network.

Phase 2 network *See* AppleTalk extended network.

Primary time server A server that determines the time by polling one or more Primary or Reference servers. The Primary servers determine an average time, then all Primary servers adjust their time to approach that average. If a Reference server exists, the Primary servers approach the Reference server's time. *See also* Time synchronization.

Print form A style of paper defined for a printer to use. Examples of print forms might be pre-printed invoice forms, paychecks, or legal-sized paper.

Print job configuration A template that indicates how a print job should be printed. Creating a print job configuration can simplify a user's task of selecting print options such as the designated printer, whether or not to print a banner page, and the type of paper on which to print.

Print queue A network directory that temporarily stores print jobs from any number of network users. The print queue stores the jobs in a first-in, first-out order, and waits for the print server to take the jobs and send them to the printer.

Print Queue object An NDS object that represents a NetWare print queue.

Print server A software program (PSERVER.NLM) that controls network printing. The print server takes print jobs from the print queue and forwards them on to a printer. It controls the order in which the print jobs are printed, and other aspects of network printing.

Print Server object An NDS object that represents a NetWare print server.

Print spooler, AppleTalk A feature of NetWare for Macintosh that appears to a Macintosh workstation to be a regular Apple printer, so the workstation will send the print job to it. The print spooler then sends the job to the NetWare print queue, where it waits in line to be processed by a print server. When users look for printers in the Chooser, they will see the AppleTalk print spooler name instead of a printer name.

Printer object An NDS object that represents a NetWare printer.

Property A piece of information that defines some characteristic of an NDS object, such as a full name, ID number, phone number, e-mail address, or access rights to other objects. Properties are also called attributes. Each type of object, such as a Server or Printer object, may have different properties than another type of object.

Profile login script A login script that applies to several users who don't necessarily have to be in the same container. The profile login script is a property of a Profile object, which defines a list of users who belong to the Profile. A user can have only one profile login script execute upon login. *See also* Login script.

Profile object An NDS object that contains a login script that executes for all users who are members of the Profile.

Protocol A set of defined rules that controls how processes or machines communicate. A protocol regulates how the processes perform activities such as making contact, transferring packets of data, and terminating the contact. There are many different types of protocols that have been developed by various organizations to control how information is exchanged across a network. NetWare 4.1 supports many of these protocols.

Protocol driver A software program that enables the LAN driver to communicate with a protocol, such as IPX or TCP/IP. IPXODI.COM is the protocol driver used to support the IPX protocol (the default protocol for most NetWare networks). The protocol driver is placed in the NWCLIENT directory by the NetWare DOS Requester installation.

Purge To remove a deleted file from the server's hard disk. Deleted files are saved in a salvageable state until they are either salvaged or purged by a user, or until the server runs out of disk space and purges them to gain more disk space.

Reference time server A server that sets the time on a NetWare 4.1 network. It is similar to a Single Reference time server, but used on larger networks where additional Primary servers are desired. Primary servers migrate their time to match the Reference server's time. If more than one Reference server exists, they must all be synchronized with the same external time source, such as an atomic clock. *See also* Time synchronization.

Remote Console A NetWare feature that allows you to temporarily transform your workstation into the server's keyboard and monitor. With the remote console running, you can type console commands from your workstation just as if you were using the server's real keyboard and monitor. You can use the Remote Console feature over a direct connection to the network, or via asynchronous lines through a modem.

Repeaters Network cabling hardware that regenerates the signal and passes it on, thereby extending the normal limits of the network.

Replica A copy of a Directory partition. Replicas of a partition can be stored on different servers. Then, if one server goes down, all the other servers can still access the NDS database from another replica of the database. *See also* Partition, directory.

Replica, master A replica that contains all the partition's object information. Any Directory partition changes, such as adding, merging, or deleting replicas, must be done from this replica. There is only one master replica per partition.

Replica, read-only A replica from which you can read NDS object information but to which you cannot make changes. Any number of these replicas can exist on a network.

Replica, read-write A partition replica from which you can make changes to NDS objects. Any number of read-write replicas can exist on a network.

Replica, subordinate reference A replica that exists on a server if that server holds a replica of a parent partition, but does not hold a replica of the child partitition. The subordinate reference replica provides pointers to the objects in the real child partition.

Resource fork The portion of a Macintosh file that contains information about the file, such as the application used to create the file (which lets you autolaunch a file by double-clicking its icon). In addition, the resource fork includes information about the type of icon that should be displayed for the file, and so on. DOS, OS/2, and Unix files don't have resource forks. *See also* Data fork.

Restore To retrieve files from a backup copy and put them back on the network. *See also* Backup.

Rights, effective The rights that the user can ultimately execute, after determining any inherited rights, rights blocked by the IRF, direct trustee assignments, and security equivalences to other objects.

Rights, file system Assigned to users and groups to control what each user or group can do with a file or directory. Also called trustee rights.

Rights, inherited Access rights you inherit from a parent container object or a parent file system directory. *See also* Inheritance.

Rights, object Access rights that control how the user works with an NDS object but don't affect whether the user can see or work with the object's properties.

Rights, property Access rights that control whether the user can see and work with an NDS object's properties.

RIP (Router Information Protocol) A routing protocol used by NetWare's IPX network protocol. RIP allows NetWare routers to create and update a router table (or database) of current information about other routers on the internetwork. Routers send periodic broadcasts of RIP packets to other routers on the network to keep all routers on the network synchronized.

Root object The highest point of the Directory tree. It contains no information.

Router A router transfers data from one segment of a network to another, but unlike a bridge, a router also calculates the most efficient route for the data to travel. *See also* Bridge.

Router Information Protocol *See* RIP.

Salvage To retrieve a deleted file from the server's hard disk. Deleted files are saved in a salvageable state until they are either salvaged or purged by a user, or until the server runs out of disk space and purges them to gain more disk space.

SAP (Service Advertising Protocol) A service advertising protocol used by NetWare's IPX network protocol. Servers advertise their services on an internetwork by periodically broadcasting SAP packets. Routers use the SAP packets to update their router tables.

Schema *See* NDS schema.

Search drive A special drive mapping to a network directory. When a search drive is mapped to a directory, the system will look in that directory for executable files if it can't find them in a user's current directory. Search drive mappings are added to the workstation's DOS path commands.

Secondary time server A server that obtains the time from another time server. Secondary servers do not participate in determining the time; they merely obtain it for their own use and to provide the time to their workstations. *See also* Time synchronization.

Security equivalence Assigning one user to have all of another user's rights. When you are given security equivalence to another user, you receive the same rights that the other user was explicitly granted. When you add a user to a group membership list or to an Organizational Role object's list, the user really becomes "security equivalent" to that Group or Organizational Role object.

Seed router An AppleTalk router that has network numbers and zone names specifically configured for it. Other AppleTalk routers can then "learn" their configuration from this seed router. Each network needs at least one seed router.

SERVER.EXE The executable file that runs the NetWare 4.1 operating system on the computer, turning the computer into the NetWare server.

Service Advertising Protocol *See* SAP.

SFT III (System Fault Tolerance Level III) NetWare 4.1 SFT III is a form of NetWare 4.1 that lets you install the operating system on two identical servers, which work in concert with each other. If one server fails, the other takes over seamlessly and continues to run the network. Although the SFT III capability is built into NetWare 4.1, you cannot access it unless you have purchased the SFT III licensed version of NetWare 4.1.

Single Reference time server The sole server that maintains the network time, often used on small NetWare networks. All other servers are Secondary time servers. Single Reference servers provide the time to workstations and Secondary time servers. *See also* Time synchronization.

STARTNET.BAT A batch file created by the NetWare DOS Requester installation. It is located in the NWCLIENT directory and can be edited with a text editor. STARTNET.BAT sets the workstation's language and loads LSL.COM, the LAN driver, and protocol driver files. Then it executes VLM.EXE, which loads all necessary VLMs.

STARTUP.NCF A server boot file that automates the initialization of the NetWare operating system. It loads disk drivers, loads name space modules to support different file formats (Macintosh, OS/2, or NFS), and executes some SET parameters that modify default initialization values.

Suballocation *See* Block suballocation.

Surge suppressor A device installed between a workstation or peripheral and the regular electrical outlet. It can help prevent electrical surges from damaging the equipment.

System login script A login script that is a property of a container object. The commands in the system login script execute for every user in that container who logs in. (It is also called a container login script.) *See also* Login script.

TCP/IP (Transmission Control Protocol/Internet Protocol) A suite of network protocols developed for use on the Internet that allows nodes on a Unix-based network to communicate. TCP operates at the equivalent of the session and transport layers of the OSI Reference Model, and IP works at the equivalent of the network layer.

Template *See* User template.

Terminator Special connectors attached to the open ends of cables. Terminators keep stray signals from causing interference on the network.

Time synchronization A NetWare 4.1 feature that ensures that servers on a network maintain the same time so that network events occur in the correct order. With NetWare's time services, you assign servers different time synchronization functions so that some servers can set the time, others can average the time together, and still others can simply receive the time from other servers.

Token Ring A network cabling architecture, which is cabled like a star but acts like a ring. When data flows from workstation to workstation, it goes through the central point each time as it makes its way around the whole network. Token Ring networks generally work well in situations that involve heavy data traffic because Token Ring is reliable. It is also fairly easy to install, but it is more expensive than either ARCnet or Ethernet networks.

TokenTalk Apple Computer's Token Ring implementation.

Topology The format in which a network is laid out, such as a bus format, a ring format, or a star format. Variations or combinations of these topologies are also commonly used.

Transaction Tracking System *See* TTS.

Tree *See* NDS tree.

Trunk cable The main cable system that forms the backbone of the network. All other nodes (workstations, servers, and so on) are connected to this trunk.

Trustee A user, group, or other object that has been granted rights to an object, file, or directory.

Trustee rights *See* Rights, file system; Rights, object; and Rights, property.

TTS (Transaction Tracking System) A NetWare feature that protects database transactions. With TTS turned on, if a transaction is caught only half-completed by a problem such as a power outage, the transaction is completely backed out so that the database isn't corrupted. When a transaction is backed out it is restored to its original state as it was before the transaction began.

Unicode files Files used to help the NetWare client software run on machines that use different country-specific keyboards and language-specific versions of DOS. These files are placed in the NWCLIENT\NLS subdirectory by the NetWare DOS Requester installation.

UPS (uninterruptible power supply) Hardware that provides the server with a backup battery in case of a power outage, allowing the server enough time to shut itself down cleanly, leaving no open files exposed to corruption.

User login script A login script that is a property of an individual User object. You store user-specific drive mappings, and so on, in the user login script. If the user does not have a specific user login script, a default login script will execute instead, setting up the most basic drive mappings. *See also* Login script.

User object An NDS object that represents a NetWare user.

User template A template you can set up to automatically apply default properties to any new user you create. (It will not apply those properties to any users that existed before you created the user template.) A user template is actually a regular User object that you create and name USER_TEMPLATE. You can have a different template for each container.

User Tools *See* NetWare User Tools.

VLMs (Virtual Loadable Modules) Files that are placed in the NWCLIENT directory by the NetWare DOS Requester installation. They control the workstation's communication and activities on the network.

Volume The highest level in the file system hierarchy (similar to a DOS root directory). It contains directories and files. Each NetWare server has at least one volume, SYS, which contains all of the NetWare files and utilities. You can have additional volumes on a server if you want; in fact, a NetWare server can have up to 64 volumes.

Volume object An NDS object that represents a NetWare volume.

Volume segment A disk partition that forms part of a volume. Each volume can have up to 32 volume segments, which can all be stored on the same hard disk or scattered across separate disks. Letting volume segments reside on different disks lets you increase the size of a volume by adding a new hard disk. One hard disk can hold up to eight volume segments that belong to one or more volumes. By putting segments of the same volume on more than one hard disk, different parts of the volume can be accessed simultaneously, increasing disk input and output.

Workstation A computer with NetWare client software installed, which users use to access and work on the network. Workstations on a NetWare 4.1 network can be DOS, Windows, OS/2, Unix, or Macintosh workstations.

Zone *See* AppleTalk zone.

Index

B

C

D

E

F

G

H

I

K

L

M

N

O

P

R

S

U

V

W

Z

IDG BOOKS WORLDWIDE LICENSE AGREEMENT

Important — read carefully before opening the software packet(s). This is a legal agreement between you (either an individual or an entity) and IDG Books Worldwide, Inc. (IDG). By opening the accompanying sealed packet containing the software disk(s), you acknowledge that you have read and accept the following IDG License Agreement. If you do not agree and do not want to be bound by the terms of this Agreement, promptly return the book and the unopened software packet(s) to the place you obtained them for a full refund.

1. License. This License Agreement (Agreement) permits you to use one copy of the enclosed Software program(s) on a single computer. The Software is in "use" on a computer when it is loaded into temporary memory (i.e., RAM) or installed into permanent memory (e.g., hard disk, CD-ROM, or other storage device) of that computer.

2. Copyright. The entire contents of the disk(s) and the compilation of the Software are copyrighted and protected by both United States copyright laws and international treaty provisions. You may only (a) make one copy of the Software for backup or archival purposes, or (b) transfer the Software to a single hard disk, provided that you keep the original for backup or archival purposes. The individual programs on the disk(s) are copyrighted by the authors of each program respectively. Each program has its own use permissions and limitations. To use each program, you must follow the individual requirements and restrictions detailed for each in the Appendix of this Book. Do not use a program if you do not want to follow its Licensing Agreement. None of the material on the disk(s) or listed in this Book may ever be distributed, in original or modified form, for commercial purposes.

3. Other Restrictions. You may not rent or lease the Software. You may transfer the Software and user documentation on a permanent basis provided you retain no copies and the recipient agrees to the terms of this Agreement. You may not reverse engineer, decompile, or disassemble the Software except to the extent that the foregoing restriction is expressly prohibited by applicable law. If the Software is an update or has been updated, any transfer must include the most recent update and all prior versions.

4. Limited Warranty. IDG warrants that the Software and disk(s) are free from defects in materials and workmanship for a period of sixty (60) days from the date of purchase of this Book. If IDG receives notification within the warranty period of defects in material or workmanship, IDG will replace the defective disk(s). IDG's entire liability and your exclusive remedy shall be limited to replacement of the Software, which is returned to

IDG with a copy of your receipt. This Limited Warranty is void if failure of the Software has resulted from accident, abuse, or misapplication. Any replacement Software will be warranted for the remainder of the original warranty period or thirty (30) days, whichever is longer.

5. No Other Warranties. To the maximum extent permitted by applicable law, IDG and the author disclaim all other warranties, express or implied, including but not limited to implied warranties of merchantability and fitness for a particular purpose, with respect to the Software, the programs, the source code contained therein and/or the techniques described in this Book. This limited warranty gives you specific legal rights. You may have others which vary from state/jurisdiction to state/jurisdiction.

6. No Liability For Consequential Damages. To the extent permitted by applicable law, in no event shall IDG or the author be liable for any damages whatsoever (including without limitation, damages for loss of business profits, business interruption, loss of business information, or any other pecuniary loss) arising out of the use of or inability to use the Book or the Software, even if IDG has been advised of the possibility of such damages. Because some states/jurisdictions do not allow the exclusion or limitation of liability for consequential or incidental damages, the above limitation may not apply to you.

7. U.S.Government Restricted Rights. Use, duplication, or disclosure of the Software by the U.S. Government is subject to restrictions stated in paragraph (c) (1) (ii) of the Rights in Technical Data and Computer Software clause of DFARS 252.227-7013, and in subparagraphs (a) through (d) of the Commercial Computer—Restricted Rights clause at FAR 52.227-19, and in similar clauses in the NASA FAR supplement, when applicable.

Disk Installation Instructions

The entire text of *Novell's NetWare 4 Administrator's Handbook* is stored on the floppy disk that comes with this book. The text appears in Microsoft Word, WordPerfect, and MS-DOS Text (ASCII) formats so that you can retrieve the text in the format that is most convenient for you. To install the files on your hard disk, follow these instructions:

For PC Users

1. Insert the diskette in your disk drive.
2. In the File Manager, select Run from the File menu.
3. If you inserted the disk in drive A:, type **A:\BOOKA** in the command line. If you inserted the disk in drive B:, type **B:\BOOKB** in the command line. A new directory called BKTEXT will automatically be created on your hard disk, and the Microsoft Word and WordPerfect files will automatically decompress in that directory.
4. Press the F5 key to see the new directory and files in the File Manager.
5. Double-click on BOOKTEXT.DOC to open the book text in Microsoft Word for Windows, or double-click on BOOKTEXT.WPD to open the book text in WordPerfect for Windows.

For Macintosh Users

1. Insert the floppy disk in your disk drive.
2. Double-click on the diskette's icon to begin installation. (On certain systems, Macintosh users may need the freeware program PC Exchange in order to use this disk.)

Note: Because this diskette was prepared before the book was printed, graphics and final revisions of the text could not be incorporated into these files. Also, you may experience a delay the first time you scroll through the book while the text is repaginated.

IDG BOOKS WORLDWIDE REGISTRATION CARD

RETURN THIS REGISTRATION CARD FOR FREE CATALOG

Title of this book: Novell's NetWare 4.1 Administrators Handbook

My overall rating of this book: ❑ Very good [1] ❑ Good [2] ❑ Satisfactory [3] ❑ Fair [4] ❑ Poor [5]

How I first heard about this book:

❑ Found in bookstore; name: [6] ❑ Book review: [7]

❑ Advertisement: [8] ❑ Catalog: [9]

❑ Word of mouth; heard about book from friend, co-worker, etc.: [10] ❑ Other: [11]

What I liked most about this book:

What I would change, add, delete, etc., in future editions of this book:

Other comments:

Number of computer books I purchase in a year: ❑ 1 [12] ❑ 2-5 [13] ❑ 6-10 [14] ❑ More than 10 [15]

I would characterize my computer skills as: ❑ Beginner [16] ❑ Intermediate [17] ❑ Advanced [18] ❑ Professional [19]

I use ❑ DOS [20] ❑ Windows [21] ❑ OS/2 [22] ❑ Unix [23] ❑ Macintosh [24] ❑ Other: [25]__________ (please specify)

I would be interested in new books on the following subjects:
(please check all that apply, and use the spaces provided to identify specific software)

❑ Word processing: [26] ❑ Spreadsheets: [27]

❑ Data bases: [28] ❑ Desktop publishing: [29]

❑ File Utilities: [30] ❑ Money management: [31]

❑ Networking: [32] ❑ Programming languages: [33]

❑ Other: [34]

I use a PC at (please check all that apply): ❑ home [35] ❑ work [36] ❑ school [37] ❑ other: [38] __________

The disks I prefer to use are ❑ 5.25 [39] ❑ 3.5 [40] ❑ other: [41]__________

I have a CD ROM: ❑ yes [42] ❑ no [43]

I plan to buy or upgrade computer hardware this year: ❑ yes [44] ❑ no [45]

I plan to buy or upgrade computer software this year: ❑ yes [46] ❑ no [47]

Name: Business title: [48] Type of Business: [49]

Address (❑ home [50] ❑ work [51]/Company name:)

Street/Suite#

City [52]/State [53]/Zipcode [54]: Country [55]

❑ **I liked this book!** You may quote me by name in future IDG Books Worldwide promotional materials.

My daytime phone number is __________

IDG BOOKS
THE WORLD OF COMPUTER KNOWLEDGE

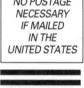